BEGINNER'S GUIDE TO
DRAWING MANGA

3dtotal Publishing

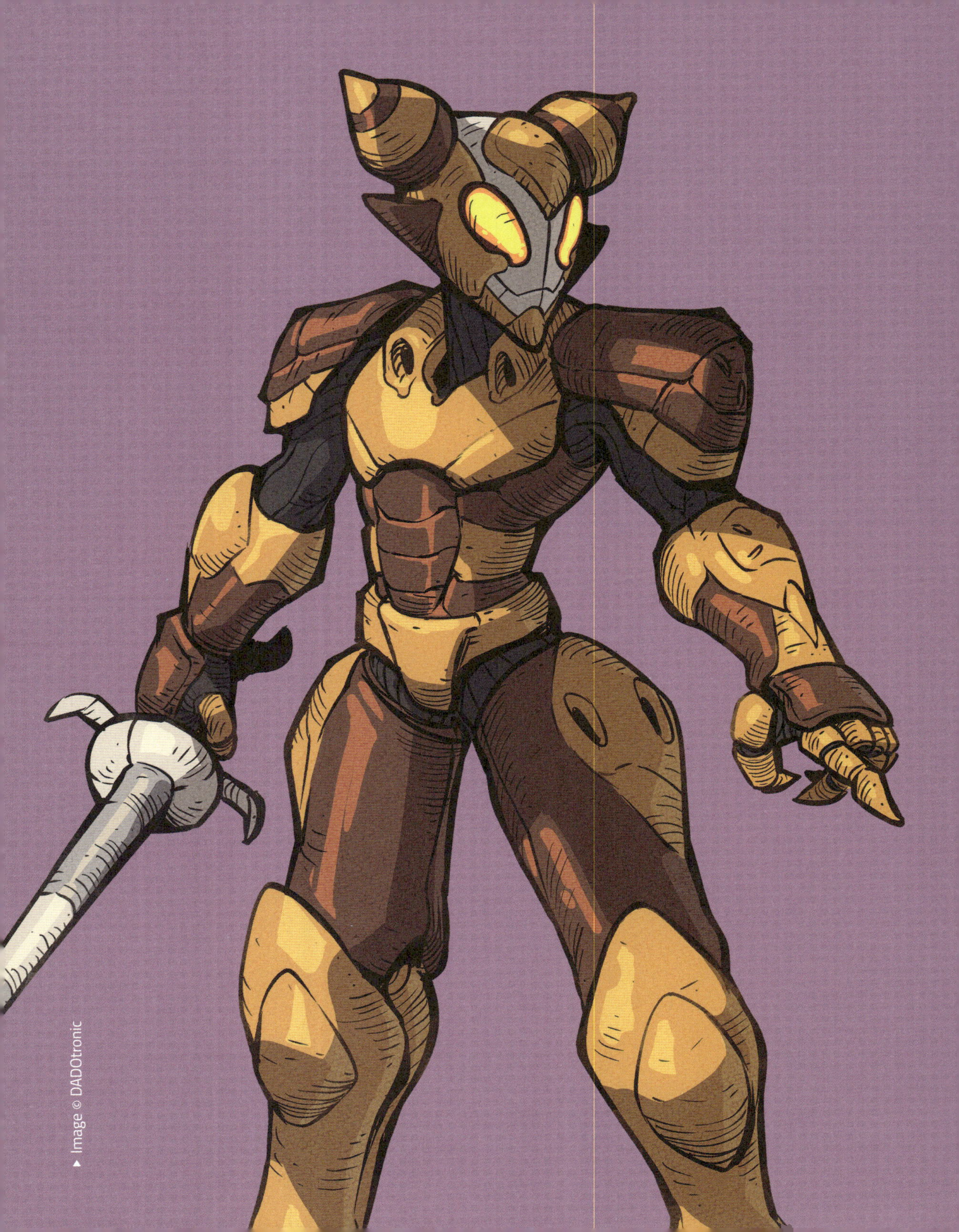

BEGINNER'S GUIDE TO

DRAWING MANGA

3dtotalPublishing

3dtotalPublishing

Correspondence: publishing@3dtotal.com
Website: www.3dtotal.com

Clip Studio Paint is developed by Celsys, Inc. Clip Studio Paint and Clip Studio are the trademarks or registered trademarks of Celsys, Inc. www.clipstudio.net/en

Every effort has been made to ensure the credits and contact information listed are present and correct. In the case of any errors that have occurred, the publisher respectfully directs readers to the www.3dtotalpublishing.com website for any updated information and/or corrections.

First published in the United Kingdom, 2023, by 3dtotal Publishing.

Address: 3dtotal.com Ltd, 29 Foregate Street, Worcester, WR1 1DS, United Kingdom.

Soft cover ISBN: 978-1-912843-71-8
Printed and bound in China by C&C Offset Printing Co., Ltd

Visit www.3dtotalpublishing.com for a complete list of available book titles.

Managing Director: Tom Greenway
Studio Manager: Simon Morse
Lead Editor: Samantha Rigby
Lead Designer: Joseph Cartwright
Editor: Philippa Barker
Designer: Matthew Lewis

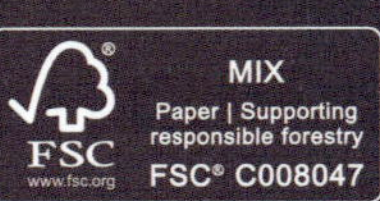

Front cover artwork by Miyuli, based on designs by individual artists as listed throughout the book. Back cover artwork © Individual artists as listed throughout the book.

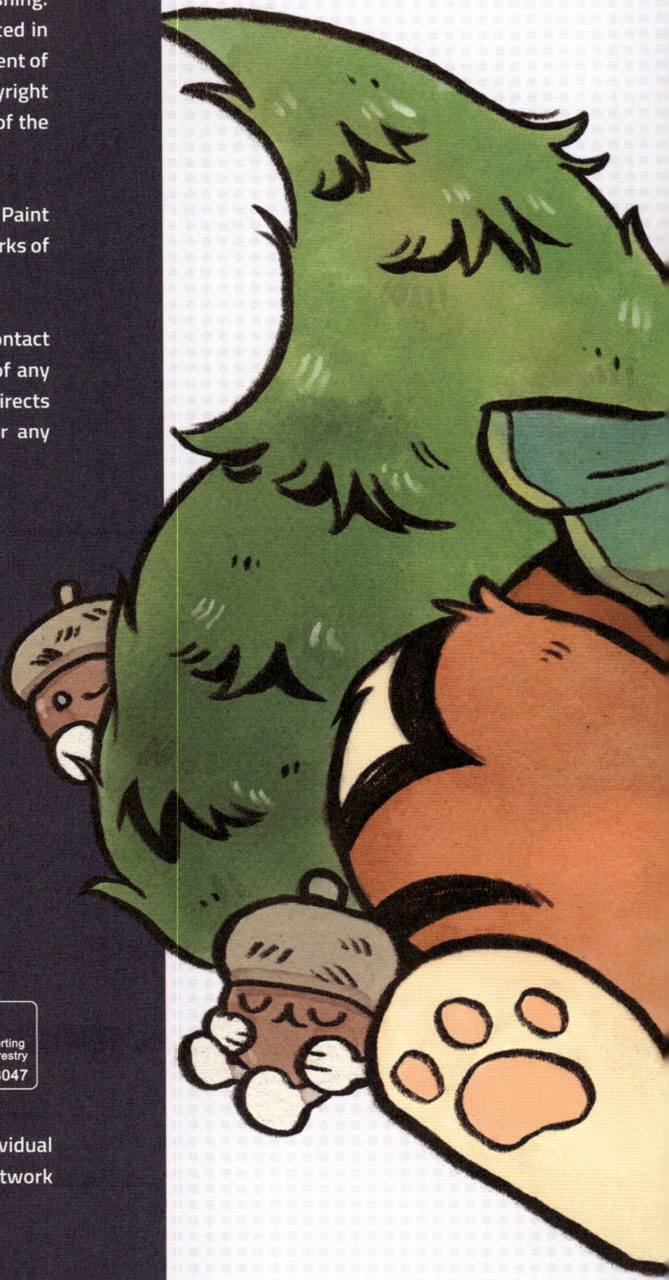

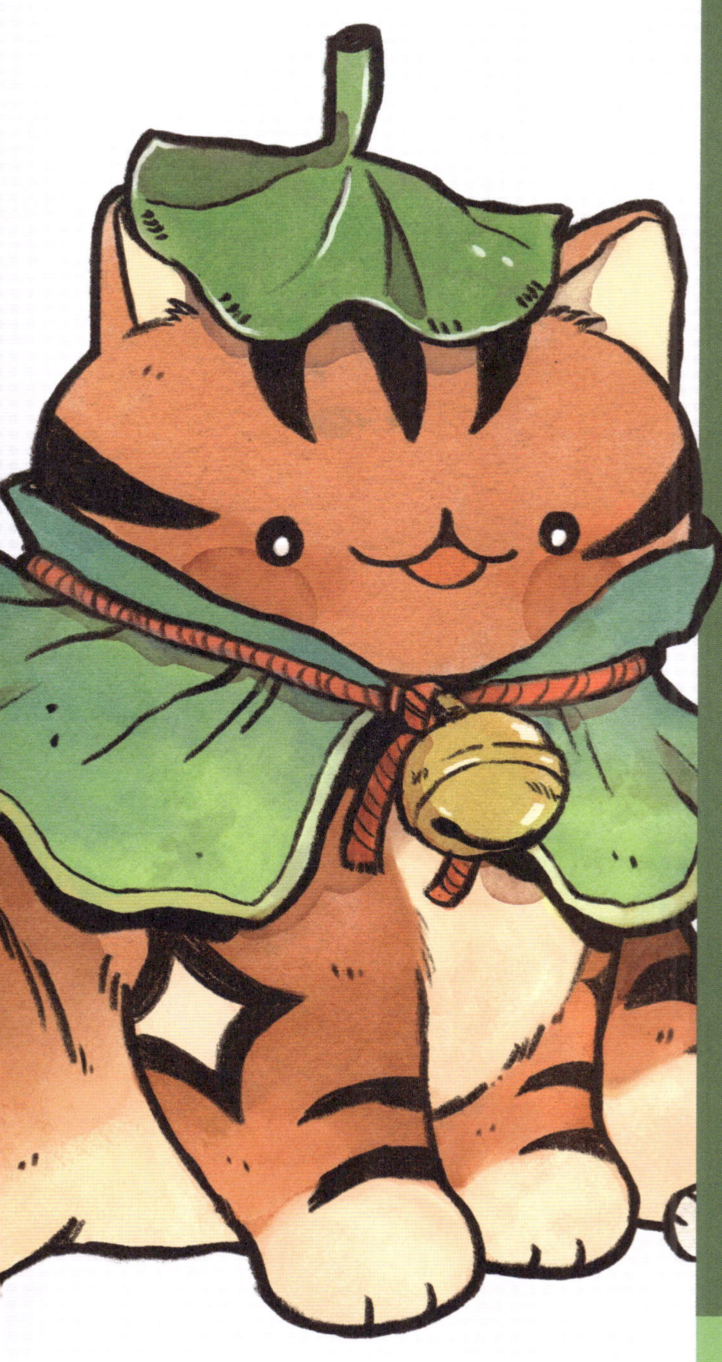

50%
of net profits donated
TO CHARITY

In 2022, 3dtotal Publishing became successful enough to make a pledge to donate **50% of its net profits to charity**. This continues to be possible due to the incredible support from all our customers, employees, and partners.

We focus our giving on three charitable areas: **environmental**, **humanitarian**, and **animal welfare**. We use organizations such as Effective Altruism and Founders Pledge to guide who we help within these causes. Some ways of doing good are over 100 times more effective than others, so donating this way hugely increases the impact of our contributions.

We also **plant one tree for every book sold** by partnering with reforesting charities and donating the required amounts. This is just one of the things we do in our aim to become a carbon-neutral publisher, to help balance the damage caused by the publishing, shipping, and retail industries.

See **3dtotal.com/charity** for full details.

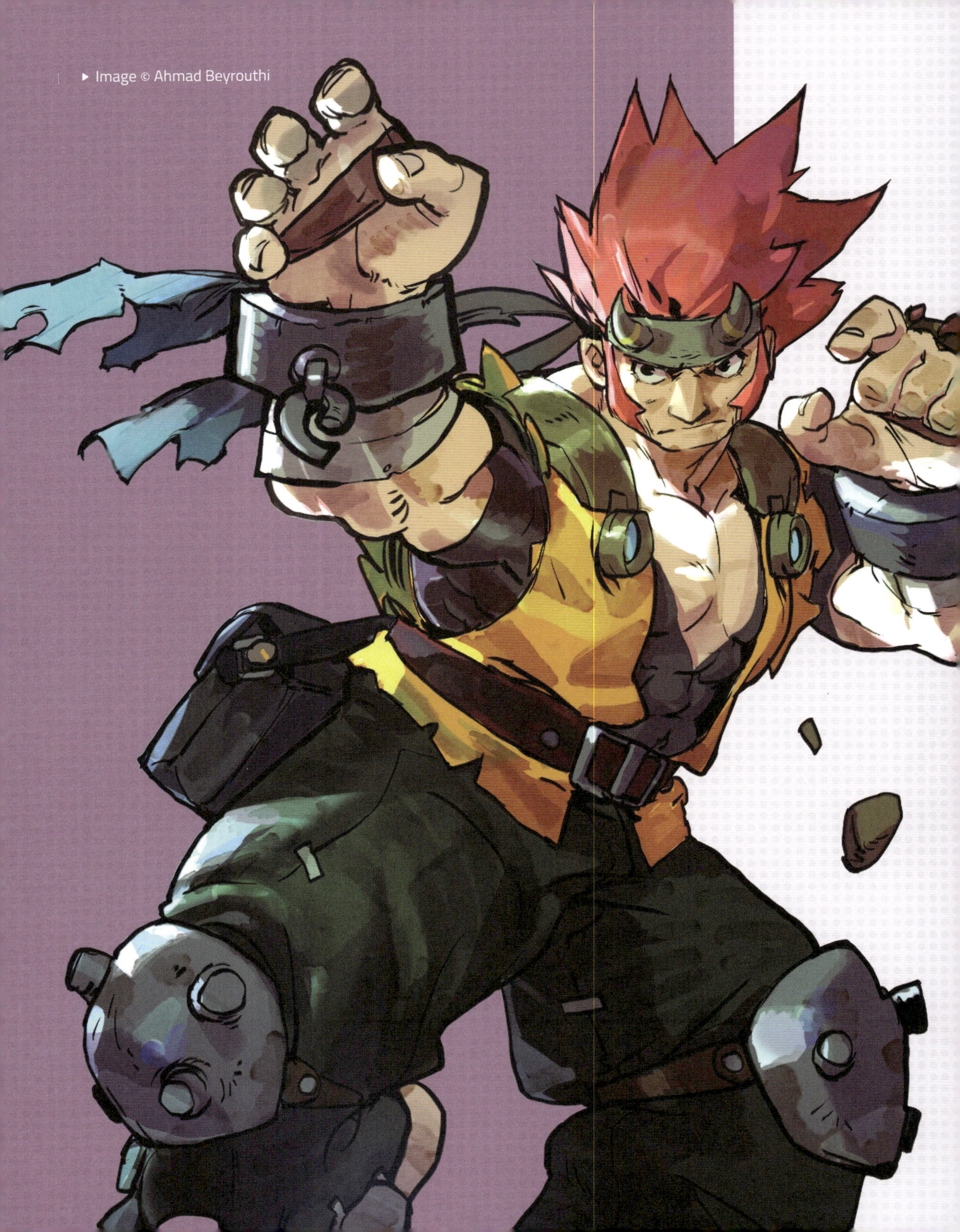
Image © Ahmad Beyrouthi

CONTENTS

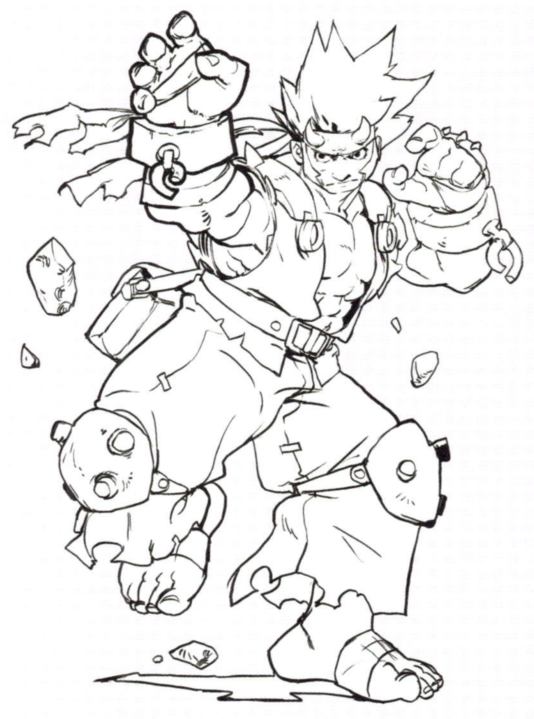

INTRODUCTION

The term 'manga' originates in Japan and roughly translates as 'cartoonlike pictures'. It typically refers to sequential art that tells a story and is used interchangeably with the word 'comic' in Japan. Why some artwork is referred to as 'manga style' while other artwork is simply called 'comic style' comes down to cultural and stylistic traits. The manga style has a long history of traditional Japanese picture books from the Edo period, which over time has been influenced by Western art. The combination of traditional aesthetics with foreign artwork has slowly developed into its own recognizable art style. Because of this, some people will only use 'manga' when talking about comics published in Japan with their industry standards and procedures.

Does this mean people who publish their work in other countries shouldn't refer to their art as manga? Does the country you come from dictate the art style you use? Nowadays, thanks to the internet and the digital market, the line between manga and comics has become increasingly blurred, resulting in a mix of both created by artists all over the world. Today manga-style artwork features heavily in graphic novels, animation, and video games.

When drawing in your personal art style, you make choices about what to emphasize and simplify. This book will explore the artistic decisions you can make to give your artwork and characters the popular manga look. Manga contains many different genres, target audiences, and art styles. The examples in this book are simply guidelines to help you get started rather than unshakable rules. The more you study your favourite manga art styles, the more variation and creativity you will find.

We hope the following chapters will prove helpful on your journey into the world of manga art!

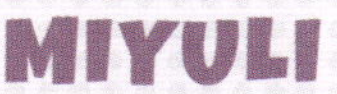

MIYULI
Comic artist & illustrator

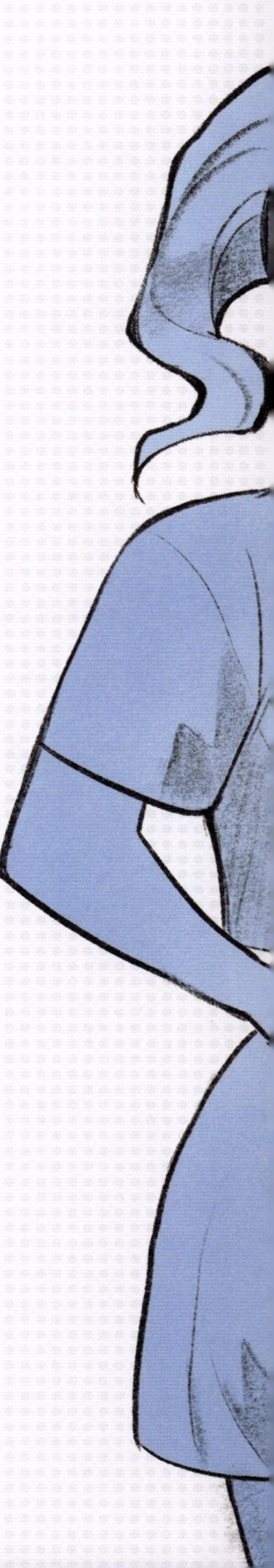

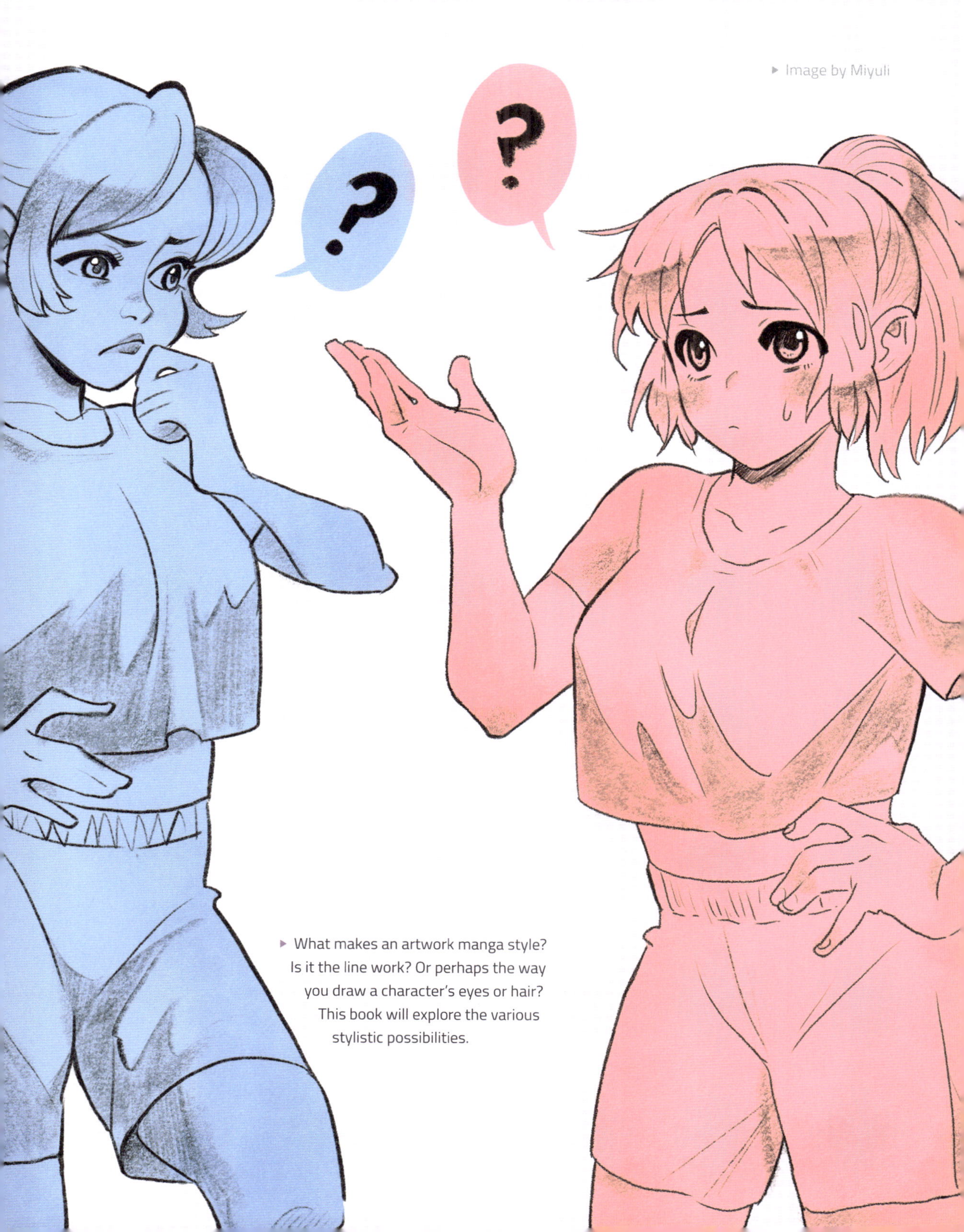

▶ What makes an artwork manga style? Is it the line work? Or perhaps the way you draw a character's eyes or hair? This book will explore the various stylistic possibilities.

GETTING STARTED

Before you set pencil to paper, it's a good idea to learn the basics of drawing. What tools and shading techniques will you need to bring your manga characters to life on paper or screen? What do you need to know about the manga style and genre? What design techniques, from pose to lighting set-up, will help you to elevate your artwork? And how can practices such as research, thumbnailing, and storytelling benefit your creation process?

This invaluable chapter is split into four sections, each of which will provide you with the foundational knowledge to prepare you for the tutorials that follow.

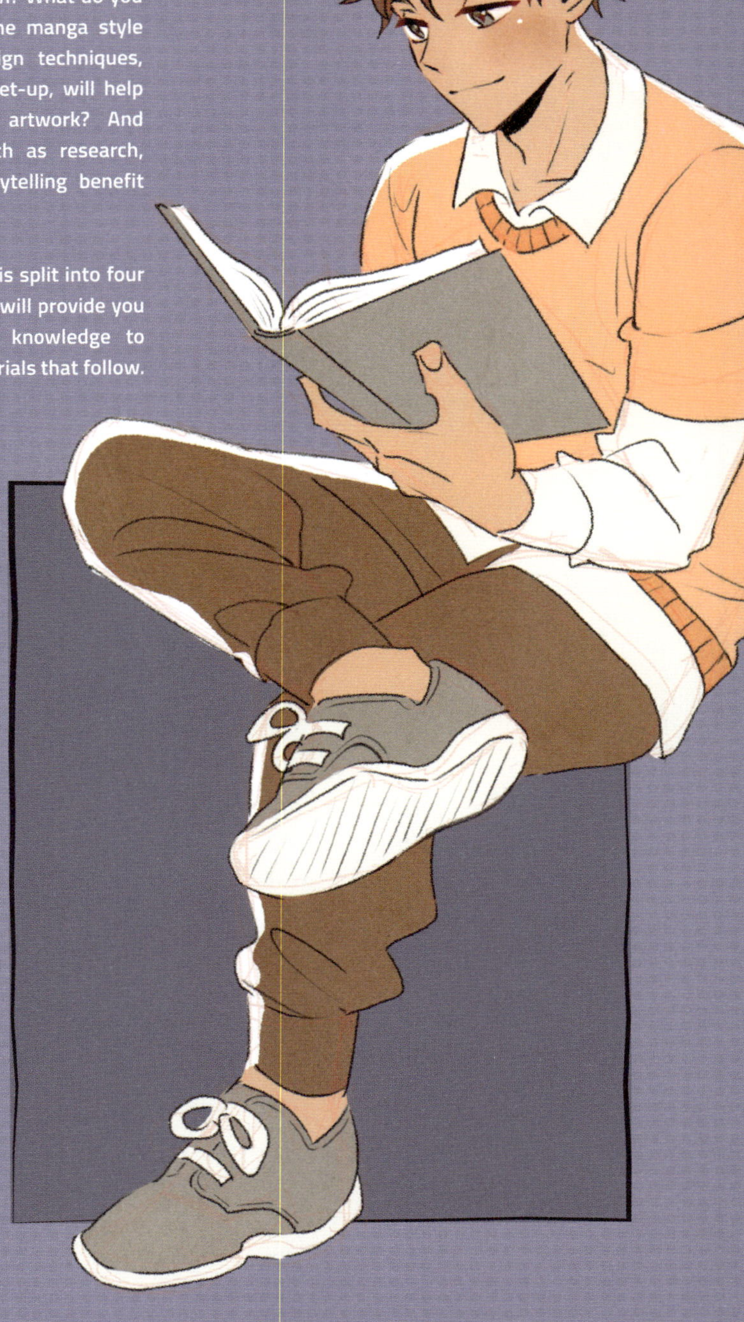

TOOLS & TECHNIQUES

BY MIYULI

Tools exist to allow you to express yourself artistically. While it's perfectly possible to use the cheapest pencils to create beautiful art, it's good to experiment and familiarize yourself with a variety of different materials. This will enable you to discover which tools you most enjoy using, and those that are best for making your ideas a reality. This chapter will explore some commonly used drawing tools and their purposes, as well as the different techniques that will help you to bring your manga characters to life on the page.

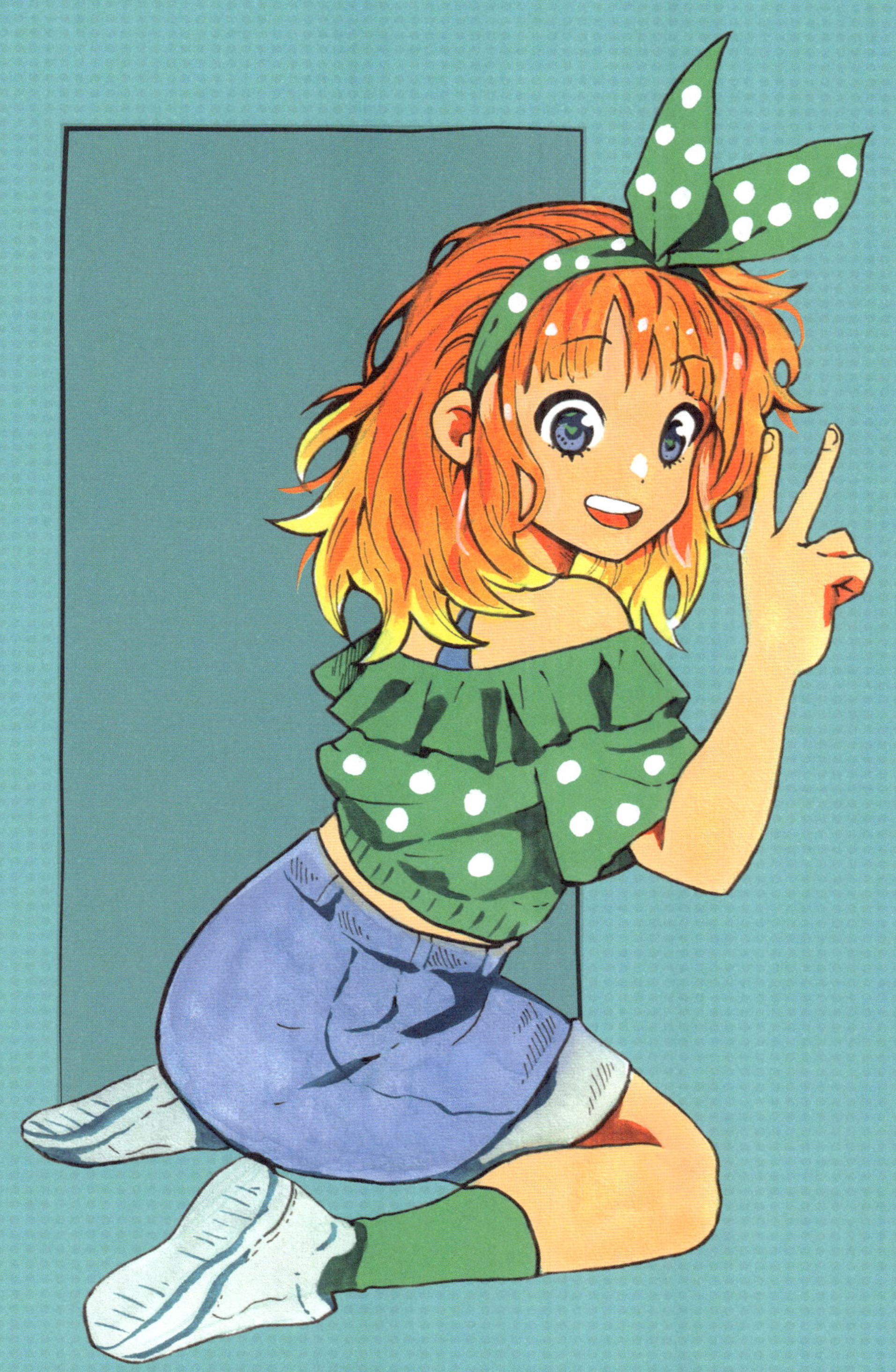

DRAWING TOOLS

TOOLKIT

- ▶ Paper
- ▶ Pencils
- ▶ Erasers
- ▶ Chalk pastel
- ▶ Pens
- ▶ Dip pens
- ▶ Brushes
- ▶ Markers
- ▶ Watercolours
- ▶ Screen tone
- ▶ Pen tablet and/or display
- ▶ Clip Studio Paint

Your choice of tool should ideally become an extension of your drawing arm, rather than an obstacle. Find out what other artists use and try out as wide a range of materials as you can, but never feel pressured to follow a trend if it hinders your artistic vision. If you feel overwhelmed, stick to one simple tool and take things one step at a time. You don't need to master every tool out there to become a successful artist.

PAPER

There are many different types of paper available in various weights and textures, bound in sketchbooks or sold in blocks. Your choice of paper will depend on the tools you use. For example, water-based tools require thick, sturdy paper that will hold the water well. Markers and ink perform well on smoother, coated paper that doesn't let ink bleed across the page. As smooth paper allows you more control over line work and creates less texture, this is what is usually recommended for drawing manga.

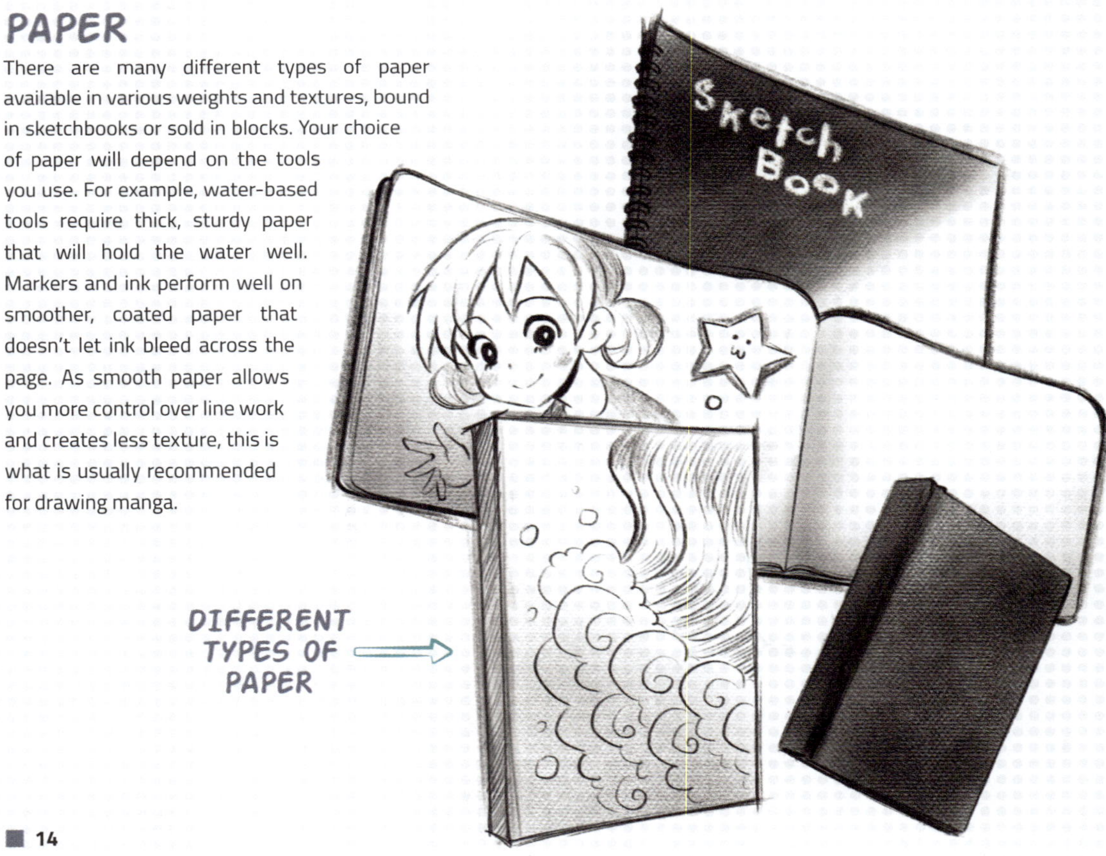

PENCILS

Since pencils are mostly used for drawing rough sketches, you don't need to worry too much about the end result. Refillable mechanical pencils often produce the quickest and cleanest results. If using wooden pencils, opt for an H or HB grade to avoid smudging. If you want to create texture and use smudging as a stylistic choice, choose softer B pencils. This also applies to coloured pencils and coloured leads.

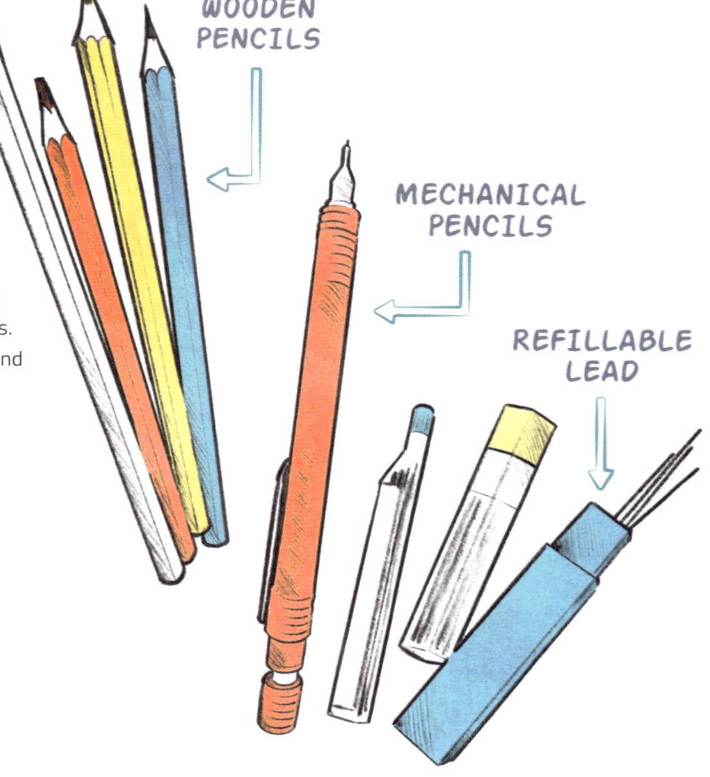

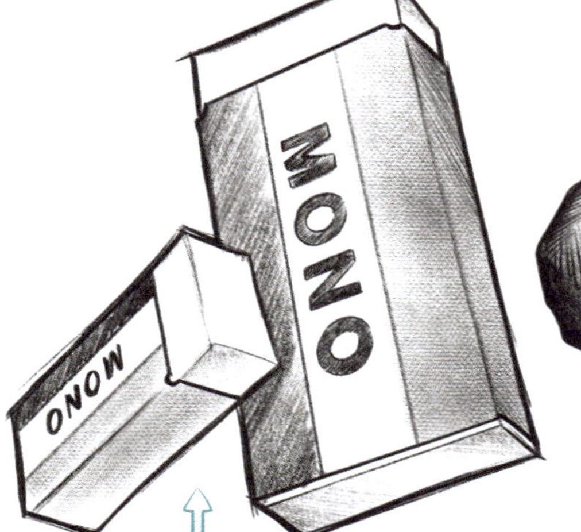

KNEADED
ERASER

PLASTIC
ERASERS

ERASERS

The eraser's task is to remove pencil lines without leaving smudges or damaging the paper. The Tombow MONO plastic eraser is a popular choice with many artists, as its sleeve protects the eraser from picking up dirt. Kneaded rubber erasers are often used to lighten pencil or chalk lines. Erasers can also be used to add details and highlights to a near-final pencil illustration.

PENS

For personal studies or sketchbook doodles, a common ballpoint pen might be all you need. This will allow you to create rough sketches by lightly pressing on the paper, or applying more weight to draw line work. Multiliners can be used to create a cleaner, more precise look. Available in a variety of sizes and colours, they are great for controlled line work. As pen drawings can't be erased, you will have to use correction fluid to fix any mistakes.

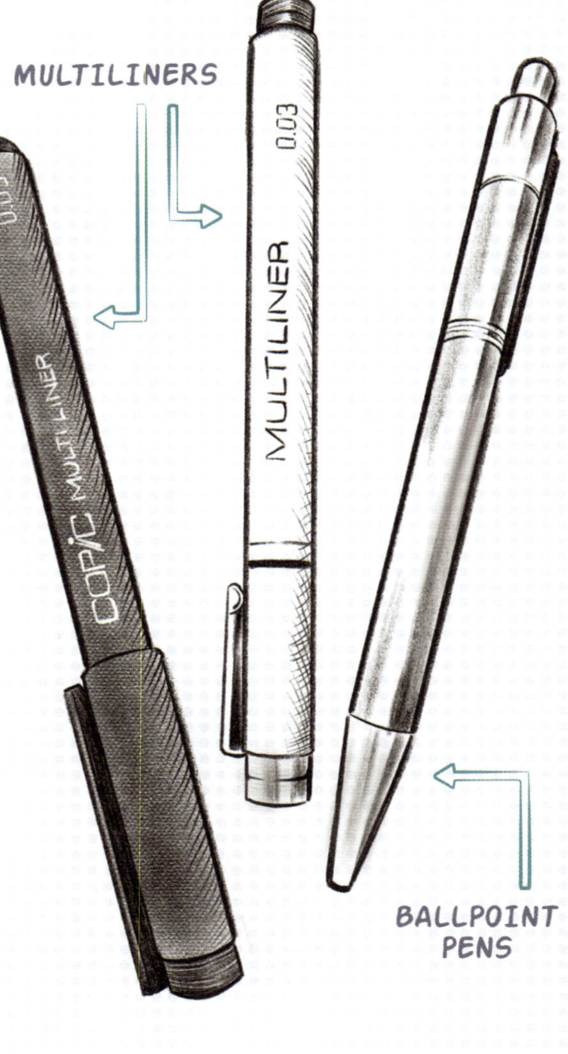

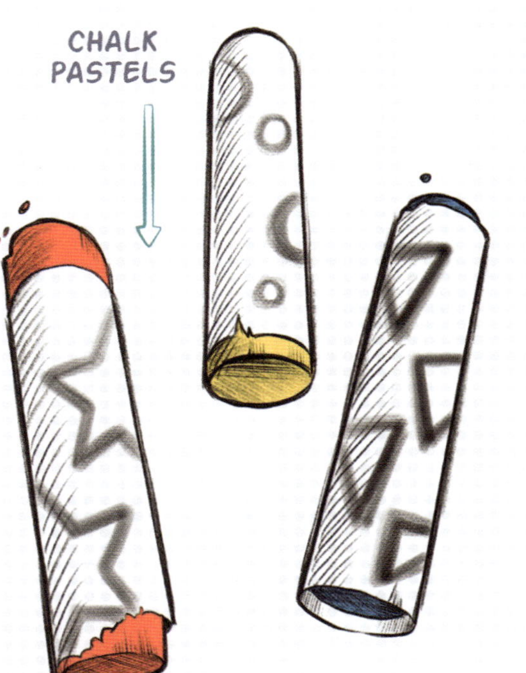

CHALK PASTELS

Hard chalk is great for creating texture, whereas soft chalk works best for blending and smudging to produce soft, gradual transitions. Chalk pastel can still be erased, so it's a safe, non-permanent method for adding colour. Use a transparent container or fixative spray to protect your finished artwork from accidentally smearing on contact with another object.

DIP PENS

Dip pens come with various nibs and can be made of different materials, though they are typically metal. They can be a little hard to control at first, so practice is needed. Flexible G-Pen nibs allow you to create both thick and thin lines, while a Maru pen is perfect for drawing very fine, thin strokes. There are plenty of cheaper pen nibs available to get you started, but it's important to make sure they fit into a suitable pen holder. There are also different types of ink. Some create a deep black, while others show more texture or mix with other materials. Some are waterproof and work well with markers. Read up on the inks available to you to ensure you select one that works well with your other chosen tools.

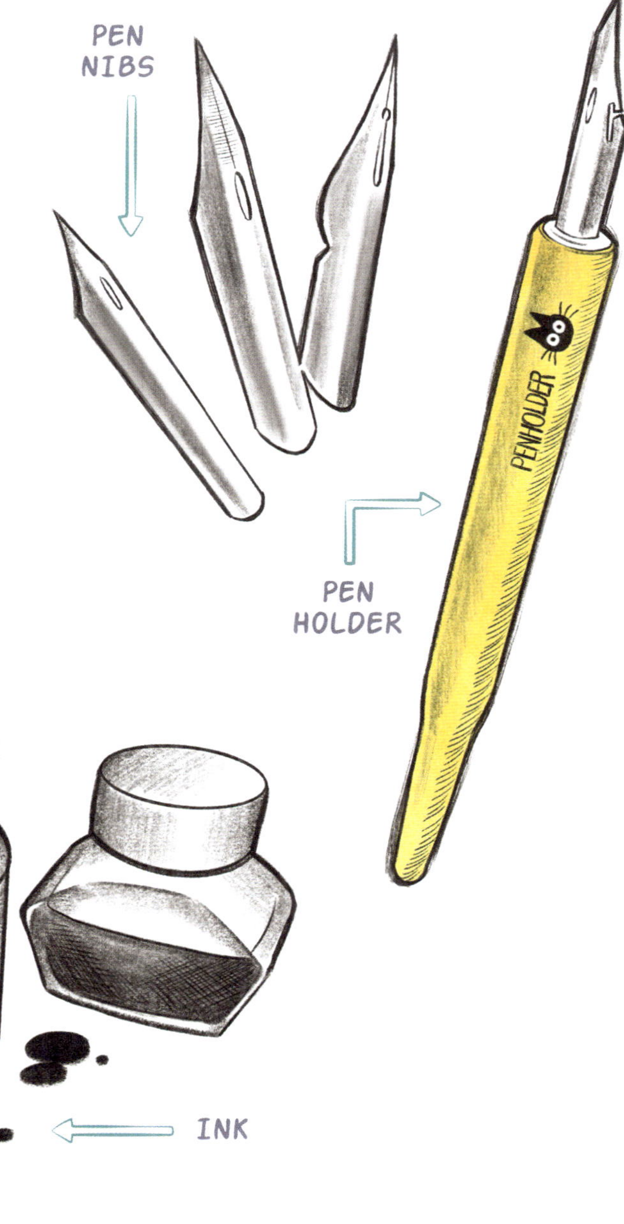

BRUSHES

Brushes are one of the most flexible drawing tools. Natural-hair brushes typically create the smoothest and most controlled results, from very thin to very thick brushstrokes. Practice is key to being able to control the size of your mark-making. Dry brushes, for example, can be used to create textured, rough effects. Brushes that hold water or ink inside are useful for travelling, as you don't need to repeatedly dip them into water.

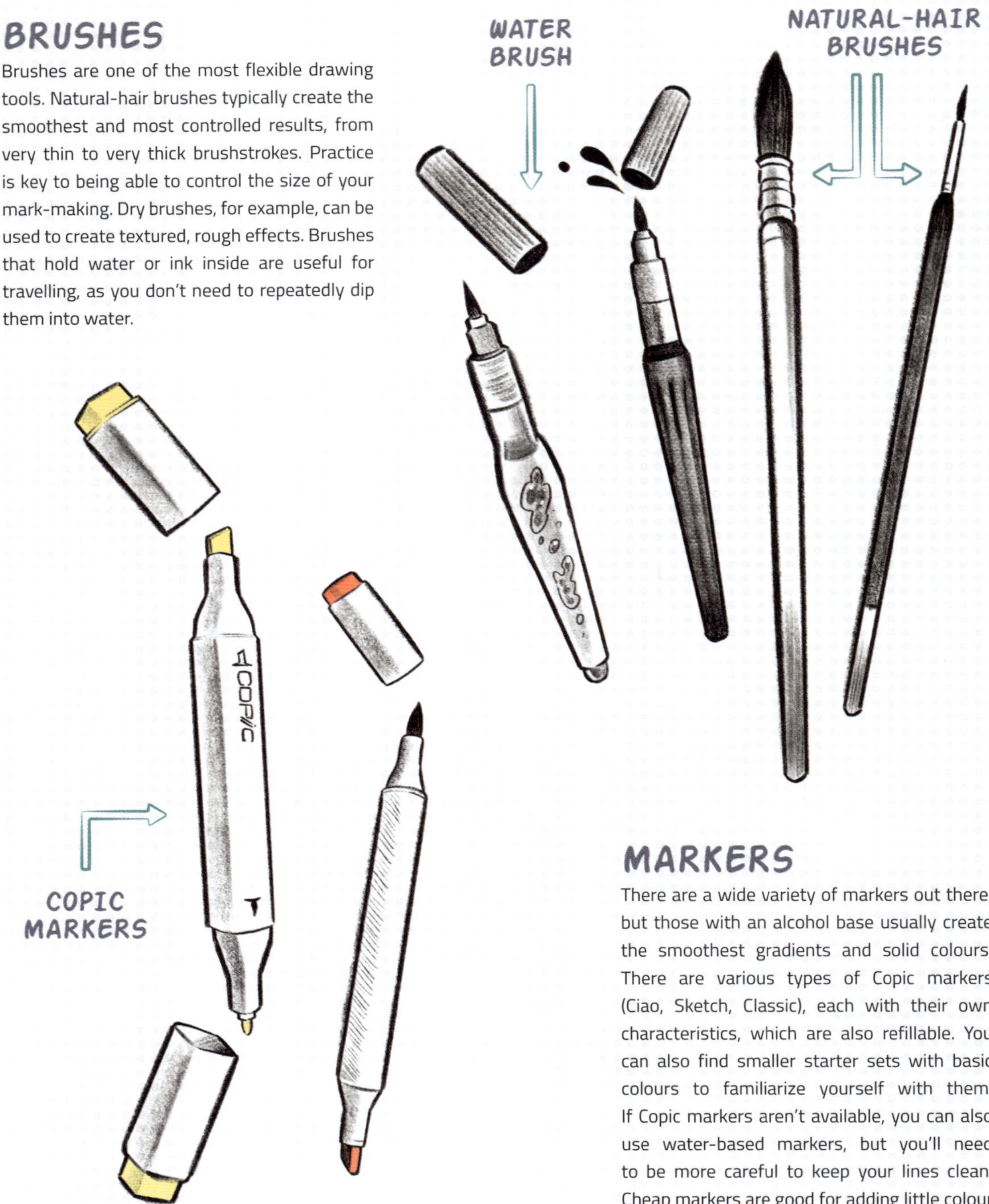

MARKERS

There are a wide variety of markers out there, but those with an alcohol base usually create the smoothest gradients and solid colours. There are various types of Copic markers (Ciao, Sketch, Classic), each with their own characteristics, which are also refillable. You can also find smaller starter sets with basic colours to familiarize yourself with them. If Copic markers aren't available, you can also use water-based markers, but you'll need to be more careful to keep your lines clean. Cheap markers are good for adding little colour accents in sketchbooks.

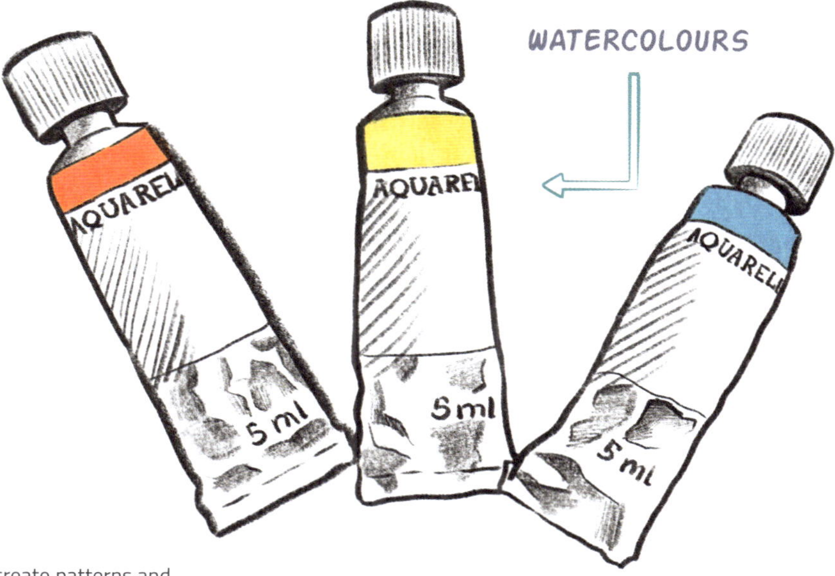

PAINTS

Watercolours allow you to create patterns and gradients by mixing colours and adding water. You can produce unique textures by combining wet and dry brush techniques. For an opaquer result, you can try acrylics, poster colours, and gouache. These provide more vibrant pigments and create solid shapes. Mixing gouache or poster colours with more water can make them behave similarly to watercolours, making them a flexible tool to have in your toolkit.

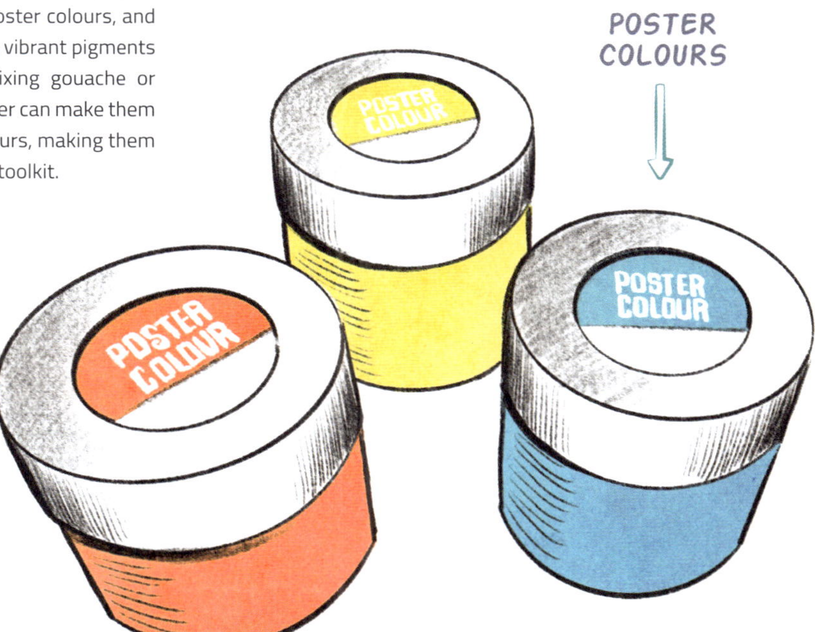

SCREEN TONE

Most manga is printed in black and white to save on printing costs, so screen tone is used for shading and applying different textures, effects, and patterns. A physical screen-tone sheet contains pre-printed patterns or textures that can be transferred onto your paper by sticking it down, rubbing the back, and peeling off the backing layer – like a T-shirt transfer. This process can be quite exhausting and expensive, so a cheap alternative is to use digital screen tone in software such as Clip Studio Paint.

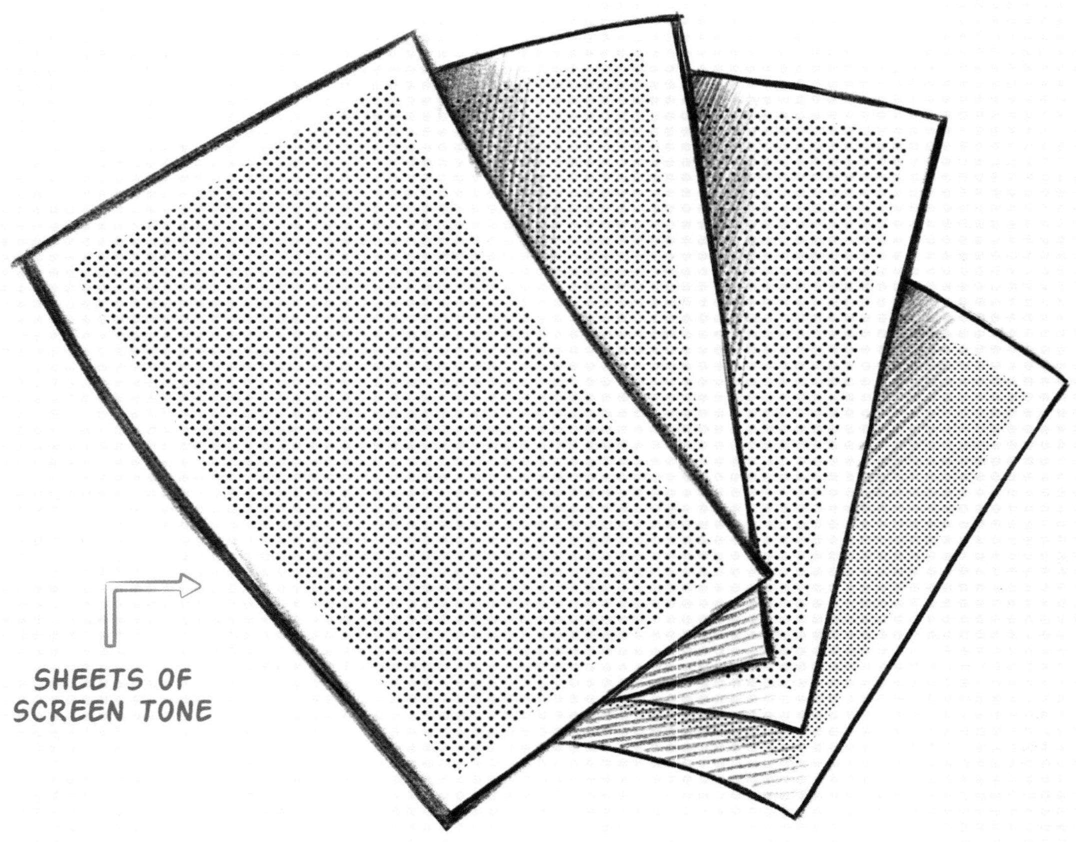

SHEETS OF
SCREEN TONE

PEN TABLETS

Nowadays there are many pen tablets and pen displays available at different prices. A pen tablet doesn't have its own screen, so needs to be used with a computer. A pen display has its own screen onto which you can draw directly. While Wacom is the most expensive brand, popular with many professionals, a small, cheap pen tablet is a good way to start. This will allow you to familiarize yourself with digital drawing before considering display tablets. You don't need the fanciest tools for digital painting – take it one step at a time!

CLIP STUDIO PAINT

Clip Studio Paint is a great program for beginners and professionals alike. It has all the tools you need to create illustrations and comics, plus the brush engine has a great intuitive feeling. (There are even some animation tools too!) It works well on most computers, tablets, and phones. You might want to experiment with free alternatives, such as Krita, before purchasing a paid program. Or Clip Studio Paint do offer free trials for three or six months, depending on your operating system.

PENCIL TECHNIQUES

The pencil is a good basic starting tool, allowing you to create smooth and clean or rough, textured lines. As pencils are often only used for loose sketches that are later erased when the line work is drawn over the top with pen, these sketches don't need to be especially pretty. Exploratory sketches are a good way to quickly capture ideas to use later. You can also use pencils to try out different shading techniques for a final illustration.

TECHNIQUES

- ▶ Line weight
- ▶ Blending
- ▶ Smudging

LINE WEIGHT

A hard wooden pencil or mechanical pencil can be used to create thin steady lines that don't smear easily, which are ideal for producing a clean initial sketch. You can then vary the line weight with a thicker and softer pencil to create a more dynamic drawing. Make use of this technique when working on pencil illustrations to create a variety of interesting and contrasting lines. Your sketches don't need to stay clean – wild lines can convey a lot of emotion.

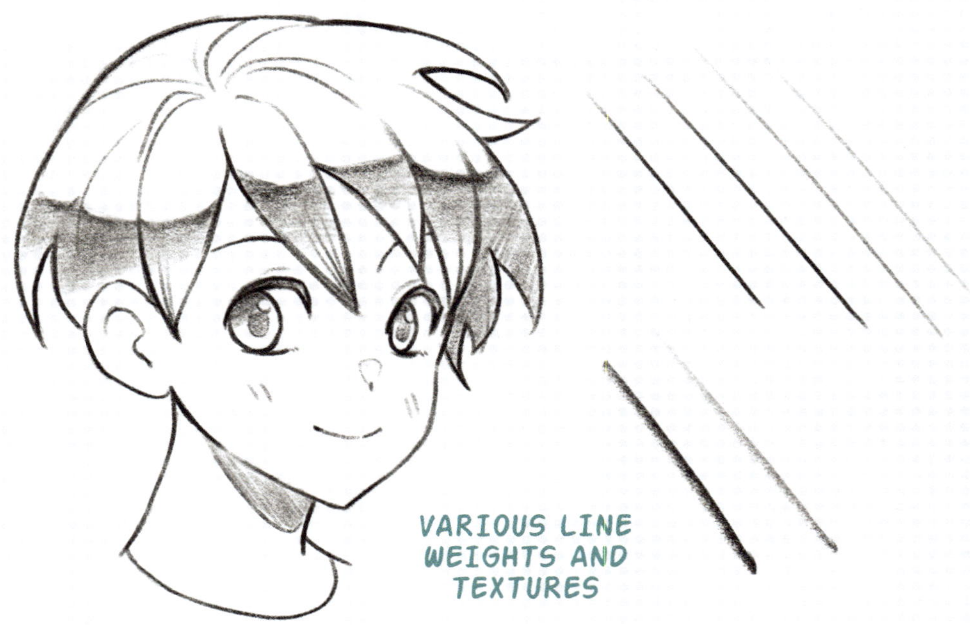

VARIOUS LINE WEIGHTS AND TEXTURES

BLENDING

Coloured pencils can be blended to create somewhat smooth transitions that have organic textures. By tilting the pencil you can create wider, softer lines, which combine to create visually pleasing gradients. Using different line weights can further increase or decrease the intensity of the colours. Cross-hatching is another way of blending pencil lines, producing a rougher transition and texture. Experiment with different techniques and see which best suit your drawings.

SMUDGING

If you want to create soft transitions, you can try smudging the pencil strokes with your fingertip. This also works well with charcoal and chalk pastels. Practise creating a steady, gradual smudge to avoid unintentional stains. You may not want to use this technique if you're using pencil as a base for a pen drawing, as the pen ink won't sit well on top of the smudging.

BLENDING

CROSS-HATCHING

SMUDGING

PEN TECHNIQUES

Pens can be used to create dynamic lines to convey drama, or to produce thin, precise lines for small details. They allow for a range of interesting hatching techniques and can create texture too. Even if your goal is a coloured illustration, manga-style drawings often have crisp, expressive line work, drawn with pen. What's more, traditional manga is often printed in black and white, so pen techniques are some of the most important skills to learn.

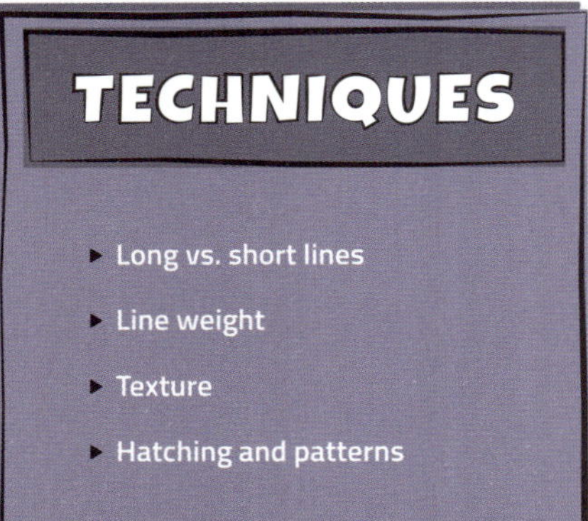

TECHNIQUES

- ▶ Long vs. short lines
- ▶ Line weight
- ▶ Texture
- ▶ Hatching and patterns

LONG VS. SHORT LINES

Practise creating long, confident pen strokes, as these can hold a lot of energy. Long lines can make your drawing look more professional; short ones can often look like the artist was hesitant and uncertain. Instead of going back and applying line after line, try to be confident and decisive. Of course, short strokes can be a stylistic choice if the situation requires it, but you must first learn how to use the length of your lines with purpose.

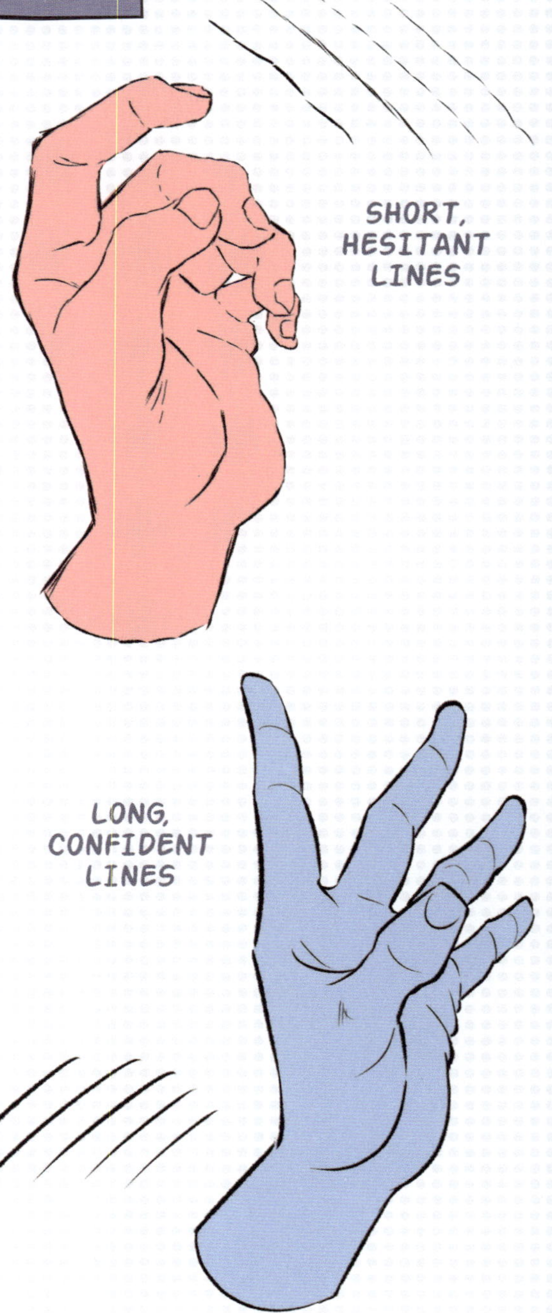

LINE WEIGHT

As with pencil, pen allows you to create a variety of line sizes by applying weight to your drawing hand. Very soft tools, such as brushes and nib pens, enable you to produce a vast variety of line weights. The lines you create can be dynamic, wild, and very expressive. It's good to practise controlling the line weight to enable you to use it with purpose. However, it can also be a stylistic choice to completely avoid line weight and stick with consistently steady lines. You often see this in animation, as it allows the artists to focus on the movement they're drawing instead.

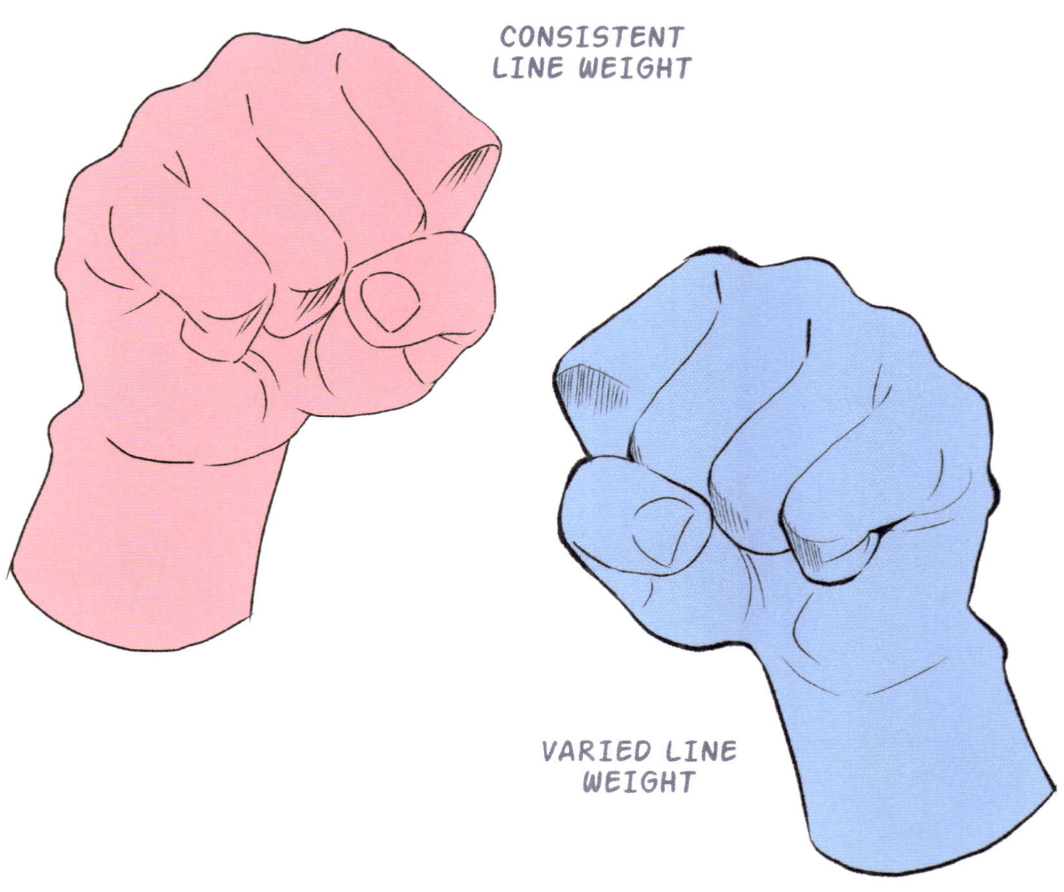

TEXTURE

Wet and dry brush pens can be used to create jagged or flowing texture for dramatic effect, or to add texture to clothes, environments, or even a character's face. Purposeful use of this technique can appear bold and expressive, but don't overuse it or you risk lessening the effect, and it could even be seen as messy and clumsy. Textured brush-pen technique is especially good for capturing organic forms such as hair or plants, as they don't need to be perfect.

HATCHING & PATTERNS

Creating patterns with your lines is a common technique for black-and-white images, but may also be used with colour. There are many variations of hatching that can be used to create a textured gradient, or to give clothes and background elements an organic feel. Hatching usually requires a very fine tool to create thin, delicate lines. As it uses short, quick strokes, it can be quite strenuous on the wrist, so be careful not to overdo it.

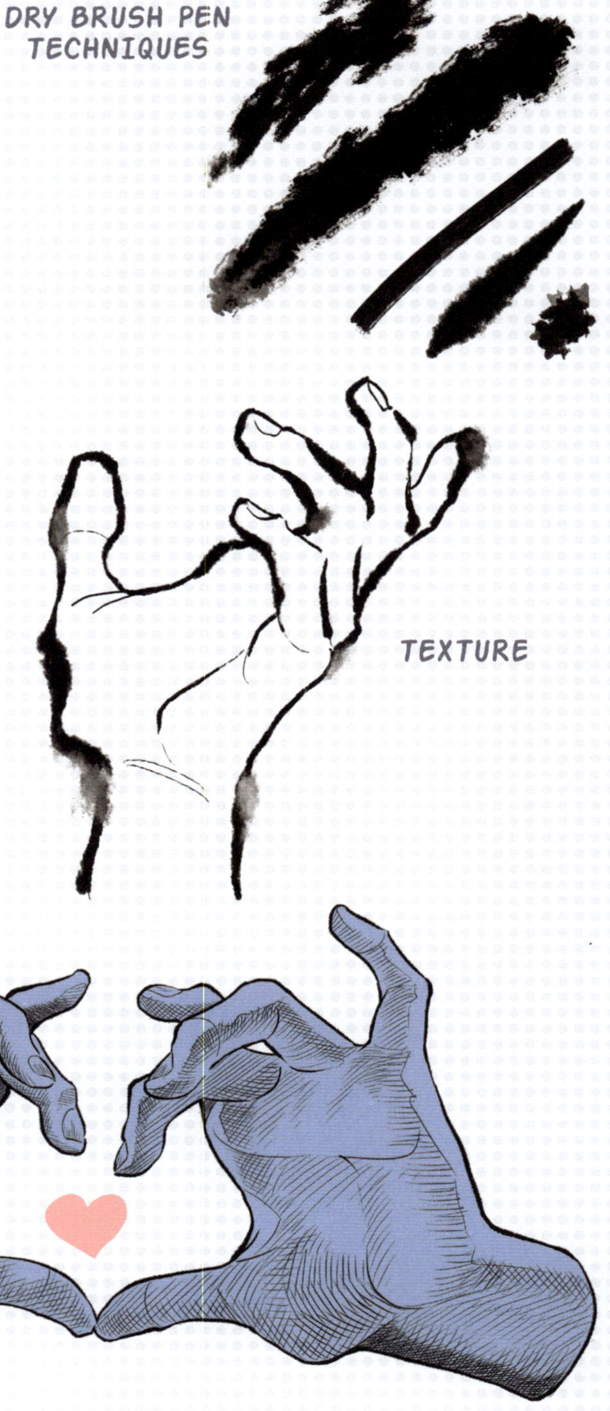

DIGITAL DRAWING IN CLIP STUDIO PAINT

Digital drawing can simplify and speed up the artistic process. Rather than having to scan your drawings into the computer, you can create them directly on the screen. Another advantage is that you don't need to refill your tools or buy new paper or ink. Software such as Clip Studio Paint provides all the tools you would ever want to use ... and more! This can be a little overwhelming at first, so take your time getting to know all that the program has to offer.

When creating artwork in digital software, you draw on layers. This allows you to easily separate your sketch, line work, and colours, enabling you to edit each layer without affecting the others. Once you've understood that concept, you can experiment with Clip Studio Paint's various preset brushes or try out the countless custom brushes you can find on the internet. The software also offers an assortment of useful rulers and effects, as well as helpful references with 3D models. Enjoy exploring what digital shortcuts are available to help you on your art journey.

If you want to print your artwork, you should draw at a minimum of 300 dpi for coloured illustrations and approximately 1200 dpi for monochrome artwork (such as manga pages). The bigger your canvas, the better the quality will be. When you upload your artwork to the internet, however, you can size it down to 72 dpi.

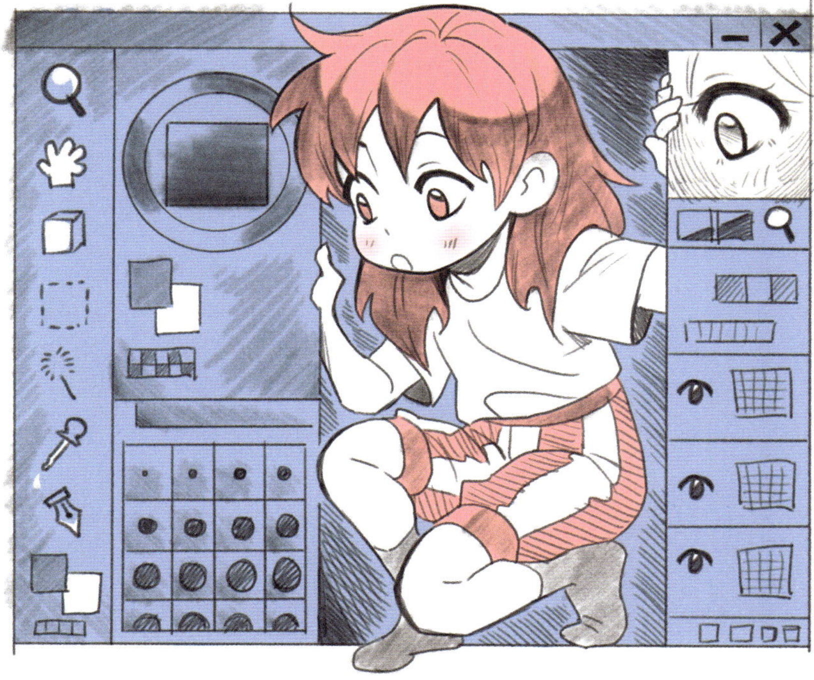

TAKE SOME TIME TO FAMILIARIZE YOURSELF WITH THE CLIP STUDIO PAINT INTERFACE

LIGHT & SHADOW

An attractive element of manga drawings is their ability to 'pop' and stand out. This can be achieved not only through using the right colours (see page 30), but also by paying attention to light and shadow. If you remove the colours from your drawing, what's left are called 'values'. These are the different shades from black to white. You need to learn how to control values with whichever style you decide to paint in. Even when adding colour, the light plays a big role in how you shade, creating several different types of transition and shadow. This section will explore a few useful scenarios to demonstrate how light can affect the drawing.

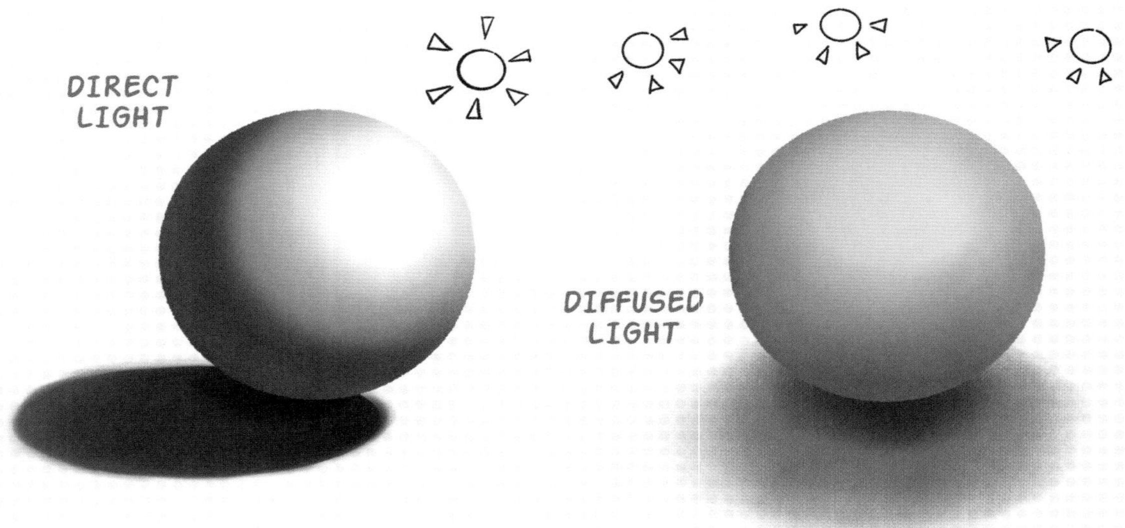

DIRECT LIGHT

A direct spotlight, such as direct sunlight, creates a clear line between light and shadow. Though it's rarely the sole light source, it's the strongest one and creates a bold image. Sometimes the lit area can seem almost white. There might be lighter areas within the shadow, caused by the reflected light all around the object. Due to the high contrast, direct light is a popular light source when drawing manga, as it allows you to create dark, crisp shadows and to use the lighting to tell a story.

DIFFUSED LIGHT

Diffused light comes from many directions and is generally weaker than a direct light source. While direct light creates hard edges where the shadows start, diffused light produces a very soft transition and rounds out the forms. This can create a much gentler image. An overcast rainy day creates a perfect diffused lighting situation where colours aren't affected by strong sunlight and can be seen in a more neutral situation.

WARM & COLD LIGHT

In addition to intensity, light can also have temperature. If opting for a warm light, giving the shadows a cooler tone will make for a more pleasant image. Conversely, if using a cool light, try introducing warmer shadows. Perceived light temperature during a sunny day with a clear sky might be cooler than during a sunset or campfire. Light and colour temperature can also be a matter of perspective and should be compared to the surroundings to make a definite judgement.

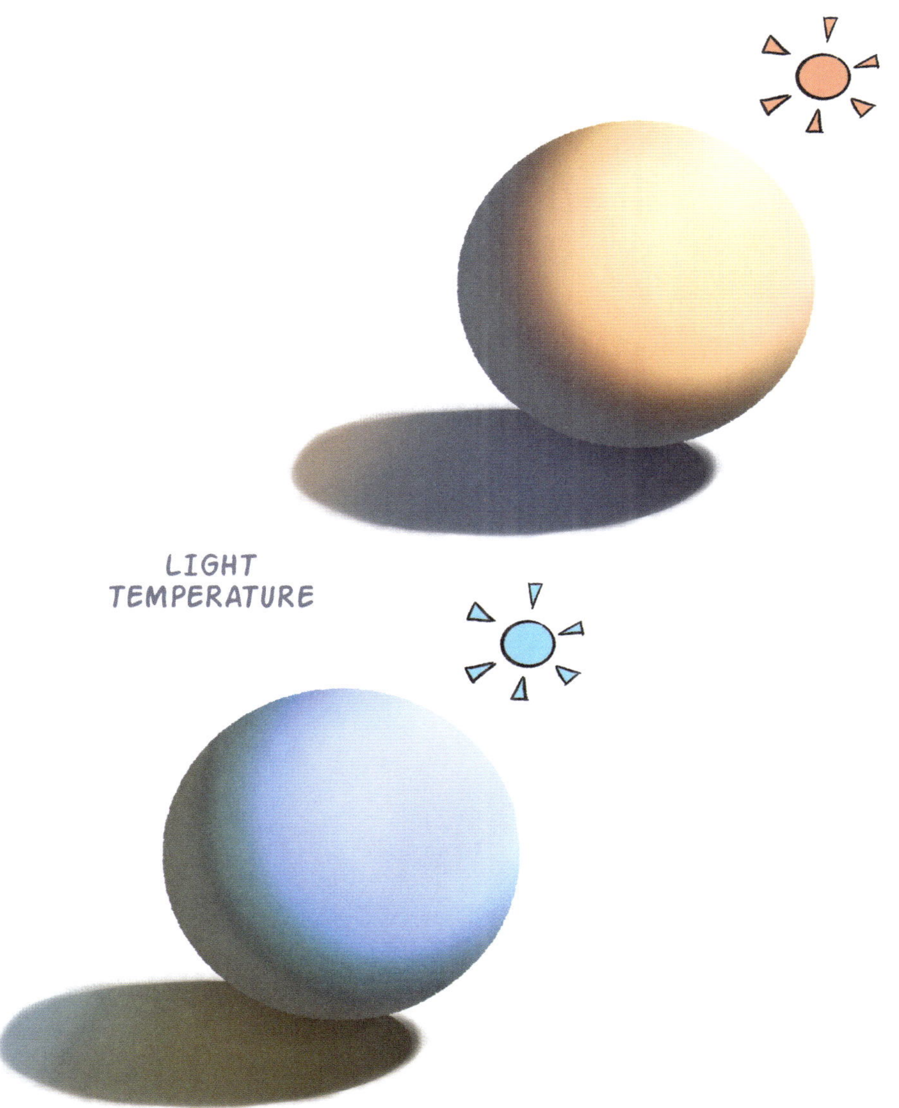

COLOUR THEORY & SYMBOLISM

Different colours have different meanings and can be used to create specific moods. Depending on culture, knowledge, and background, colours can mean different things to different people, but there are general themes that can be drawn. While the mood and personality you want to create can help you to choose colours, how do you know which colours work well together? This is where colour theory can help.

COLOUR WHEEL

The colour wheel allows you to see the relationships between colours. One half of the colour wheel is made up of warmer colours, while the other half contains cooler colours. There is also the hierarchy of the three core **primary** colours, followed by the colours that are created by mixing them together to create **secondary** and **tertiary** colours. When choosing a colour palette for your manga artwork, it's a good idea to first decide on a dominant colour. You can then explore the relationships it has with other colours on the wheel.

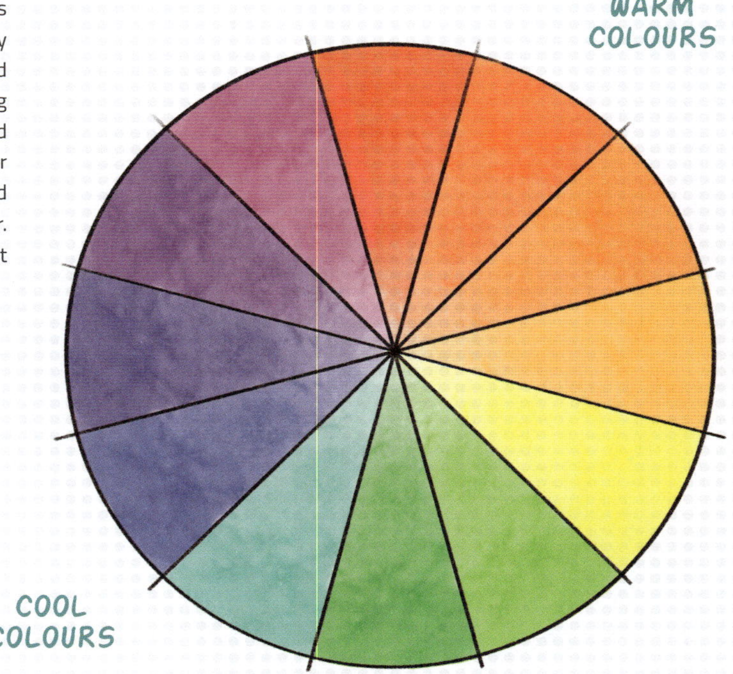

COLOUR HARMONY

Instead of choosing colours randomly, take the time to learn various colour harmonies that work well together. The more colours you want to include in a palette, the more careful you need to be when choosing. Made up of similar colours, **monochrome** is the easiest colour scheme to work with, but risks looking a little boring. **Analogous** describes three colours that sit adjacent to one another on the colour wheel, so you can already see how they work together. **Complementary** colours sit on opposite sides of colour wheel and contrast with one another. **Triadic** palettes are made up of three colours evenly spaced around the colour wheel, while **tetradic** combines four colours, again evenly spaced around the wheel.

MONOCHROME

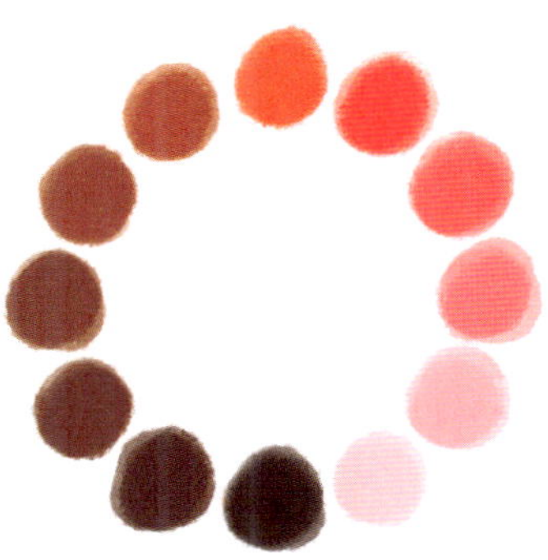

ANALOGOUS

COMPLEMENTARY

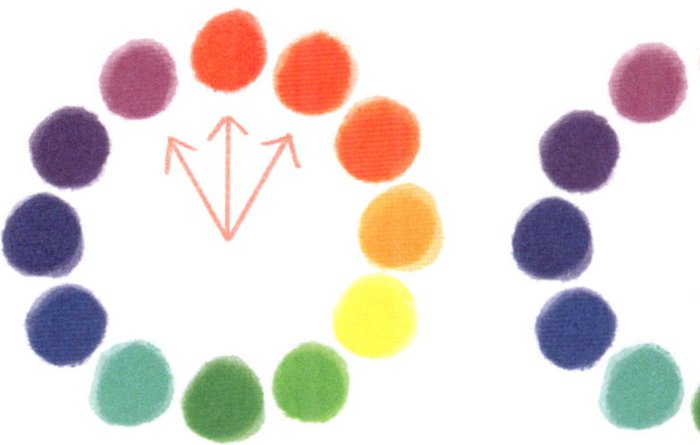

TRIADIC

TETRADIC

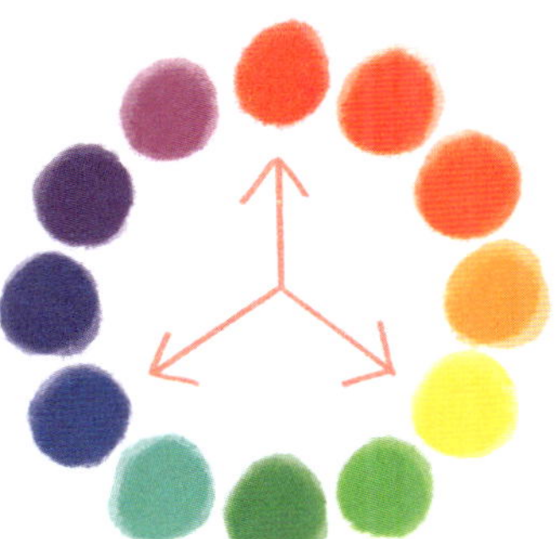

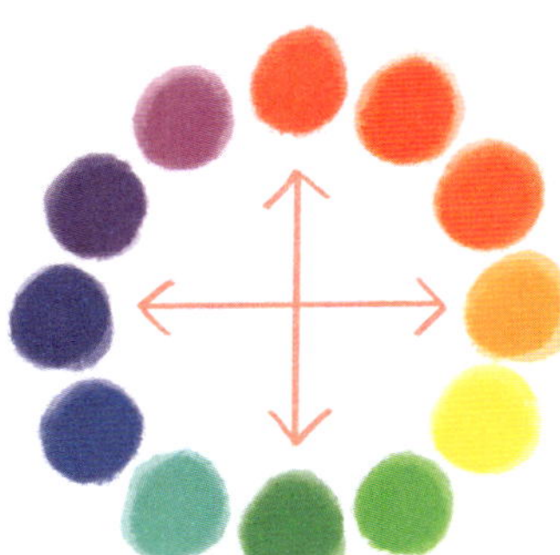

GREYS

If you find that none of your chosen colours look good together, even though you've tried using the harmonious colour schemes listed above, another approach is to choose one dominant colour and tone the other colours down to greys. Combining vibrant colours with grey tones can make the vibrant colours pop even more, whereas too many saturated colours can compete for attention. As grey is a neutral colour, it will not compete in the same way, but can provide a pleasing balance.

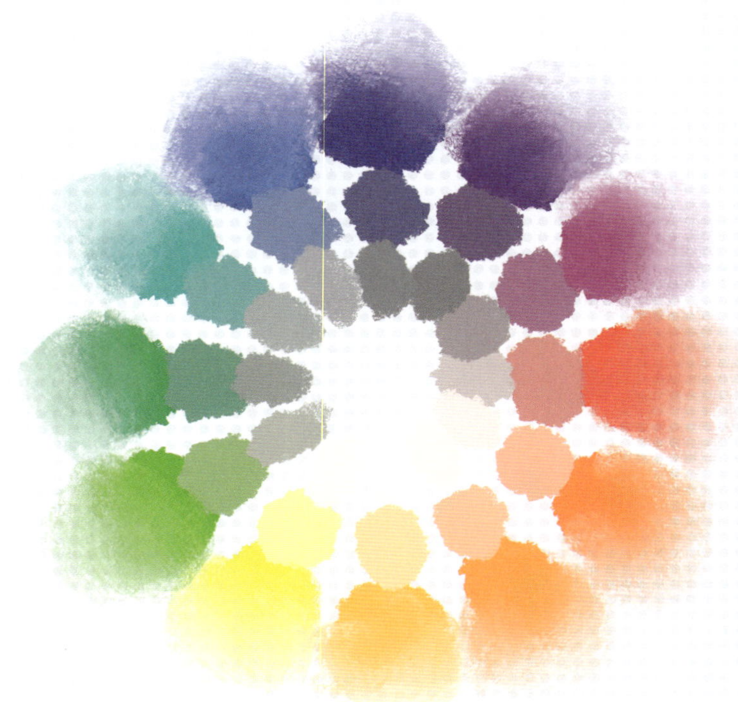

SYMBOLISM

RED

One of the three primary colours, red is very powerful and recognizable. It has both positive and negative uses. It can symbolize danger, aggression, anger, dominance, and power. Conversely, it can also be used to convey excitement, romance, passion, and love.

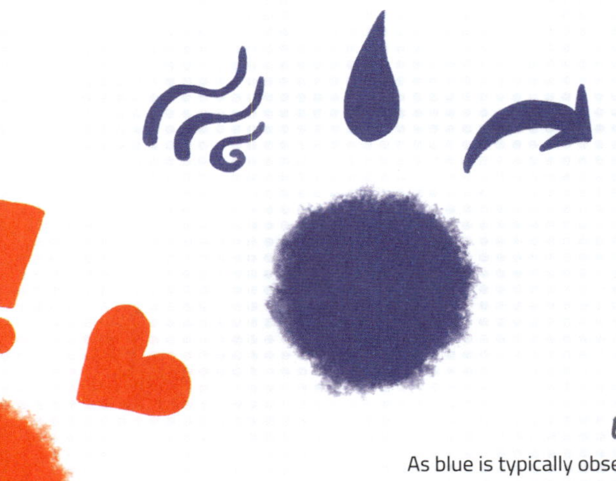

BLUE

As blue is typically observed in water and the sky, it often has a calming effect. It can also conjure moods that are sad and melancholic, or clean, calming, quiet, and serene.

YELLOW

Yellow is an easily recognizable colour that is often used for warning or danger signs. Its brightness can also remind you of a sunny day and can convey optimism, happiness, and energy.

PURPLE

Purple is rarely found in nature, which is why historically it often symbolized royalty, nobility, and wealth. It can also be used to convey wisdom, mystery, magic, and spirituality.

GREEN

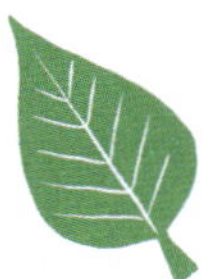

As green can be found all around us in nature, it has a fresh, organic feeling, symbolizing new beginnings and growth. However, it can also be used to symbolize jealousy and envy.

NEUTRAL COLOURS

Beige, grey, brown, black, and white are considered neutral colours and can convey a natural, simple, and calm look. They can work well in combination with more vibrant colours, allowing brighter shades to stand out.

BLACK & WHITE

Black is often used interchangeably with darkness and can convey a range of meanings, from sadness and mourning to elegance, sophistication, and formality. Meanwhile, white is the lightest shade and is often associated with purity, cleanliness, simplicity, and innocence.

ADDING COLOUR USING TRADITIONAL TOOLS

There are a range of different ways to apply colour that can produce a variety of results. Manga-style illustrations often use the cel-shading colouring technique typically seen in anime. This is where solid colour is applied to individual shapes to save time and resources, making the objects appear flatter, but also stylized and iconic.

Coloured pencils and watercolours provide an alternative approach, allowing you to create soft transitions and gradients for a more rounded and rendered look. Both methods have their merits.

OPAQUE SHADING

Creating solid forms with opaque materials, such as acrylics, poster colours, or gouache, can achieve a bold, eye-catching result. As it's opaque, keep in mind that using traditional media for this style requires a steady hand. Keeping it simple will help you to create a bold and expressive image; other than the flat colours, you don't want to busy the illustration with too much information. This allows you to concentrate more on the line work and overall design. Mistakes are fairly easy to fix with the opaque shading technique, as you can simply apply more colour on top.

▶ Opaque shading with gouache before the line work is added

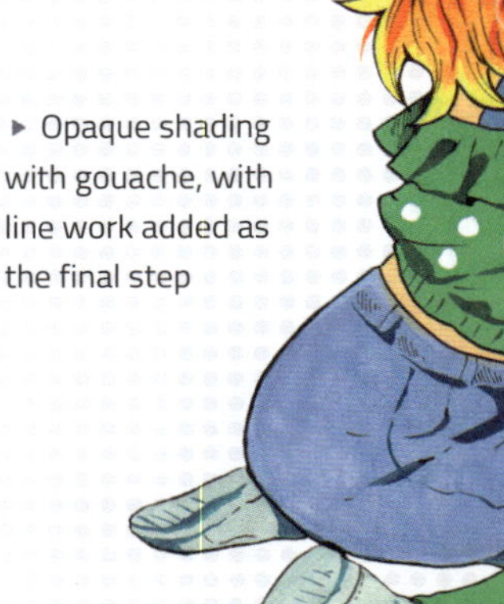

▶ Opaque shading with gouache, with line work added as the final step

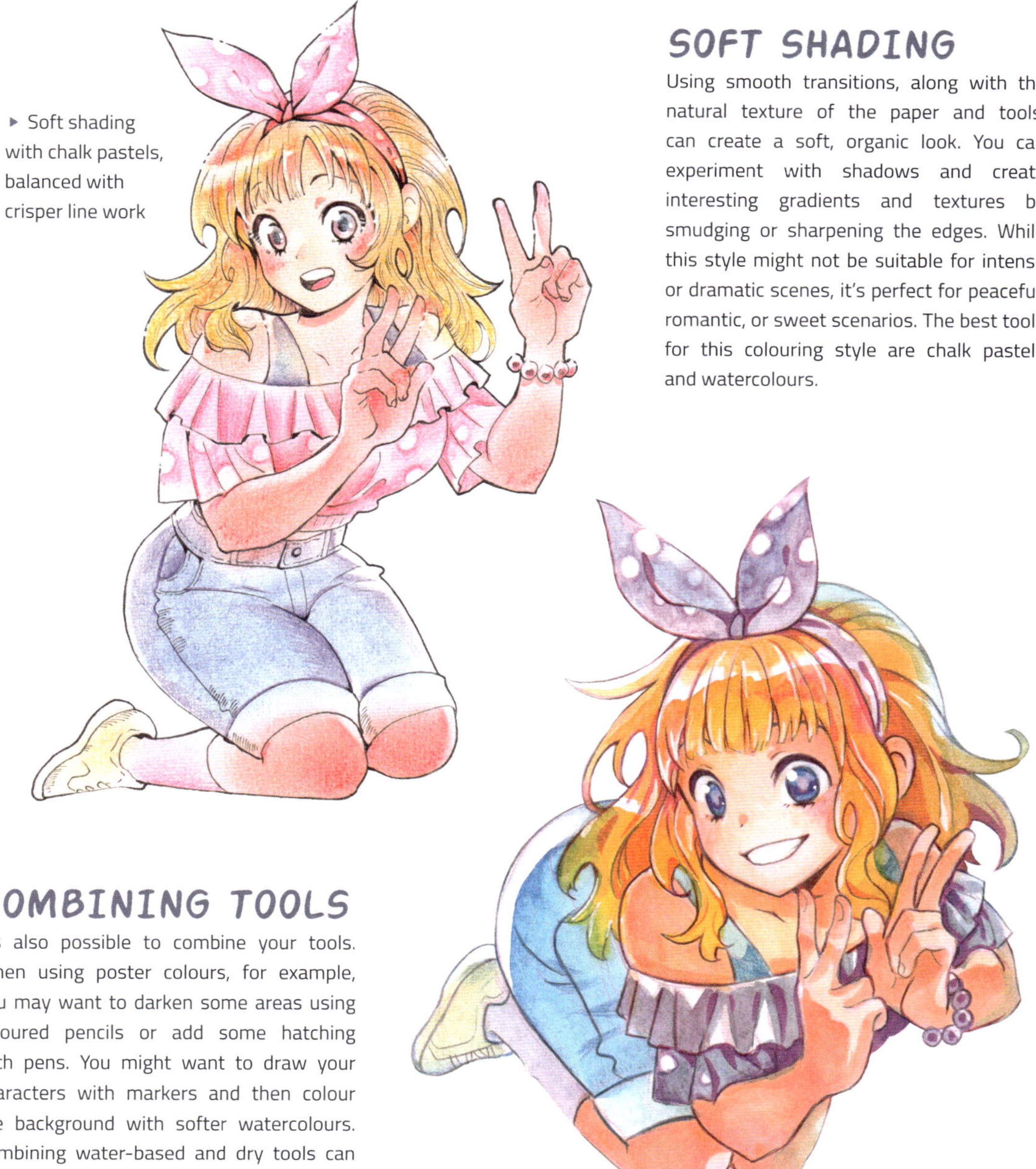

▶ Soft shading with chalk pastels, balanced with crisper line work

SOFT SHADING

Using smooth transitions, along with the natural texture of the paper and tools, can create a soft, organic look. You can experiment with shadows and create interesting gradients and textures by smudging or sharpening the edges. While this style might not be suitable for intense or dramatic scenes, it's perfect for peaceful, romantic, or sweet scenarios. The best tools for this colouring style are chalk pastels and watercolours.

COMBINING TOOLS

It's also possible to combine your tools. When using poster colours, for example, you may want to darken some areas using coloured pencils or add some hatching with pens. You might want to draw your characters with markers and then colour the background with softer watercolours. Combining water-based and dry tools can create an interesting texture, but make sure to test out how well the tools work together on a spare piece of paper first, or invest in paper specifically designed for mixed media.

▶ A combination of Copic markers and watercolours, plus a little gouache – the line work consists of simple pencil lines, strengthened by coloured pencils

ADDING COLOUR IN CLIP STUDIO PAINT

Digital tools are useful for speeding up the colouring process. You don't need to prepare your brushes, mix colours, and clean up afterwards. When drawing digitally, everything is ready for you on the screen. This might seem overwhelming at first, but you can still follow the same colouring techniques discussed for traditional media. While some of them might be easy to recreate digitally, others will lose their traditional texture if you're not careful. The processes differ a little, so you will need to experiment and choose the style suited to the manga character you wish to create.

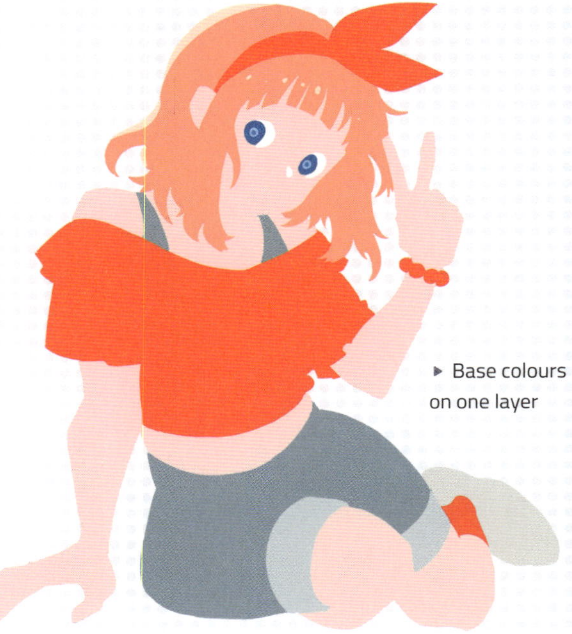

▶ Base colours on one layer

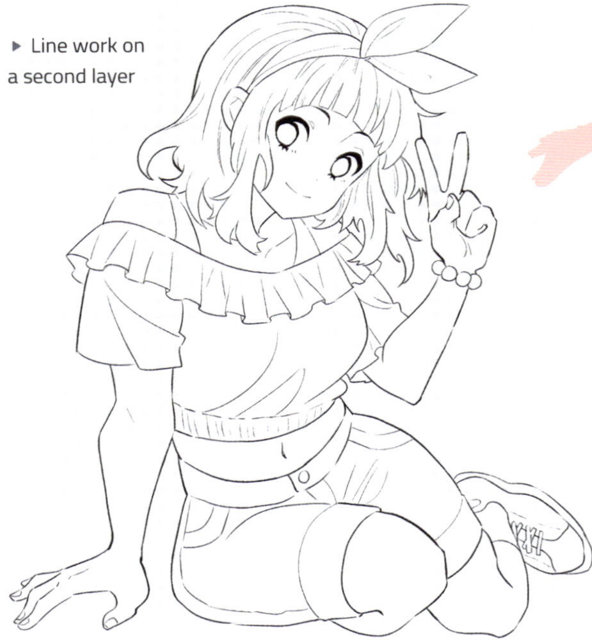

▶ Line work on a second layer

DIGITAL CEL SHADING

With digital cel shading, the Paint Bucket tool will become your best friend. Simply fill the spaces inside your line art with colour and then add shading on a separate layer. This style creates a simple but bold look. You can then combine it with different layer styles or add glowing effects to make it more detailed. Compared to traditional media, cel shading is especially easy to create digitally, as you hardly need to make any brushstrokes.

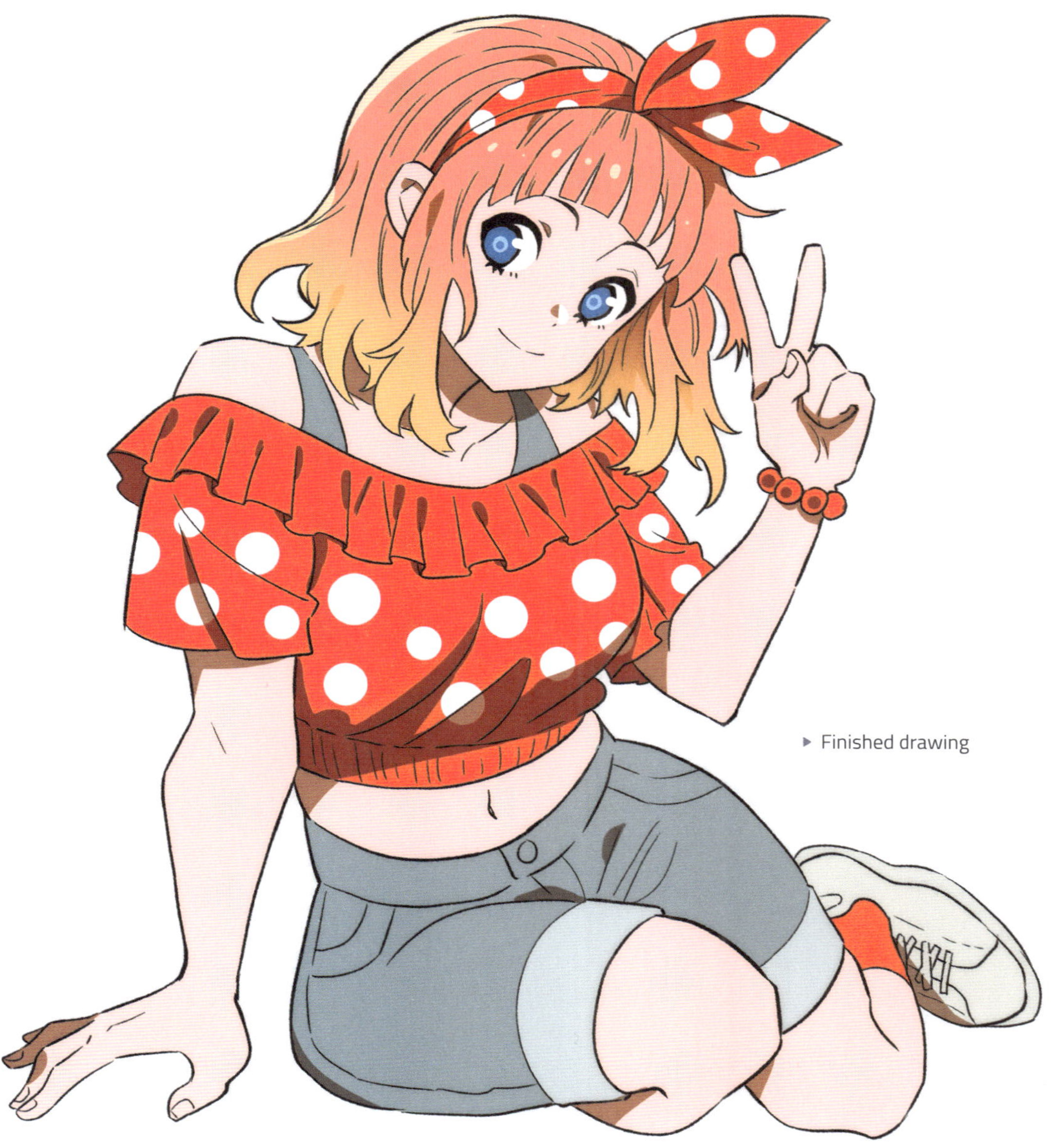

▶ Finished drawing

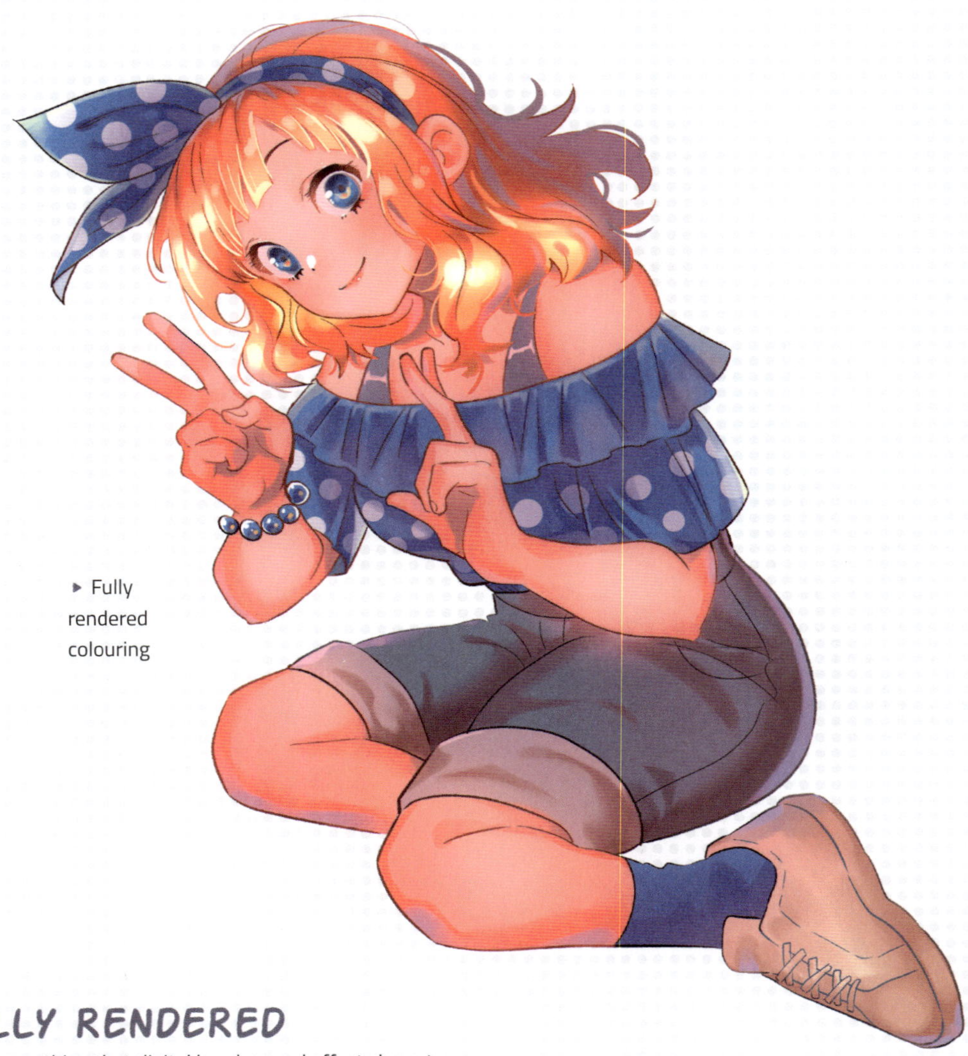

► Fully
rendered
colouring

FULLY RENDERED

Using everything that digital brushes and effects have to offer can create a more painterly or even a photographic look. In animation, it's common to see a combination of painterly backgrounds with cel-shaded characters. In illustration, you might see especially detailed character drawings that look like they might walk out of the screen. Check out speed paintings and drawing-process videos from your favourite manga-style artists to learn their processes.

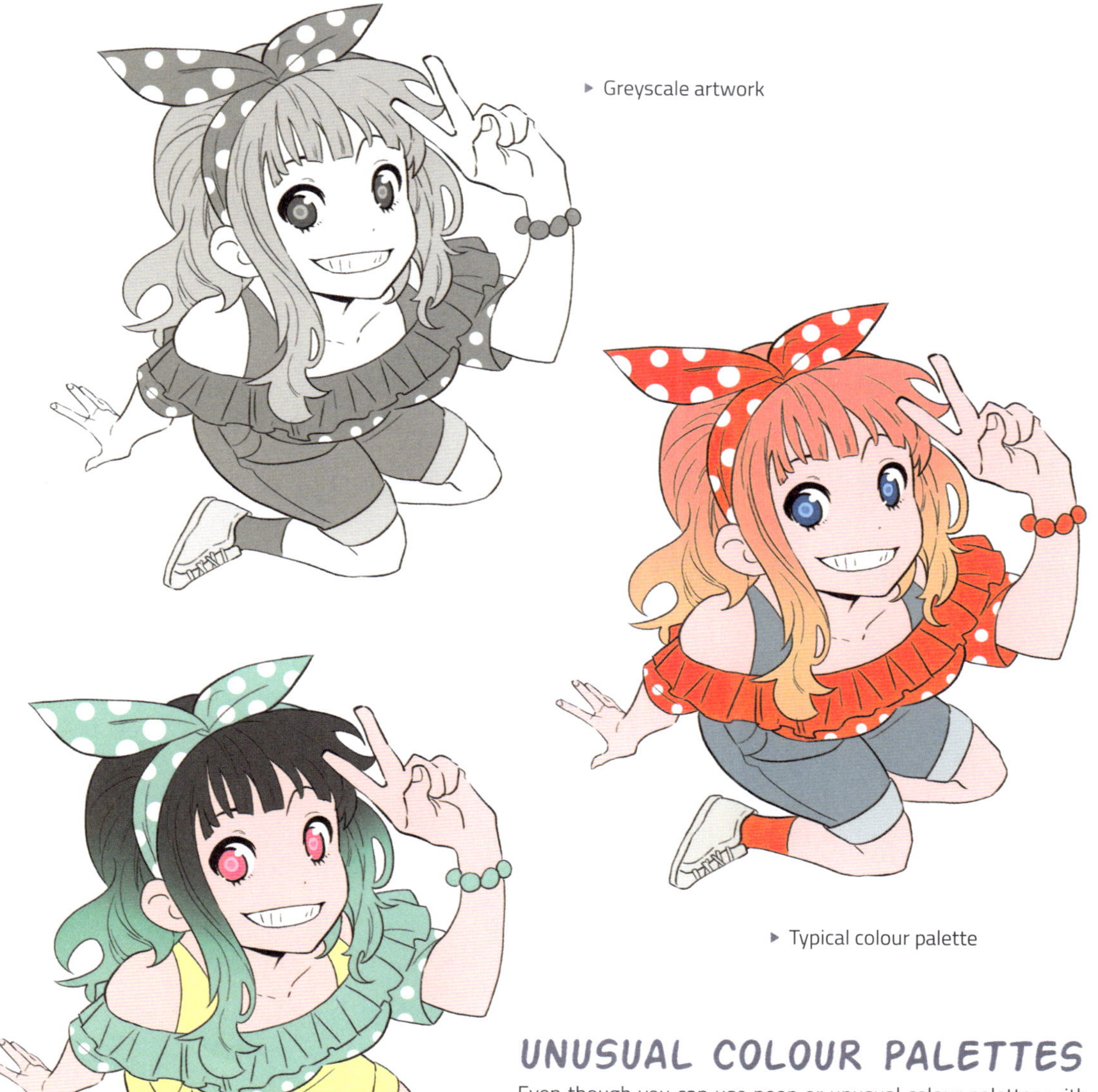

▸ Greyscale artwork

▸ Typical colour palette

▸ Neon colour palette

UNUSUAL COLOUR PALETTES

Even though you can use neon or unusual colour palettes with traditional tools, it's much quicker and easier to experiment in this way when using digital software. You can easily turn a greyscale painting into a coloured image, or choose colours that might be challenging to reproduce in watercolour. Take care when printing your work, as colours can look different on screen than in print. This is because screen displays use the RGB colour mode, but colours are translated to CMYK mode for printing with ink. Always run a few test prints first.

MANGA STYLE BASICS

BY MIYULI

Drawing in the manga style is often about taking something realistic and exaggerating or simplifying it. When it comes to the human figure, you can exaggerate the length of arms and legs, or simplify the shapes of the body so they represent body parts, rather than looking exactly like they do in real life. You can even go as far as 'super deformation', where the body is very different to how it looks in reality, and characters look cute and squishy. This chapter will go into more detail about how to draw characters in the manga style.

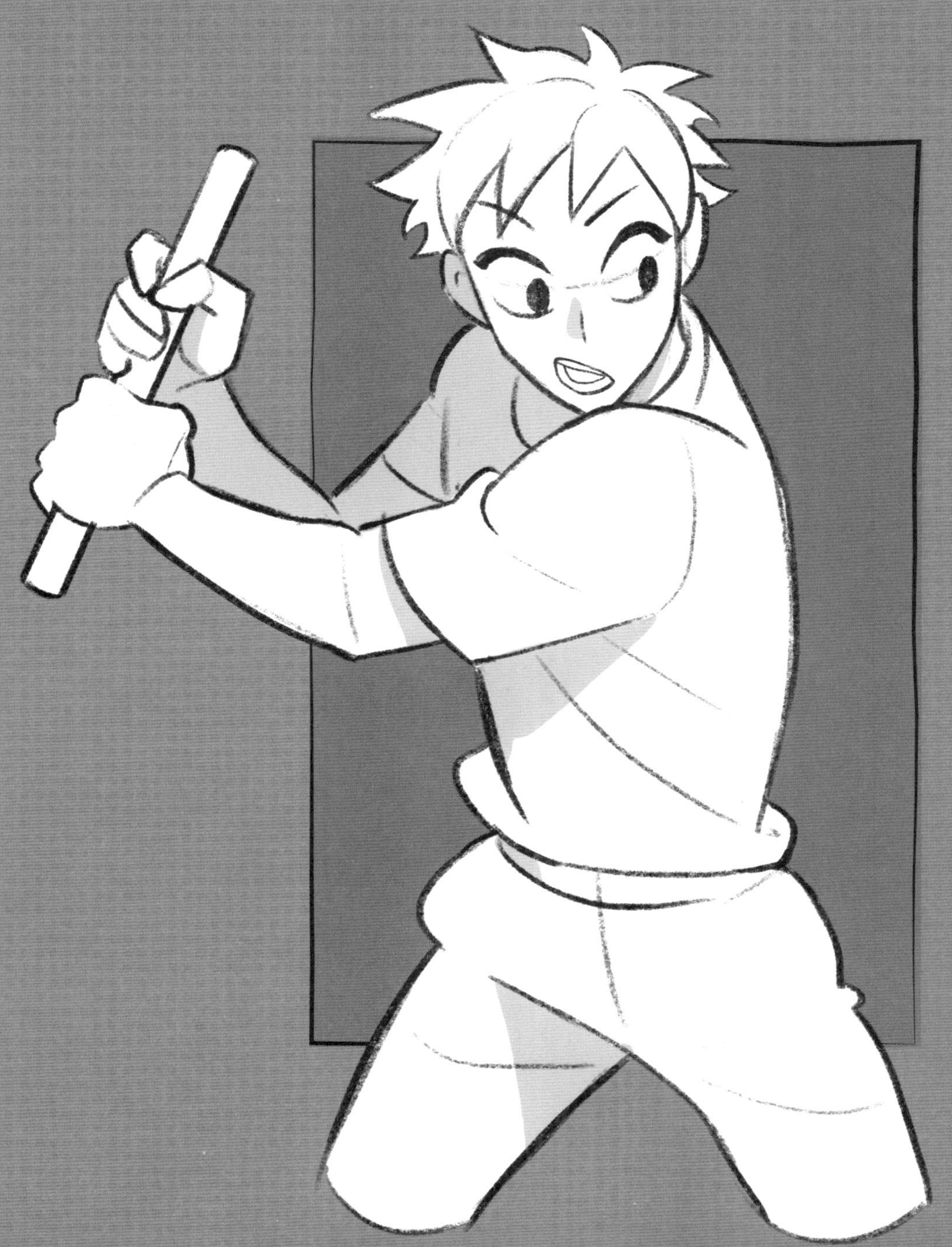

ANATOMY BASICS & BODY TYPES

Drawing a human-like character in a manga style is fairly similar to drawing a character with realistic anatomy. You look at the general body and face proportions of a person, then interpret them in your own style. This is why it's helpful to have a solid understanding of basic anatomy before drawing in a style like manga. Here are some tips to help you on your way.

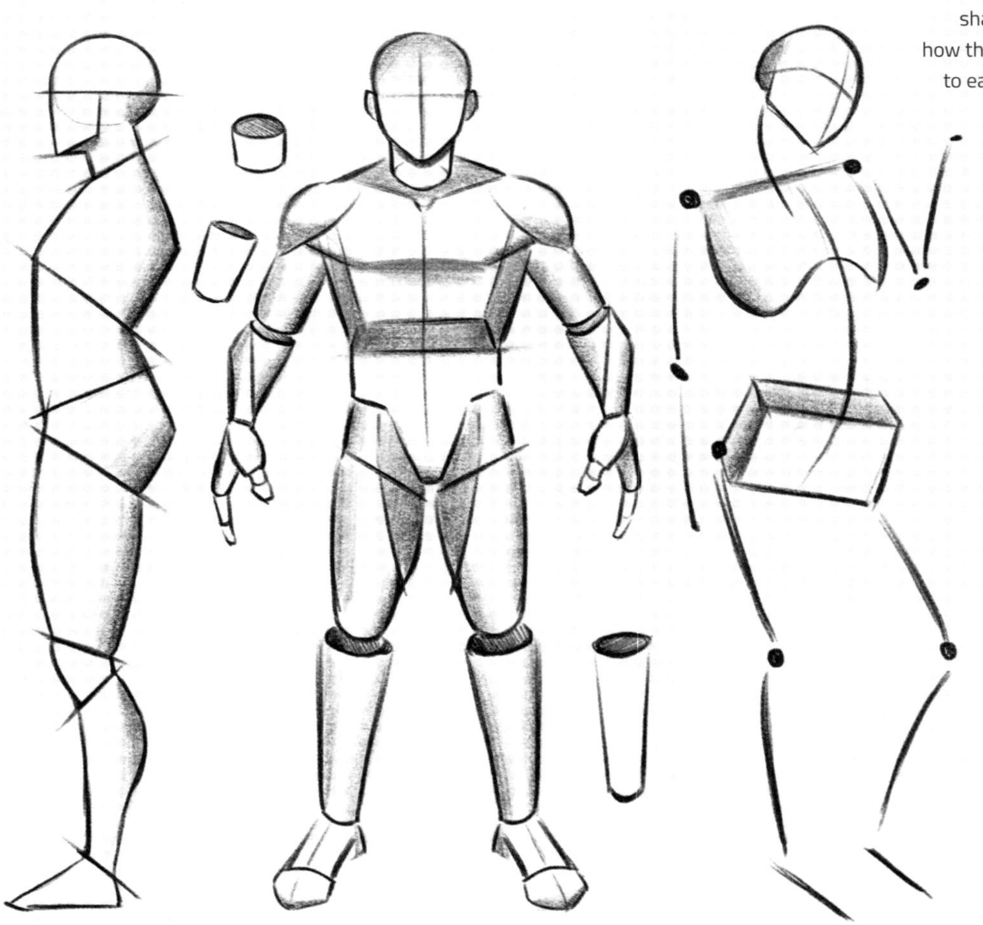

▶ Basic body shapes and how they relate to each other

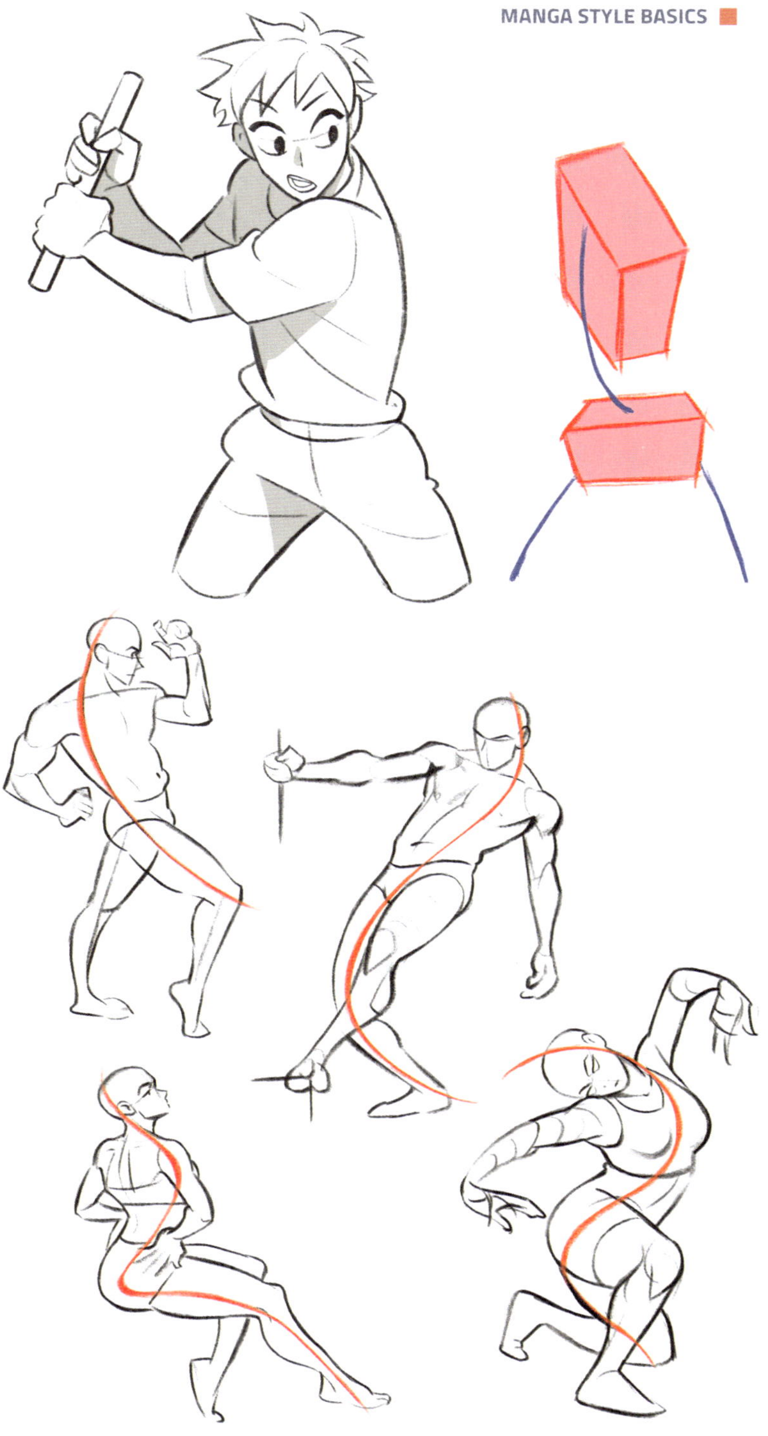

BASIC SHAPES

Human anatomy is pretty complicated, so it's useful to simplify the basic shapes into spheres, boxes, and cylinders to allow your brain to visualize and remember them more easily. It's also important to look at how all of the shapes work together. First, look at where the body parts meet – their tilts and twists balance each other out to create a sturdy and stable form.

Next, observe how the largest body parts, such as the rib cage and the hip area, are connected and interact. These areas are crucial when it comes to movement and balance. Looking at the connection between two specific body parts at a time is an effective way to learn about anatomy.

LINE OF ACTION

It's easy to get a little overwhelmed when focusing on individual elements of the body, so it's a good idea to train your eyes to see the complete picture. The 'line of action' is the body summarized in one dynamic line. It's not necessarily the outline, but the movement you're trying to capture and emphasize. Once you have the line of action in place, you can start to construct the body around it. Silhouettes and posing will be discussed in more detail later, but for now just remember that the body must work as a whole.

MEASURING WITH HEADS

An easy way to judge how tall a character should be is by looking at the height of their head. A very idealized proportional body height is eight times the height of the head, but in reality it's more common to see a body height of six or seven heads. Using the head-height guidelines, you can work out what size to draw each part of a body. The hips are usually in the centre. If your character is seven heads tall, then the torso, including the hips, should be around three and a half heads tall. The legs would be three and a half heads tall, too.

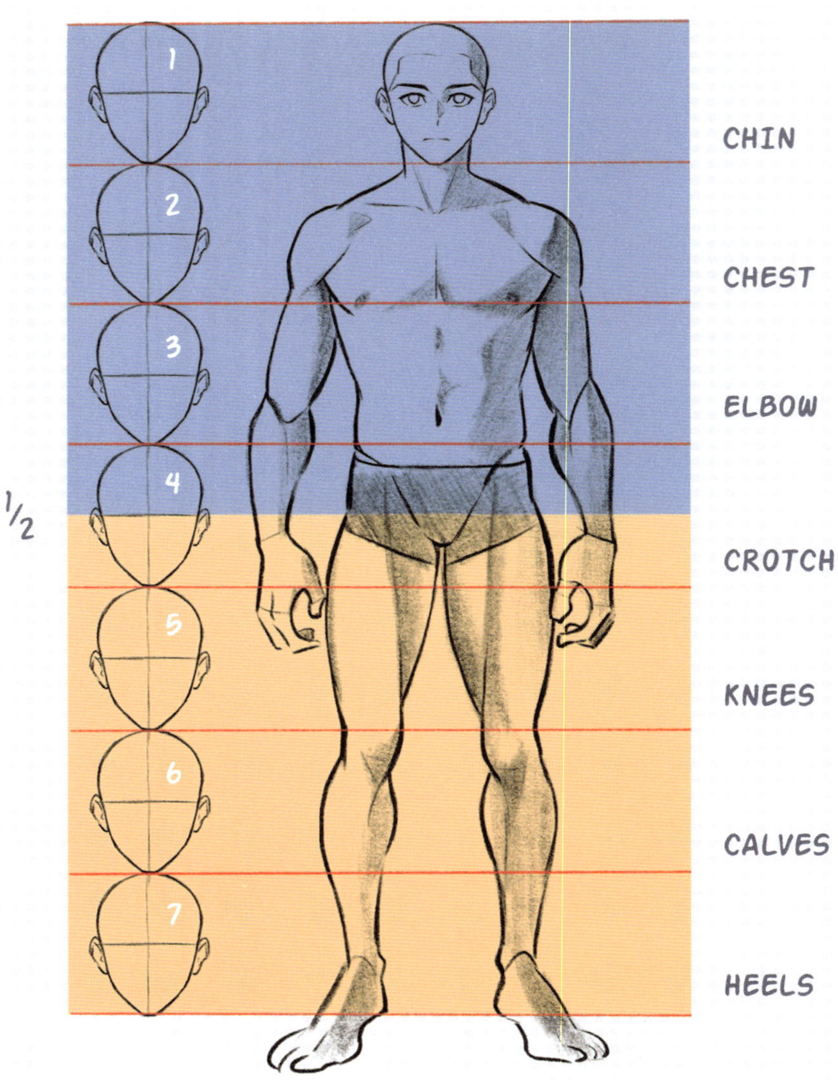

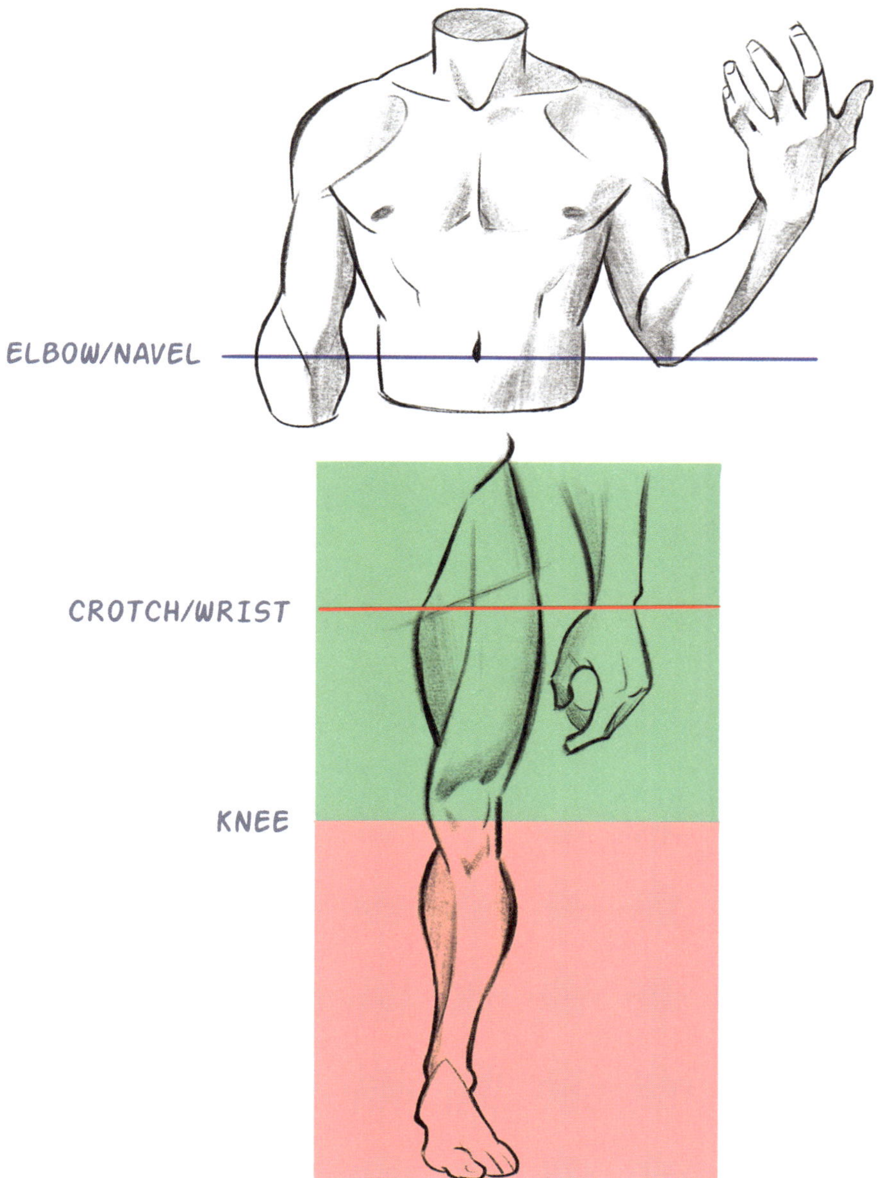

Use landmarks on the body to guide you in how long various body parts should be. For example, the elbows usually come to the same height as the belly button, while the wrists rest at the same height as the crotch. The knee sits halfway between the top of the hip and the bottom of the foot. Looking at the body parts in relation to each other is a great way to study them.

BODY TYPES

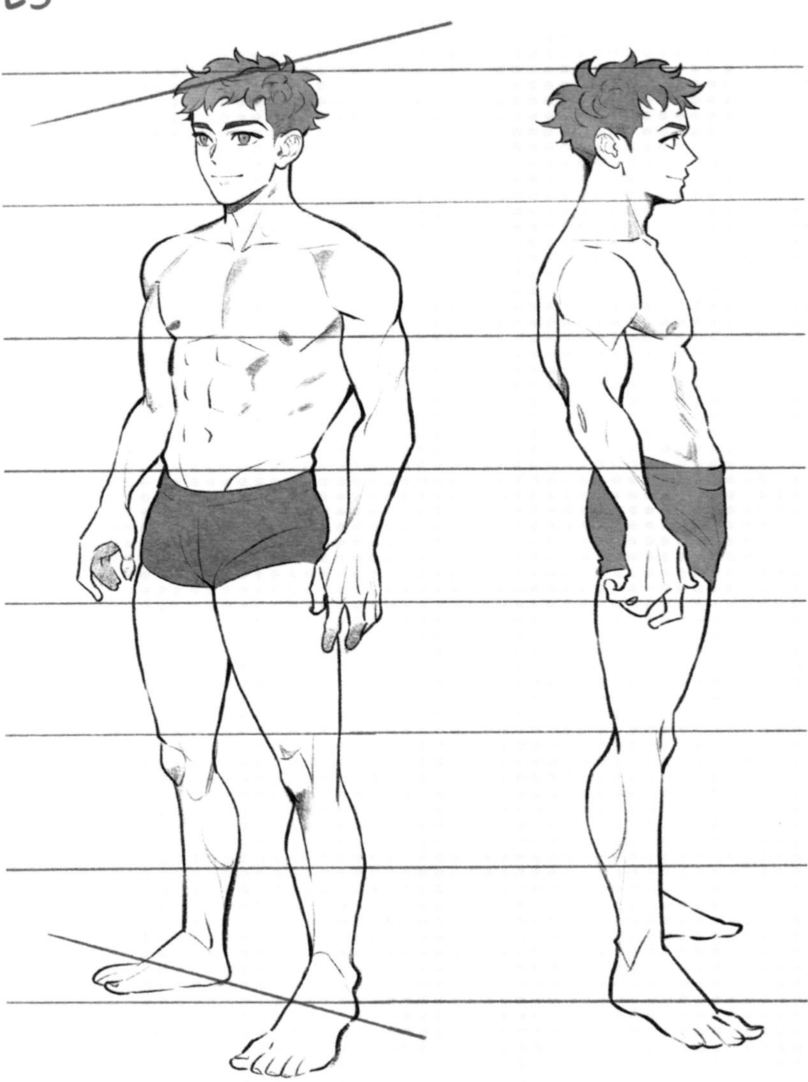

MALE

Typical characteristics found on a male body might include a thicker neck, wider shoulders, and narrower hips. Because of the shoulder and hip width, the arms and legs might face outwards a little. These are generalizations and might not always be the case, of course. Artists tend to emphasize the parts they like, for example making the shoulders wider or the legs longer than you would normally see. You can be flexible with reality, as long as you stay roughly consistent within your own fictional universe.

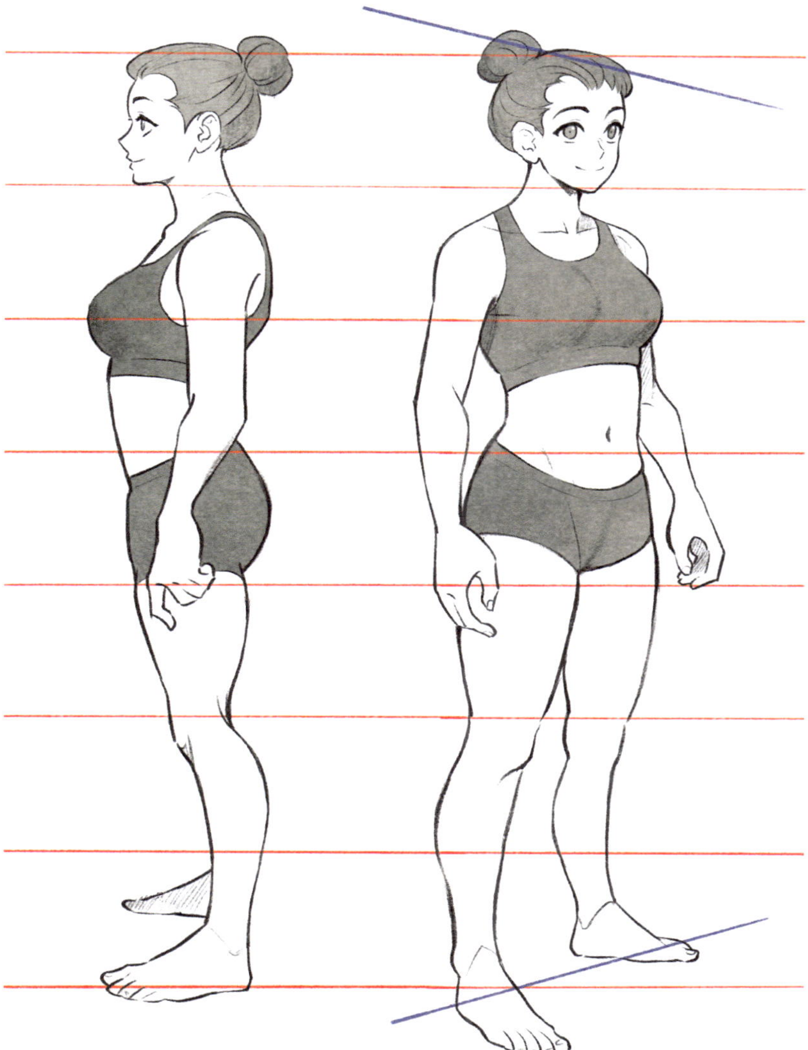

FEMALE

On a female body you might expect to see softer and rounder curves, a slimmer neck, narrower shoulders, and wider hips. Hands and feet may also be a little smaller. The female hip structure often causes the legs to turn inwards slightly.

The fat distribution on a typical female body is different to the male's. While men tend to store fat in the upper body, women tend to store more in their hips and thighs.

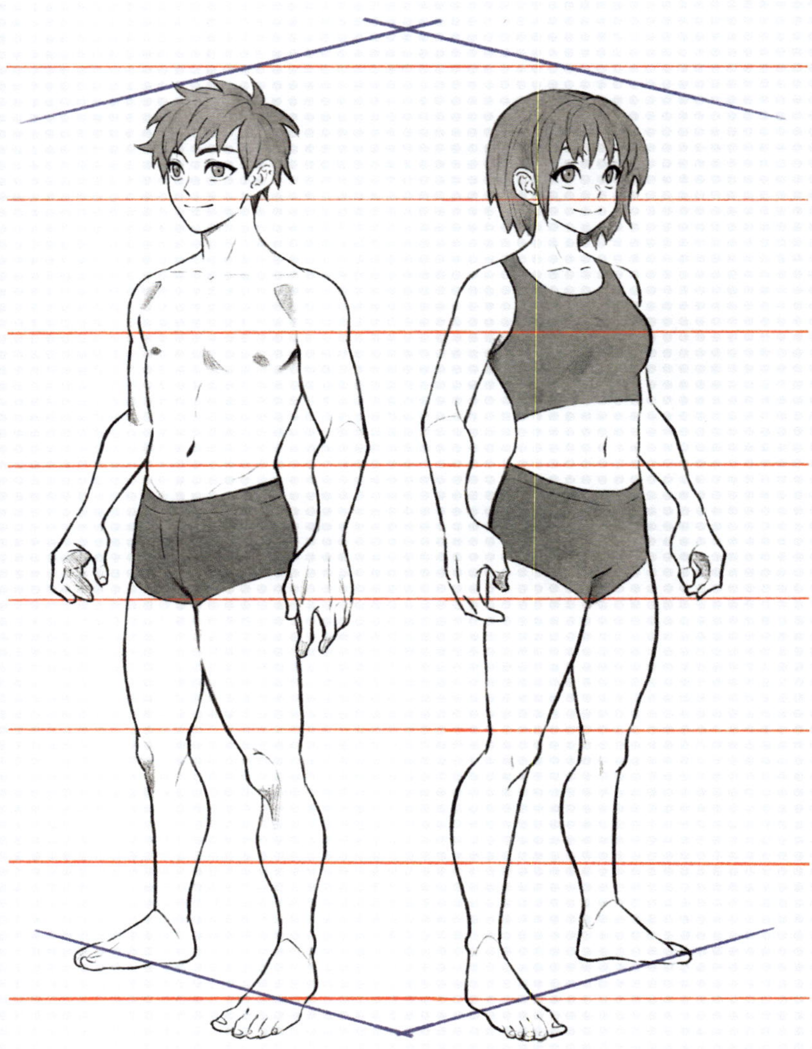

TEEN

Since bodies change a lot during the teenage years, you will see different proportions and fat distribution in younger people. They might already be as tall as an adult, with a height from six to seven heads. Shoulders and hips might not be as wide as their adult counterparts. Since the manga style can be quite varied, it may be difficult for your audience to recognize the age of an isolated character. Ensuring the adults, teens, and children in your artistic universe have noticeable differences will give the viewer a good reference point.

CHILD

As you might have guessed already, younger characters have much smaller bodies than adults. Children could be drawn with a height of four or five heads, but this can vary. The younger the characters are, the fewer differences you will see between boys and girls. Some structural differences might start to show when puberty begins, but until then you can just work with round, plump shapes for any gender, since children still have a lot of their baby fat.

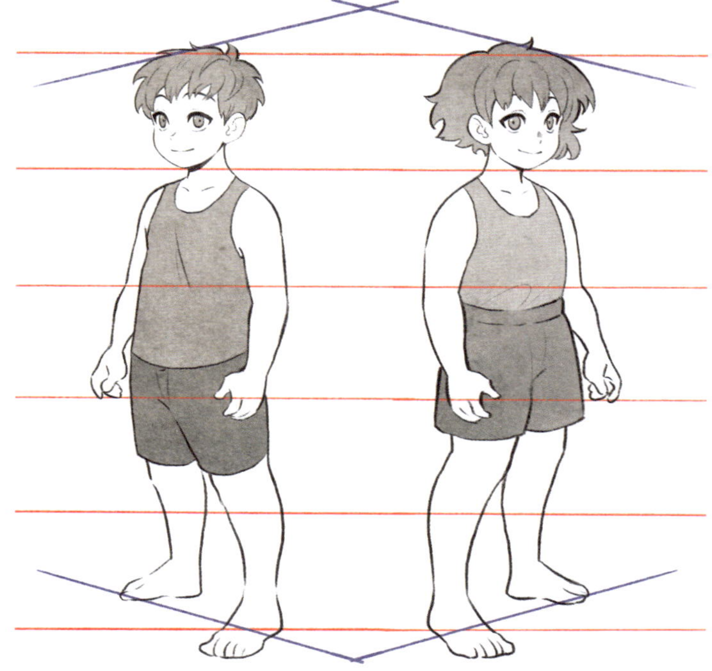

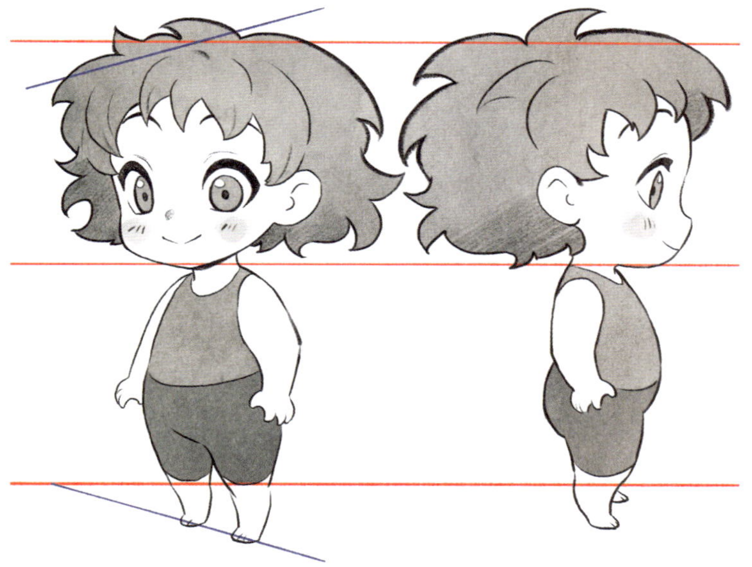

CHIBI

Manga is well known for its extremely deformed proportions. This is described as 'super deformed', or SD for short, and is used in the chibi style. The body is only the height of two heads, which makes the head appear gigantic. Cute proportions are pushed to the max, and the body is much more simplified. This form can be quicker and easier to draw than more realistic characters, and it's often aimed at younger audiences.

FACE & HAIR

A character's face and hair are probably the most important elements of the body in the manga style, as they evoke the most expression. Many manga artists focus on the eyes, as they hold a lot of emotion and grab the viewer's attention. Other artists will simplify the eyes and hair, focusing instead on action and detailed backgrounds, depending on the genre of manga. Either way, there is undoubtedly a lot of stylization involved when it comes to drawing the face, with some parts being simplified and others more emphasized. The manga style you end up drawing depends on your own preference; this chapter features some common stylization methods you can practise.

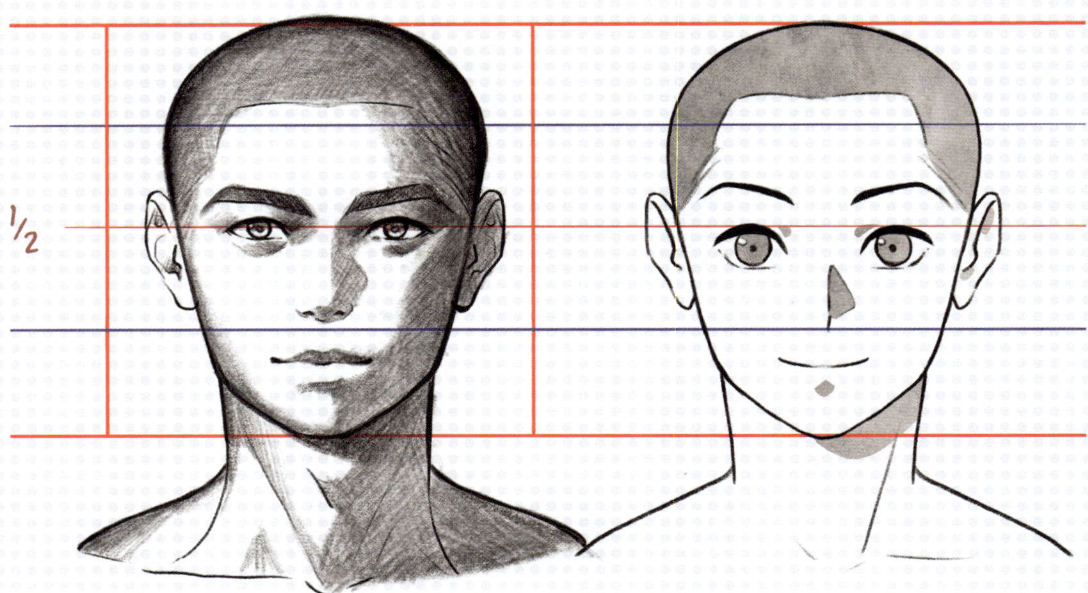

REALISM VS. MANGA

It only takes a few simple changes to make a realistic human face look like a manga-style one. The eyes sit a little lower, as they do on a child's face, and are generally made larger. This makes the face look cuter and more youthful. The nose and mouth are reduced to very simple lines, and the eyebrows are made thinner and more defined. The manga style also uses a lot less shading, instead opting for a cleaner look with a few defined shadows. Since there are many different manga styles, these general proportions may not apply to all, but shown above is the most widely recognized manga-style face.

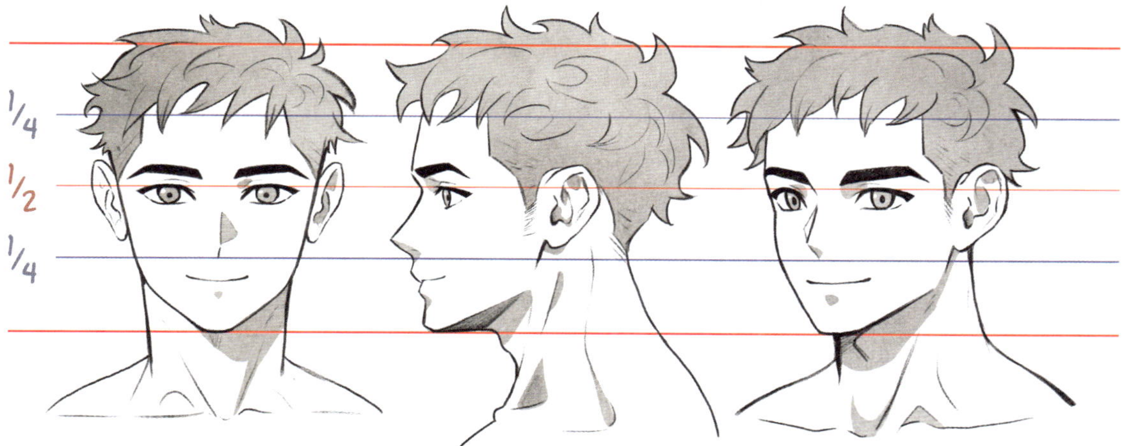

MALE FACE

To make a face look more manly, you can make the eyes smaller and move them a little higher than the halfway point of the face. The neck can be made much thicker, depending on how old your character is and how muscly they are. The eyebrows are closer to the eyes and the jawline is more pronounced. You can experiment with wider chins, though pointier chins are more common in the manga style. A man's nose is usually longer than a woman's, and you might want to add facial hair.

FEMALE FACE

For a more feminine face, round out the face and the jawline. Make the eyes a little bigger and the shading around the mouth more subtle. The hair is often more voluminous and may slightly affect the proportions of the face. You can also add more detail to the eyes and eyelashes. All these elements separately could be found on any face, but putting them together makes it easier for your audience to read your character as female. Once you feel more confident in your skills, you can play around with these typical features and subvert expectations.

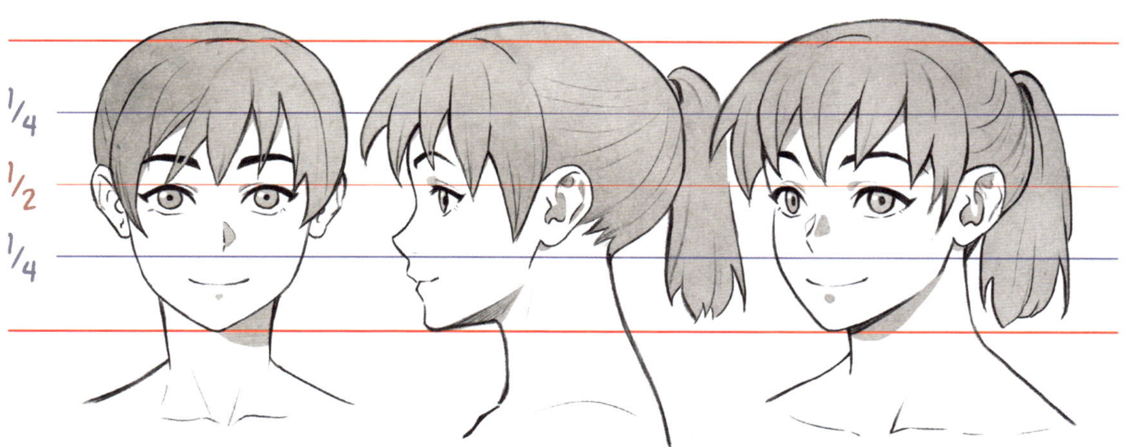

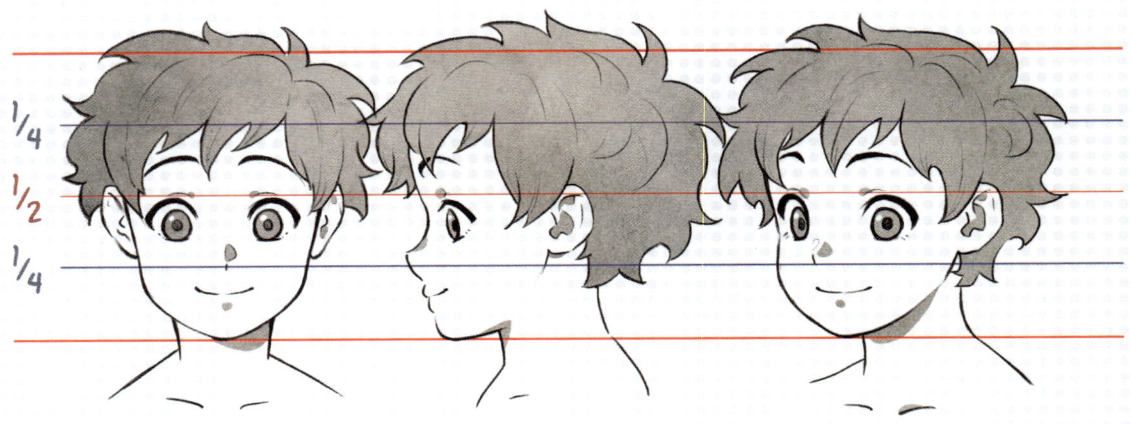

CHILD & CHIBI FACE

A child's face (shown above) is much more rounded than an adult face. The cheeks are chubbier and the jawline and chin may appear very soft. The nose is usually pointed upwards, which creates a cute profile. The eyes are bigger and appear way below the halfway point of the face. The neck is slimmer and shorter, as it has yet to grow. With the chibi style (shown below), you can take all these elements to the extreme and exaggerate them as much as you like.

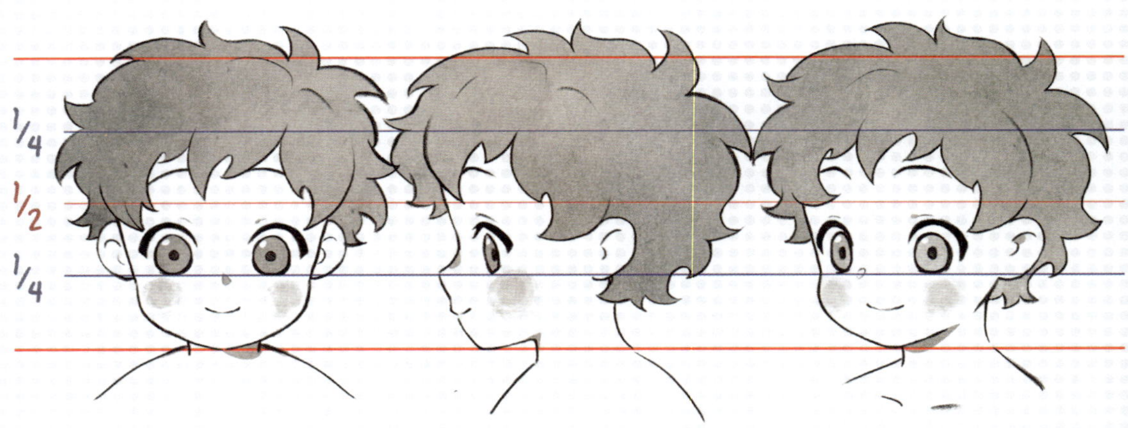

EYES

Even though manga-style eyes might seem very stylized and simple, their core foundation still lies in a realistic eye shape. You can choose which part of the eye to emphasize and which to leave out completely. You don't have to stick to one stylization method for all your characters; you can play around with different styles, even within a single universe. Parts that are typically emphasized are the eyelashes on the upper lids – and sometimes the lower lids. Be sure to design your eye shapes with different angles in mind, looking at your real eyes in a mirror for reference.

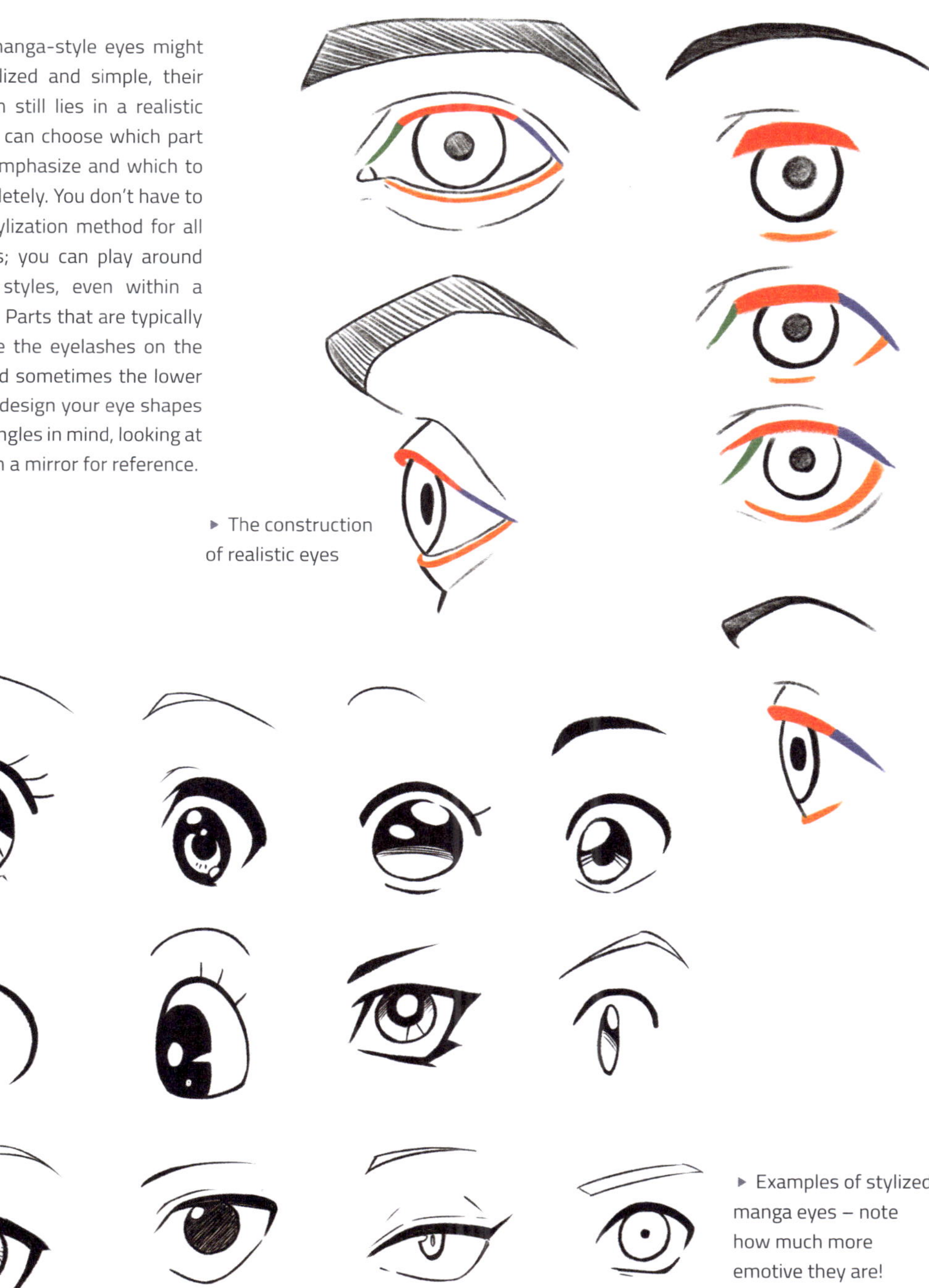

▸ The construction of realistic eyes

▸ Examples of stylized manga eyes – note how much more emotive they are!

PUPILS

The pupils of the eyes are often very stylized in manga artwork. Sometimes, these are given intense focus in close-up drawings during very emotional scenes in a story. The eyes are essential in showing a character's expression, and the pupils alone can create an impactful emotion. If you would prefer to concentrate on other parts of the face when drawing a character, you can leave the pupils as simple as possible, but it can be fun going into more detail and creating expressive close-up moments.

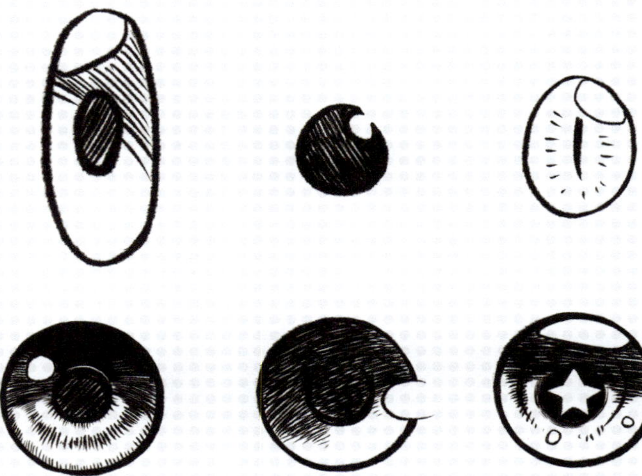

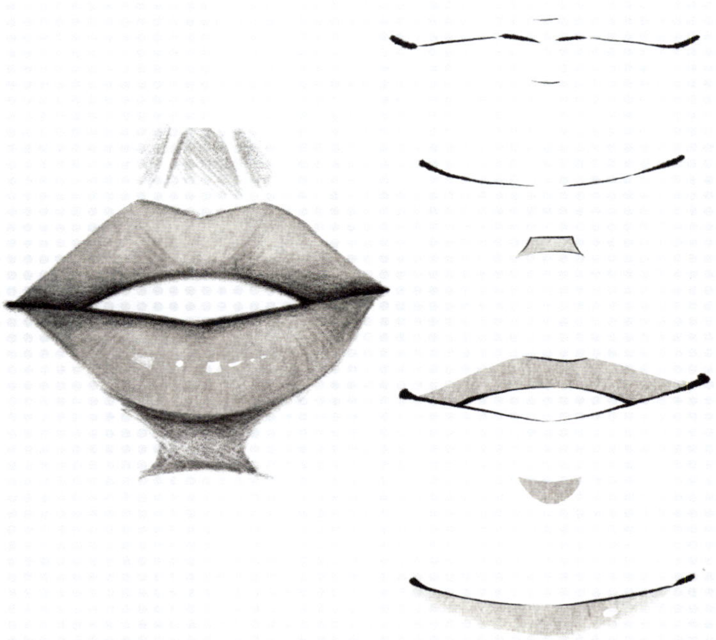

MOUTH

The mouth is typically very simplified in manga art. The lips are only usually drawn if the character is wearing lipstick, and a little glossiness is added to the bottom lip. There are some Korean manhwa styles where fuller lips are the norm, but often the shape of the mouth can be simplified into one single line. It's up to you how detailed you want your character's mouth to be, but a simplified version is most common.

TEETH

Manga teeth are usually kept quite simple. Characters typically have slightly pointy teeth, and if they smile, you may only notice a canine peaking out. In some manga styles, you might see slightly more realistic teeth, but even then, the lines between individual teeth are usually left out. It can be helpful to know the shapes of the different types of teeth – incisors (shown in red), canines (in yellow), premolars (in blue), and molars (in green) – and draw the correctly shaped ones depending on what's visible in your character's mouth. Even if the teeth are very simplified, this will help your character to look convincing.

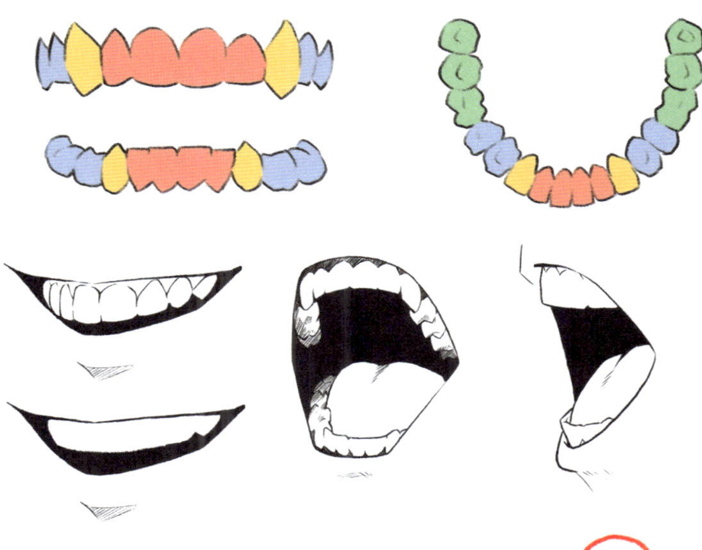

EARS

The ears don't usually have much of an impact on the expression or the emotion of the face, so they are often kept quite simple. They could be drawn realistically, or just with one line; it really depends on how important they are to your personal manga style. Spend some time studying the ear shape from different angles, as that will make your drawings more convincing, whether realistic or simplified.

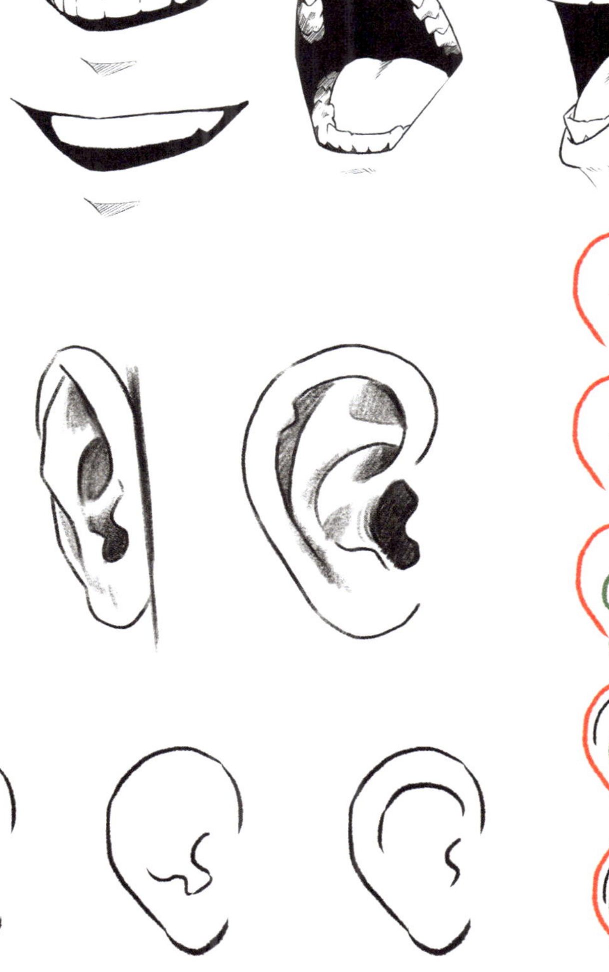

NOSE

The nose is one of the least important elements of the face in manga. Sometimes, just a simple dot represents the tip of the nose, and sometimes the nose is defined only by shadow. You can choose if you want to draw the nostrils or leave them out completely, or if you wish to draw shadows on the side and under the nose to give it some shape. The closer you zoom in on the face, the more detail you might want to show.

HAIR

Hair in manga is often very detailed, and even loose strands and locks may be emphasized. It can be helpful to think of the hair in three simple sections: the fringe, the side strands, and the back of the hair. With these sections in mind, you can build up most hairstyles. All of the sections can vary in length and shape – curly or wavy hair will have more volume than straight hair. Of course, you can also highly stylize your characters' hair if you wish, creating shapes that you might not see on real-life people.

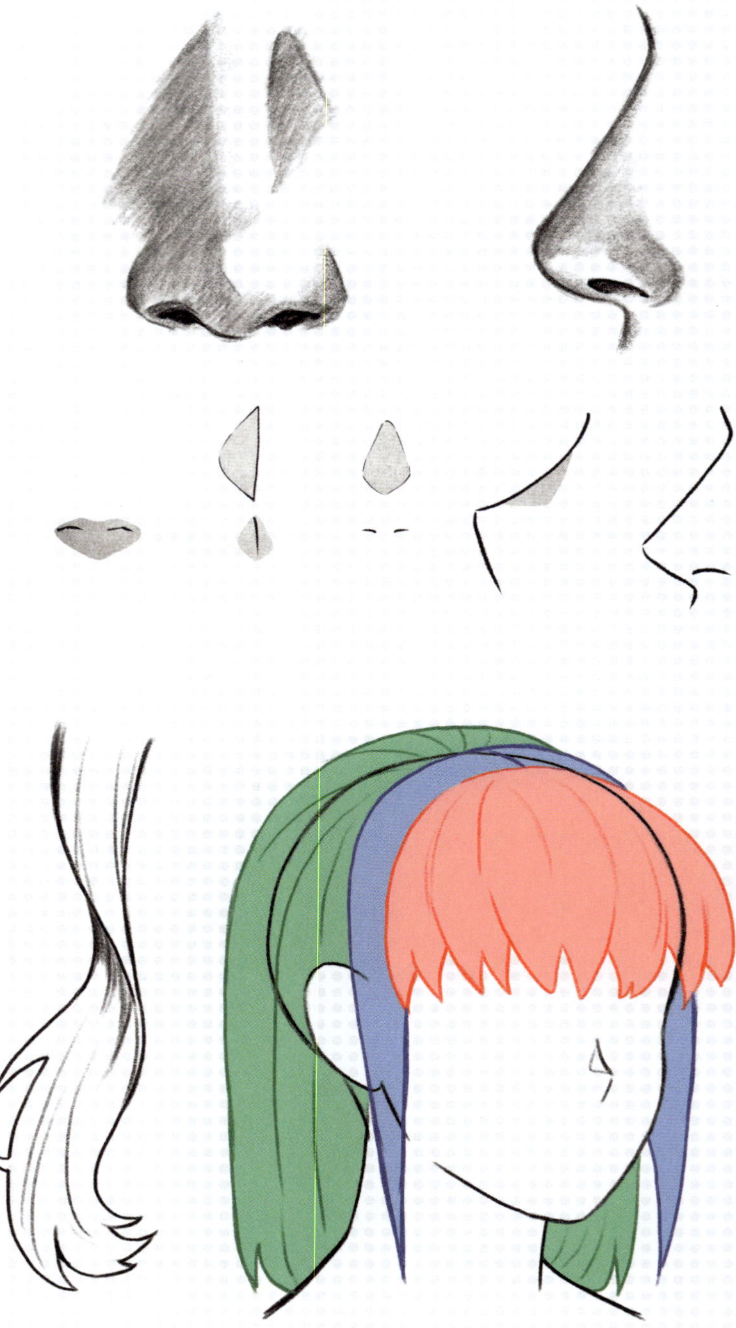

SHORT HAIR

When drawing short hair, it's important to decide a location for the hair whorl (or crown). This is the point on the head from which strands of hair grow outwards in a circular motion. You also need to decide if the hair will be straight, wavy, or curly, as this affects the overall shape. Pay attention to the edges of the hair, especially around the ears and the back of the neck — according to the character's personality, they may have it shaped or cut in various ways.

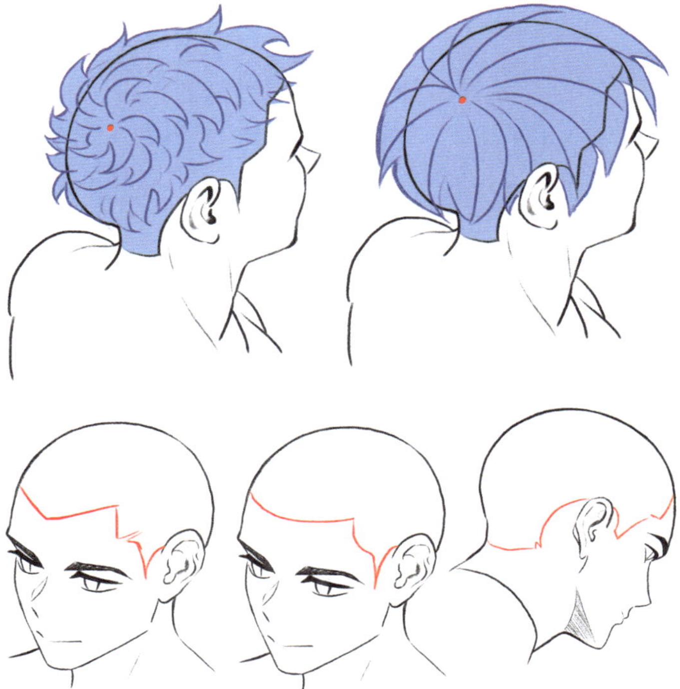

RENDERING HAIR

There are many ways to draw and colour hair. It might help you to think of individual strands as ribbons that twist and reflect light. Straight hair is usually quite shiny, so you can include plenty of highlights. In a black-and-white image, you could use a brush to paint entirely black hair as one solid shape, using the tip of the brush to create fine points. For curly hair, you could use a dry brush to swirl paint around. If you use digital brushes, you can find many that are custom made especially for certain types of hair.

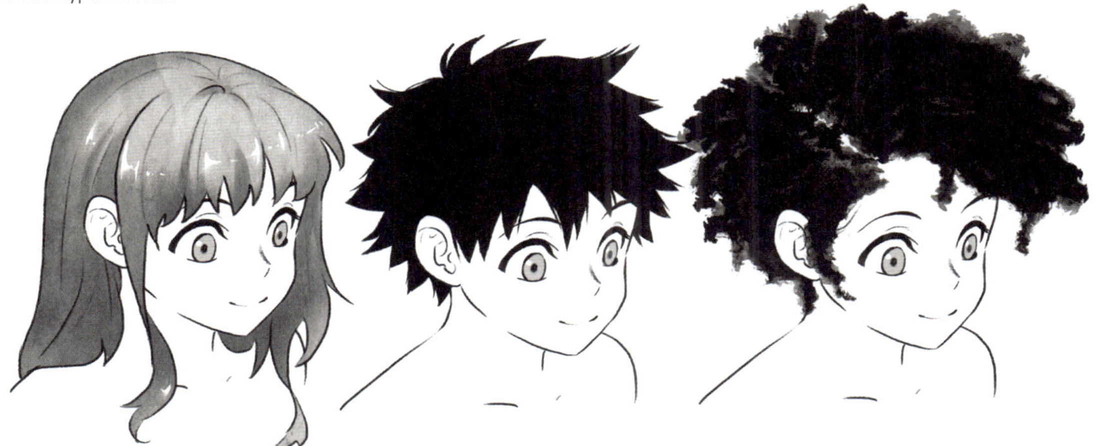

EXPRESSIONS

The face is where you usually observe reactions and emotions, so being able to draw expressions in a clear and readable manner is very important. To do this, you need a good grasp of the facial structure and an understanding of which parts to move to enhance any expression. In manga, you can also use stylistic additions, such as sweat drops, to emphasize an expression and keep it loose and fun. The level of deformation or realism depends on how you wish to draw. Some artists like to go wild with a deformed style, while others tend to show emotion in a more realistic and subtle way. This section covers some common approaches.

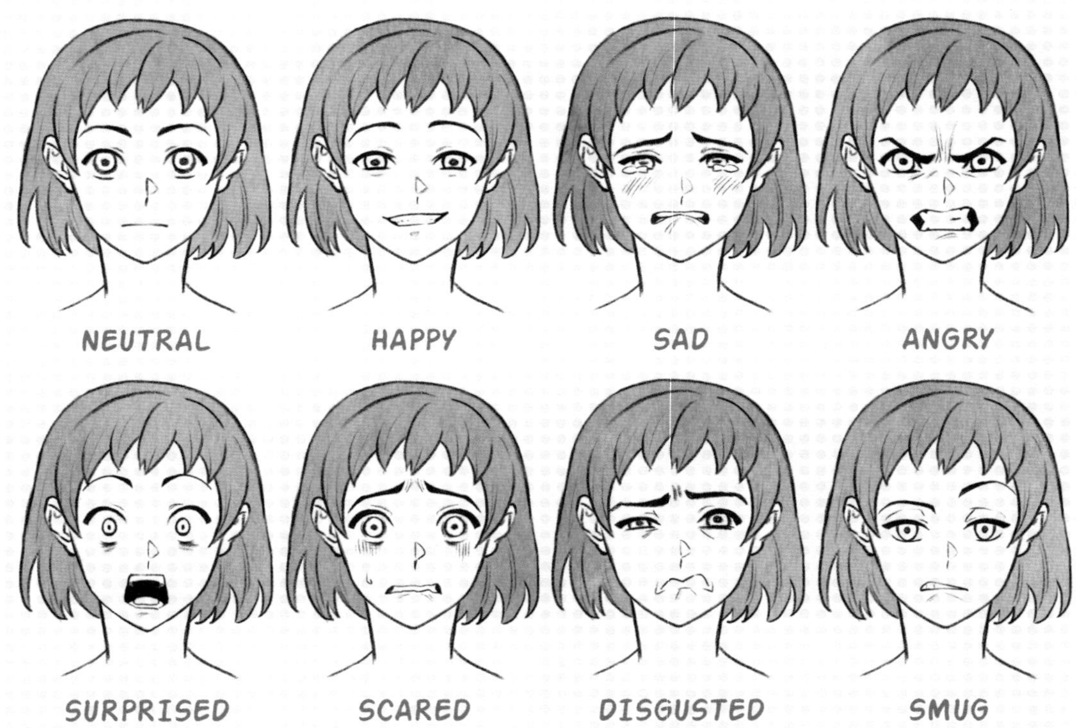

UNIVERSAL EXPRESSIONS

There are eight set expressions (including a neutral face) that you can observe in any type of character. There may be cultural differences that come into play, but these eight (shown above) are a good basis for studying expressions and finding ways to stylize them. The biggest emotion indicators are the eyes (eyebrows and eyelids) and the mouth (corners and lips). You don't see much expression happening around the nose area in manga artwork, but there can always be exceptions to this.

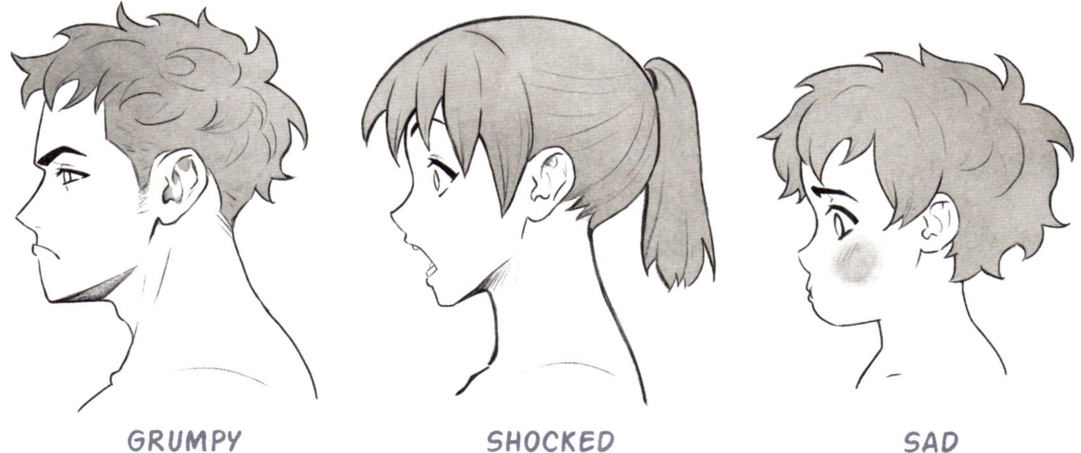

GRUMPY   SHOCKED   SAD

PROFILE VIEW

It's good practice to try drawing different expressions in a profile view (from the side), as shown above. From this angle, the eyebrows and jaw are key to showing emotion, as they shape and change the profile depending on the expression. Since you can't show as much information in profile as you can in a more frontal view, emotions might be half as readable. However, you can improve this by making things more obvious – for example, have the eyes looking right up or down depending on the character's mood, or make the lips stick out in a big pout, or pull them right back in a smile.

STYLISTIC SYMBOLS & EXAGGERATION

In order to convey an expression as fast as possible, as is often required in manga comics, you can use stylistic symbols such as sweat drops, angry veins, blushing cheeks, darkening eyes, and many more exaggerations that would usually look out of place. Depending on your individual manga style, you might want to use these elements often, or only occasionally for comedic effect. You will need to find a balance, as the contrast between more realistic characters and funny deformations can either enhance the comedy or break readers out of the moment, ruining the fantasy of the story. It depends on what your readers are used to seeing in the particular genre you work in, and also on your artistic choices. Sometimes, you just have to try things out to see if they resonate with other people.

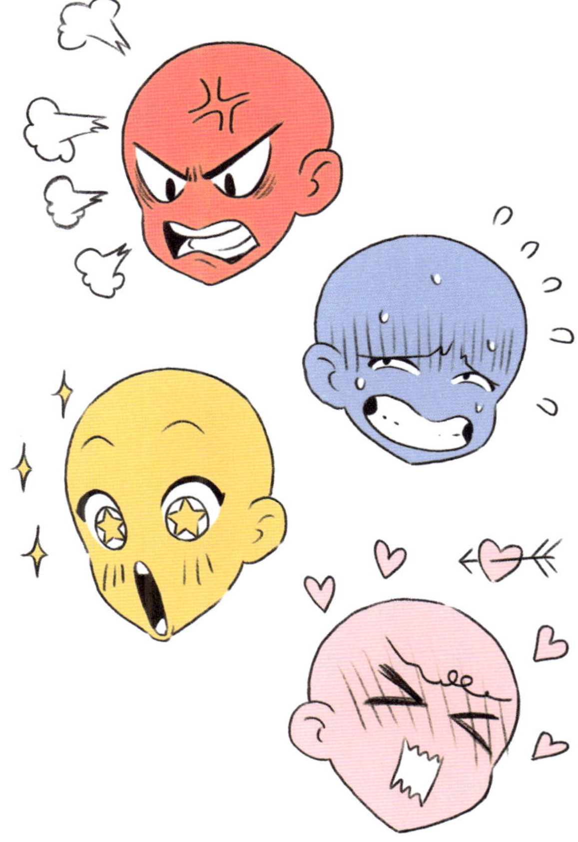

DESIGN TECHNIQUES

BY MIYULI

Designing original manga characters can be incredibly fun and rewarding. There are several ways to proceed and a few tricks you can use to enhance the final image. While other drawing styles, such as fashion design, often use very flat drawings of figures to concentrate more on the clothing, with manga you want to design a character with personality that inhabits a sense of three-dimensional space. Another important factor is the general design language you use and how you communicate with your audience. It's essential that you learn how to use your tools with intent.

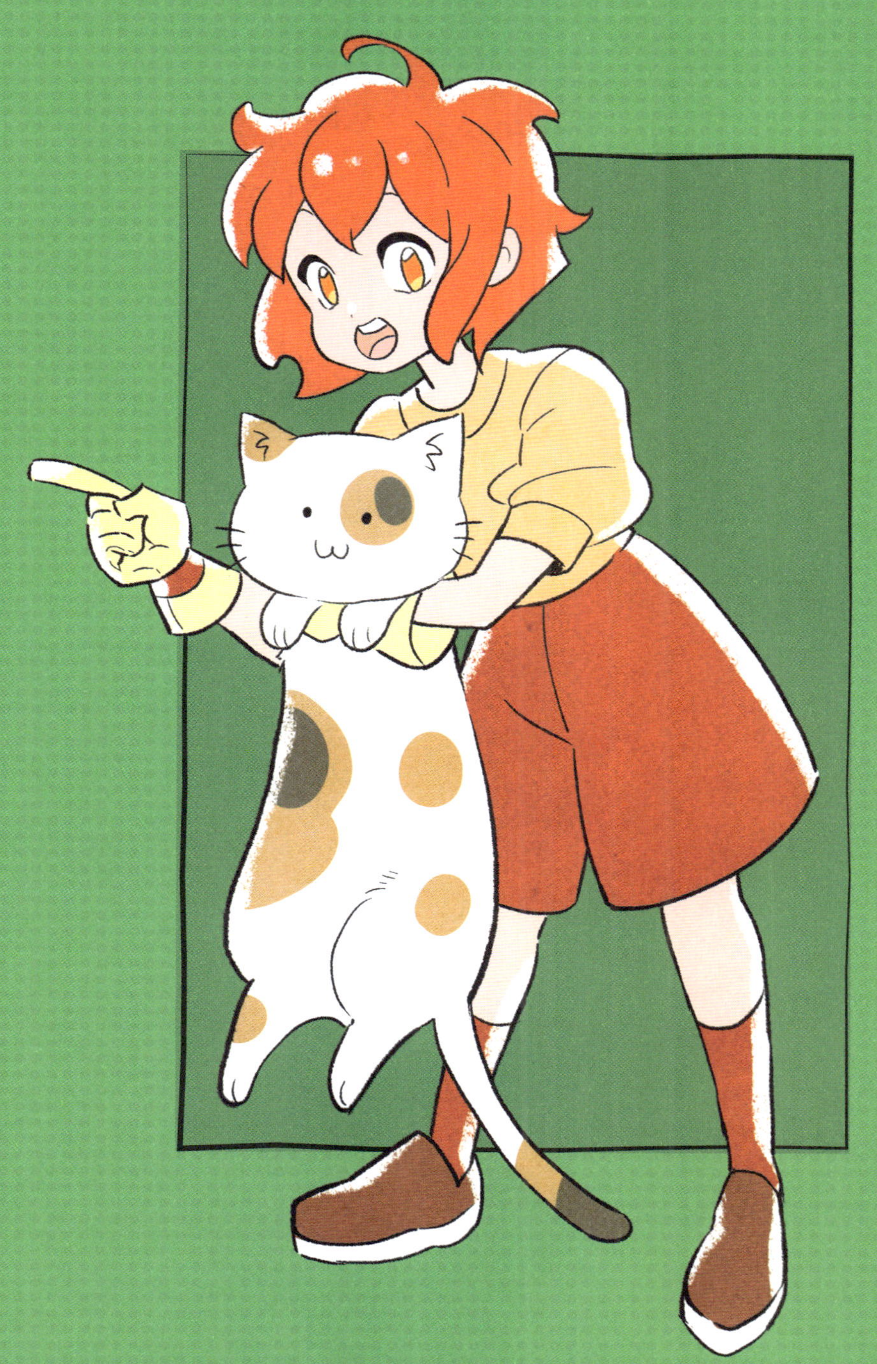

FORESHORTENING & PERSPECTIVE

Perspective is not only shown with parallel lines and vanishing points, but also through foreshortening the forms of the character or object. Your brain will usually straighten things out, ignoring how the proportions are distorted to such a small size when facing away from the viewer. In photography, you can influence the intensity of the foreshortening by using different camera lenses. It's a good reference point to compare long and wide lenses and how they affect the presentation of a figure. It takes a lot of practice to correctly estimate how much to shorten and deform the elements you draw. Both your hand and eyes have to adjust to the information.

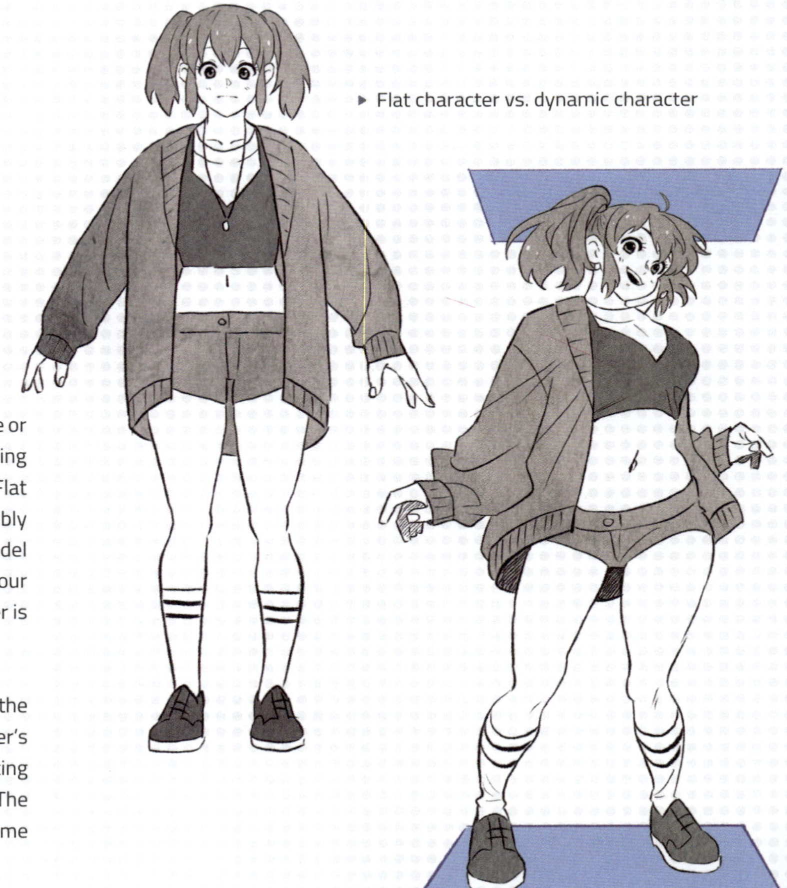

▶ Flat character vs. dynamic character

DYNAMIC ANGLES

Flat figures that show no perspective or foreshortening are useful for designing clothes, armour, and tattoos. Flat character drawings are also incredibly useful if you want to build a 3D model for games or animation based on your design, as every part of the character is visible in its true proportions.

Dynamic figure drawings, on the other hand, show off a character's personality and are useful for creating memorable scenes full of narrative. The proportions are distorted and some elements of the design are hidden.

CAMERA LENSES

A long-angle camera lens has vanishing points that are far apart, which is great for capturing natural proportions with minimal distortion and a normal amount of foreshortening. In contrast, a wide-angle camera lens captures much more of the environment because the vanishing points are much closer together, which also creates more intense foreshortening and a more distorted view of the object. The wider the camera lens, the more distorted the elements at the corners of the image become. With an extreme wide-angle lens, whatever is closest to the camera appears much bigger, while elements further away appear much smaller.

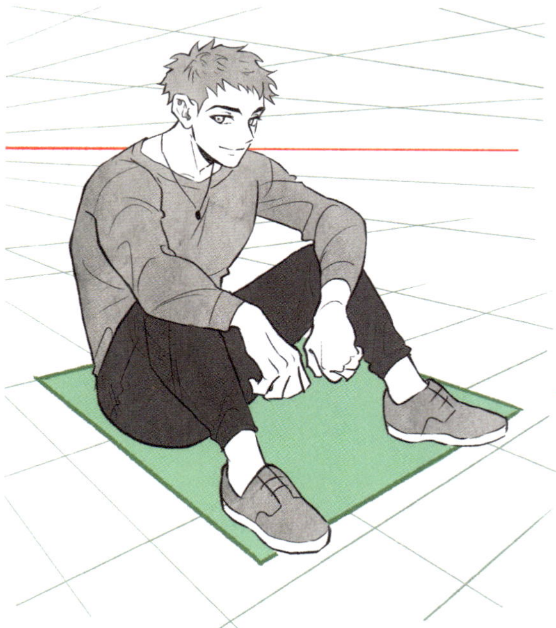

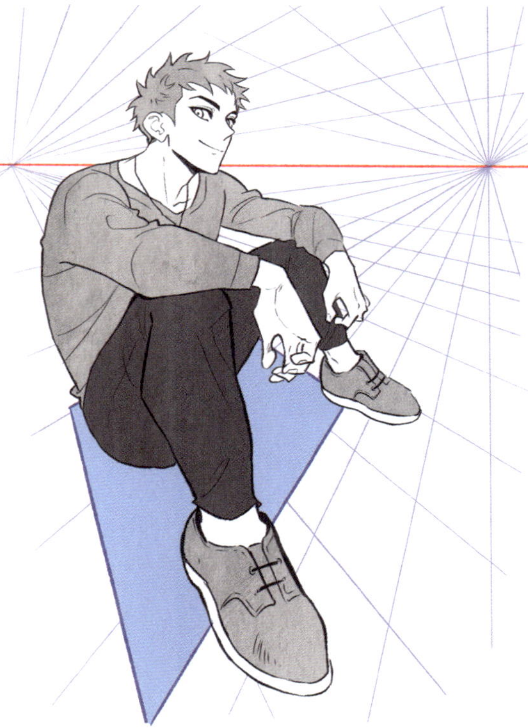

▶ Long lens vs. wide lens

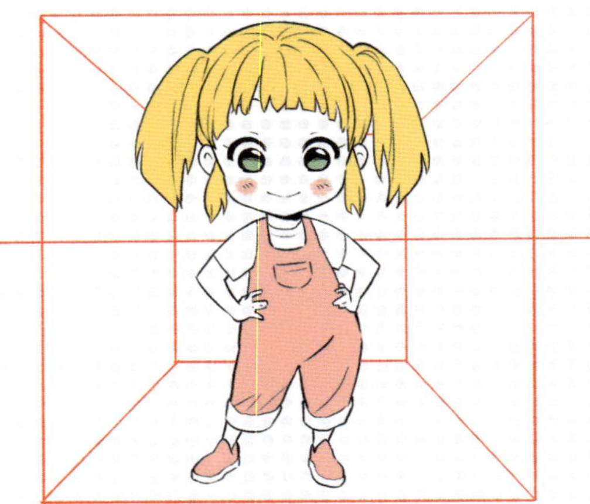

ONE-POINT PERSPECTIVE

With one-point perspective there is only one vanishing point. The lines that don't meet the vanishing point appear to be parallel. Depending on where you crop an image, one vanishing point might be all you need. The further an object is from the vanishing point, the more distorted it looks, so be careful as to where you place your character. This kind of perspective often creates interesting patterns and symmetries. It's great for front-facing characters positioned in the centre.

TWO-POINT PERSPECTIVE

Two-point perspective places two vanishing points on the horizon line, creating harmonious and undistorted results. As long as the character stays close to the viewer's eye level, this type of perspective will usually be all you need. How far away the vanishing points are from one another will control how more or less distorted the figure may look.

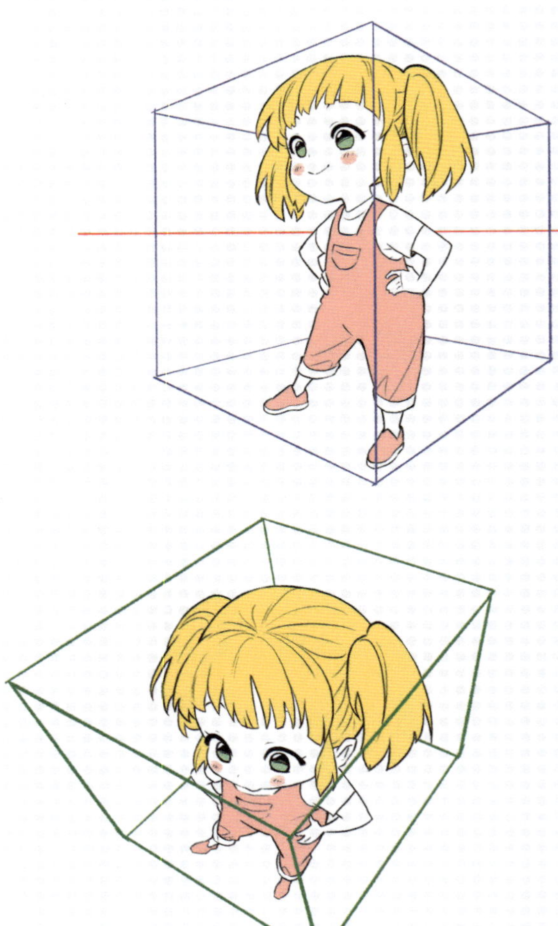

THREE-POINT PERSPECTIVE

Three-point perspective is required when looking up or down at an object. In such cases, another vanishing point is needed either above or below the horizon line. Three-point perspective is the most dynamic type and is often used in fast-paced action scenes. The viewer is more likely to feel drama and intensity when looking at a character from an unusual perspective they're not used to seeing. These unusual angles may also be slightly harder to draw until you get used to the foreshortening involved ... so get practising!

POSE & SILHOUETTE

When designing characters, one way to make them more recognizable and interesting is to give them a clear silhouette that is unusual yet coherent. It must be interesting enough to catch the viewer's eye, while also giving them an idea of what to expect. Silhouettes and poses are great for designing a character line-up. The more the silhouettes differ from each other, the easier it will be to differentiate between the characters. In a fantasy manga setting you might take the opportunity to push anatomical boundaries, or you may choose to stay on the side of realism and give all of your characters a recognizably human shape.

PERSONALITY IN POSES

Everyone has a different way of carrying themselves, which is no different for original characters. Even when designing a simple standing pose, you can communicate something about the character's personality, mood, physical health, and sometimes even age. Is the character hunched over or standing with perfect posture? Are they slouched and relaxed, or upright and tense?

No two characters should be standing in exactly the same way if you want to make them interesting and unique. There might also be a specific pose they're known for, almost like a catchphrase; body language or a gesture they enact so often, viewers instantly associate it with them. It might be an unusual fighting stance, a characteristic cheering pose, or the cute way they flick their magic wand. When designing poses for your characters, consider their backstory, occupation, and hobbies to understand how they use their body.

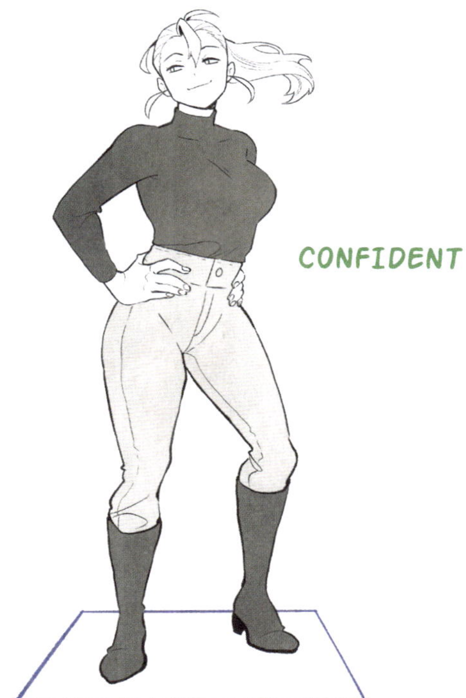

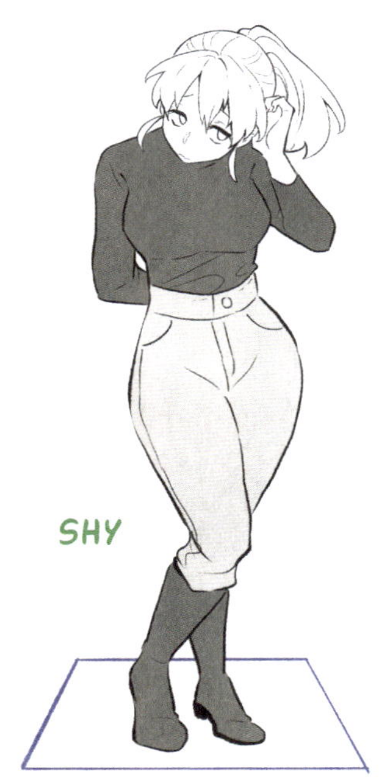

MOVEMENT

Whether walking or running, fighting or hugging, characters will need to perform a variety of different movements over the course of your manga stories. You may choose to design each of these from scratch, capturing the unique way your character performs each movement. Or, you may find designing every single movement too time-consuming. An alternative approach is to think of generally feminine or masculine movement patterns, as there is a lot of reference material available for this. It can also help to observe people moving in real life. You can choose what level of typically feminine or masculine movement to give your characters.

HANDS

As a beginner, you may tend to ignore hands or try to hide them altogether, but don't underestimate their expressiveness. Hands can contribute to the overall flow of the whole pose, as well as providing crucial information about the character's personality. Try to avoid giving all of your characters the same hand shape. Some people have short, thick fingers, while others have long, slender, or bony fingers. Nails can be short and clipped or long and artificial. Look at how age and fat distribution affects the overall hand shape as well.

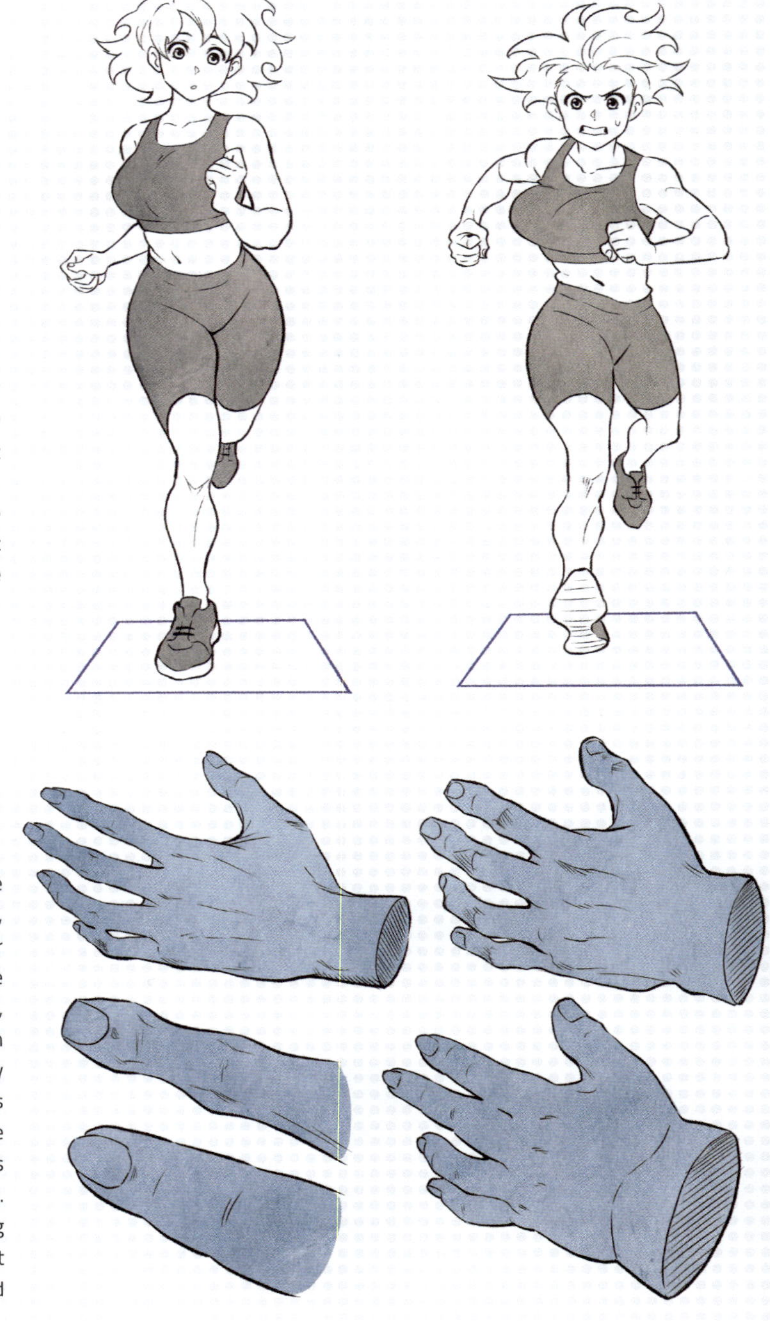

CHOOSE A CLEAR SILHOUETTE

When it comes to the most famous manga characters, you can usually recognize who they are by their silhouettes alone. This is no coincidence, but an intentional part of their design that contributes to their success. When you focus on the silhouette, you can concentrate on the shape language of your character. Their clothes, hair, body, and pose all contribute to creating a readable yet interesting form.

In comics, animation, and video games alike, it's crucial that viewers are easily able to recognize at least the main characters to ensure they don't get unnecessarily confused about who's who, or who is performing what action. The angles and poses you choose will read much more clearly when you can tell what the character is doing without having to rely on the finer details.

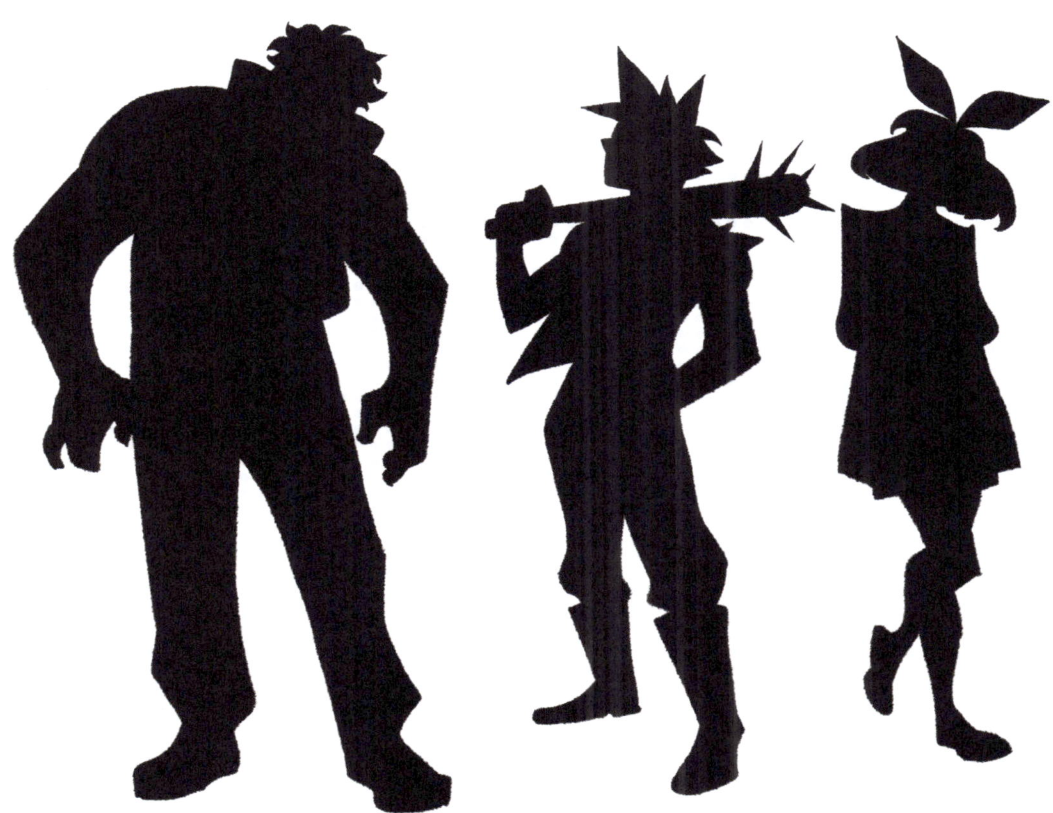

LIGHTING

Lighting plays a big part in storytelling, as characters can be presented completely differently in different lighting set-ups. Dark and light areas create their own shape languages, which you can design for your own purposes. The colour of light can also greatly impact the mood of the scene.

While the different types of light sources and how they affect forms may seem a little intimidating at first, the trick is to keep things simple when starting out. This section will cover the most common lighting situations that you will find useful.

SPOTLIGHT

When first introducing a character, this is typically done in a well-lit environment or under a spotlight shining from above. The character becomes the whole focus of the scene, while everything else that's not important is pushed into shadow. The spotlight can have a small range and only illuminate the character's head, or it can have a wider range so that the whole body is clearly visible. Place key information you want to show and emphasize to the viewer in the light, while moving unimportant or mysterious elements into the shadows.

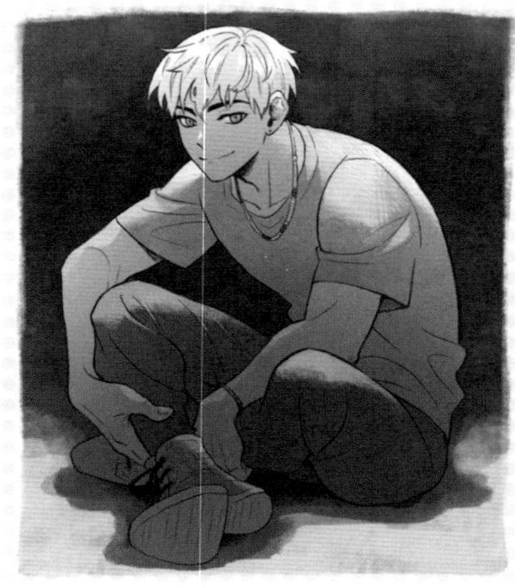

LIGHT FROM BEHIND

Light shining from behind the character, also called 'contre-jour', usually emphasizes their outline. The character is obscured in shadow, while the background is overly bright. This is one way to draw attention to the silhouette, as basic shapes are emphasized while details are hidden in shadow. This can be useful for a mysterious but generally gentle introduction to a character. The viewer might not have all the information clearly, but there is enough to form a good idea of what they're looking at.

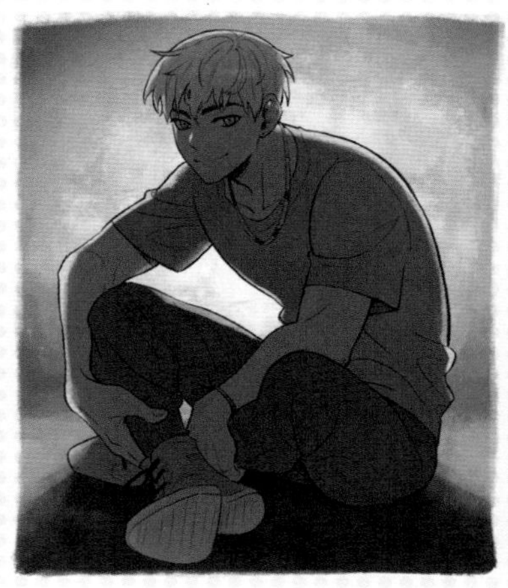

LIGHT FROM BELOW

Light shining from below is very unusual in nature. Perhaps you have shone the light of a torch upwards from below your chin when telling spooky ghost stories. This type of lighting set-up emphasizes something unnatural and slightly unsettling. It can look mysterious and magical, but it can also cast odd shadows on the face, which is what makes it appear distorted and scary. You can also create contrast with funny situations in this kind of lighting. Avoid overusing it in normal scenes or you might unintentionally make the viewer feel uneasy.

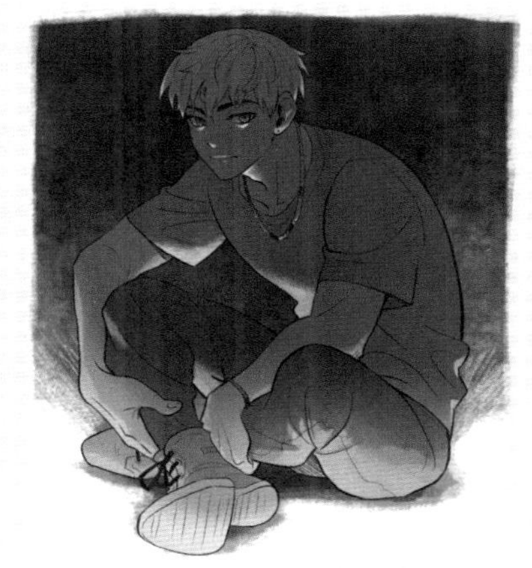

OVEREXPOSURE

Using methods from photography, you can overly expose the scene by only using very light values to create a soft, peaceful mood. If there is too much white light, however, it risks creating a very blinding effect. There is also the risk of details getting lost in the areas that are the most lit, while you will notice the most information in the unusually light shadows. Use this method for celestial, ethereal, and godly characters that step into the light and yet potentially have things to hide in plain sight.

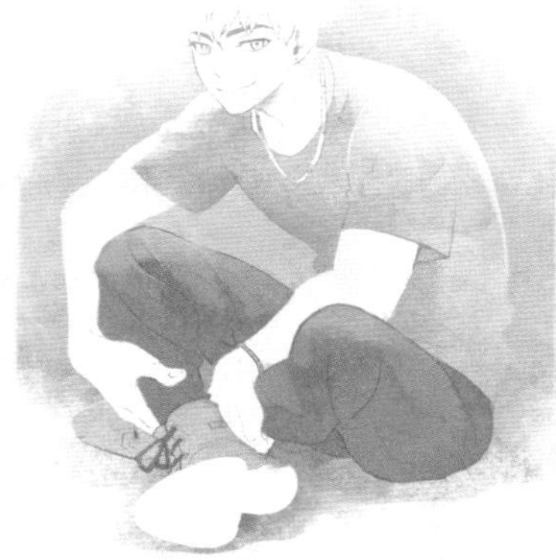

UNDEREXPOSURE

The opposite of overexposure is underexposure. This is when everything appears too dark. The light source is very weak, so you can hardly make out any information at all. Use this method when you want to hide information from the viewer and make them strain their eyes to work out what's going on. For example, when you want to make characters appear scary, dark, and mysterious. Only use this method very intentionally, as it's usually a bad idea to make an image so hard to see without a deeper meaning behind it. If all of your artwork is too dark, your audience will likely become frustrated and move on to something brighter, so make sure you use it with purpose.

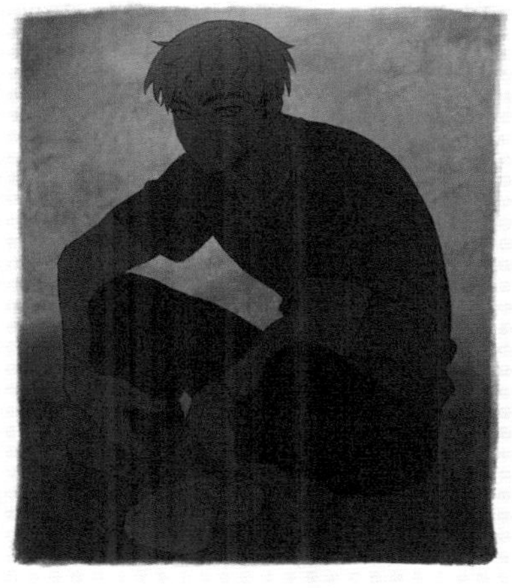

DESIGN VARIATIONS

Manga styles are typically influenced by their intended audiences. Sales and viewership numbers often dictate which styles and genres become more prevalent and successful than others. Sometimes the similarities and differences between styles depend on the tools used to create the artwork. For example, you see softer shading and thinner lines in manga art styles aimed at women, and bolder lines with harder edges in manga art styles aimed at men. There will always be exceptions within each style and you are free to experiment with combining styles and genres. This section will provide you with an introduction to the distinctions that can be made between the five main types.

SHOJO

The shojo style is aimed at a young teenage female audience. It typically has a lot of details with thin, delicate lines. Since emotions are very important in shojo, the characters typically have big, detailed eyes and colourful pupils. The hair is also often quite detailed, with individual strands breaking up the outline, and colours are both vibrant and gentle. Shojo often uses traditional media, such as watercolour or similar effects, to add texture to the drawings.

JOSEI

Josei is a manga style that aims to appeal to adult women. Because of its target audience, it features more adult characters with a grounded look and covers more mature themes. It relies less on symbolism and magical effects, and more on visuals based in reality. Characters may still contain plenty of details, but nothing that will distract the audience too much. The josei genre often makes use of digital colouring techniques to create an engaging and effective colour palette.

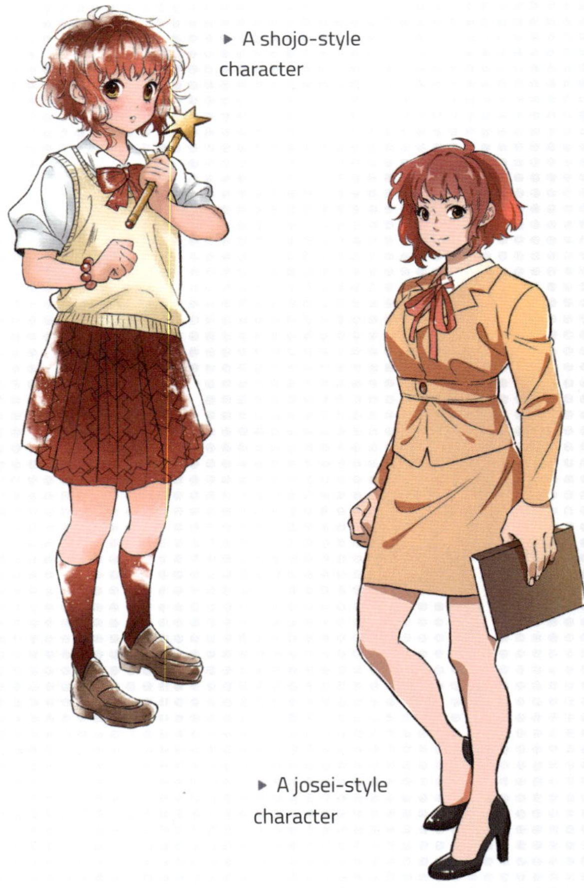

▶ A shojo-style character

▶ A josei-style character

SHONEN

The shonen manga style typically prioritizes action, strong emotions, and principles such as determination, heroism, and teamwork. The line work might be rougher, thicker, and more energetic. You will observe dynamic angles and impactful gestures. Eyes and hair are often kept simpler, with bold shapes and vibrant colours. As the target audience is mainly teenage boys, important scenes are made to look cool and flashy. Traditional colouring tools, such as Copic markers, have typically been used, but there is now an increasing amount of digital colouring being utilized to create a more vibrant and powerful look.

SEINEN

The seinen genre is aimed at adult men, covering heavier topics and more mature characters. The action is less flashy, replaced by more grounded and serious movement, or very violent, bloody conflict. The art style tends to be slightly more realistic, with smaller eyes, more wrinkles, and more realistic shading. You will also sometimes observe experimental techniques, such as expressive brushwork, and the colours might generally be less saturated. As with the connection between shojo and josei, there might be some similarities and intersection with the shonen style.

KODOMO

Manga art styles that are aimed at children might be referred to as kodomo or kodomomuke, known for their cute and easily recognizable character designs. The colours are bright and saturated, which is what makes them so popular with a young audience. Cute animals and young children typically feature as the main characters. Kodomo also features chibi-style characters, where the characters' proportions are simplified and made rounder and cuter, with big expressive eyes and simple shapes (see page 49).

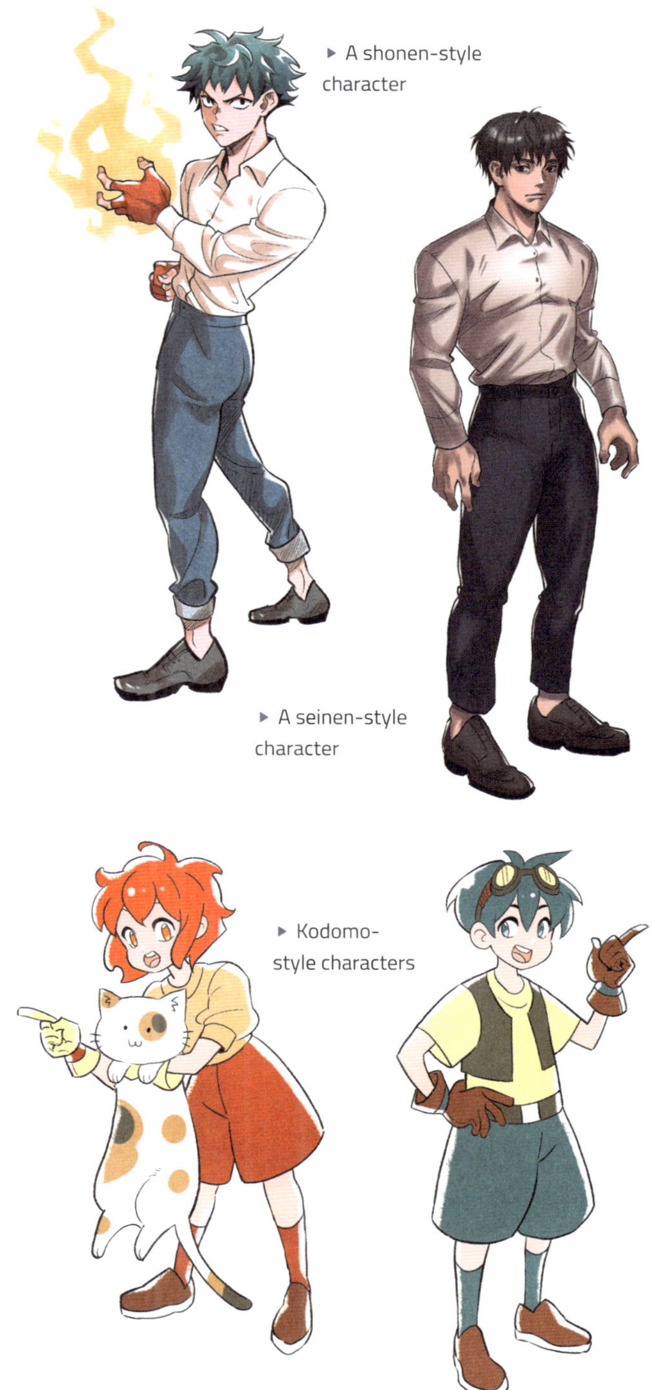

▶ A shonen-style character

▶ A seinen-style character

▶ Kodomo-style characters

PROCESS TIPS

BY MIYULI

Creating new manga characters and worlds requires both your mind and body, so it's important that you take care of yourself to ensure you're able to unleash your full creative potential! When you're young, it's all too easy to overestimate your own physical and mental abilities and regularly push yourself, or even worse, neglect certain areas of your health. This chapter contains some reminders and tips on how to keep your body and mind in good shape to make sure you can carry on creating art for years to come.

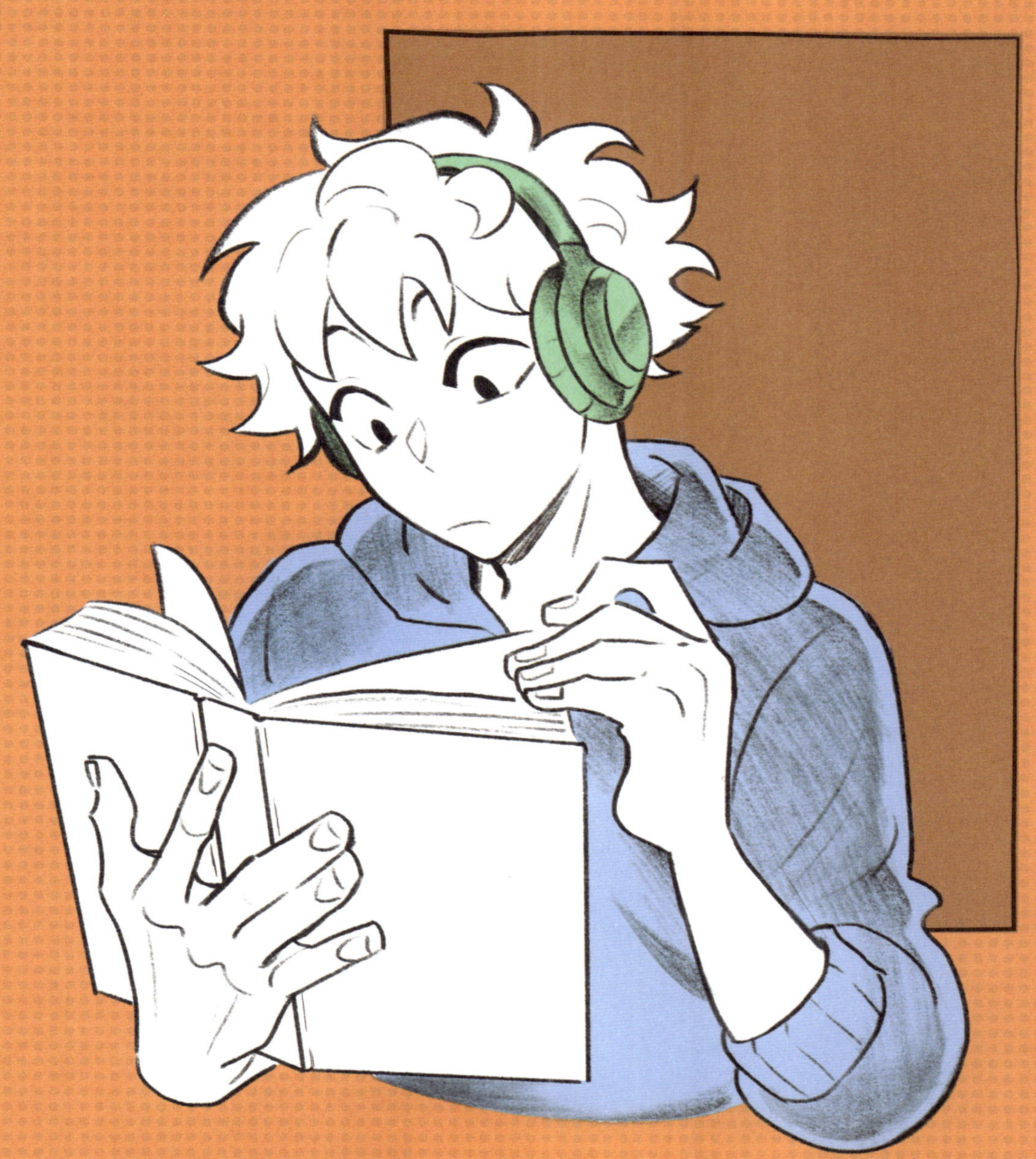

DRAWING HABITS

The way you approach the drawing process can have a huge impact on your concentration, level of enjoyment, and the quality of your work. Small actions, such as frequently drinking water or taking regular breaks to stretch your legs, can make a big difference, so it's helpful to pick up good habits as early as possible. You might be fine pulling an all-nighter or sitting awkwardly today, but in a few years' time your body and mind will start to complain. Making sure you integrate healthy habits into your daily routine will allow you to keep creating for as long as possible.

POSTURE & CHAIRS

Don't underestimate what time and bad posture can do to your body. The 'text neck' has already become a problem for people who spend too much time looking down at their phones, which is the same position artists adopt when working hunched over a drawing. You can prevent this by looking straight-on at your paper or screen and letting your arms and legs rest at comfortable angles. Don't clench your drawing hand; practise making smooth, relaxed movements with your wrist. Don't forget your spine! One of the most important purchases for artists is a good ergonomic chair that supports your back.

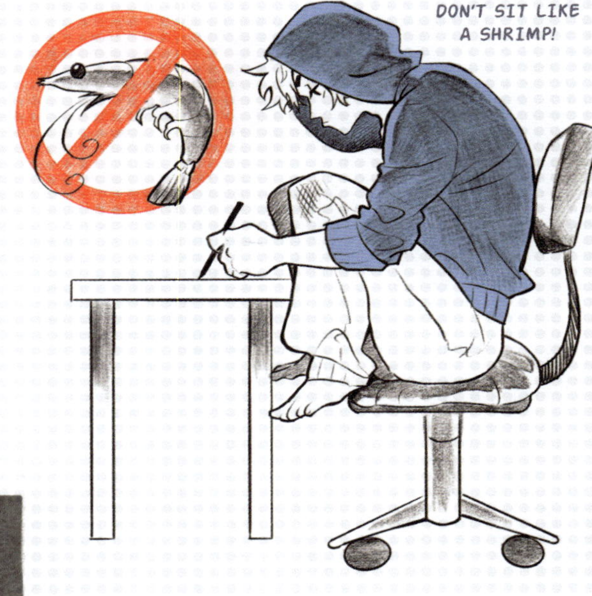

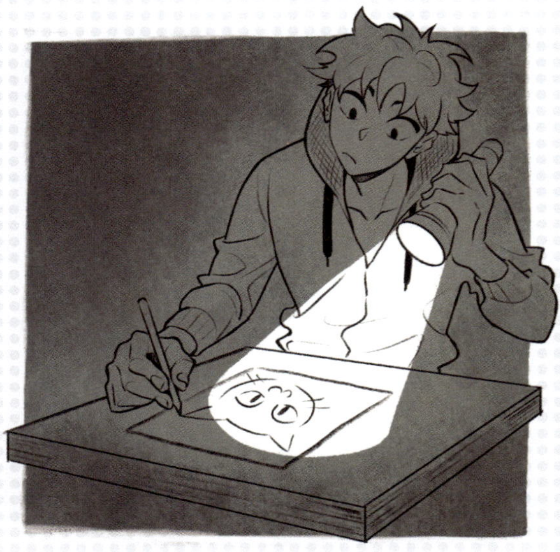

GOOD LIGHTING

When drawing with traditional materials, it's important to keep your workspace illuminated to make sure no unnecessary shadows get in the way of the drawing. You might think that lighting doesn't matter if you draw digitally, as the screen is already lit, but drawing on a bright screen in a dark room will only strain your eyes. Make sure your room is well lit and turn on your device's blue-light filter when working late. Sleep is a crucial part of the creation process, so make sure you take enough time to rest.

EXERCISE

Drawing and creating requires a strong body, but when you sit and draw for long periods of time, your other muscles can feel neglected and slowly become weaker with disuse. Stress accumulates in your muscles and joints, so you will find it beneficial to let it out regularly through exercise, yoga, and meditation. If you make a habit of trying to free your body and mind of stress regularly, rather than only when you feel pain from the lack of movement, this will aid your creative practice.

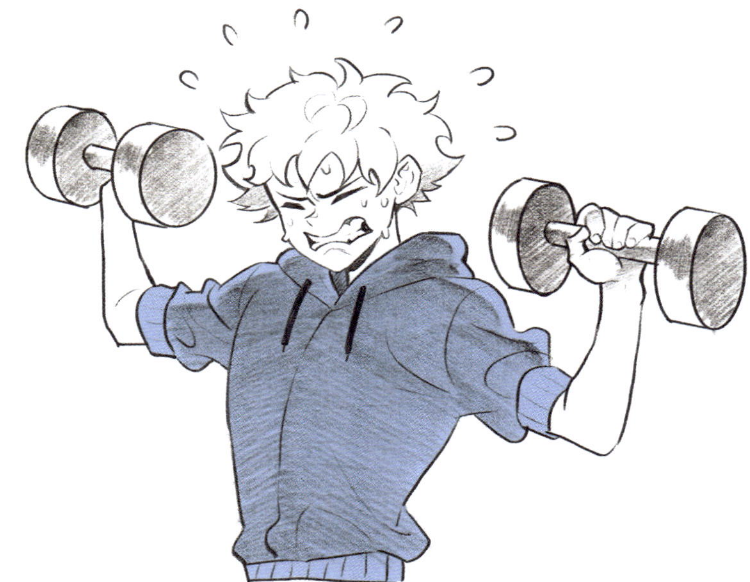

WARM-UP

As an artist, it's important to keep your muscles supple and mobile. Just as it can be helpful to undertake some light full-body stretches or exercise before and after a drawing session, you should also warm up your hand before you start drawing. When a deadline is nearing, artists will sometimes count the first few hours of actual work as their warm-up. However, it can often prove helpful to do some warm-up exercises in the form of quick studies, or to practise drawing dynamic lines with a relaxed grip. When working over long hours, your grip tends to tighten and tense around the pencil. Always remind yourself to refer back to your relaxed grip or, better yet, take a break!

GESTURE DRAWING

One fun and useful warm-up practice is creating gesture drawings. Ideally you should create gesture drawings from real life, but if this isn't possible, look at photography online or videos of athletes and dancers. Chronophotography can also be useful for showing the sequence of movement. Even if you don't work in animation, the ability to draw characters that look like they're about to jump out of the canvas is an incredible skill.

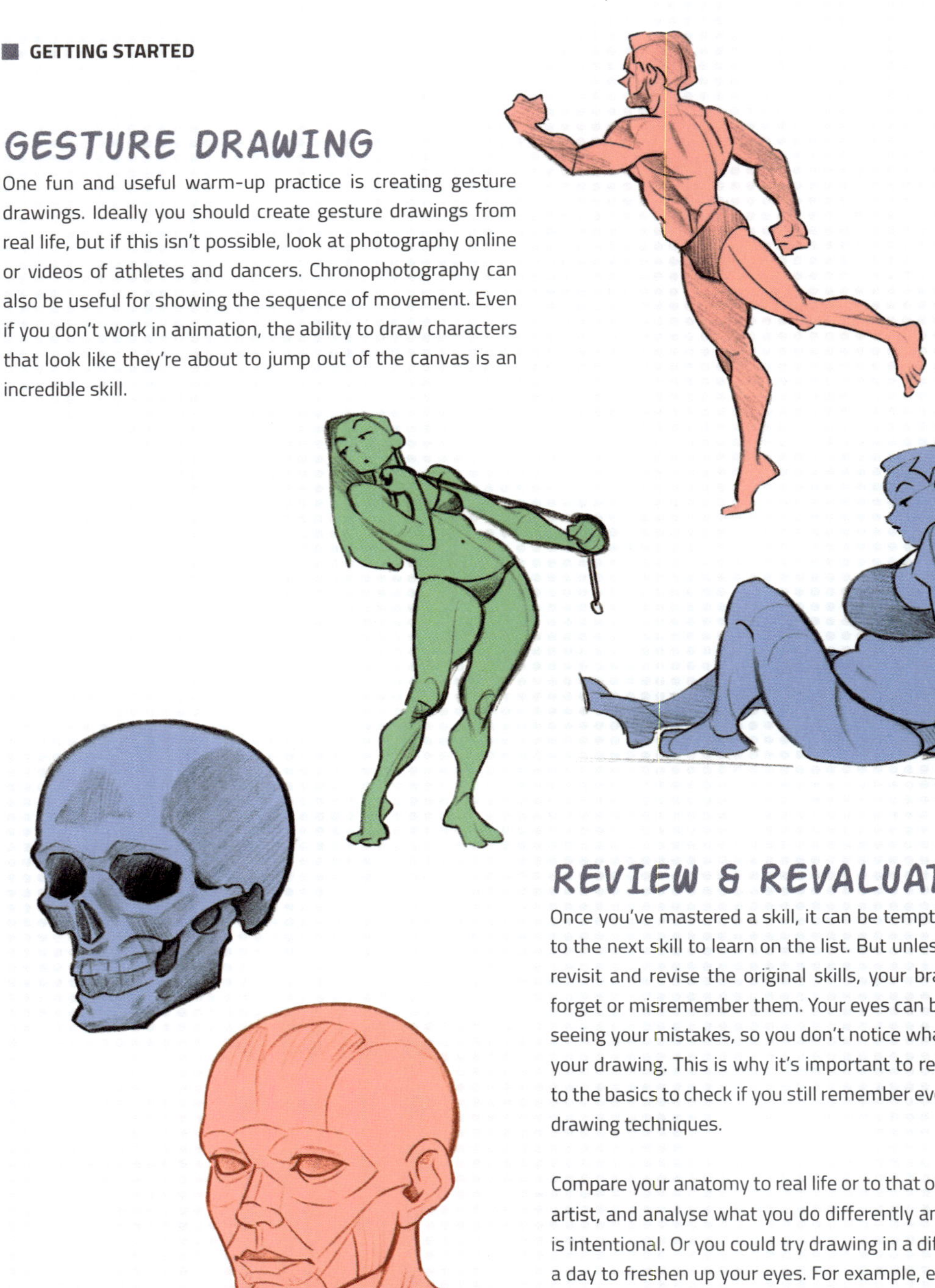

REVIEW & REVALUATE

Once you've mastered a skill, it can be tempting to move on to the next skill to learn on the list. But unless you regularly revisit and revise the original skills, your brain may slowly forget or misremember them. Your eyes can become used to seeing your mistakes, so you don't notice what's wrong with your drawing. This is why it's important to regularly go back to the basics to check if you still remember even the simplest drawing techniques.

Compare your anatomy to real life or to that of your favourite artist, and analyse what you do differently and whether this is intentional. Or you could try drawing in a different style for a day to freshen up your eyes. For example, experiment with a more realistic manga style, or a more cartoonlike chibi-style, or even another genre altogether. You might find that you discover different skills to experiment with, while the basics become less daunting.

RESEARCH

Research and reference material are essential for drawing. You have to feed your mind with information before you can start to imagine and interpret things in your own personal and creative way. Don't limit your research to online search engines. Seek out inspiration and reference in the real world and in physical media too. Even the simple acts of people-watching or engaging people in conversation can provide boundless insight and new ideas.

DRAWING FROM LIFE

You might wonder why you would ever need to draw from life when photos can capture a moment so perfectly. But life drawing is a great way of teaching you to see from a natural perspective in a three-dimensional space. Getting used to using the lenses of your own eyes will help you to better understand material captured via a camera lens.

Try to position your subject matter in a three-dimensional space and work out where potential vanishing points could be. How does your position influence the drawing? Can you use the background to help with perspective? Any information from real life can be a great resource for your drawings.

VARIETY IS KEY

You likely started drawing because something inspired you. Always be on the lookout for new ideas to keep your mind fresh with new material. Whenever you catch yourself enjoying something, take the time to ask yourself why this is. Obviously, you should never copy the work of other creatives, but do analyse what elements particularly speak to you. What kind of structures do you observe in different pieces of media and how could you potentially use them in your own work?

Look at different types of art – comics, video games, animation, live action. Restricting yourself to just reading manga and watching anime will make your ideas limited to certain tropes and visuals. Combining various looks from different media can give your art a unique and interesting appeal.

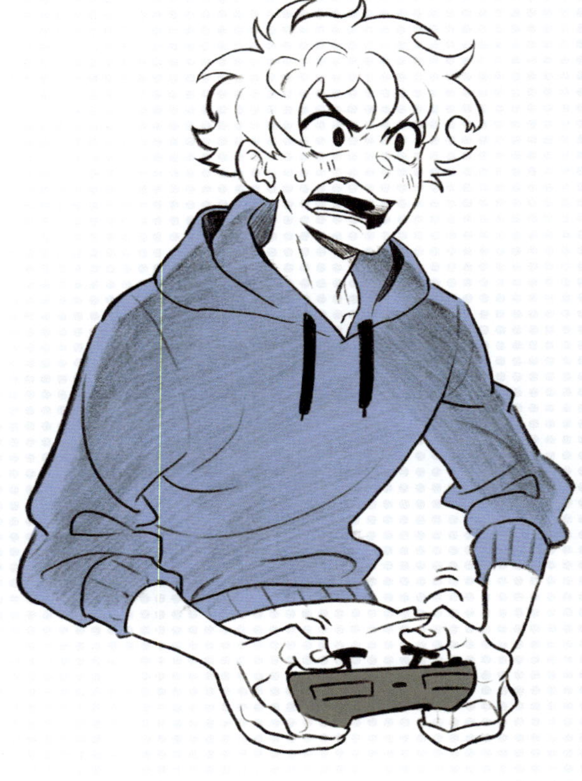

BOOKS & MUSIC

Reading stimulates the brain in a slightly different way to looking at images, so it's important to do both when thinking up new ideas for your manga artwork. Non-visual media, such as music, is also useful for providing inspiration. If you plan to study animation or gaming, a soundtrack will play a big part in the process. But even if you choose to create comics, you can still find ways to work with music, be it as a source of inspiration or by new technologies, such as adding music in webtoons. Going to concerts or live music bars can inspire new ideas and experiences that could be great material for your artwork and stories.

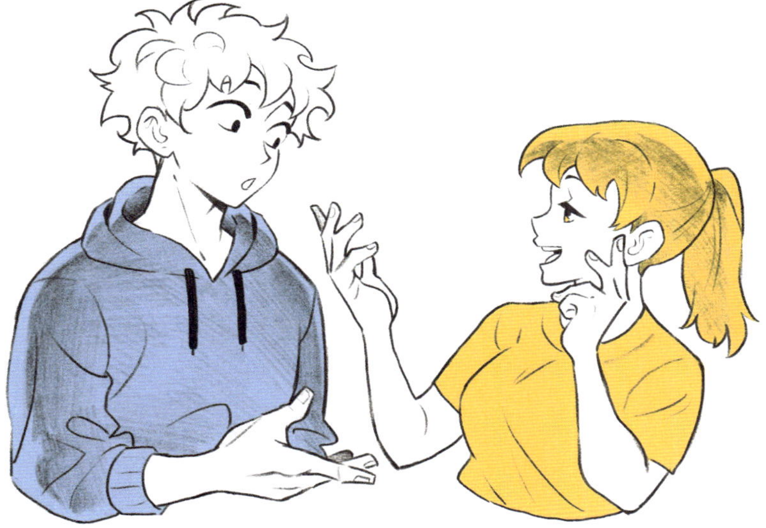

TALK TO PEOPLE

Talk to fellow creators to find out how they got started and what inspires them. You might learn invaluable tips and form great friendships. Avoid only talking about your interest in manga, though. And don't just listen to one single person or artist; make sure you check out several perspectives to inform your own opinions. Creating well-rounded characters requires a good understanding of people and the human experience. Take the time to talk to your friends and family, then when you create your characters, give them elements that reflect the people you love to make them feel real.

CHALLENGES & TRENDS

The internet is full of interesting art challenges and trending topics. These are a great way to begin building your community when you're starting out as an artist. It can give you a good idea of what audiences enjoy and how other artists approach these challenges. One example is the 'Draw This In Your Style' challenge, often seen with the hashtag #dtiys, where artists invite their audience to draw the same character in their own style. This is a fun and useful way to both practise and analyse other art styles.

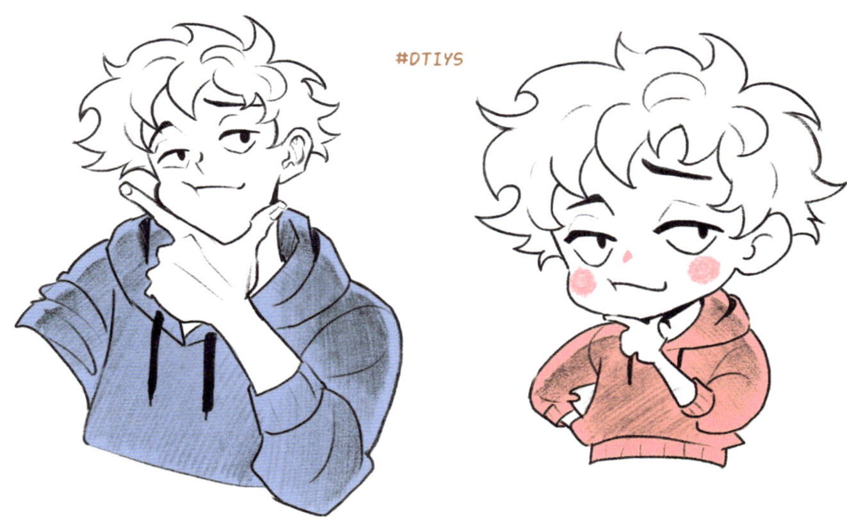

THUMBNAILS

When you start drawing, before committing to a big, detailed sketch, it can help to first create a series of small thumbnail sketches. This will allow you to quickly capture your ideas and try out numerous possibilities without committing to any. It's also a good way to take visual notes for later drawings. Sometimes it can help to take a break and step away from your ideas before you can see what it truly needs in order to shine.

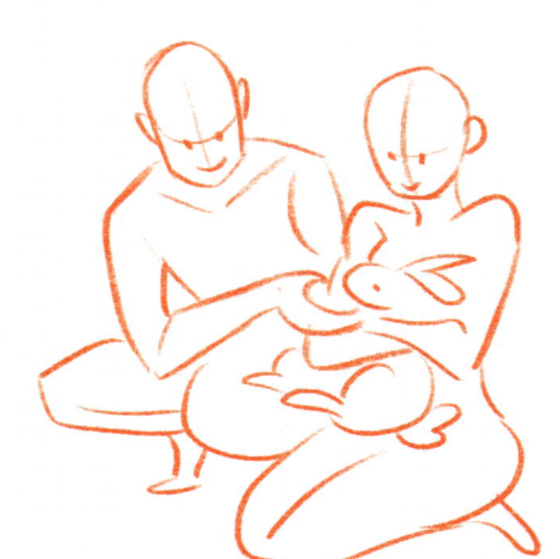

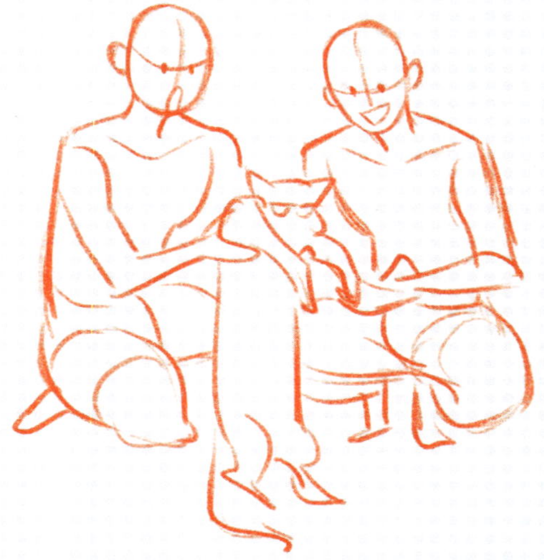

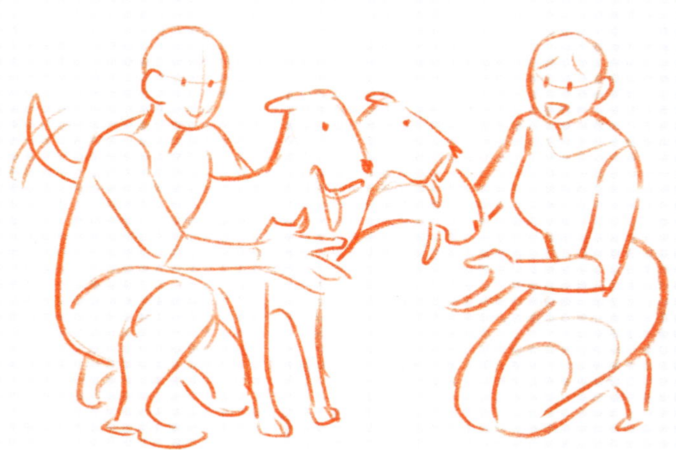

EXPLORATION

Your first thumbnail is important, as it shows your initial idea and instincts. While you may think it's your best idea, it's always worth exploring more variations, as you will often find you stumble on unexpected possibilities. Think of thumbnailing a bit like a mind map. Sometimes you need to sketch a visual before you can come up with another one. After a period of exploration, you may still decide to go with your first sketch, but as thumbnailing is a quick process, you won't have lost too much time. Plus, you can somewhat justify your decision by examining what aspects of the thumbnails do and don't work.

COMPOSITION THUMBNAILS

Thumbnails are the best way to try out compositions, allowing you to concentrate on the whole picture without the distraction of detail. Bold compositions have daring and clear forms, which can be hard to see once you start worrying about anatomy, perspective, and all the smaller yet important components of an image. Study other illustrations and film stills to sketch small composition thumbnail studies. This can help you to understand how and even *why* other artists use the shape language they do.

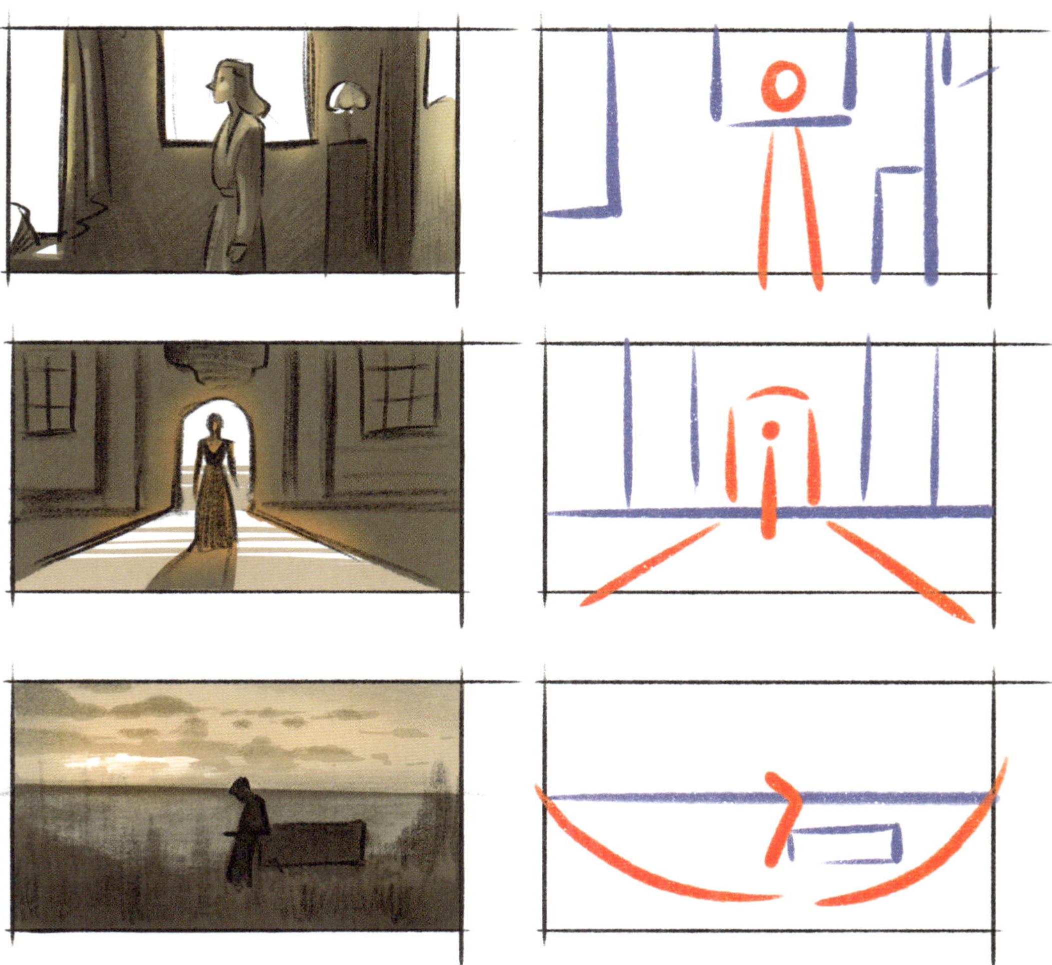

SILHOUETTE THUMBNAILS

Silhouette thumbnails enable you to concentrate on big forms. When creating a character without a background, it can be helpful to try out different silhouettes with various designs and poses before choosing colours, expressions, and details. Imagine your character is standing very far away. Will you still be able to tell who it is and what they're doing? The silhouette should always be clear and readable. Consider if the silhouette would even be engaging enough to make you notice it and try to figure out what makes it interesting.

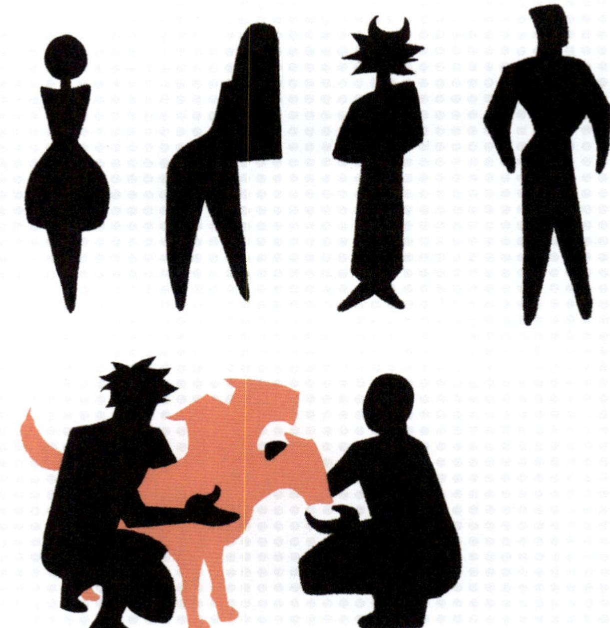

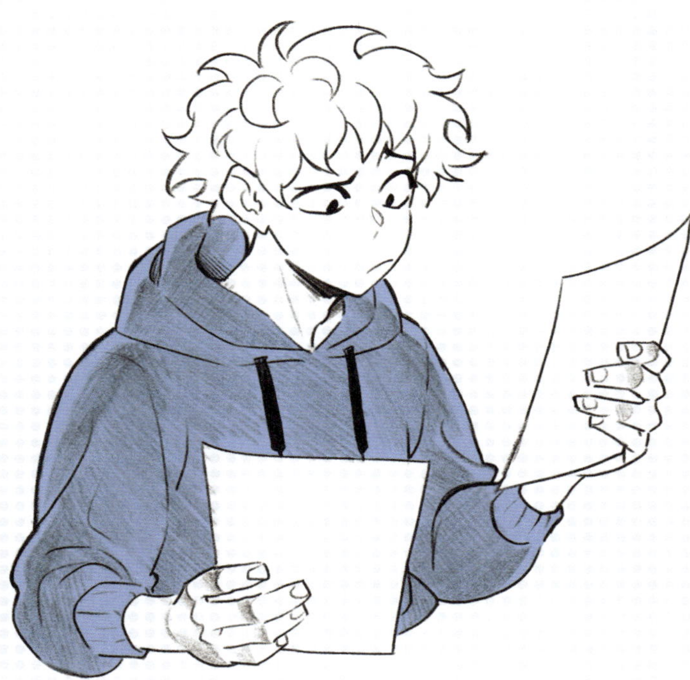

CHOOSING THE IDEAL THUMBNAIL

First decide on the purpose of what you're drawing. Is it a simple image you want to upload to share on the internet? If so, consider what format reads the clearest on which app. Sometimes a square format is best, whereas at other times a longer portrait image will better fill a whole phone screen. Is the image intended for print or on clothing? All artwork has to be slightly adjusted depending on its use, so don't be overwhelmed by the decisions you will have to make. See them as opportunities to strengthen your will and sense of aesthetics. Choose the thumbnail that works best for the platform it's intended for, as well as the one that best conveys your vision for the character.

SEQUENTIAL ART

Thumbnailing is essential for sequential art, such as storyboarding for animation sequences and comics. Here thumbnails must work in a sequence, rather than on their own, which brings its own set of challenges. The reader's eyes should be guided through the sequence without any unnecessary strain, confusion, or boredom.

Printed comics vs. online comics or those read on mobile phones have a different reading experience, which has to be considered. It's a good idea to think about these things when creating quick thumbnail sequences, as going back to change more detailed images can be much more time-consuming.

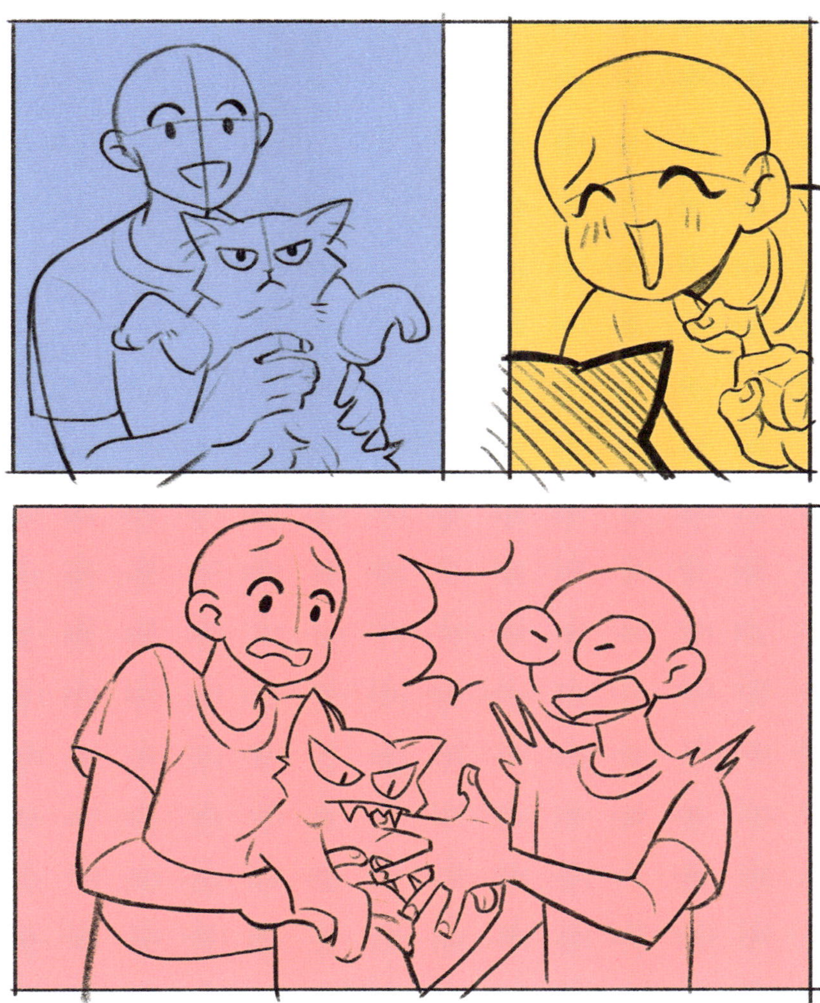

STORYTELLING & PERSONALITY

The characters you create should be full of personality. While you don't have to go overboard and add lots of details to their background, you do need to establish some kind of narrative. Here are some tips and questions you can ask yourself in order to create story in your artwork:

▶ **Set-up:** What does your character want? Why do they want that? Where do they come from? What kind of family do they have? What is it they're missing in their life? At this point you make a promise to the reader about what they can expect. The story is then about how well you can keep your promise, or maybe even surprise your audience.

▶ **Catalyst:** What moment throws their life off balance and forces them to act? Maybe they meet someone new? Explore interactions between characters.

▶ **Confrontation:** What kind of problems is your character facing? Think of the thing your character would hate the most and throw it at them to see how they react. What kind of lessons should you teach your character and possibly even your audience? No one enjoys a moral lecture, but explore possible solutions. A story can be an exploration for both you and your audience, but make sure you do make some kind of discovery or statement, otherwise the audience might feel like they're left with nothing to digest.

▶ **Resolution:** How could your character's problems escalate? Will they be able to face and overcome their faults or obstacles? How could they use what they have learned to win the day? Perhaps you could spend some time showing their new world after the conflict has finally ended.

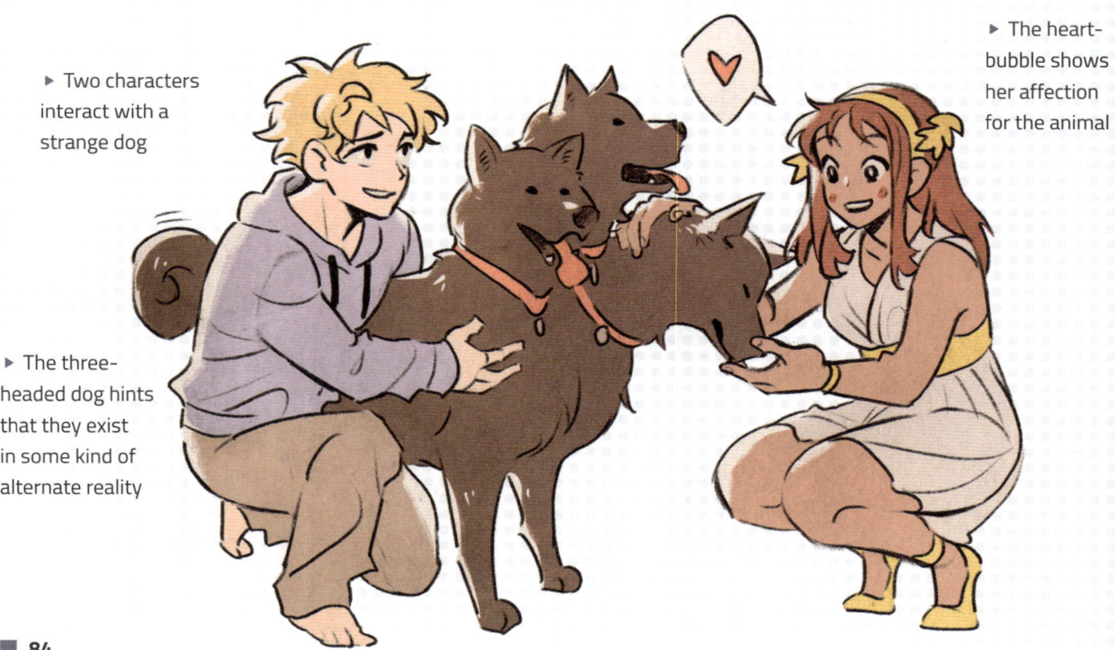

▶ Two characters interact with a strange dog

▶ The three-headed dog hints that they exist in some kind of alternate reality

▶ The heart-bubble shows her affection for the animal

MOTIVATION

What is motivating can be different for every artist. It's all too easy to fall into moments of frustration and potentially even burnout if you don't take care of yourself. Technology can be a helpful tool, but it can also eliminate a lot of what makes art enjoyable. As an artist, it's essential that you find enjoyment in the creation process, rather than focusing solely on the final result. If you feel tense and unable to concentrate, it's important to take a break, release the stress, and recharge. Knowing yourself and what your body needs will help your work greatly.

If you do feel like you lack the motivation to draw today, here are some popular sources of inspiration:

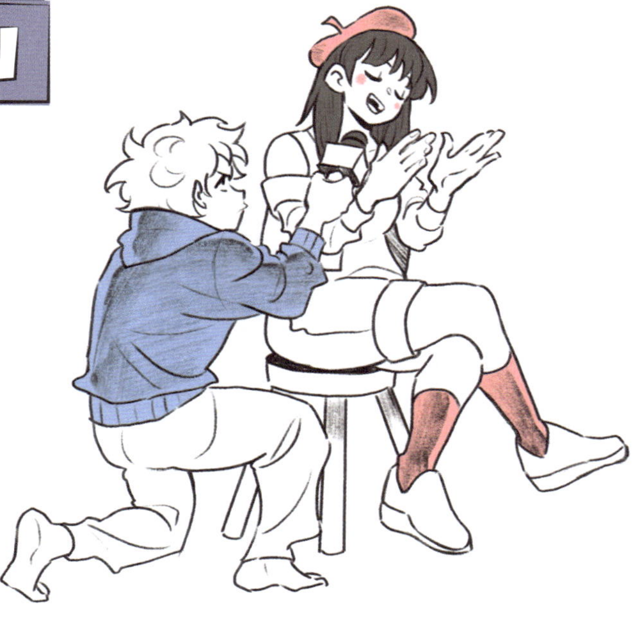

▶ **Artist interviews:** While you connect with characters and stories, it's also helpful to see where they came from. What motivated your favourite artist to create their comic or character? Every artist has their own process and it's incredibly valuable to be able to learn from other's wisdom, and even their mistakes.

▶ **Museums and art books:** Sometimes you don't need to directly interview an artist or even read their biography. Simply going to a place with a lot of information or art you enjoy – such as a library, museum, or art gallery – can help to get your creative juices flowing. Looking at art books and collections can inspire new ideas and open your eyes to new possibilities you might not have explored yet.

▶ **Remember why you started:** Why do you love art? What do you love to consume? It helps if you're a part of an audience yourself. Why do you feel motivated to read or watch something? Maybe it can be the same reason you feel motivated to create.

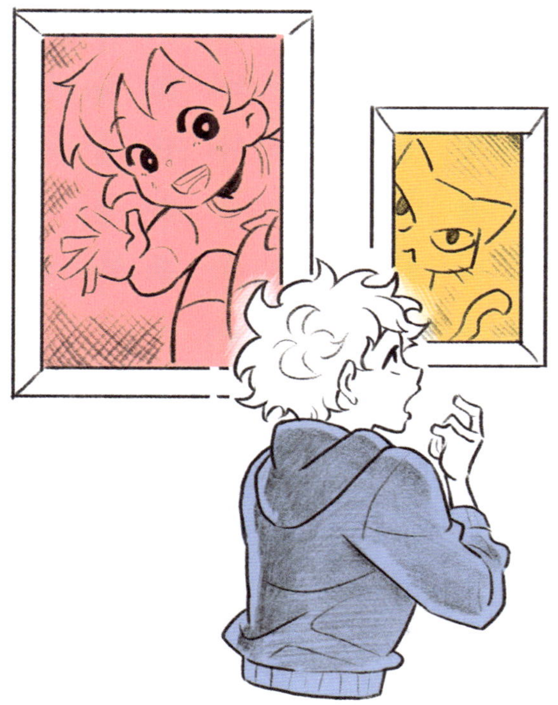

Now that you've read through the Getting Started chapters and have an understanding of the different drawing tools, design techniques, and the manga style, you can start to put your new skills into practice. The following section contains ten character tutorials by ten leading manga artists. They span a variety of different styles, mediums, and approaches, with six created using traditional media and four created digitally in Clip Studio Paint. Each tutorial follows the same steps, as described on the opposite page.

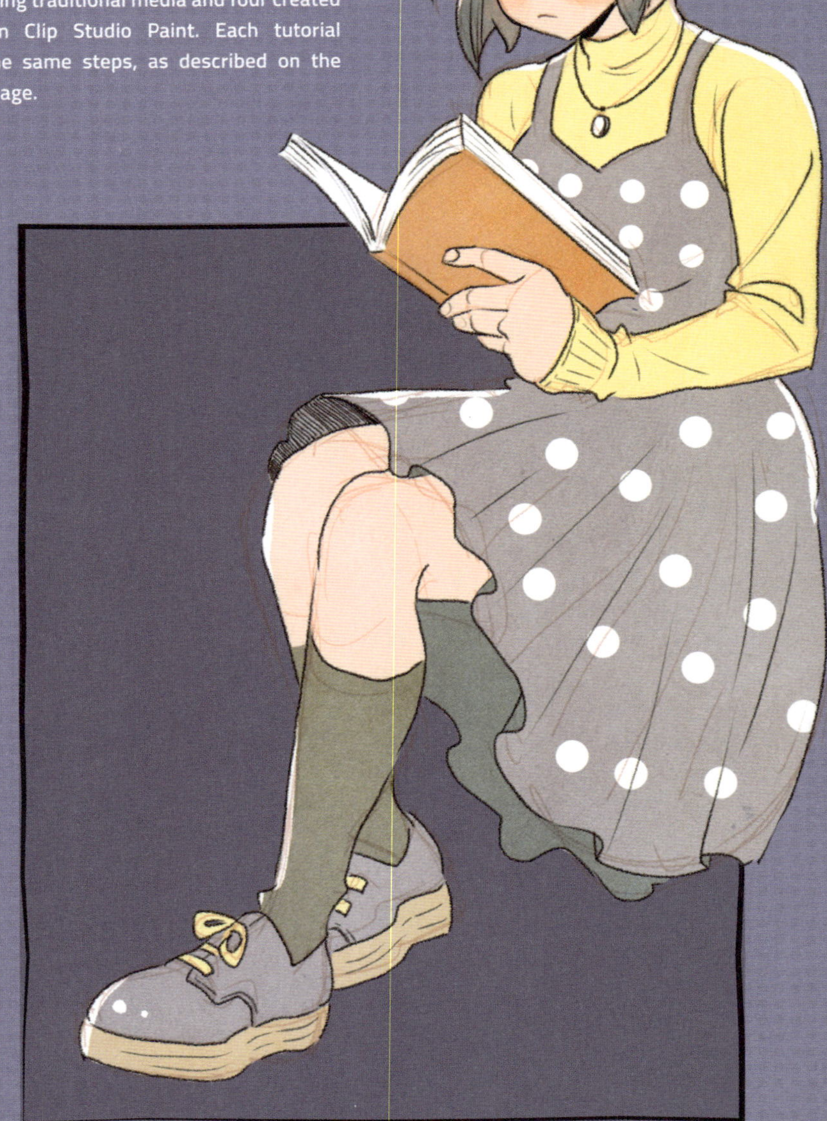

RESEARCH

Researching ideas and collecting reference material is key to creating a good character design. Look at what each artist discovers and observe how it makes their final design more interesting and believable.

THUMBNAILS

Thumbnail sketches enable you to explore various shapes, silhouettes, and compositions before selecting a favourite. Notice how each artist uses this step to refine their ideas before choosing one to develop.

FOUNDATIONS

Every good character design requires a strong foundation. See how the artists create simple building blocks for their design, ready for more details to be added later.

BUILDING UP

This step is used to draw a full-size pencil sketch on top of the foundation. Read the tips each artist offers for drawing specific areas of the design.

DESIGN FOCUS

Once you have a pencil sketch of the whole character, focus in on three key parts of their design. Note what design decisions the artist has made to ensure it reveals more of the character and their story.

IDEA INVENTORY

This step is for exploring different design variations – of a prop or costume accessory, for example – to develop the character's design. Observe how the artists use this stage to come up with new ideas.

FINAL SKETCH

Once you have finished exploring ideas, it's time to create a final pencil sketch. Watch how the artists use this step to tidy up their design in preparation for inking the line work.

LINE WORK

Draw over your pencil sketch to create clean, refined line work in preparation for adding colour. See how the artists vary the line weight in order to add depth and interest to their design.

COLOURING

Bring your character to life with colour! The artists have used a variety of different media, from watercolours and Copic markers to digital painting in Clip Studio Paint. Follow along with the tools you have, or step out of your comfort zone and experiment with something new.

DOWNLOADABLE RESOURCES

Drawing can be challenging and it's not unusual to need a little extra help and guidance. Visit **store.3dtotal.com/ resources** to discover a selection of downloadable resources to help you as you work through the following tutorials. The resources include line work for each tutorial, plus several anatomy sketches, which you can print out to provide a guide as you draw.

CHIBI FANTASY HERO

BY JHON LUIS GAÑAS 'PSYCHORAMEN'

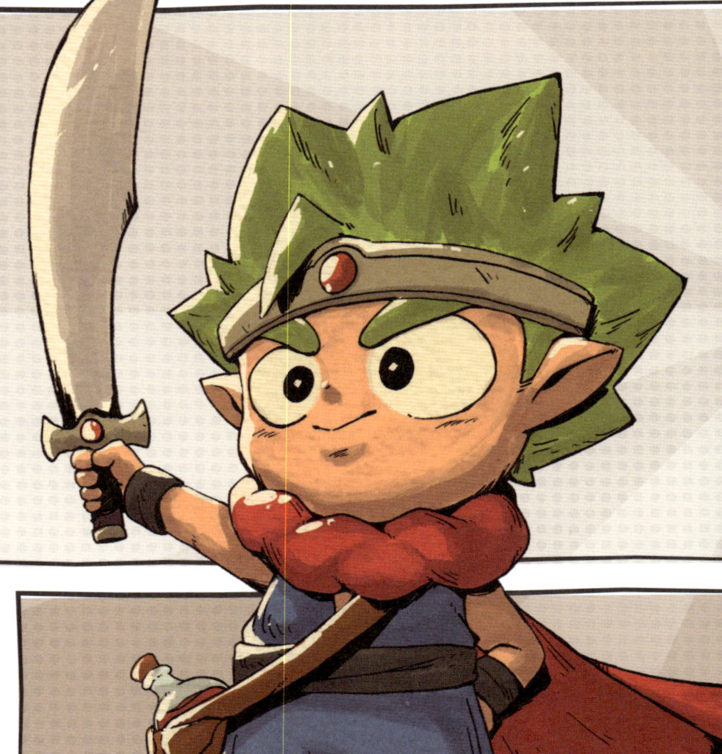

In this tutorial you will learn how to create a chibi fantasy hero. Imagine the character as a video-game protagonist, chosen to save his world. On top of looking brave and adventurous, he also has a heart of gold. By following the steps you will find out how to master the popular manga style, as well as how to draw a chibi form, which is a distinct caricature technique within the manga genre.

TOOLKIT

▸ Graphite pencil

▸ Eraser

▸ Graphic marker

▸ Fineliner pen

▸ Correction fluid

RESEARCH

Before you get going, a thorough study of typical fantasy heroes will help you to visualize your character. You can usually find good references in video games, especially Japanese role-playing games. Official art books of all varieties can be useful, and you can hunt for images using online search engines, too. Your objective is to find the essential elements that make up a fantasy hero. Use your graphite pencil to create rough sketches while you are researching.

SWORD

Every hero needs a weapon to vanquish evil, and most fantasy heroes use a sword. This weapon should be simple, but also something that would be wielded in a fantasy setting.

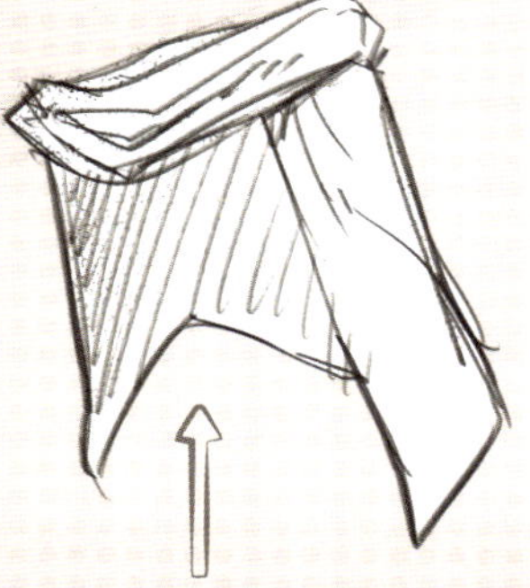

POTION

What good hero goes adventuring without a potion? This invaluable item is known to restore health upon consumption. Most potions shown in video games are stored in glass vials.

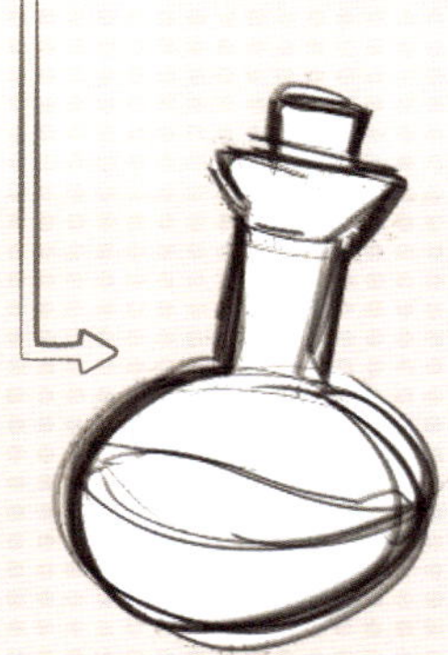

CAPE

A cape is another staple for fantasy heroes. Your character will need it for protection against weather conditions such as wind, rain, or cold.

ACCESSORIES

In fantasy worlds, accessories aren't just worn for the sake of fashion. Some can grant heroes additional abilities. Maybe your hero can wear an item like an amulet or circlet with embedded gemstones.

COMPANION

You may also give your hero a companion. They are usually tiny creatures that accompany them on their journey. Companions can range from normal creatures, such as birds or dogs, to fantastical creatures, such as fairies or spirits.

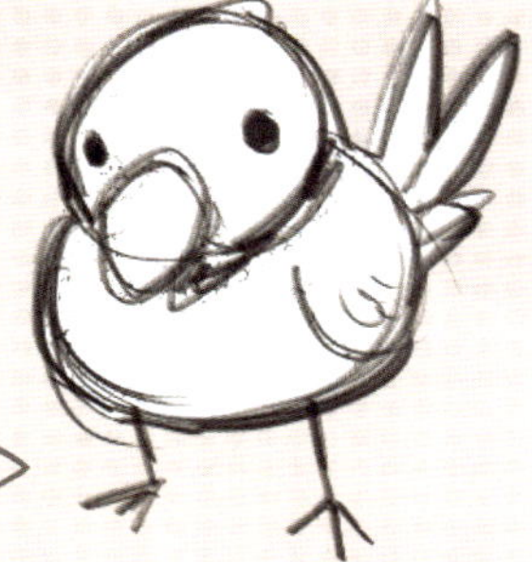

THUMBNAILS

Thumbnails are helpful for expressing ideas as you plan a character. It's important to explore poses that can appear both strong and charming. Due to his chibi form, most of the hero's features will be small and rounded, which make him look soft and harmless. However, you can counterbalance this by adding rectangular and triangular shapes to make him appear sharper and stronger. Use your graphite pencil to sketch the pose, then fill it with a grey fineliner pen to determine the thumbnail's pose and silhouette.

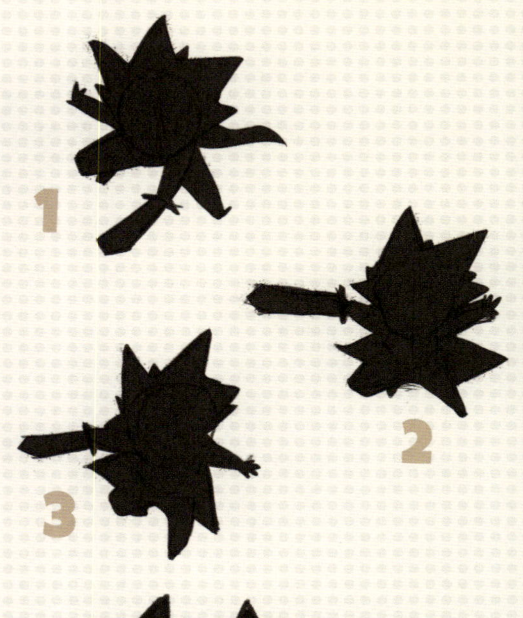
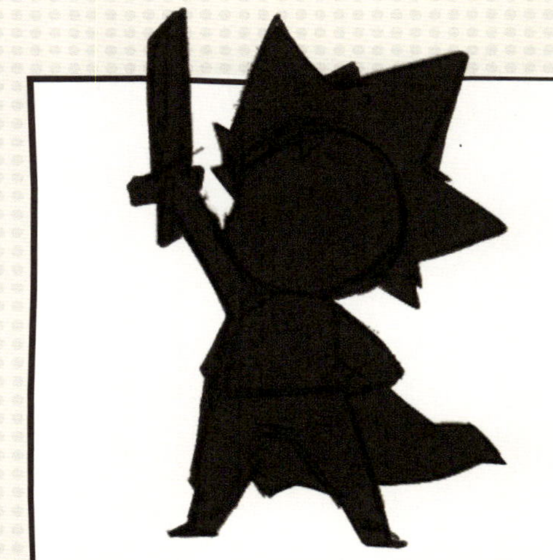
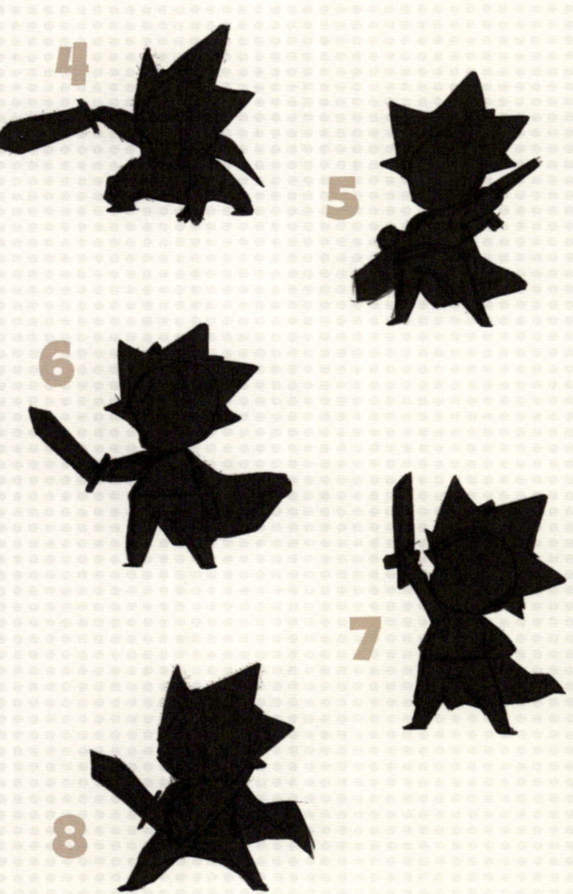

CHOSEN THUMBNAIL

The firm stance of thumbnail 7 depicts strength, while the raised sword gives the hero an air of confidence. The cape on the opposite side adds a dynamic look to the pose.

FOUNDATIONS

Now that you've selected a thumbnail, you can start recreating your hero in a respectable size. Using a graphite pencil, sketch the pose by drawing a stick figure. Draw circles for the head, joints, and limbs, then connect them with lines. A good skeleton will help you realize the overall pose of the character. After finishing the body parts, use basic shapes to continue adding other elements, such as the cape and sword.

BASE

▸ A prominent feature of the chibi art style is having a very disproportionate body. The head of your chibi fantasy hero should be a third or a half of his overall body size.

▸ Draw the arms and legs like tapering tubes, connecting the shoulder to the hand, and the hip to the foot. The hands and feet should be small to give the character a miniature feel.

▸ Add the cape by making a trapezoid with two corners connected to each shoulder. Make sure that it's formed in a diagonal direction to give it a dynamic pose.

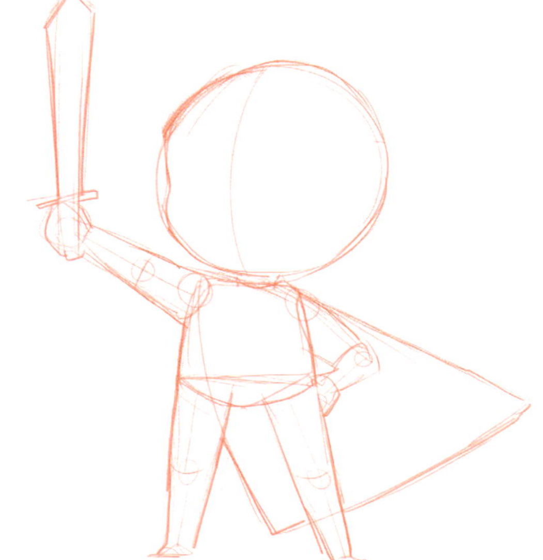

LINES

▸ Start shaping the face by drawing a rounded cheek and chin. This shape will give your hero a somewhat cute appearance. Style the hair by adding spiky shapes in different sizes.

▸ Add a collar to the cape by sketching several circles shaped like puffy clouds. To give the clothes some volume, round off the bottom so they look baggy and heavy.

▸ For more volume, add some slightly bigger details to different areas. Start by drawing a medium-sized triangle at the end of the cape to make it look like a fold, then add some spiky strands of hair around the face.

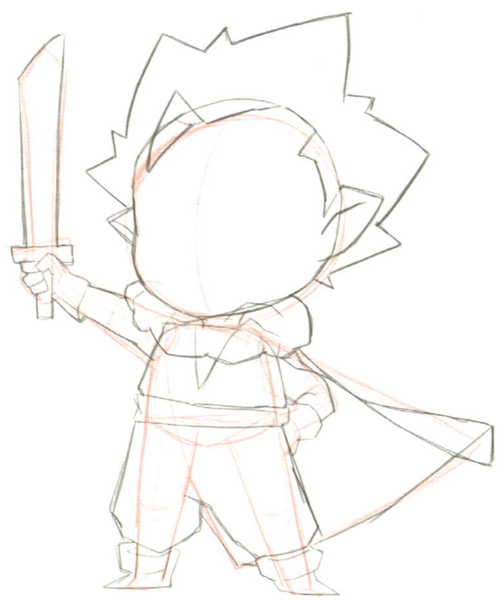

BUILDING UP

Now that the basic shapes are in place, you can add more detail to the composition. The goal here is to work out all of the parts needed for the design. Look back at the elements you researched earlier. Perhaps you can incorporate a potion bottle or some other accessory to give the character more story. The hero must look like someone with experience, but still with room for improvement. At this point in the process, apply more pressure while sketching. Keep using your graphite pencil to add various elements. Also keep in mind that you're still building the design, so it's fine for some details to be rough.

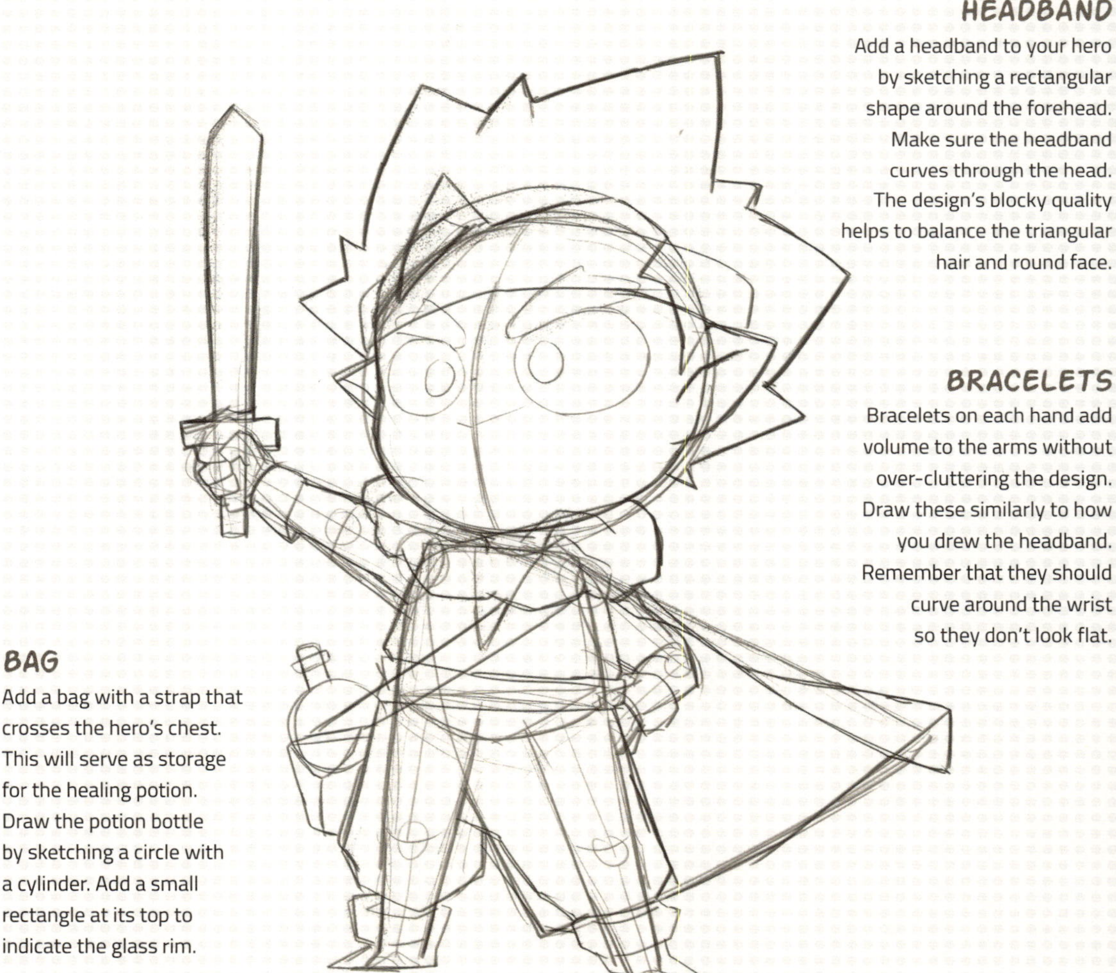

HEADBAND

Add a headband to your hero by sketching a rectangular shape around the forehead. Make sure the headband curves through the head. The design's blocky quality helps to balance the triangular hair and round face.

BRACELETS

Bracelets on each hand add volume to the arms without over-cluttering the design. Draw these similarly to how you drew the headband. Remember that they should curve around the wrist so they don't look flat.

BAG

Add a bag with a strap that crosses the hero's chest. This will serve as storage for the healing potion. Draw the potion bottle by sketching a circle with a cylinder. Add a small rectangle at its top to indicate the glass rim.

DESIGN FOCUS

HAIR

When creating similar shapes, a good habit to get into is varying the sizes to avoid making the element redundant. Draw the spiky hair by adding a medium, small, then large version of each triangle.

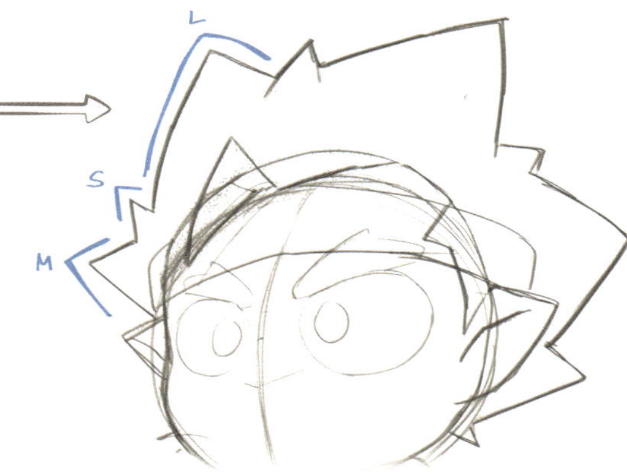

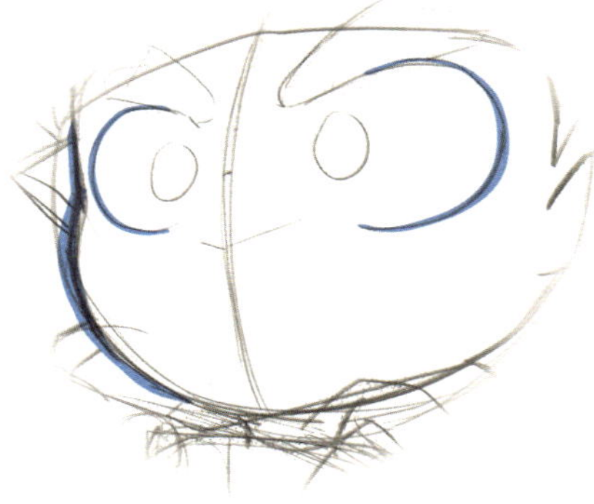

FACE

A chibi character's appeal lies in its adorable features. Achieve this look by creating round details, particularly on the facial area. Rounded cheeks and eyes create a cuter aesthetic.

TROUSERS

Make sure his trousers have a teardrop shape at the base. This will make the base of the design feel heavier, and as a result, the character's stance will appear stronger.

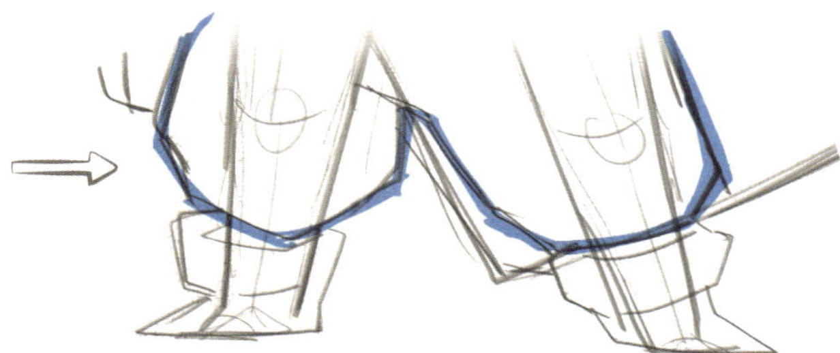

IDEA INVENTORY

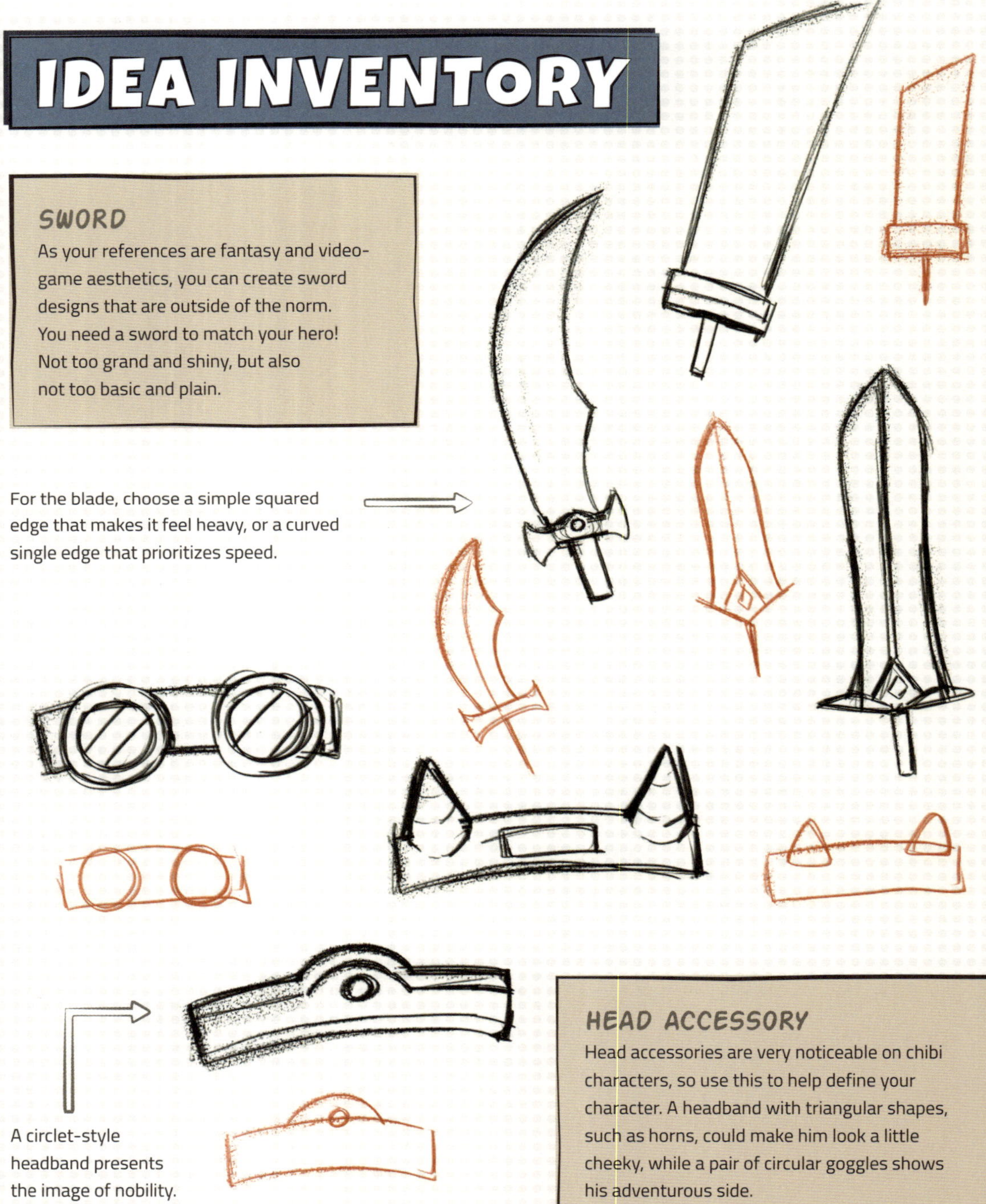

SWORD

As your references are fantasy and video-game aesthetics, you can create sword designs that are outside of the norm. You need a sword to match your hero! Not too grand and shiny, but also not too basic and plain.

For the blade, choose a simple squared edge that makes it feel heavy, or a curved single edge that prioritizes speed.

A circlet-style headband presents the image of nobility.

HEAD ACCESSORY

Head accessories are very noticeable on chibi characters, so use this to help define your character. A headband with triangular shapes, such as horns, could make him look a little cheeky, while a pair of circular goggles shows his adventurous side.

FINAL SKETCH

Now that you've assembled every part of the design, you can start finalizing the sketch by erasing unnecessary guidelines. Apply more pressure to significant details using your graphite pencil. This stage is also where you can change or add components before inking. Here, you can add the type of sword and head accessory you chose earlier. This finalized design makes the character look well-prepared for his adventure; his curved blade gives him speed and his circlet grants him additional abilities!

▶ Make the curved blade appear more striking by splitting the back of the blade into two curves. This will give the sword a tooth-like appearance. Note that both sides of the blade must be parallel and tapered towards the handle.

▶ Draw circular shapes to serve as embedded gems on the circlet and sword cross-guard. These gems will give the impression of being the sources of power for both the weapon and accessory. It also elevates the fashion of the overall design.

▶ Reposition the potion bottle to look more tilted. Slightly move the neck of the bottle backwards to create a three-dimensional look.

▶ As the puffy collar becomes one of the more prominent features of the design, you should consider giving it a bolder shape. Perhaps you can sketch a straight, zigzagging pattern on both sides, making it look like a tough fabric instead of a soft one.

▶ Your hero's face should look valiant, so tilt the eyebrows downwards to give him a determined smile. Most chibi characters don't have noses, but you can incorporate one by adding a small comma between the eyes.

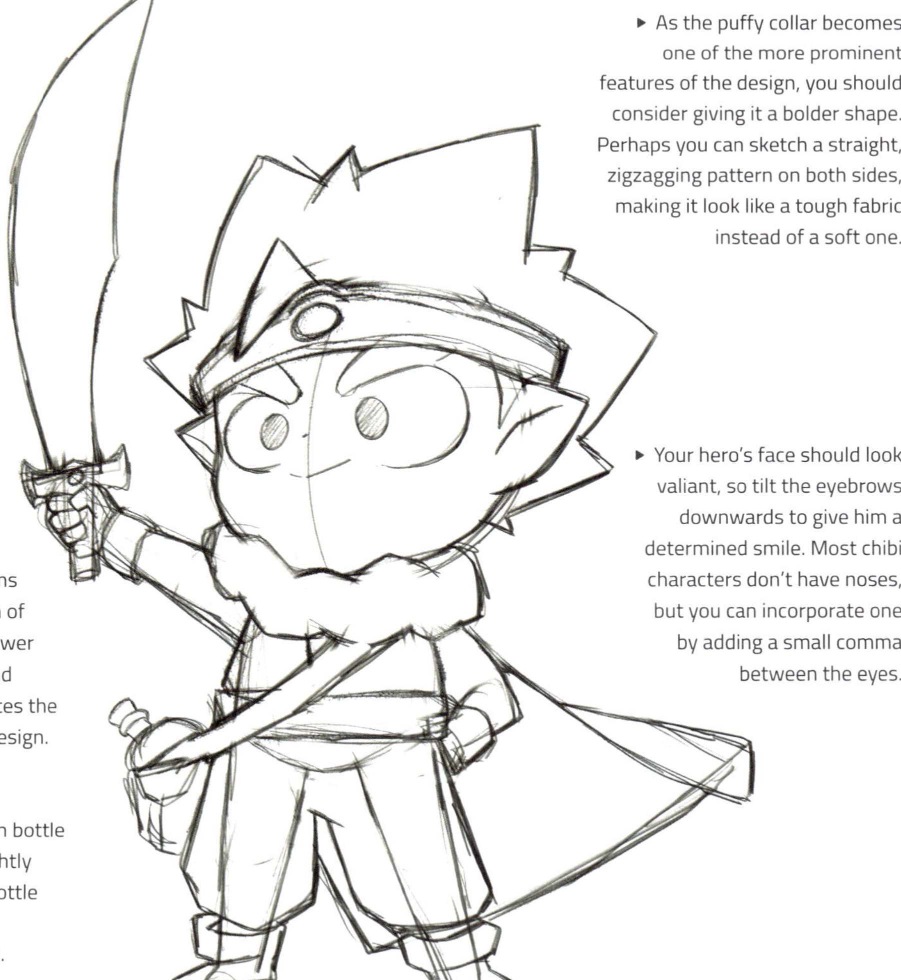

LINE WORK

For this stage, use a 0.2mm and 0.5mm fineliner pen for inking. Inking is one of the most prominent steps when creating manga, since the majority of manga has no colour and uses only black ink. Make sure to line your sketch using steady brushstrokes at a controlled pace. When dealing with lengthy lines, use your whole arm to get to the end, then use your wrist to create smaller, finer details for accuracy.

▸ Add shadows to the areas that have objects sitting in front of them, such as the hair, bag straps, sword handles, and ears. Make sure to follow the shape of the objects to create a believable shadow.

▸ Add volume to the design by using small lines that follow the outline. Not only will it create a pleasing rougher look, but it will also make the detail look textured.

▸ Remember to use thick lines for outlining, but thin lines for the smaller, finer areas. This will help to differentiate the overall shape from the details.

▸ Lines inside any shape can appear less noticeable when you use a few slant lines instead of lining them completely. Apply this to areas like the shoes and wristbands so the lines don't clutter the shape.

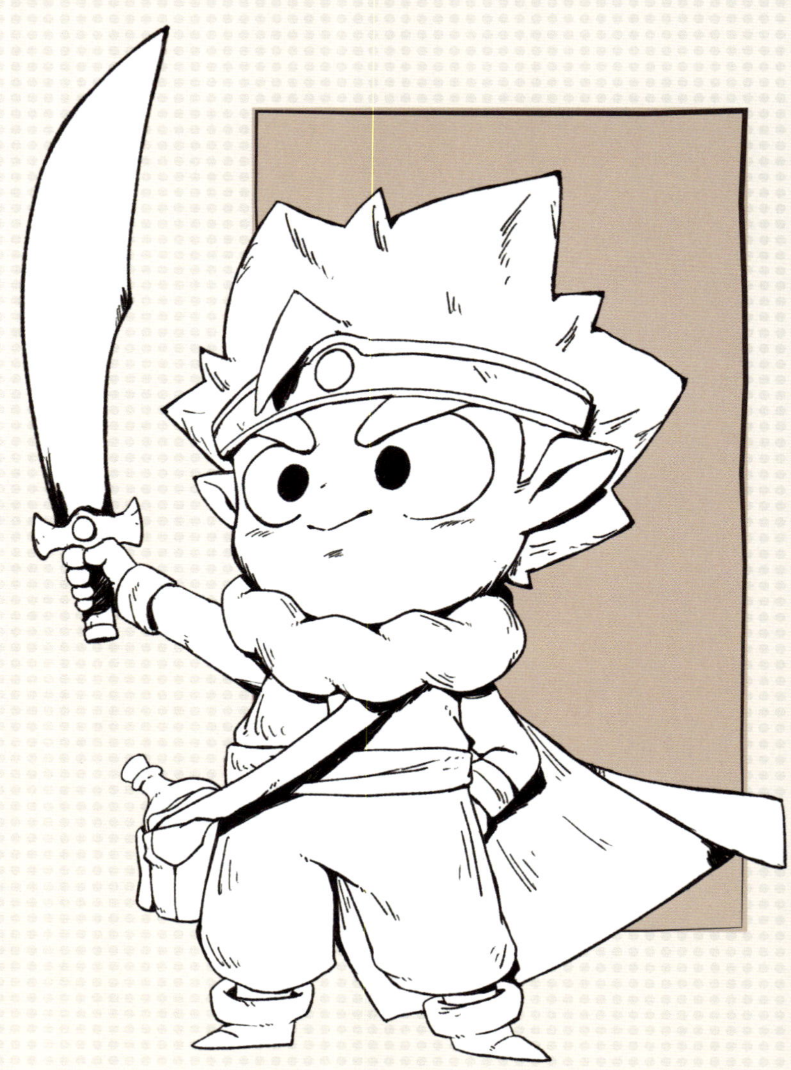

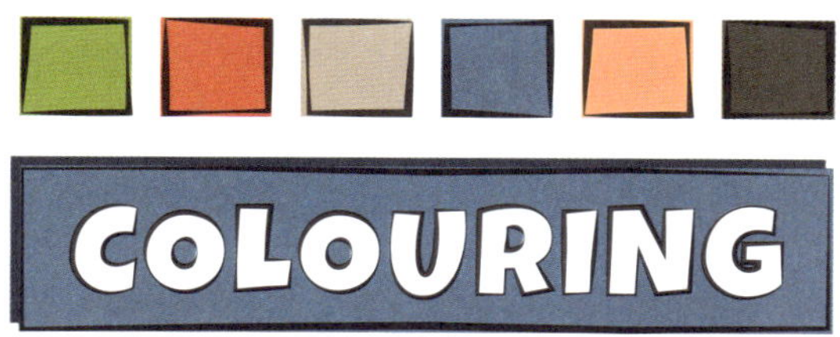

COLOURING

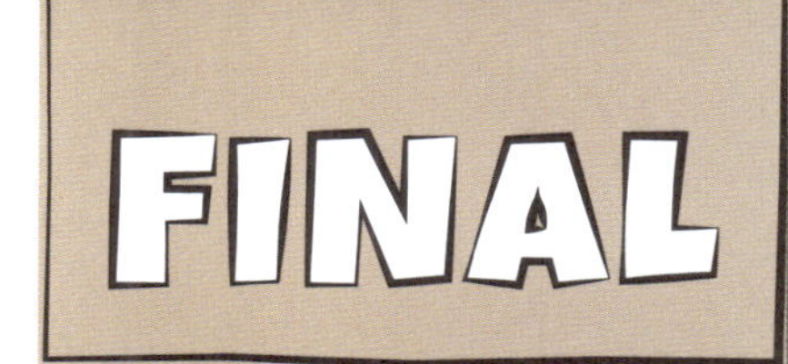

FINAL

Use graphic markers to colour your hero. A complementary palette of green, red, and blue will help him to stand out. It will also give him a noble and courageous look that defines him as a hero. Add the three colours to the most prominent features: the hair, cape, and his outfit. Use a peach colour on his face and arms, then use neutral colours for other elements, such as the circlet, boots, wristbands, and sword.

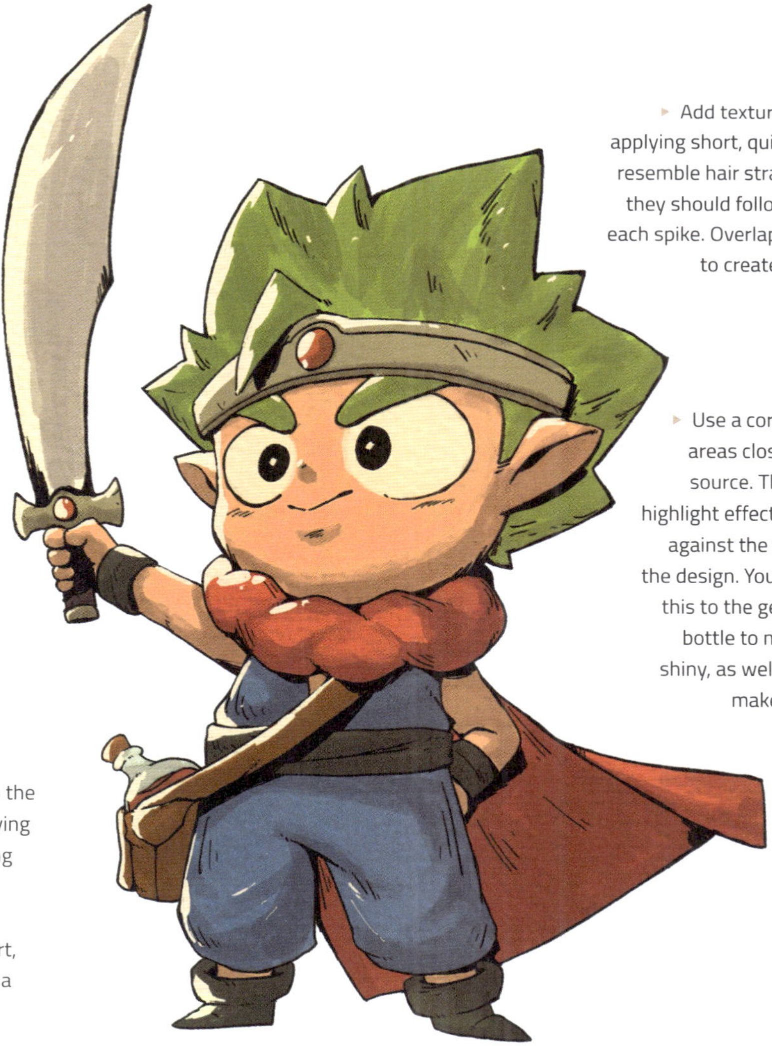

▶ Use a grey marker to add shadows. First identify the direction of the light source, then apply the shadows to the areas the light doesn't reach.

▶ Add texture to the hair by applying short, quick strokes that resemble hair strands. Note that they should follow the shape of each spike. Overlap these strands to create more volume.

▶ Use a correction fluid on areas closest to the light source. This will create a highlight effect that contrasts against the darker areas of the design. You can also apply this to the gems and potion bottle to make them look shiny, as well as the eyes to make them sparkle.

▶ For fabric texture on the trousers, start by applying long, downwards-facing tapered lines towards the centre. Next, add another layer with short, tapered lines to create a wrinkle effect.

MAGICAL ZODIAC GIRL

BY MIO

In this tutorial you will learn how to design a magical zodiac girl using traditional media. Step by step you will be guided through the creative process to build a character with the adorable traits of a cute witch in the popular shojo manga style. Typical of the 'magical girls' genre, she will have large eyes, delicate features, and soft line art to illustrate her gentle, whimsical nature. The zodiac theme – specifically the Libra sign and Air element – will help to define her aesthetic and powers, which she uses to fight alongside her friends against those who mean them harm.

TOOLKIT

- ▸ 0.5mm mechanical pencil (or graphite pencil)
- ▸ Eraser
- ▸ Black marker
- ▸ Coloured pencil
- ▸ Ruler
- ▸ 0.1mm sepia fineliner pen
- ▸ White gel pen
- ▸ Watercolour paint and ink
- ▸ Gold paint

RESEARCH

Start by figuring out your character's personality, as this information will make the design process much easier. This character will work with a team of magical friends, so it's important to give them a united theme.

Look online for inspiration for her clothing style based on the chosen theme and personality. Mix and match outfits without limiting yourself. There are plenty of possibilities in the world of fashion.

HEAD ACCESSORY

This character represents the Libra zodiac sign, communicated in this head accessory through the small scales attached to spread wings. The wings' shape makes her element more recognizable.

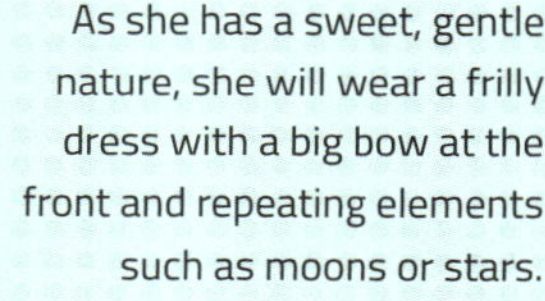

DRESS

As she has a sweet, gentle nature, she will wear a frilly dress with a big bow at the front and repeating elements such as moons or stars.

MAGICAL STAFF

She will wield a large magical staff to summon tornadoes with the help of her Air element. Try to design it to match the astrological theme.

HAIR

Long, feathery hair will give her an attractive, warm, and approachable look. Loose, wavy strokes will make the hair look like it's gently blowing in the wind.

BOOTS

She will wear special ankle boots with little wings attached that unleash her ability to fly. The dainty bows on the sides add to her overall cuteness.

THUMBNAILS

Experiment with ideas for the character's pose through a series of thumbnails. Use a black marker to roughly sketch out concepts and shapes as silhouettes. Her body language should be clearly readable and combine a balance of her confident yet reserved nature. Drawing her feet set wide apart and grounded could make her appear overly bold. Adjusting her legs closer together and positioning her arms nearer to her torso will convey a gentler vibe, yet she should still seem ready to defend against enemies.

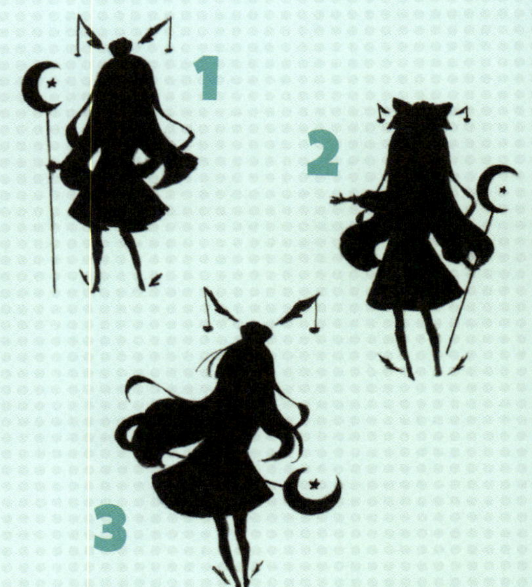

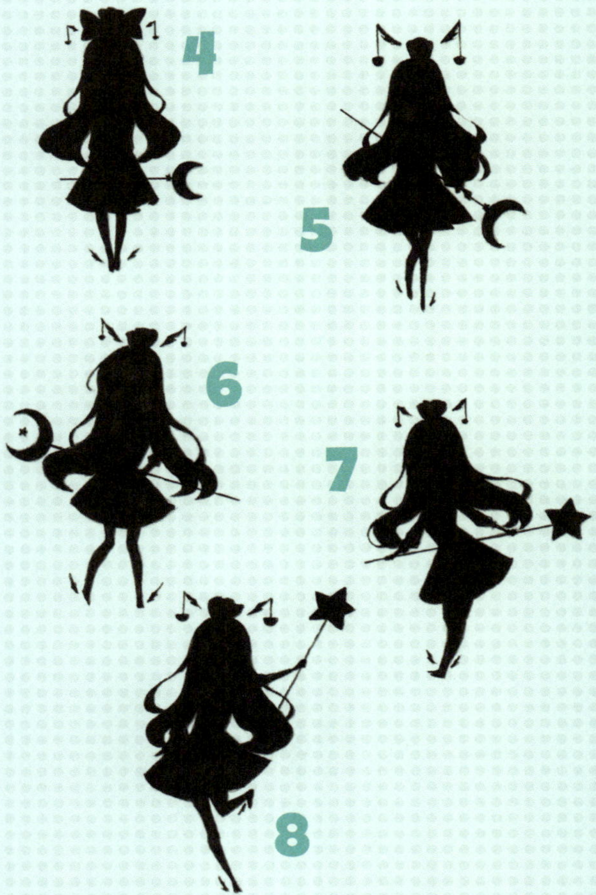

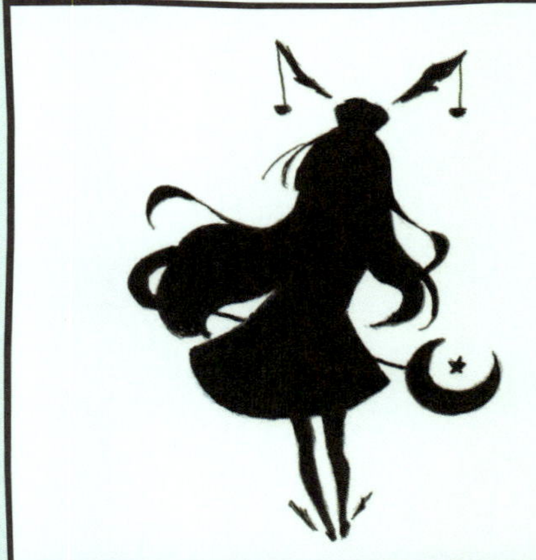

CHOSEN THUMBNAIL

The soft movement of her hair and dress in thumbnail 3 creates a dynamic pose. Her legs hang loosely below her body in a way that makes it look like she's floating, conveying her magical abilities.

FOUNDATIONS

Start by drawing a few guidelines using a coloured pencil. Simplify the character's body by sketching a simple figure made up of basic shapes. Refer back to the chosen thumbnail when positioning each shape. Draw an egg-shaped oval for the head and attach a curved line for the spine. Sketch two angled lines to mark hips and shoulders. Using simple lines, attach arms and legs. These guidelines will allow you to draw basic shapes for the arms, legs, and torso in the following steps.

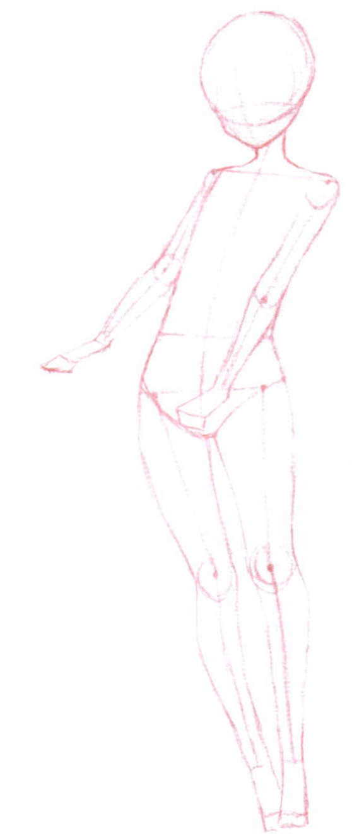

BASE

▶ To sketch the head, start by drawing a circle for the upper part. Mark a crosshair to indicate how the head is tilted slightly to the left. This will also help with drawing the details of the face. Next, add a pointy chin.

▶ Attach a narrow neck to the head. Female manga characters are typically narrower at the waist and wider at the hips, so sketch her chest area as a tapering rectangle, then draw the expanding shape of her pelvis below.

▶ To sketch her arms and legs, imagine them as curved cylinders connected by joints. Roughly indicate her hands by drawing rectangles for her palms and fingers. Repeat this step for her feet, then draw circles for the knees, elbows, and shoulders.

LINES

▶ Use a mechanical pencil to determine the position of her facial features. Lightly sketch her eyes with round shapes. Avoiding angular shapes will give the character a softer look. Sketch a kind smile and mark the nose with a dot.

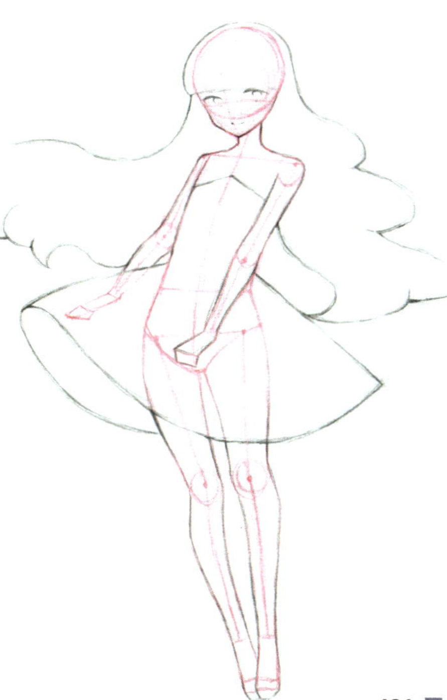

▶ To give her a dynamic, airy look, assume there's a breeze blowing from right to left. First sketch the silhouette of her hair by drawing organic, irregular shapes, then indicate her fringe with a straight line. You can define the hair strands later.

▶ Imagine the skirt's front side as a triangle, with the lower edge facing the wind direction. Curving the edges will suggest the fabric is moving in the wind. Lastly, draw the visible part of the back of the skirt.

BUILDING UP

The next stage is to define the key elements that were developed in the previous step. Use a mechanical pencil to sketch a few interesting medium-sized shapes on the dress to give it a cute, girlish look. As a reserved character, she won't wear clothing that is too revealing, so draw in an appropriate amount of fabrics on her outfit. Her hair and face are the features that should stand out the most, and these can also be used to convey her personality.

HAIR SHAPE

Instead of drawing each individual stand of hair, divide the silhouette of the hair into sections. Avoid parallel lines to make it look natural. Separate a few strands of her fringe by drawing curved V-shapes, then sketch the side strands using long, wavy lines.

DRESS

Draw elegant puffy sleeves and connect them to the upper part of the dress with a strap. Sketch a few folds in the skirt to give it a more realistic look, then draw frills along those folds to give the design more of a feminine aesthetic.

BOW & BOOTS

Draw a large bow to form the central element of the costume, then add a close-fitting fabric that's connected to the neckline of the dress. Next, define the lines of the boots.

DESIGN FOCUS

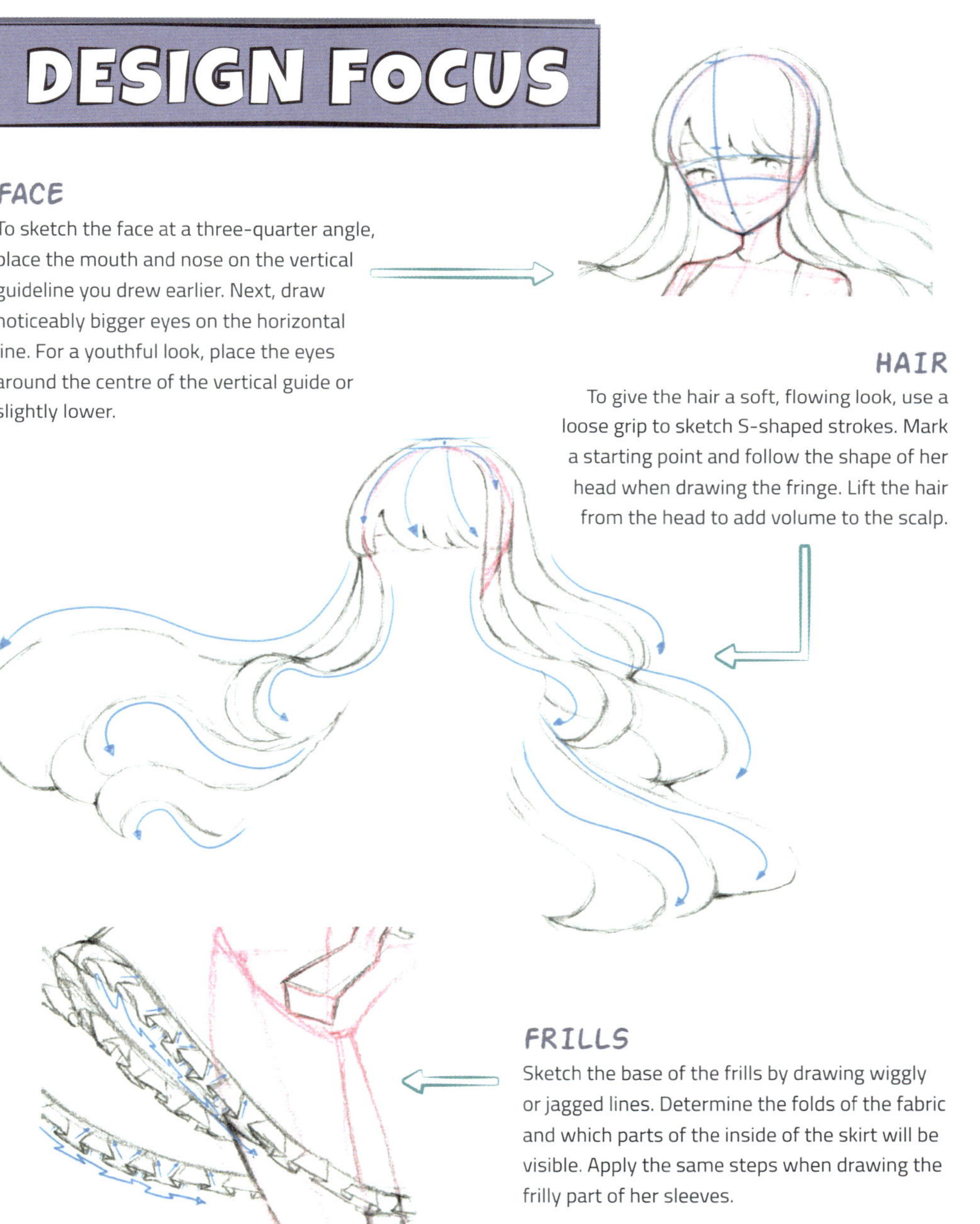

FACE

To sketch the face at a three-quarter angle, place the mouth and nose on the vertical guideline you drew earlier. Next, draw noticeably bigger eyes on the horizontal line. For a youthful look, place the eyes around the centre of the vertical guide or slightly lower.

HAIR

To give the hair a soft, flowing look, use a loose grip to sketch S-shaped strokes. Mark a starting point and follow the shape of her head when drawing the fringe. Lift the hair from the head to add volume to the scalp.

FRILLS

Sketch the base of the frills by drawing wiggly or jagged lines. Determine the folds of the fabric and which parts of the inside of the skirt will be visible. Apply the same steps when drawing the frilly part of her sleeves.

IDEA INVENTORY

MAGIC STAFF

The character will carry a large magical staff. Experiment with different designs and shapes, making sure they fit the overall zodiac theme. Use stars and a crescent moon as the focal elements, varying their size and position.

The moon stands out most in this design, enhancing the composition with its interesting asymmetrical shape.

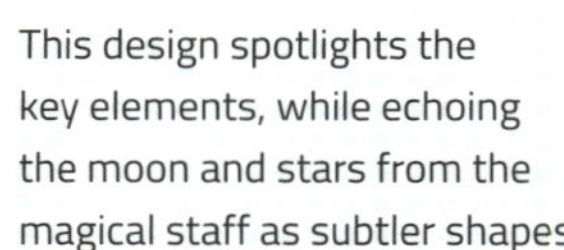

This design spotlights the key elements, while echoing the moon and stars from the magical staff as subtler shapes.

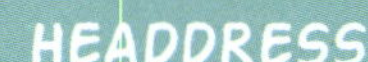

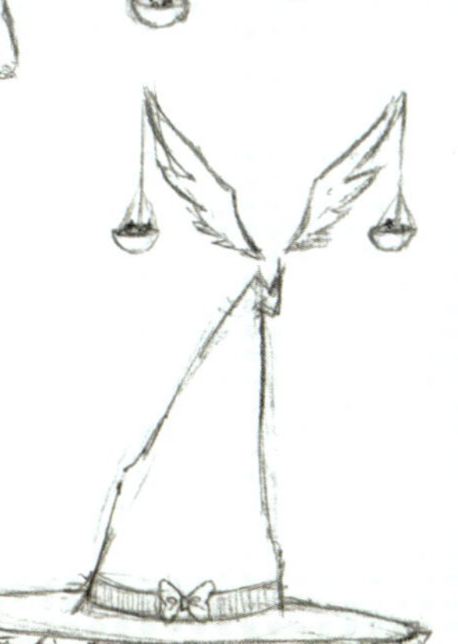

HEADDRESS

The headdress is a great opportunity to combine star sign and element. Sketch wings and scales as fixed shapes to create different variations. Keep the wings stylized and simple, making the ends point upward for a dynamic look.

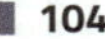

FINAL SKETCH

Increase pencil pressure when drawing the last details, such as patterns, small accessories, and decorative elements. Erase any guidelines that are no longer needed. Focus on incorporating the magical girl theme into the outfit to ensure the viewer quickly recognizes her zodiac sign. Introduce reoccurring shapes by echoing a few elements of the staff and headdress from the Idea Inventory to decorate the dress.

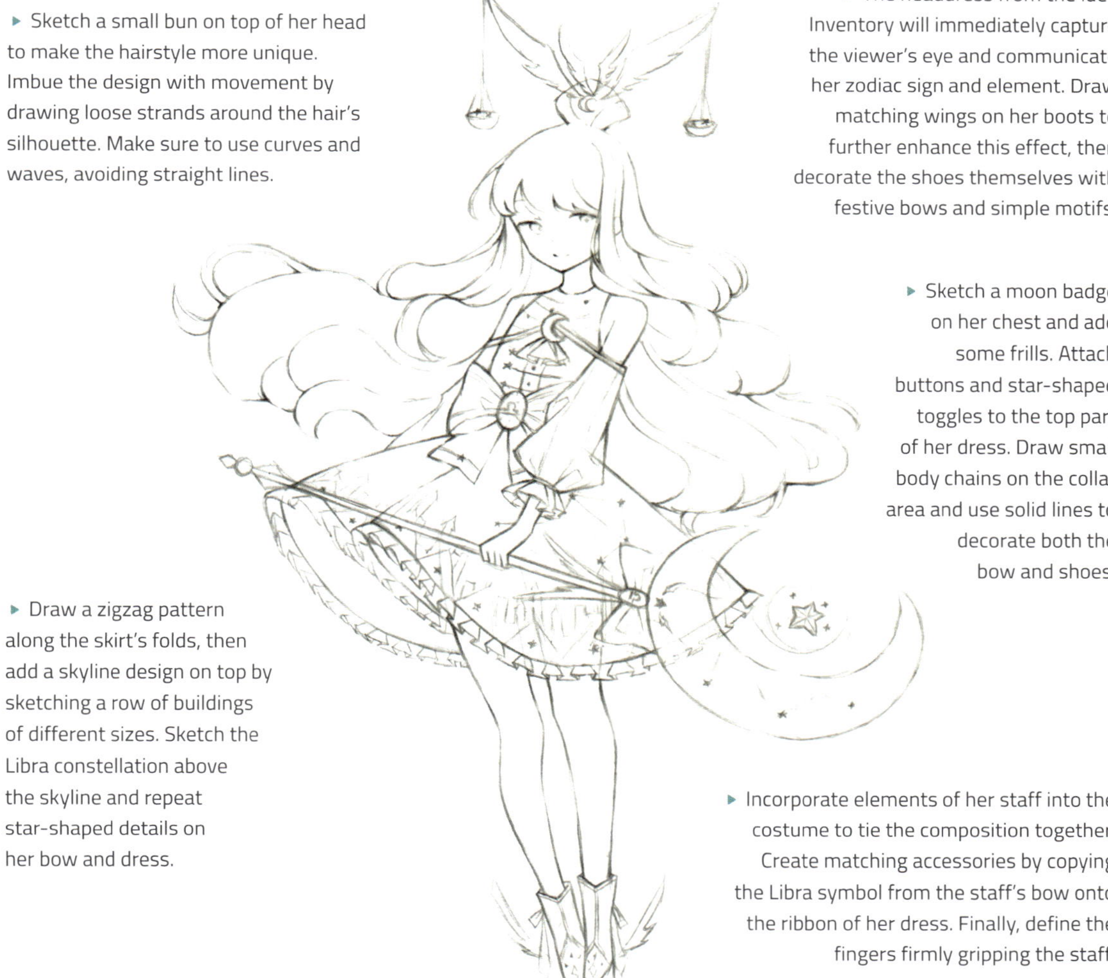

▶ Sketch a small bun on top of her head to make the hairstyle more unique. Imbue the design with movement by drawing loose strands around the hair's silhouette. Make sure to use curves and waves, avoiding straight lines.

▶ The headdress from the Idea Inventory will immediately capture the viewer's eye and communicate her zodiac sign and element. Draw matching wings on her boots to further enhance this effect, then decorate the shoes themselves with festive bows and simple motifs.

▶ Sketch a moon badge on her chest and add some frills. Attach buttons and star-shaped toggles to the top part of her dress. Draw small body chains on the collar area and use solid lines to decorate both the bow and shoes.

▶ Draw a zigzag pattern along the skirt's folds, then add a skyline design on top by sketching a row of buildings of different sizes. Sketch the Libra constellation above the skyline and repeat star-shaped details on her bow and dress.

▶ Incorporate elements of her staff into the costume to tie the composition together. Create matching accessories by copying the Libra symbol from the staff's bow onto the ribbon of her dress. Finally, define the fingers firmly gripping the staff.

LINE WORK

Use a 0.1mm fineliner to ink the cleaned-up sketch. Line the big sections first to get into the flow of inking, gripping the pen near the tip to create stable strokes. Try inking with sepia tones to make the lines look softer and to brighten up the final colours. To further enhance your line art, add tints of saturated colour on top of some parts of the lines. This will help to make your colours stand out more.

▶ Give your line art more life by varying the line thickness. When inking the hair, for example, thicken the areas where two lines meet. In contrast, capture the smaller hair strands by using thinner, looser strokes and a light pen pressure.

▶ Use thicker lines to ink the outline of her face and the upper lash line, while keeping the lines of her other facial features thin and fine. Use similarly thin strokes for other small details, such as buttons and patterns.

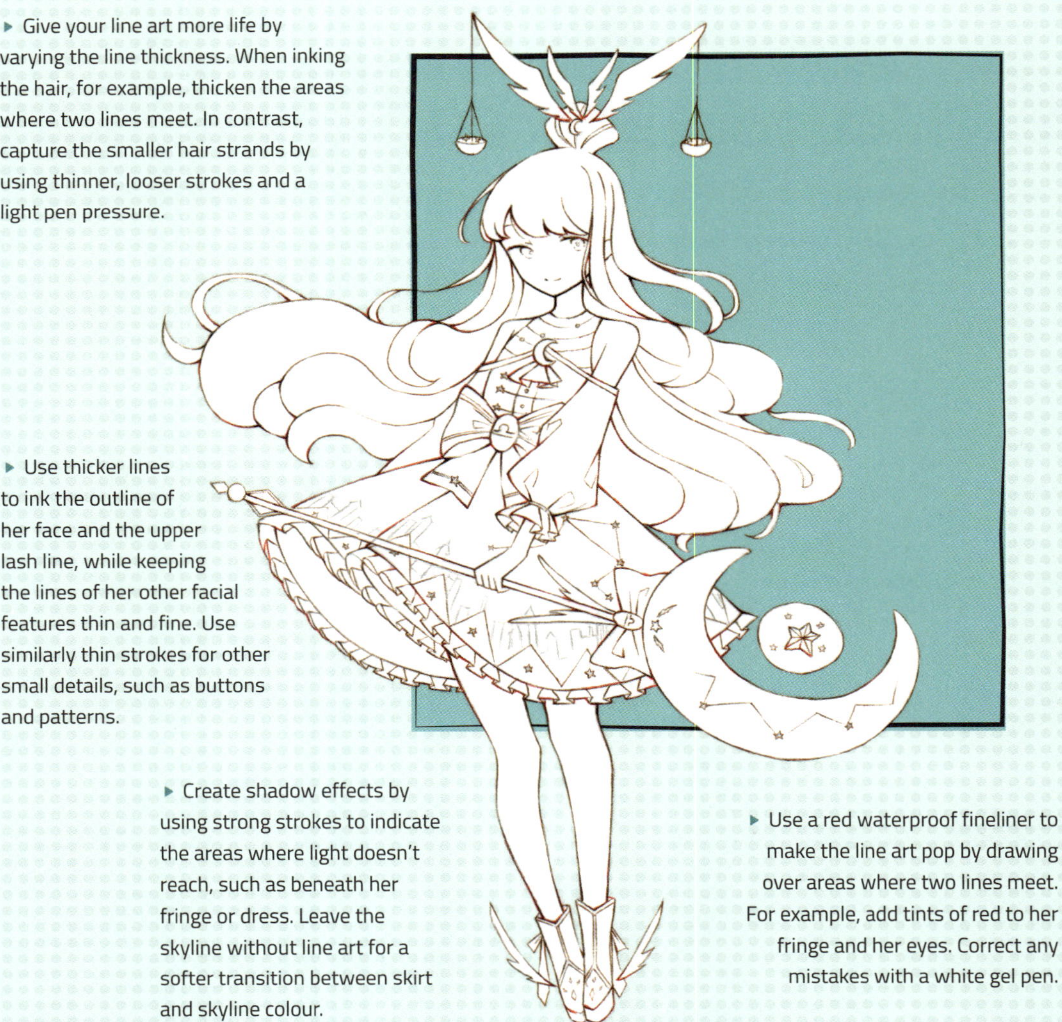

▶ Create shadow effects by using strong strokes to indicate the areas where light doesn't reach, such as beneath her fringe or dress. Leave the skyline without line art for a softer transition between skirt and skyline colour.

▶ Use a red waterproof fineliner to make the line art pop by drawing over areas where two lines meet. For example, add tints of red to her fringe and her eyes. Correct any mistakes with a white gel pen.

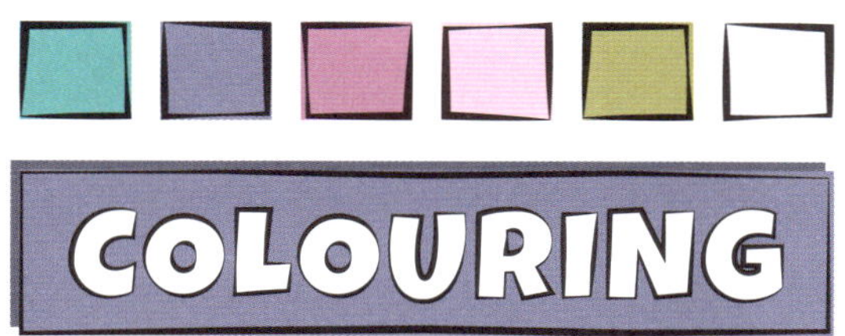

COLOURING

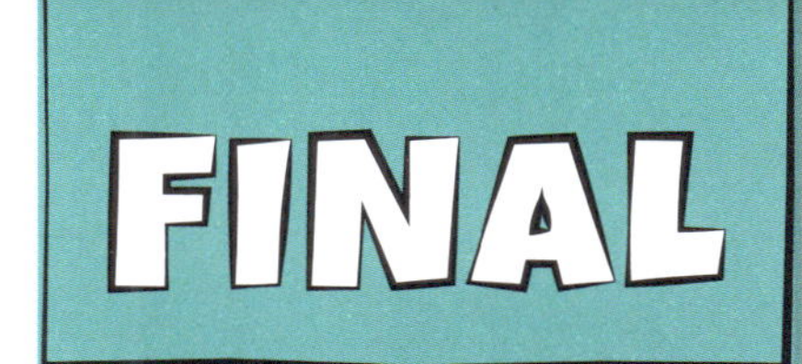

Use watercolour paint and ink to colour the character. Selecting turquoise as the dominant outfit colour will give her a calming vibe, while choosing purple tones for the bows will strike a visually pleasing contrast. Paint her hair a neutral brown, the skin a peach tone, and use yellow umber and bold red for her staff. Mix purple and turquoise to create grey shades for the white areas. Add embellishments using gold paint and draw stars on her skirt using a white gel pen.

▶ Start by creating an underpainting. Apply water to her hair and add light shades of purple and turquoise on top. Since watercolour is translucent, the underpainting will shine through the top colours, creating soft glow effects.

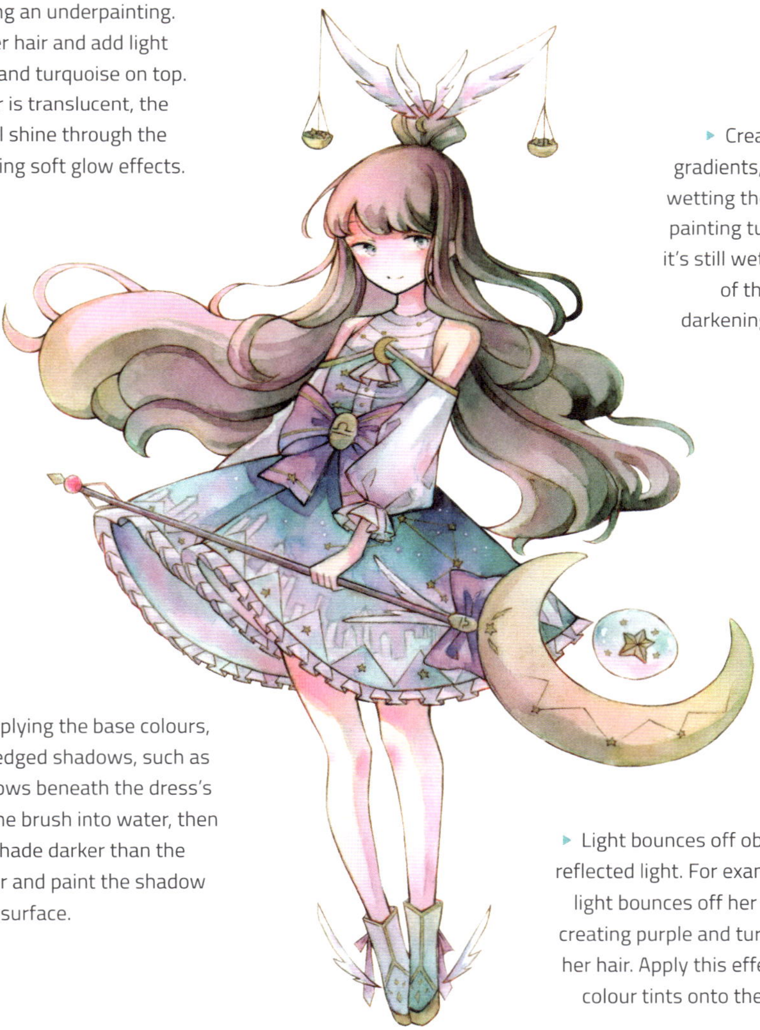

▶ Create soft shadows with gradients, from dark to light, by wetting the area of the skirt and painting turquoise on top. While it's still wet, apply more pigment of the same colour on top, darkening the upper skirt area.

▶ After applying the base colours, add hard-edged shadows, such as drop shadows beneath the dress's bow. Dip the brush into water, then choose a shade darker than the base colour and paint the shadow on the dry surface.

▶ Light bounces off objects, creating reflected light. For example, reflected light bounces off her skirt and bow, creating purple and turquoise tints in her hair. Apply this effect by painting colour tints onto the main colours.

▶ Final image © Mio

GUARDIAN OF THE FOREST

BY COCO GLEZ

In this tutorial, you will design the big, fluffy guardian of an enchanted forest, along with his little acorn helpers. This magical cat and his friends only show themselves to humans they deem worthy of their trust. The other forest inhabitants know they can rely on this friendly protector, but don't let his sweet appearance fool you! He is serious about protecting his forest home from human destruction. To bring these characters to life, you will need to use round shapes and organic lines, as well as ink and watercolour textures.

TOOLKIT

- ▸ Graphite pencil
- ▸ Eraser
- ▸ Waterproof ink and brush, or fineliners
- ▸ Watercolour paper and paint
- ▸ Brushes in various sizes
- ▸ Two jars of clean water
- ▸ Paper towels to dry your brushes
- ▸ White gouache (optional)

RESEARCH

When designing a fantasy mascot, it's helpful to learn as much as you can about their environment. Your characters live in a world of your own invention, and while the possibilities are boundless, you have to make sure your design is coherent. In this case, you will be drawing inspiration from nature and animals. Use a graphite pencil or a ballpoint pen to sketch ideas during your research.

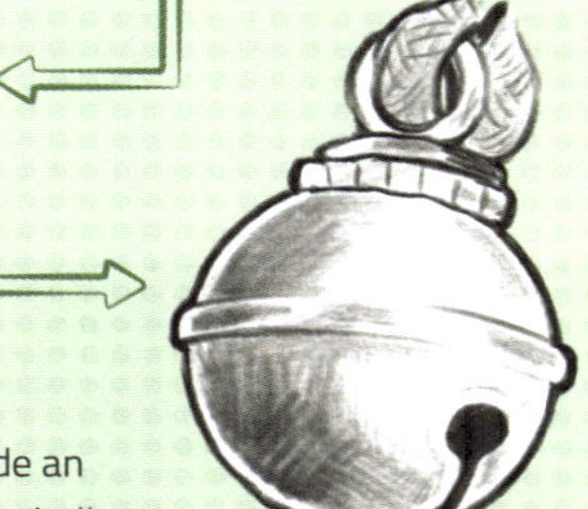

ANATOMY

Reference animal anatomies and study them from various perspectives. The key is to visualize how these creatures move and express themselves.

ACORNS

Take inspiration from nature by observing plants, especially their leaves and fruit. The concept of an acorn imbued with life is both simple and fun.

BELL

If you plan to include an ornament, such as a bell or an amulet, it's also important to study different styles and varieties of the same object.

LEAVES

Through study and practice, artists continuously add to their visual library. They learn different ways to draw various objects and elements such as leaves, which can greatly vary in shape and size.

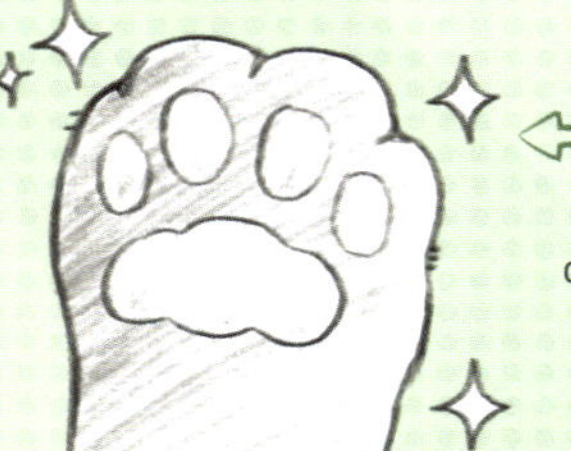

PAWS

Why not add a dash of sweetness to your design! Cat paws are universally cute, so find a pose that showcases them.

THUMBNAILS

Sketching thumbnails is a quick way to test the readability of your character design without worrying about the details. As you are combining a cat with forest elements, there are options to implement leaves, flowers, branches, or even an entire tree into your design. Using ink and a brush, try creating different silhouettes that will represent the character's personality.

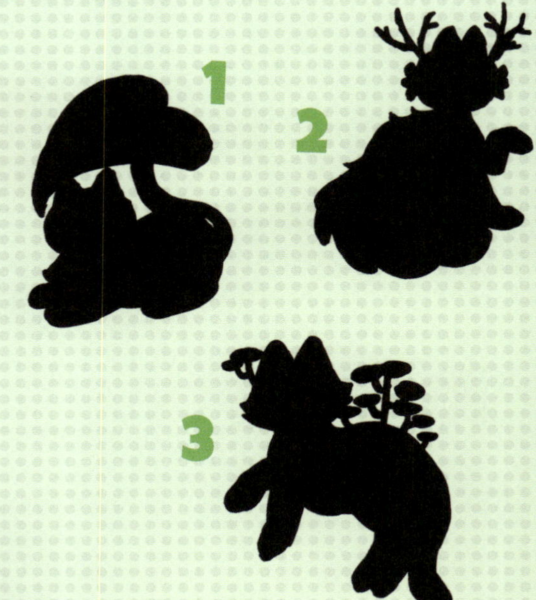

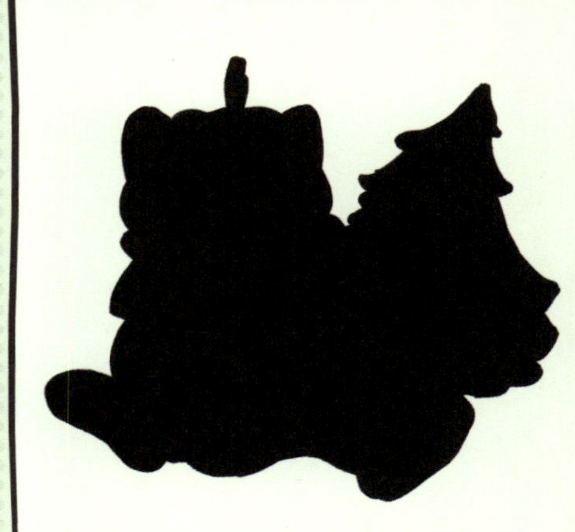

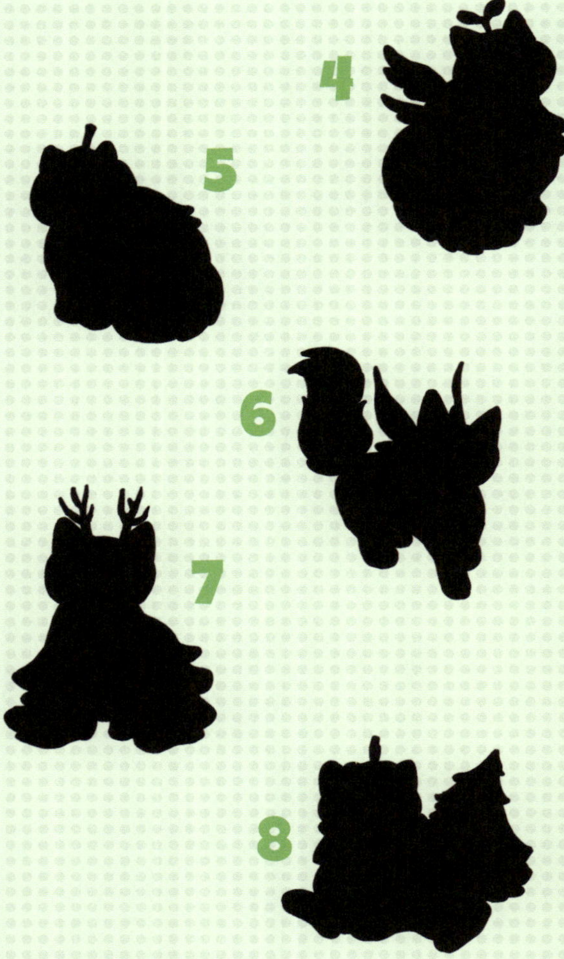

CHOSEN THUMBNAIL

Thumbnail 8 best represents this character's traits: smart, reliable, and relaxed. He is calmly watching over the forest.

FOUNDATIONS

Now start building your character from very simple shapes. Remember to take your time. If your sketch is detailed enough, the inking process will require much less improvisation. Try to keep the pencil sketch as light as possible, as you will be erasing the lines later.

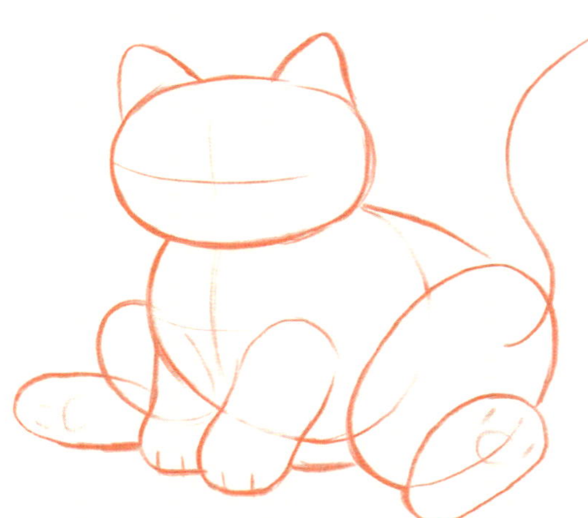

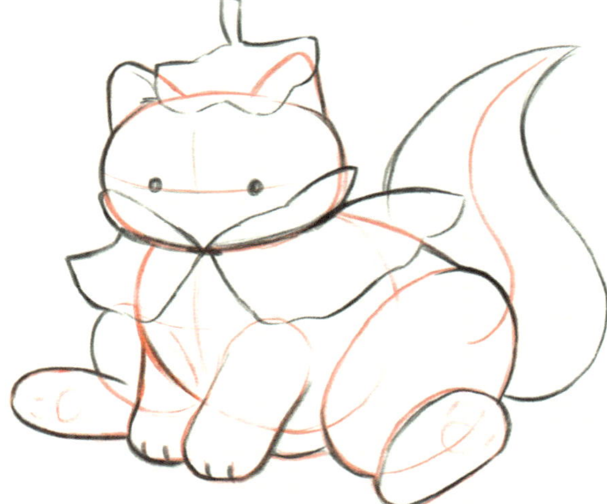

BASE

▶ To draw the cat's head, visualize a flattened sphere (similar to a macaron or a burger bun). Next, shape the torso like an upside-down egg. You can draw light section lines to help you envision how these shapes are oriented.

▶ Next, draw the cat's front and hind legs. For the front legs, create two rectangular shapes starting from the middle of the torso. Use two oval shapes for the hind legs. The smallest one will be the paw.

▶ Add the pointy cat ears and a curved S-shape tail. Connect the hind legs to the torso using another curved line and make sure to mark the placement of the toe beans.

LINES

▶ Once you give your cat some eyes, you can start building the rest! The guardian's outfit is composed of a leaf hat and a little cape. They both have an irregularly scalloped contour with a similar flow.

▶ Make sure to outline the elements that will be visible, such as the legs and the left ear. At this stage, keeping the details simple will ensure you don't lose sight of the overall composition.

▶ As you build the shape of the tail, think of a dancing flame. This will add some dynamism to the character. This subtle movement indicates that the otherwise calm forest guardian is always alert and ready for action.

BUILDING UP

Now that you have the basic elements laid down, it's time to refine the shapes and add more detail using a graphite pencil. At this stage, you can experiment with different facial expressions and find a suitable balance for the level of detail. If one area is super detailed, other areas might appear unfinished. General balance takes priority over the complexity of individual elements.

EXPRESSION

Add some more detail to the face by drawing the creature's expression. Try out different shapes for the mouth, nose, and eyes. To achieve cute, manga-inspired characteristics, an unrealistic and simplified style will do the trick.

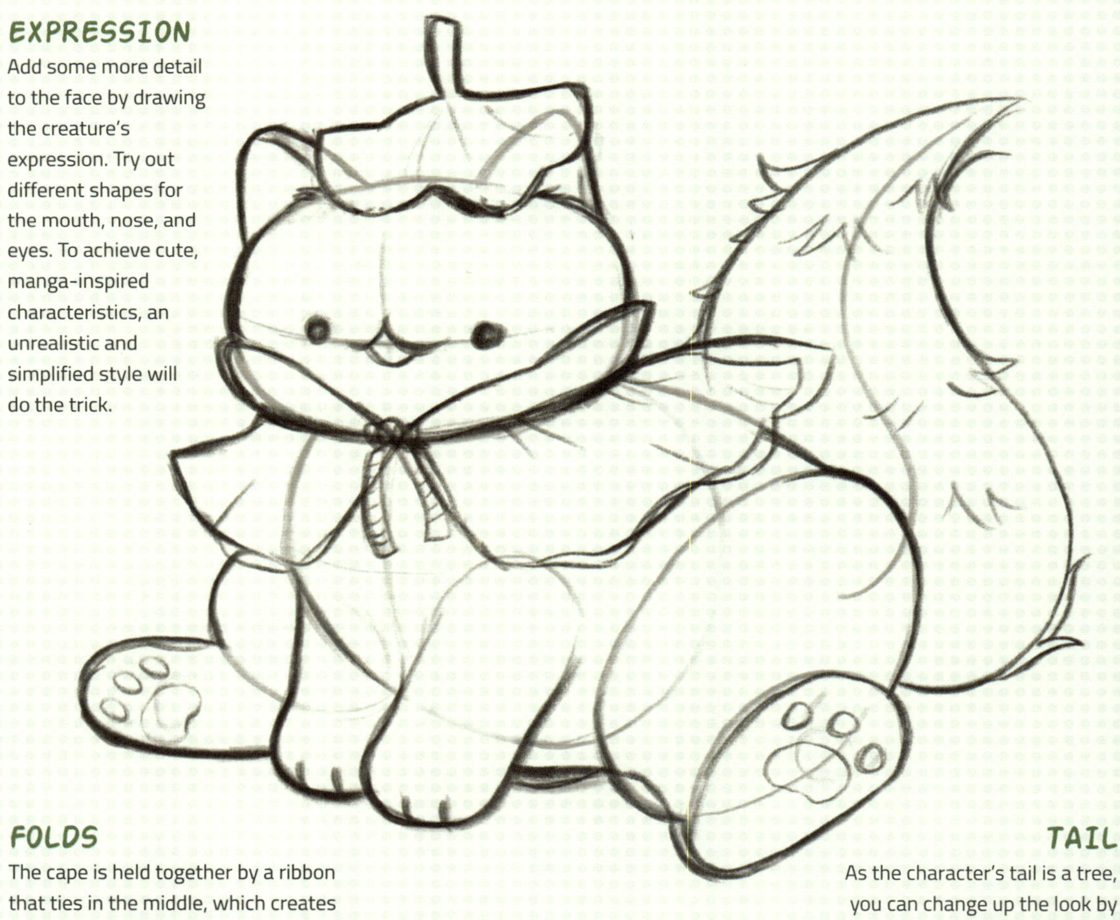

FOLDS

The cape is held together by a ribbon that ties in the middle, which creates creases and folds in the material. Figure out where to place the folds in the fabric to ensure it looks believable.

TAIL

As the character's tail is a tree, you can change up the look by using a few lines to indicate leaves. Normally, the fur would follow the direction of the tail, but here, the leaves go the opposite way.

DESIGN FOCUS

EARS

The character's right ear is partially covered by his leaf hat, but don't forget to draw the visible part! Elements like stray hair (or leaves, in this case) can add a sense of playfulness to a character.

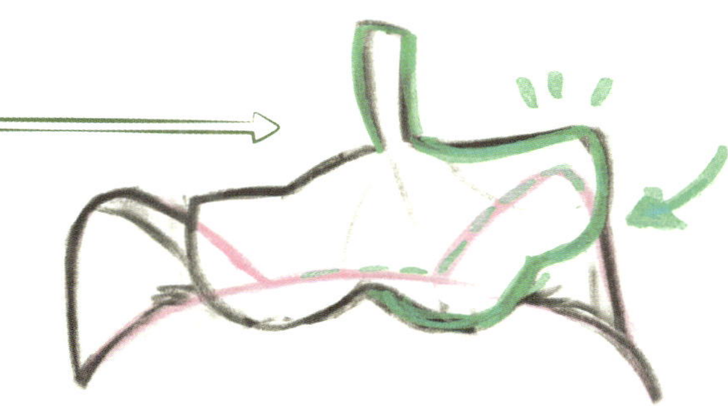

TAIL

Since the character's raised tail is made up of leaves instead of fur, make sure to draw curved V-shapes that stray against the tail's main direction.

TOE BEANS

When studying your reference photos, you'll notice that cats have four small toe beans and one big, central paw pad. In art styles that tend to simplify elements, cats are often drawn with three toe beans instead of four.

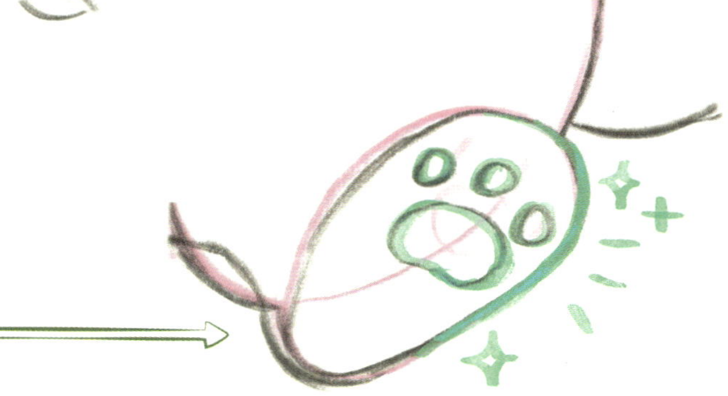

IDEA INVENTORY

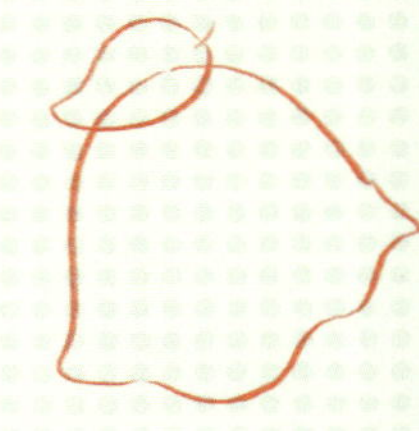

HELPERS

The forest guardian could use some little helpers! Draw a few smaller creatures to accompany your main mascot. There are many inspiring elements in fantasy forests, such as talking animals, walking objects, or even woodland spirits.

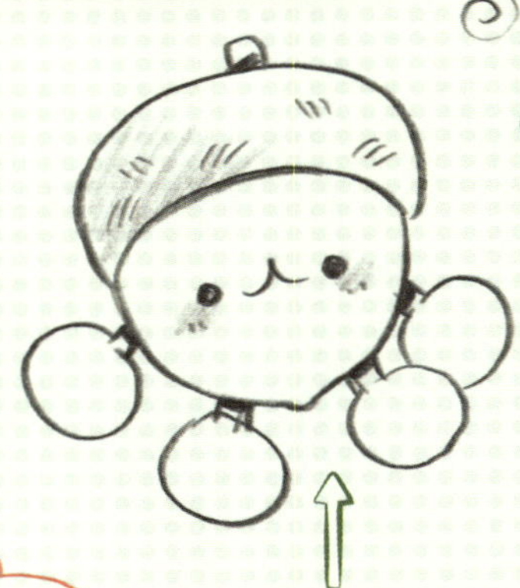

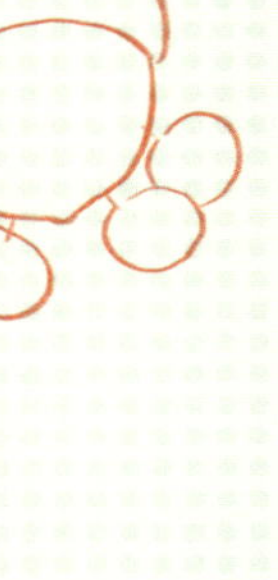

Animated acorns add another magical component to the ensemble.

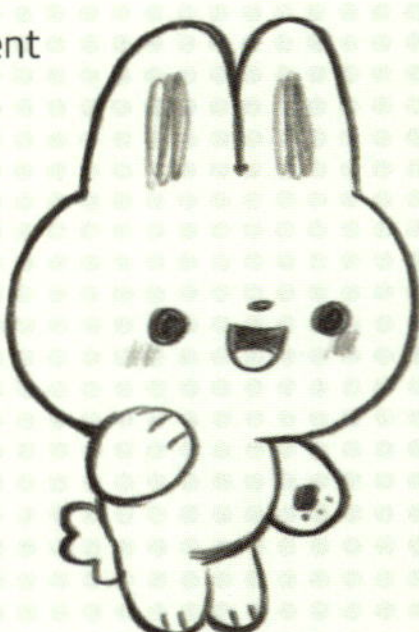

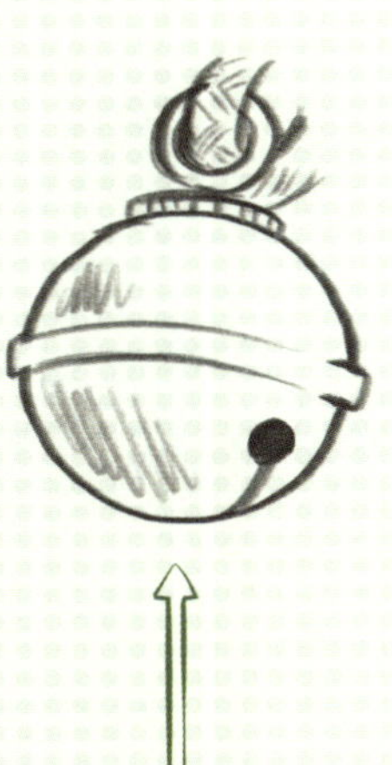

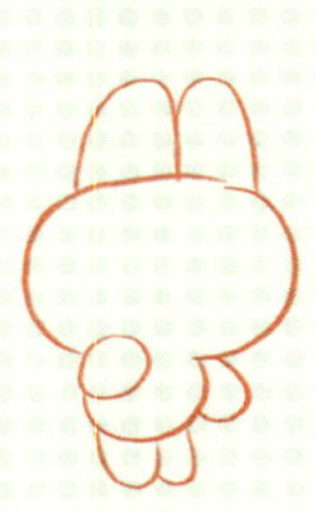

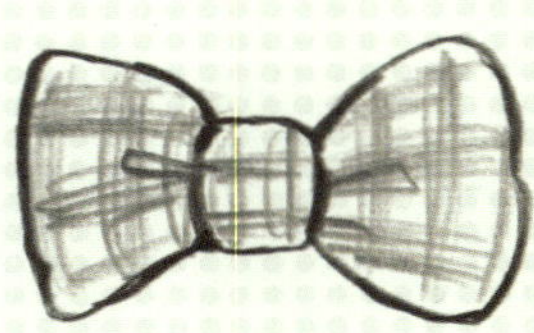

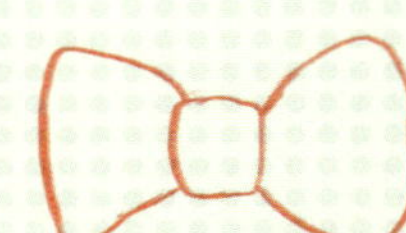

For a little twist, the forest guardian could wear a special bell that chimes when humans are near.

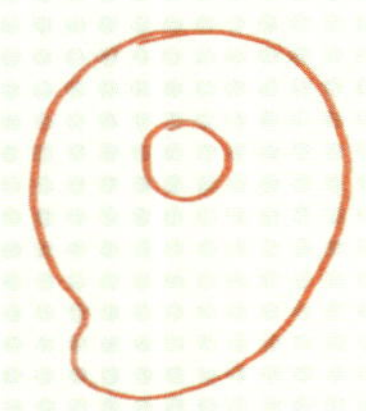

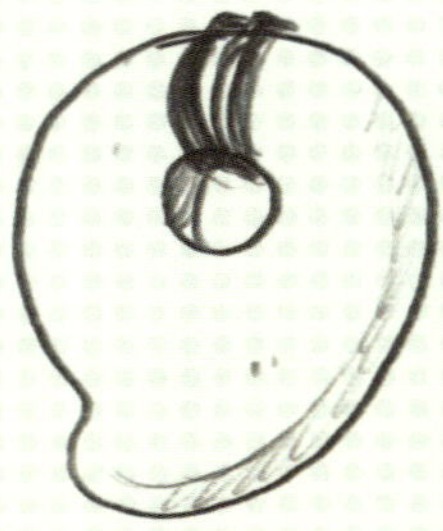

ORNAMENT

A brooch will complete the cape's design. Some possibilities include an ancient amulet (inspired by Japanese magatama), a bow tie, or a bell. People used to make cats wear bells to alert surrounding wildlife of their presence.

FINAL SKETCH

It's now time to refine the sketch and finalize your design choices. You can use a softer graphite pencil, or simply apply more pressure with your current tool to achieve darker lines for the definitive sketch. Make sure to include the little acorn companions in your final sketch – they're coming on the adventure too!

▶ Keep in mind that the viewer's eye will follow your character's gaze. To bring more attention to the smaller characters, direct the cat's gaze towards one of the acorns. This will improve the flow of the composition.

▶ It's good practice to step away from the drawing every so often – you will return to it with fresh eyes. Now that the bell is in place, it's time to rethink the ribbon and add in more detail.

▶ Take the opportunity to showcase your characters' personalities! One of the acorns seems outgoing, another is taking a nap, and the third is playing hide-and-seek. This makes the scene much more interactive.

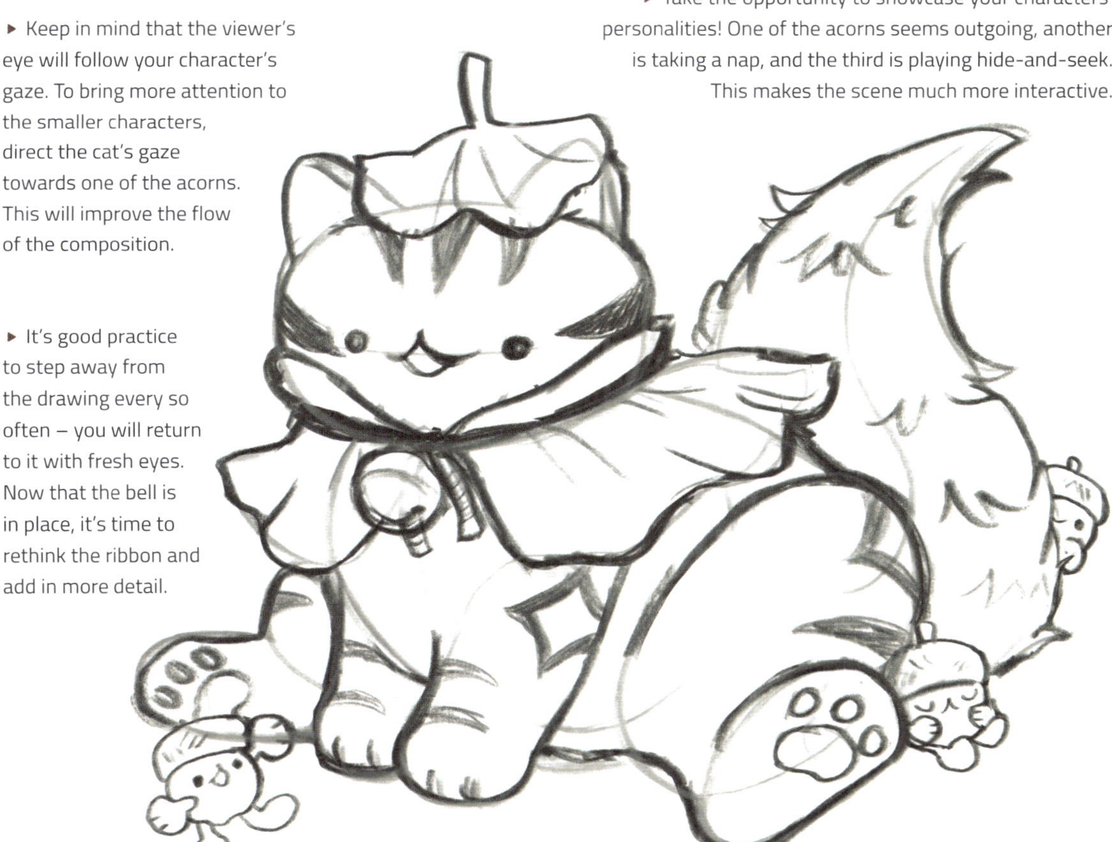

▶ Draw special fur markings to differentiate this magical cat from a normal cat. A few sparkle-shaped marks will help to emphasize his fantastical qualities.

▶ Use quick pencil strokes to apply texture to the fur and tail, avoiding the temptation to add too much detail. It's not necessary to draw each fur strand or leaf. The less detail shown, the softer the design will appear.

LINE WORK

A brush and waterproof ink is the most versatile option for inking your illustration, but you can also use a calligraphic pen or a fineliner to the same effect. However, as you will be applying watercolour, the ink should be waterproof.

Using draft paper, practise your lines and try to make long, controlled brushstrokes, adding variation to the line thickness.

▶ For areas needing contrast and texture (such as a leaf border or limb joint), add small lines in pairs or in threes. This will smooth out the transition between surfaces.

▶ Use very thin brushstrokes to create repetitive patterns, like the one shown on the cape's strings. For this purpose, a fineliner or a smaller brush can be useful.

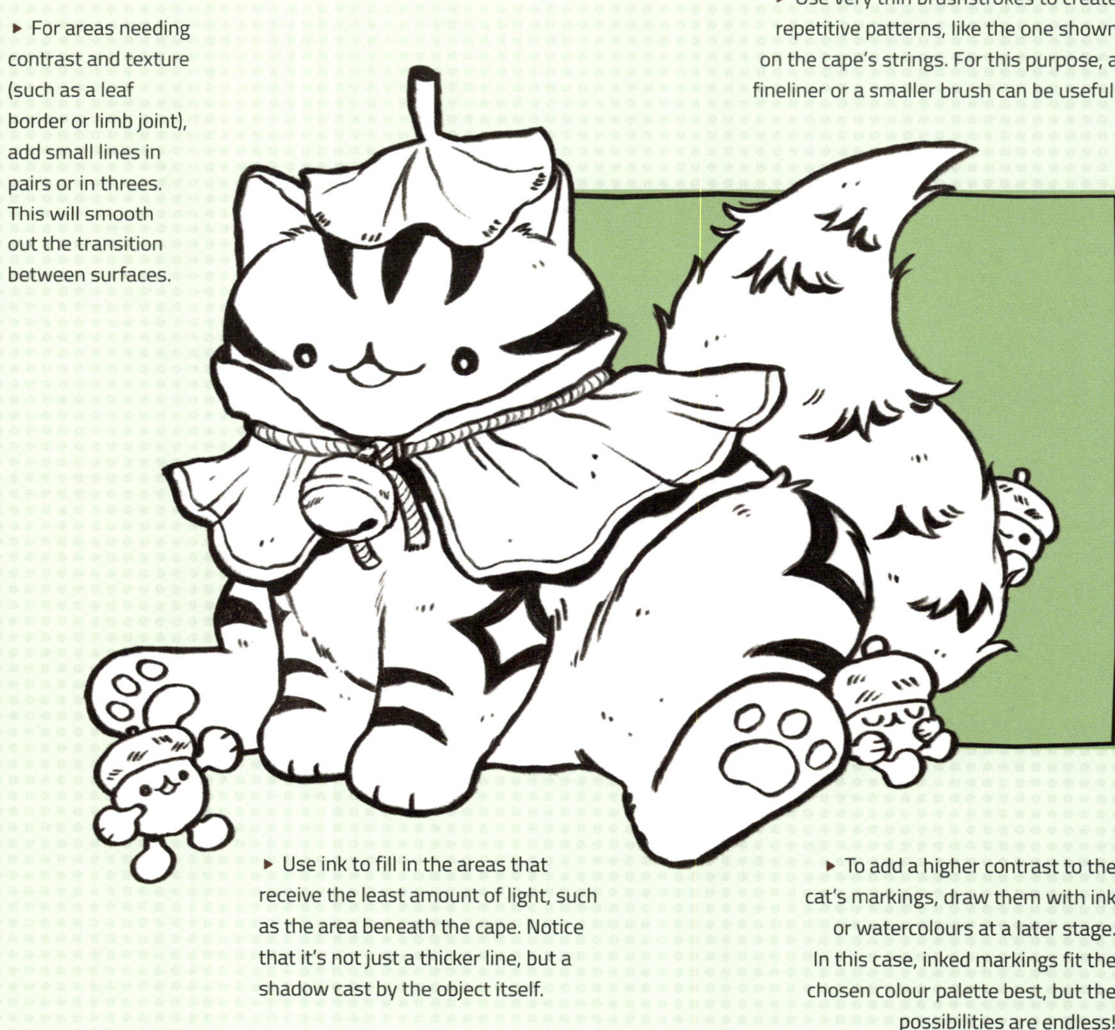

▶ Use ink to fill in the areas that receive the least amount of light, such as the area beneath the cape. Notice that it's not just a thicker line, but a shadow cast by the object itself.

▶ To add a higher contrast to the cat's markings, draw them with ink or watercolours at a later stage. In this case, inked markings fit the chosen colour palette best, but the possibilities are endless!

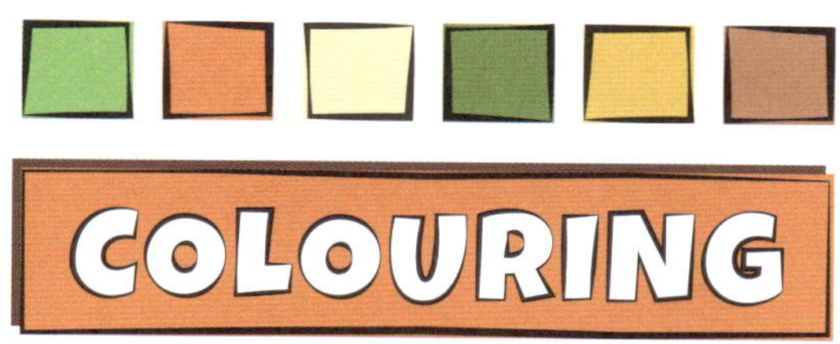

COLOURING

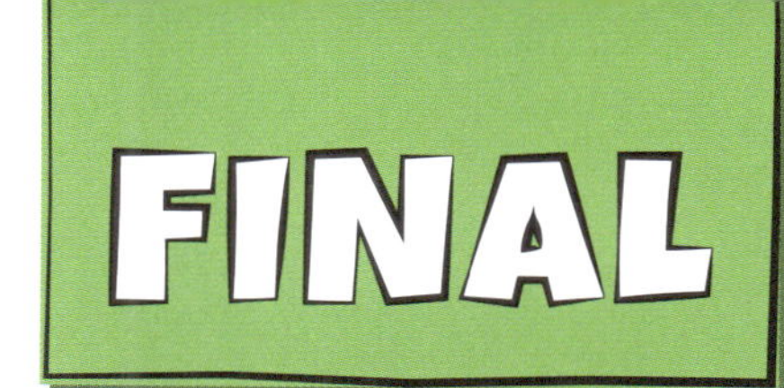

This magical cat is a guardian of the forest, so choosing an earthy palette with green accents is the best match. This is also the colour combination that will allow him and his friends to blend into their habitat. To produce a more organic look, try mixing different green tones in the same area to create gradients and add variations, as can be observed in nature.

▶ When using watercolour, work from the lightest colours to the darkest, allowing layers to dry completely before continuing. To make sure the layer is dry, touch it lightly with the back of your hand. If it's damp and cold, it's not ready yet. Don't rush the process; take your time.

▶ Once the other colours are completely dry, mix a diluted dark purple or blue tone to apply shadows under the cape and leaf. This will add extra volume and make the cape stand out more.

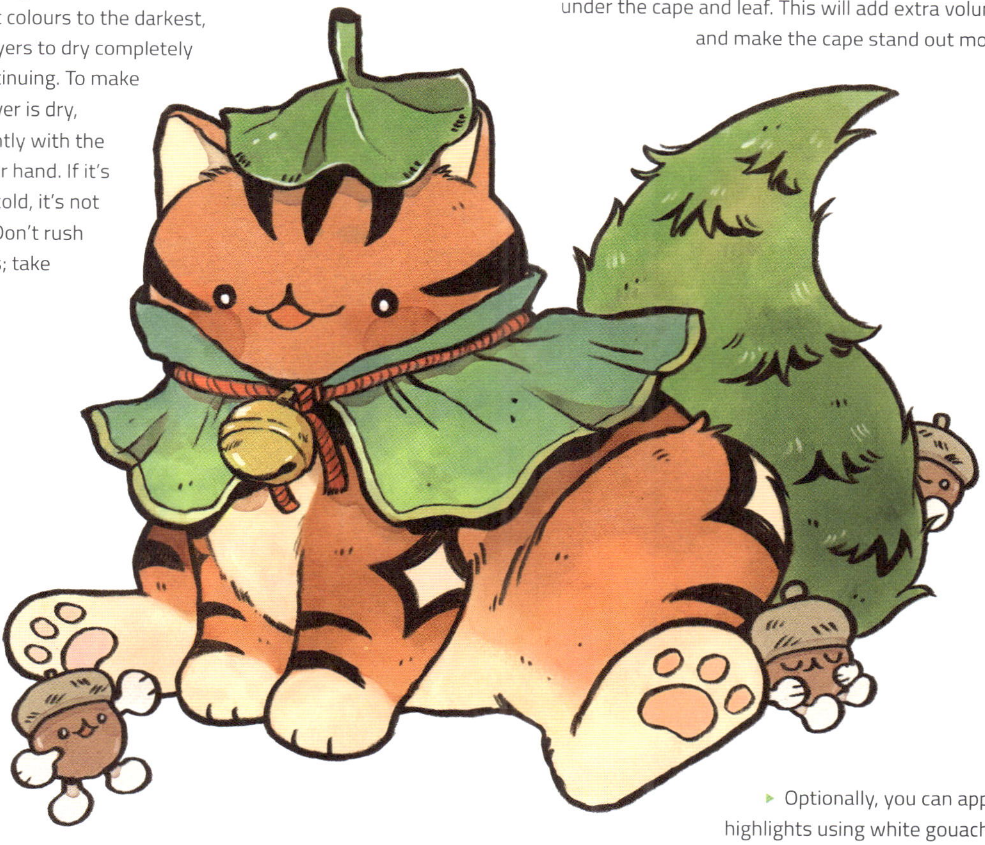

▶ Use two jars of water to clean your brushes. Always use the same jar for the first rinse, then use the clean water in the second jar to mix your paints again. This will prevent the colours from becoming muddy.

▶ Optionally, you can apply highlights using white gouache. Adding small highlights to the leaf hat or tree tail will accentuate the shininess and contrasting textures.

FOX MAGICIAN

BY PUNIPAWS

This tutorial will teach you how to draw an anthropomorphic fox magician. Simple details and an open, confident pose help to showcase this character's remarkable talents, which is often the case with other anthropomorphized manga subjects. Using pens and markers for a softer, stylized approach, you will learn how to illustrate her fun personality while keeping in line with your fox reference images.

TOOLKIT

- ▸ Graphite pencil
- ▸ Eraser
- ▸ HB coloured pencils (red and blue)
- ▸ Ruler
- ▸ Copic markers
- ▸ 0.5mm and 1.0mm multiliner pens

RESEARCH

The best way to create an anthropomorphic character is by first studying the original animal. Look up lots of fox references and focus on how you can capture their best-known traits. Think fluffy faces, long ears, and bushy tails. Use the same method for capturing a magician's unique elements, such as a cape, wand, and top hat.

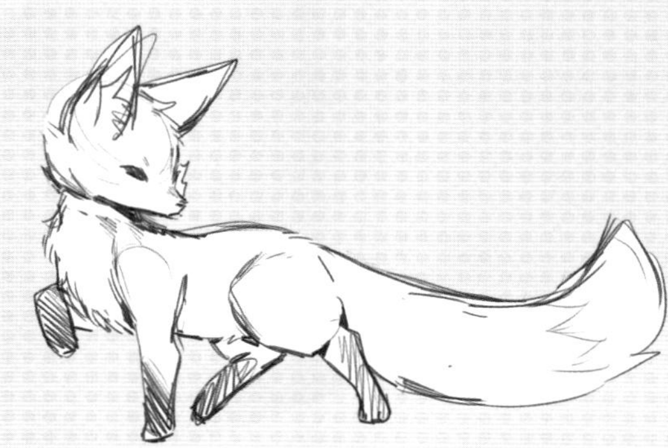

HEADSHOT

A fox's most recognizable features are its large ears and long nose. In the modern manga style, big, soft, round features are typically used to turn animals into anthropomorphic characters.

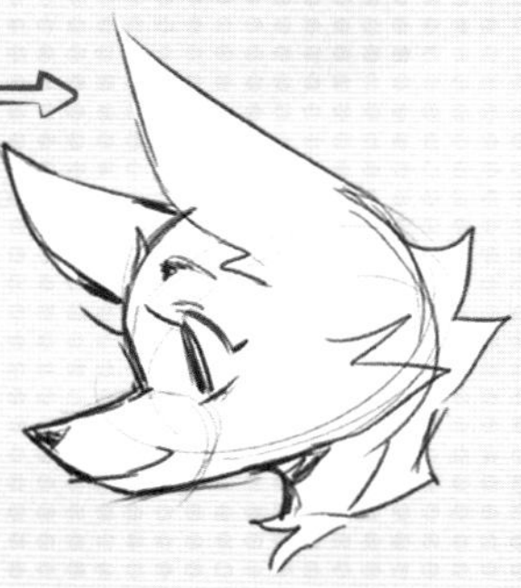

BODYSHOT

Take the classic bushy fox tail and place it on a more humanlike torso. Elongate the legs to make them look more human, too.

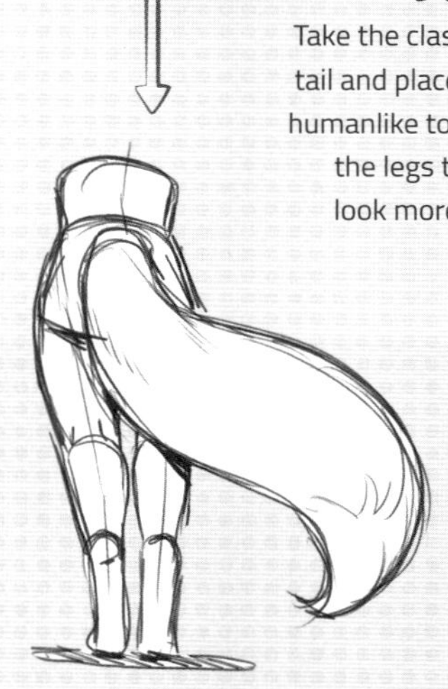

PAW HAND

Since foxes don't have palms or thumbs, it's important to figure out how the paws will look on your anthropomorphic character. Locate the main traits – the claws and toe beans – and adapt them to a human hand. In manga, paws have stretched digits to make them look human without compromising the character's style.

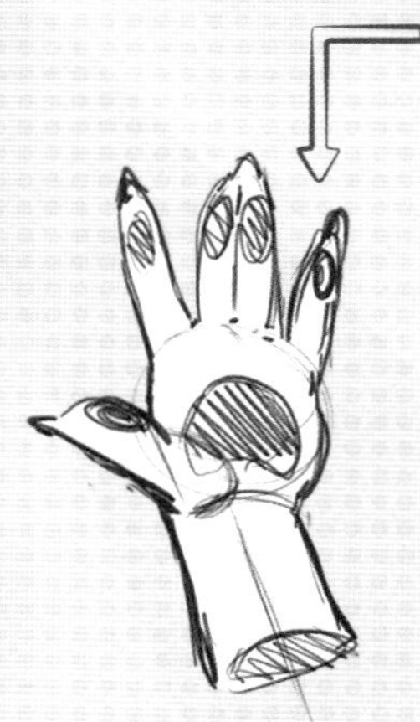

FURRY LEGS

Transforming the legs is easier than you think. Just imagine the fox is standing on its hind legs. Keep the elongated ankles, feet, and four-toed paws.

THUMBNAILS

It's important to test out different poses for your character. Using a graphite pencil, experiment with ideas until you find a dynamic pose that appropriately conveys the thrill and excitement of a magician performing on stage. When deciding on a final thumbnail, think about what inspires you the most.

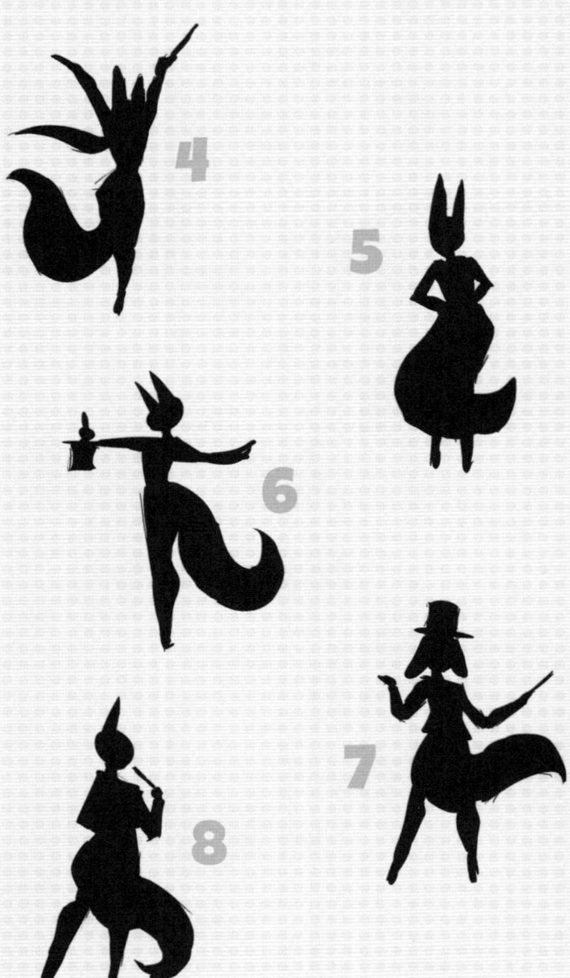

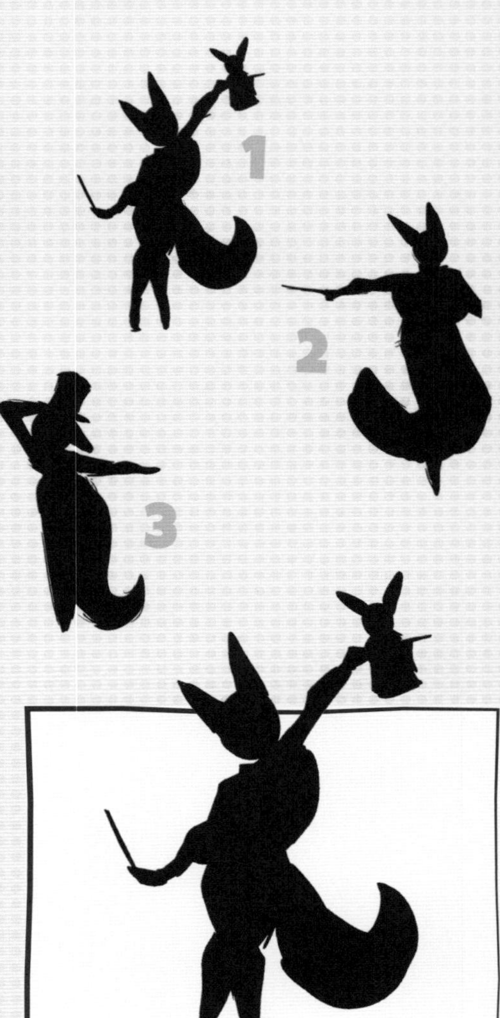

CHOSEN THUMBNAIL

The first thumbnail is the best option as it shows the clearest silhouette of a magician performing a magic trick. The dynamic pose leaves little room for misunderstanding, especially as the hat, rabbit, and wand are visible.

FOUNDATIONS

This step will help you to flesh out the overall design. Use a graphite pencil for the base drawing, keeping the sketch loose and undetailed. Think about how your character would stand, and the positioning of their arms.

BASE

▸ Using a red HB pencil, start by drawing a loose circle for the head and a square shape for the torso. A slight bend in the lines will indicate the character is leaning backwards.

▸ To add a sense of showmanship, extend the arms and make sure to have one stretch above her. Use simple triangles to block out the hands and ears. This charismatic pose is commonly found in shonen manga, as it shows off a character's energetic personality.

▸ Sketch grid lines to break up the torso. Use three triangles for the hips and more circular shapes for the knees and tail.

LINES

▸ The round, flowing shape of the skirt and cape adds to the character's magical appearance. It also fits well with her pose and fox tail. The movement in the skirt emphasizes her soft look and spirited personality. It's important to keep the intended shonen manga energy.

▸ To form the magician's vest, follow the character's simple shape and sketch over the red HB pencil with a graphite pencil. Draw lines to define the cape's collar.

▸ Next comes the iconic rabbit in the hat! Using basic square and circular shapes, sketch the prop at a slight angle to convey its weight as it rests in the magician's hand.

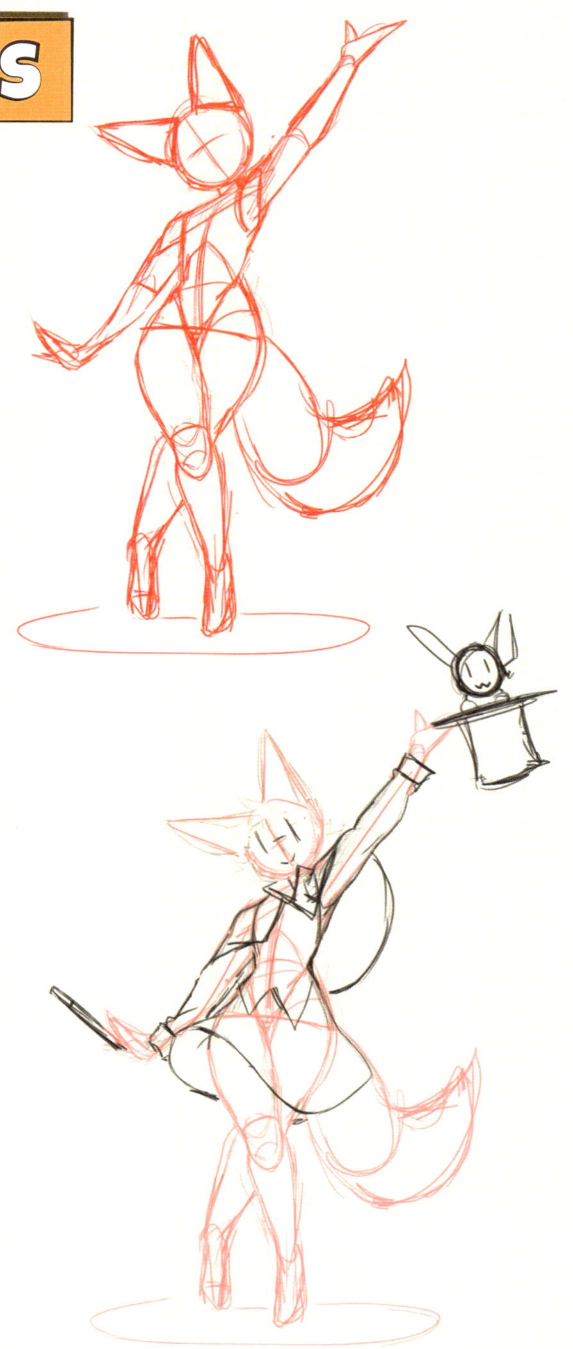

BUILDING UP

The next stage is about following the thumbnail's general layout without spending too much time on detail. For now, focus solely on the overall shape and pose. Use a graphite pencil to loosely place down less intricate details, such as the bow tie, hat ribbon, tail tip, and any facial features. This will help later when it's time to add in fine detail.

UNDERSHIRT

For the undershirt, simply add an overlay sketch on top of the arms. With a ruler, draw lines to indicate where the elbow bends, and make sure to add folds and creases to the shirt sleeves to make them look more realistic.

SKIRT

Make sure the skirt doesn't look overly simple or flat. Using the graphite pencil, define the legs and tail underneath the skirt by lightly tracing over the outline you made during the breakdown stage.

EXPRESSION

Using the guidelines you established earlier, sketch defined expressions for the magician and the rabbit. Even with the pointed tufts of fur, their round faces give off an illusion of softness that fits with the overall theme. The fur also prevents the faces from looking too flat. When there is more than one anthropomorphic subject, different types of fur can help to distinguish characters.

DESIGN FOCUS

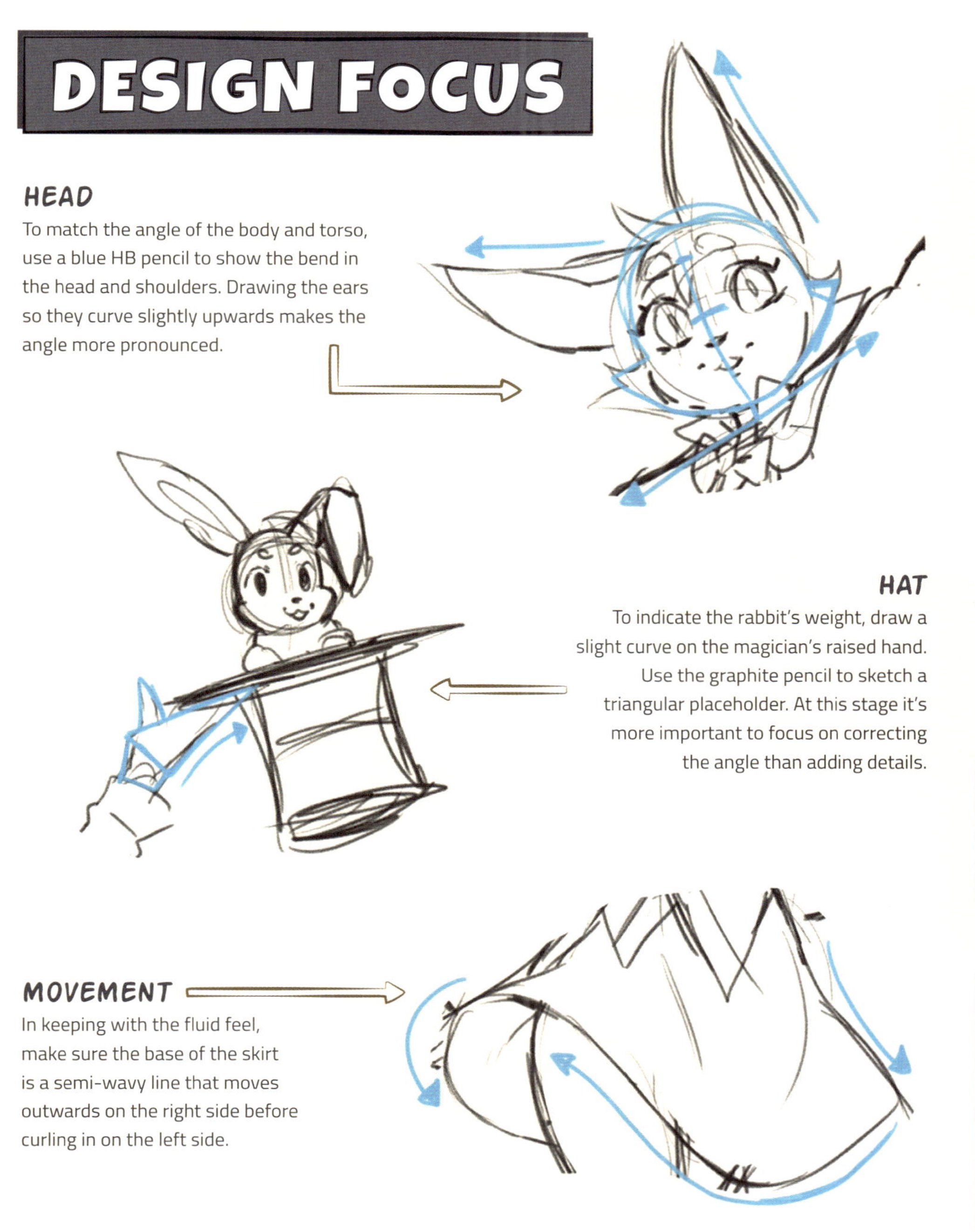

HEAD

To match the angle of the body and torso, use a blue HB pencil to show the bend in the head and shoulders. Drawing the ears so they curve slightly upwards makes the angle more pronounced.

HAT

To indicate the rabbit's weight, draw a slight curve on the magician's raised hand. Use the graphite pencil to sketch a triangular placeholder. At this stage it's more important to focus on correcting the angle than adding details.

MOVEMENT

In keeping with the fluid feel, make sure the base of the skirt is a semi-wavy line that moves outwards on the right side before curling in on the left side.

IDEA INVENTORY

WAND

A wand is an essential tool for a magician, helping to solidify the magical theme of the character. Using a graphite pencil, sketch different styles of wand and see which design suits your character.

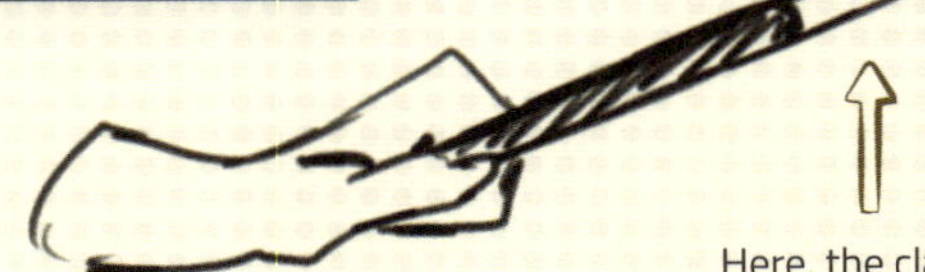

Here, the classic wand works best as it's both simple and effective.

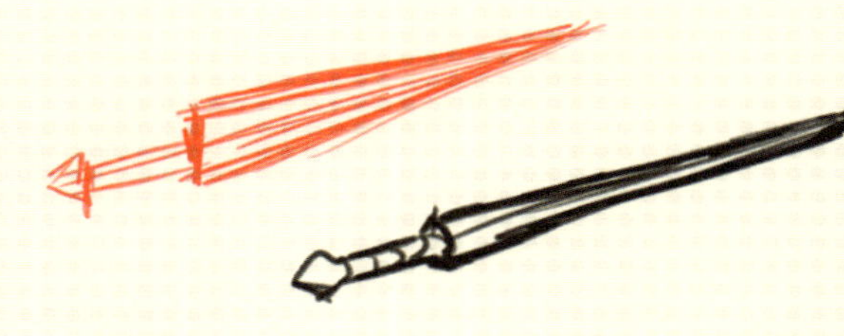

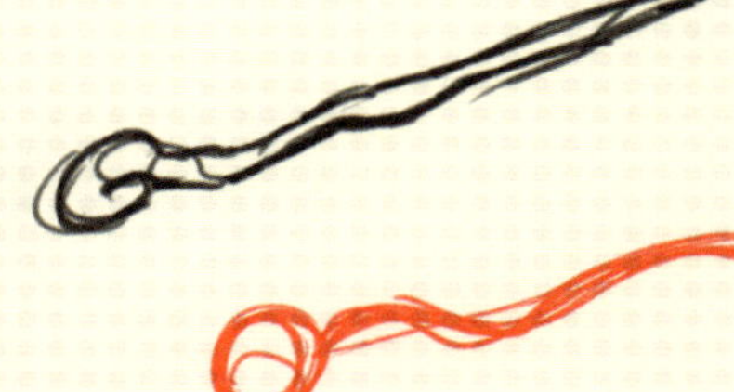

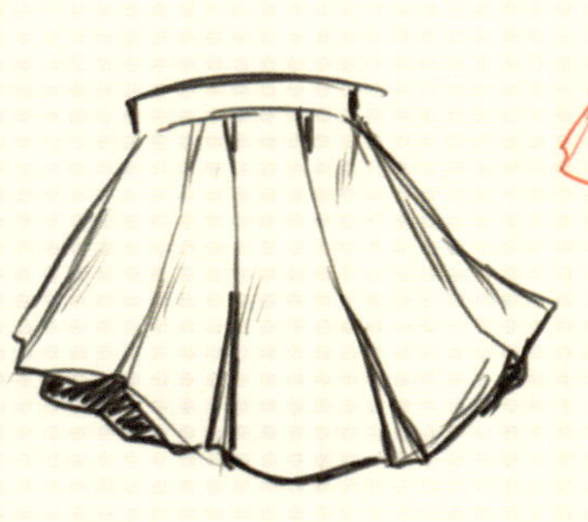

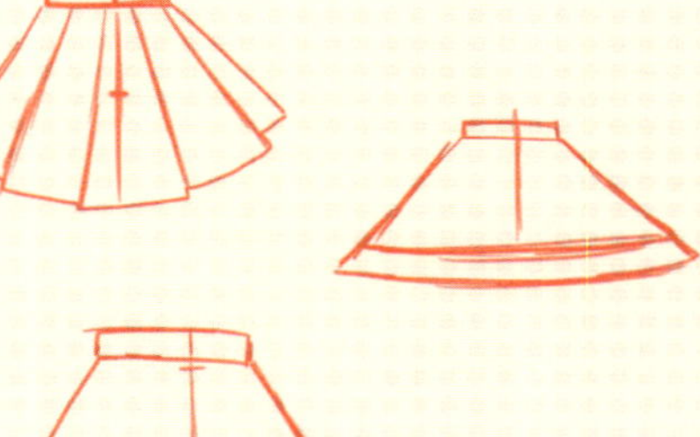

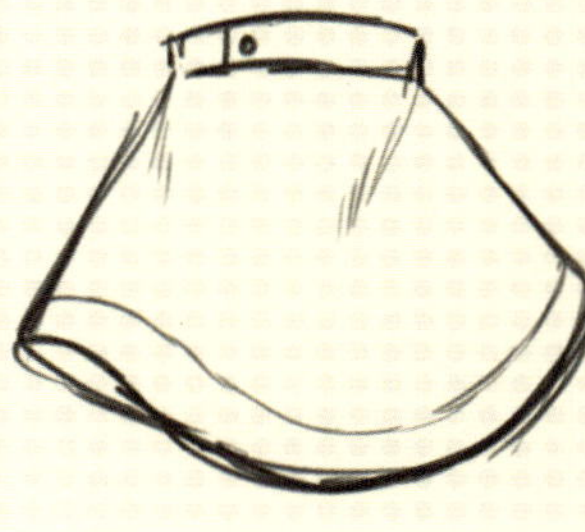

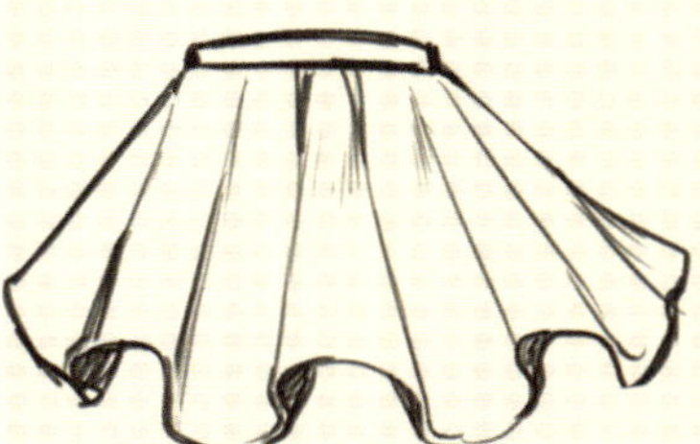

▶ Make sure the skirt will bend around the tail and legs to create a sense of depth.

SKIRT

As a magician's outfit is another key component, it can be helpful to sketch multiple designs before you choose one. Think about how different folds, flats, and angles work with your furry character.

FINAL SKETCH

As you clean up the final sketch, use an eraser to remove any lines or shapes that are no longer needed. Use a graphite pencil to darken any areas where line art will have a thicker line width. Clean up the guidelines for the shoulders, hips, and tail to ensure you don't lose the angles when lining the sketch. Add elements such as the bow tie and the detailing on the hat and vest to show changes in fabric or pattern.

▸ Give your magician more personality by defining her face. Add a cute, cheerful smile and big, wide eyes. For her hair, draw a small tuft of fur on top of the head that matches the fur on her cheeks. Sketch a small bun on top of her head to make the hairstyle more unique. Imbue the design with movement by drawing loose strands around the hair's silhouette. Make sure to use curves and waves, avoiding straight lines.

▸ It's time to add detail to the magician's vest. With your graphite pencil, design a simple sweater pattern with big black buttons and a thin trim along the sides and bottom. This gives the outfit more flair and elevates the illustration.

▸ Referencing the Idea Inventory, decide which skirt option fits best with the rest of the outfit. Next, add details such as a ribbon or trim along the bottom edge.

▸ Now apply the same changes to the rabbit. Add a smile, round eyes, face fluff, and a cute little bow tie to give the animal more personality. In manga, round eyes are often used for cutesy characters who have upbeat, joyous personalities, while sharper features are shown on characters who appear moody, bold, or disinterested.

▸ Take a step back and view the overall sketch. Keep using the graphite pencil to add more line depth in certain areas. This step will come in handy when you get to the line-art stage.

LINE WORK

Start by using an eraser to lighten the sketch without erasing it completely. With your 0.5mm liner, trace the sketch to create a thin base. Next, switch to the 1.0mm pen to thicken the areas where you added depth in the previous step. This will give the line art different variations of weight, which is pleasing to the eye.

▸ Add more line depth around the character's form to enhance the design. Variation in line weight will prevent your character from appearing too one-dimensional and flat. Use thicker lines to define the shadow beneath the skirt, along the vest, and along her rear leg.

▸ Fold lines give the outfit texture, as shown on the cape, shoulders, and inner skirt. However, make sure to keep it simple. One or two lines is all you need to create this effect.

▸ Make sure to keep the character's form soft and round, especially in the face and tail. This also applies to the rabbit.

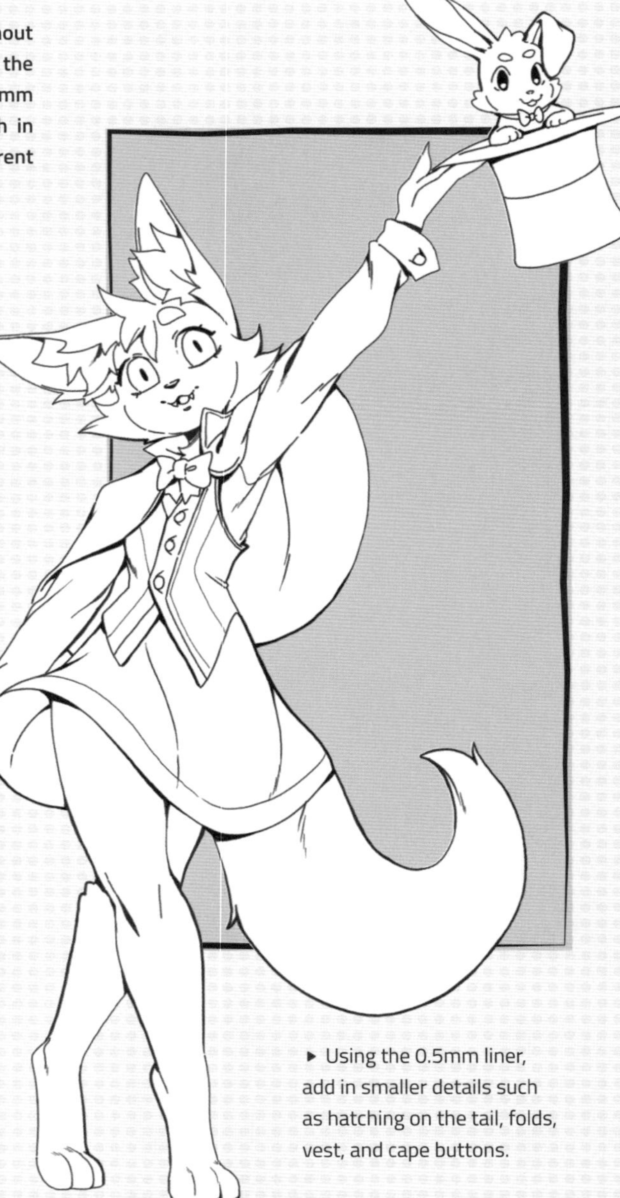

▸ Using the 0.5mm liner, add in smaller details such as hatching on the tail, folds, vest, and cape buttons.

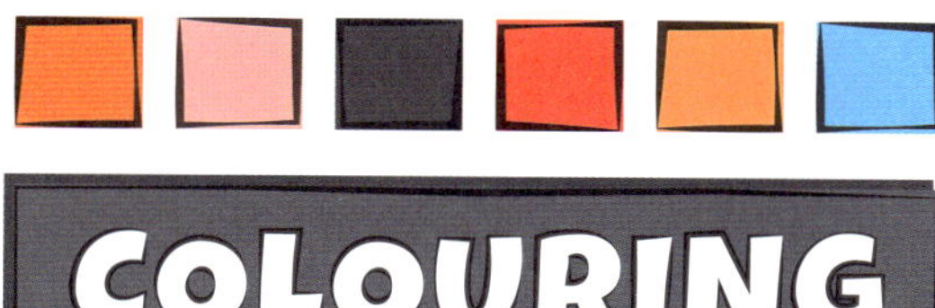

COLOURING

Now it's time to add colour. Use Copic markers to fill in base colours for the fur, clothes, and various other details. Make sure to leave the white areas of the fur visible. Once all the solid colours are laid down, use darker shades to indicate shadowed parts of the body. This includes the shadow from the skirt and cape. Adding these shades creates colour depth and makes the character appear more dynamic.

▸ Use a bright blue Copic marker for the eye base, followed by two deeper blues to add depth. Leave three areas white for a shimmering eye effect. Shiny eyes are used in manga for friendly characters, as it adds a sense of brightness.

▸ To create a simple, shiny effect on the hat, use navy-blue and red Copic markers to colour each side. Make sure to leave a gap in the middle for the original base colour to show through.

▸ In keeping with the skirt's movement, shade alongside the curves and folds of the line art. As the inner skirt is a darker colour, use the same Copic marker for the top and sides to show the slight bend from the legs and tail underneath.

▸ For the shading on the fox's body, keep in line with the orange-and-red fur palette. Use two darker Copic markers that contain deeper reddish-orange and brown hues. Apply the shading to the tail and legs.

MARTIAL ARTS FIGHTER

BY AHMAD BEYROUTHI

This tutorial will walk you through the process of creating a male martial artist in the shonen manga art style. Existing in the nineties anime video-game era, this beat-up character has seen many battles and tournaments. His outfit is torn and tattered; the broken handcuffs are there to remind him that breaking free and conquering fear is the key to winning any challenge! The following pages will teach you how to build up a character through basic shapes, develop visual elements that fit the character, and select a striking colour composition.

TOOLKIT

- ▸ 0.5mm mechanical pencil
- ▸ Eraser
- ▸ Brush pen
- ▸ Coloured pencils
- ▸ Coloured marker pens

RESEARCH

As you begin to explore ideas for your character, think about what unique quality you can bring to each element, including the face, outfit, accessories, and weapons. Whether you want to create a hero or villain, the more unique the design, the more they will feel like a main character. Some exaggeration of the anatomy – such as bigger fists, feet, and eyes – will contribute to creating a memorable design with a strong shonen manga look. Understanding and controlling the combination of these features will guarantee a visually engaging design.

FACE

Designing the face is key to creating a likeable character. Focus on the hairstyle and facial features, and convey personality, whether through a confident smirk or determined eyes.

BANDANA

The bandana is a strong design feature for this character because it emphasizes the toughness and focus in his eyes. You can make it look even more powerful by adding elements such as horns.

ACCESSORIES

Accessories are optional, but they can help to tell your character's story, as well as creating a more interesting silhouette.

KNUCKLES

The broken handcuffs add force when delivering punches, plus the chains will make a dramatic clinking sound!

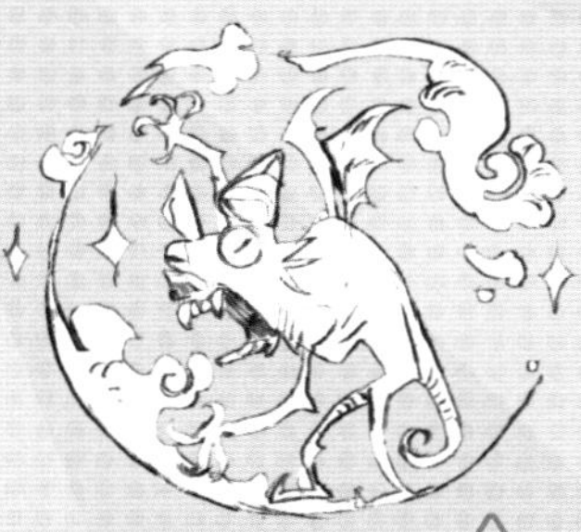

EMBLEM

Whether as a tattoo, shirt design, or country mascot, an emblem will add richness to the character's backstory.

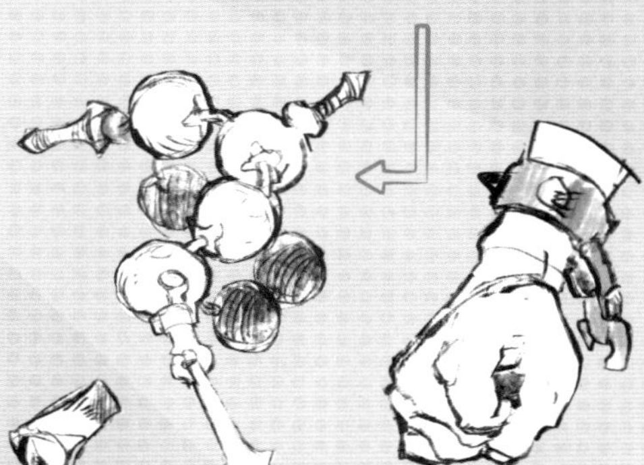

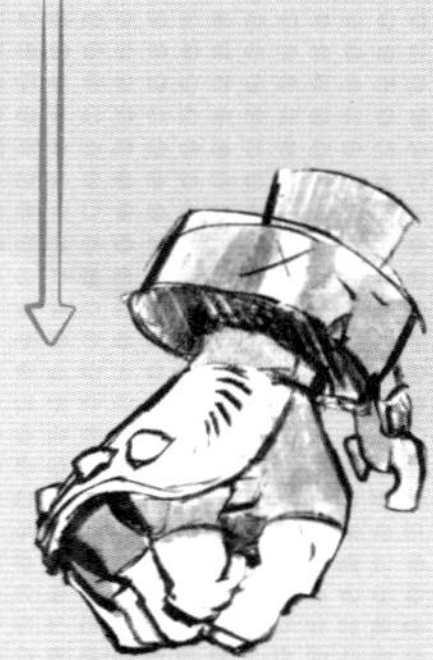

THUMBNAILS

Thumbnailing is the quickest way to see if your overall idea has potential. The poses for a martial artist should be firm, strong, and confident. The elements you're thinking of adding to the character – such as a bandana, large backpack, or even a weapon – shouldn't get in the way of your general design, but should be readable through the silhouette. Keep the character description in mind when creating the thumbnails to ensure you don't drift away from it.

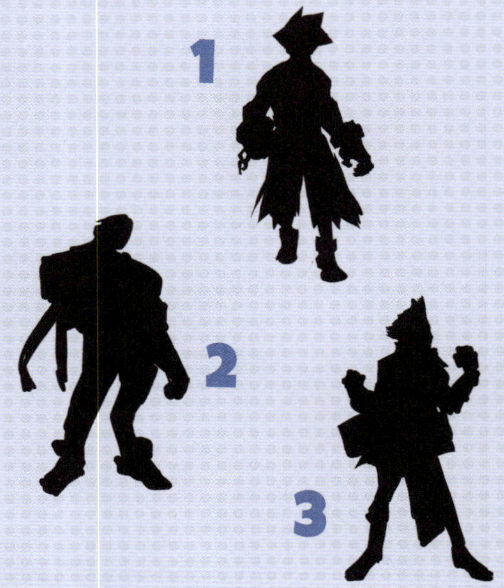

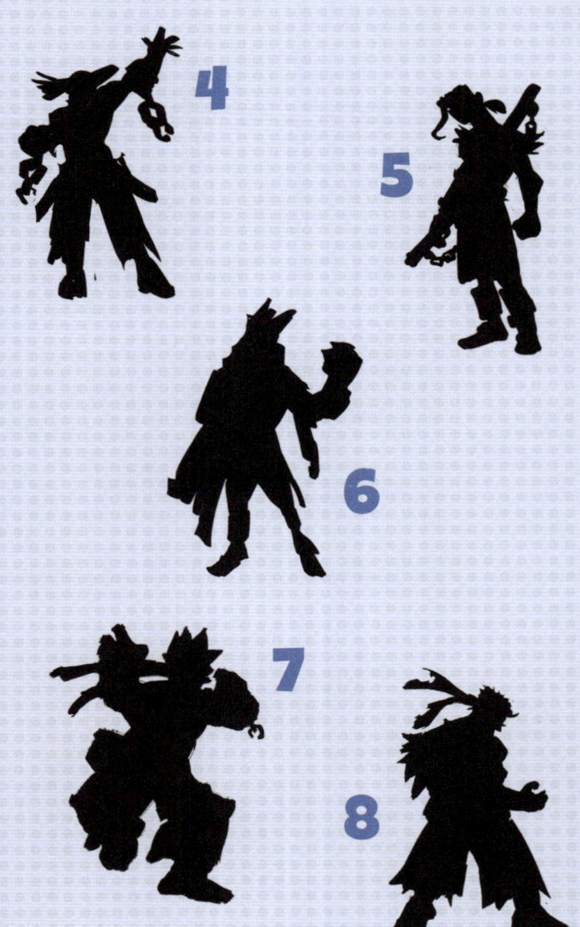

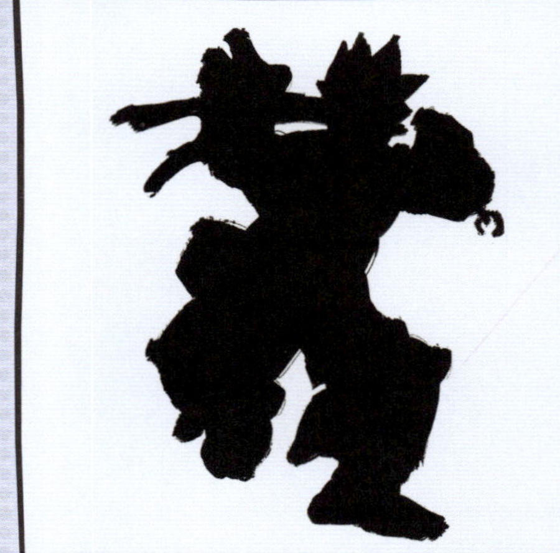

CHOSEN THUMBNAIL

Thumbnail 7 is the most interesting, as it is the most confident pose. The strong angular shapes capture the strong will of the character.

FOUNDATIONS

Use your chosen thumbnail as a base as you develop it into a more constructed design. Use a coloured pencil to map out the basic shapes that make up the character's body and their pose. Start with a rough skeleton, which can be as basic as a stick figure. Once you've sketched the skeleton in the chosen pose, begin to build basic geometrical shapes – such as cuboids, cylinders, and spheres – on top. You may find it helpful to draw a simple grid beneath the character to place his feet in perspective.

BASE

▶ Start by drawing a circle for the head, then sketch a line for the neck, and continue down to create a basic skeleton. This will help to set up the proportions.

▶ Designing a fighter is mainly focused on the muscles. Using cylinders for the arms will help to convey their thickness as well as keeping the pose in perspective. Don't worry about drawing the individual muscles at this stage.

▶ Practise drawing geometric forms in perspective. This will help you to construct the basic shapes of your character as a warm-up before starting the build-up.

LINES

▶ Start with the head, before adding any other details, as this will be the focal point. Next, fill in the anatomy. This character has an athletic body with large, muscular arms, spiky hair, and a bandana.

▶ Roughly sketching in the eyes and facial features will allow you to see the character progressing, despite the early stage. Draw the handcuffs as basic cylinders, again making sure they're in perspective.

▶ Sketch the trousers and belt with rectangular shapes. You can add more details, such as damaged material or folds, at a later stage. This step is simply for blocking out the key elements.

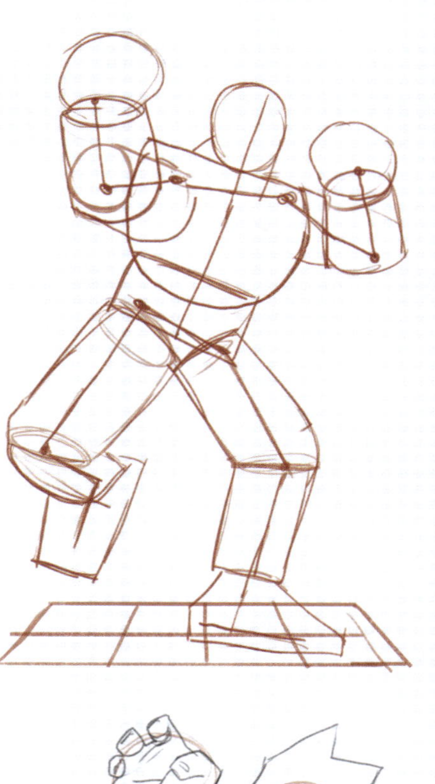

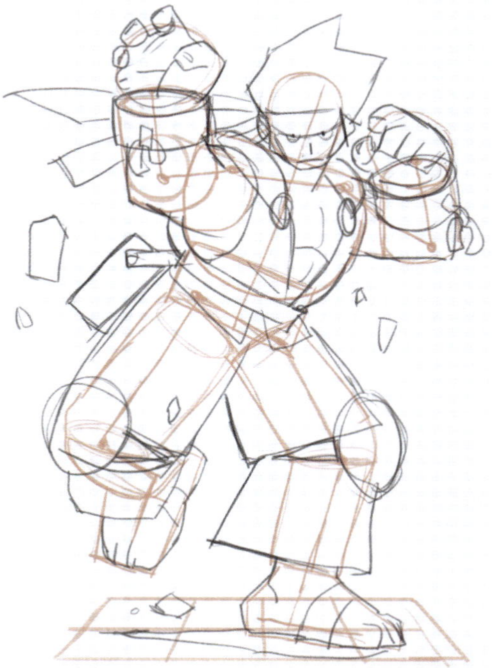

BUILDING UP

The foundation drawn in the previous step forms the base of your character's design. Anything new that is introduced must support it visually. Consider the small, medium, and large elements that you need to add and ask yourself questions as you develop the character. For example, what is the main shape pattern? And can you repeat it throughout the design? Here the repeated pattern is the spikes. Both his hair and trousers have an angular shape, but with different intensities.

SHAPE

As the arms are cylinders, the shirt needs to have a rounded shape as it wraps around them. The same with the trousers. Start to sketch the shapes of the muscles where they are visible through the fabric.

SHADING

When shading, sketch some hatched lines that follow the geometrical shape of the object to add more volume to the shaded areas.

BANDANA

Begin to introduce rough details throughout the design. Starting with the bandana, make sure it follows the curved sphere of the head.

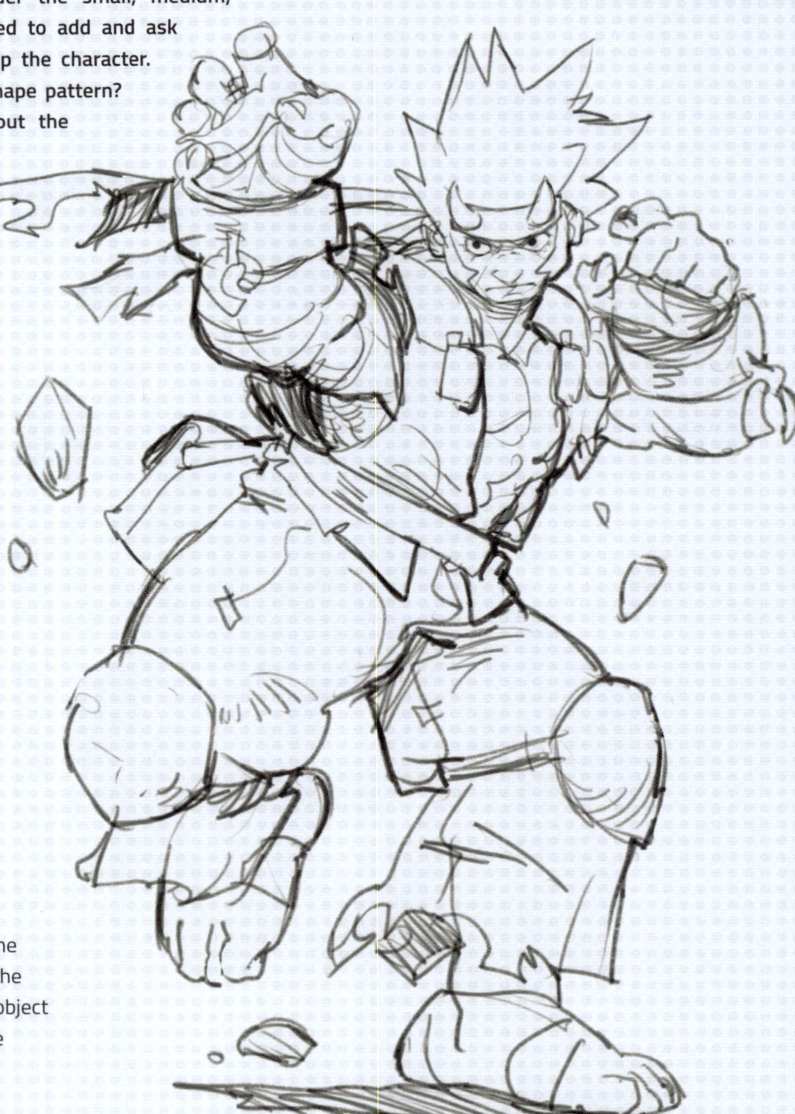

DESIGN FOCUS

BALANCE

Try to incorporate a balance of straight and curved lines into the character's design. The thumb-side of the hand is curved, while the side with the fingers forms a straight line.

FACE GRID

Try using a face grid to help you place the eyes, nose, and mouth in the correct position, especially if the head is tilted or front-facing. The lines are curved because of the head tilting in perspective.

STRAIGHT VS. CURVED

Carry the straight vs. curved line contrast into other areas of the body. Here the heel of the foot is curved, while a straight slope down to the angular toes provides a nice contrast in shape.

IDEA INVENTORY

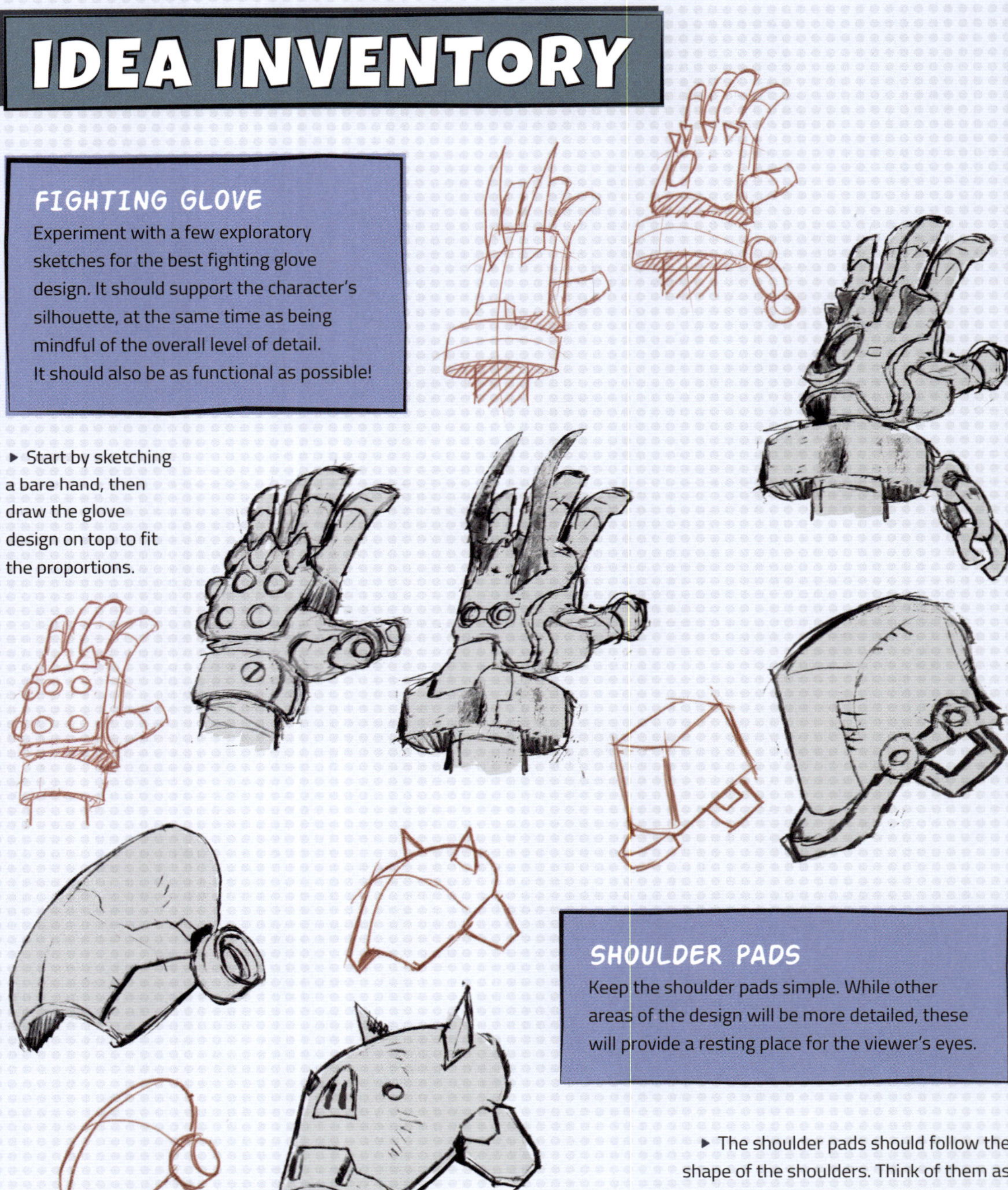

FIGHTING GLOVE

Experiment with a few exploratory sketches for the best fighting glove design. It should support the character's silhouette, at the same time as being mindful of the overall level of detail. It should also be as functional as possible!

▶ Start by sketching a bare hand, then draw the glove design on top to fit the proportions.

SHOULDER PADS

Keep the shoulder pads simple. While other areas of the design will be more detailed, these will provide a resting place for the viewer's eyes.

▶ The shoulder pads should follow the shape of the shoulders. Think of them as geometric basic shapes, then build on top by subtracting the shoulder shape out of them.

FINAL SKETCH

Begin to refine the details, applying a slightly stronger pressure on the pencil. Rushing at this stage will only cause problems, so be patient and take your time. Finish shape by shape and don't try to clean up your drawing all at once.

Erase any mistakes that might occur along the way, along with the basic guidelines beneath once they are no longer needed. Feel free to sketch in environmental elements, such as small rocks, to give the design a boost of energy.

▸ The bandana has its own line of action that gives the character more speed. It also creates a dynamic X shape when combined with the arm as a focal point.

▸ The character's sharp, spiky hair has a dynamic look to communicate his intensity. Drawing the spikes one line at a time will help to capture the energy and speed of your stroke.

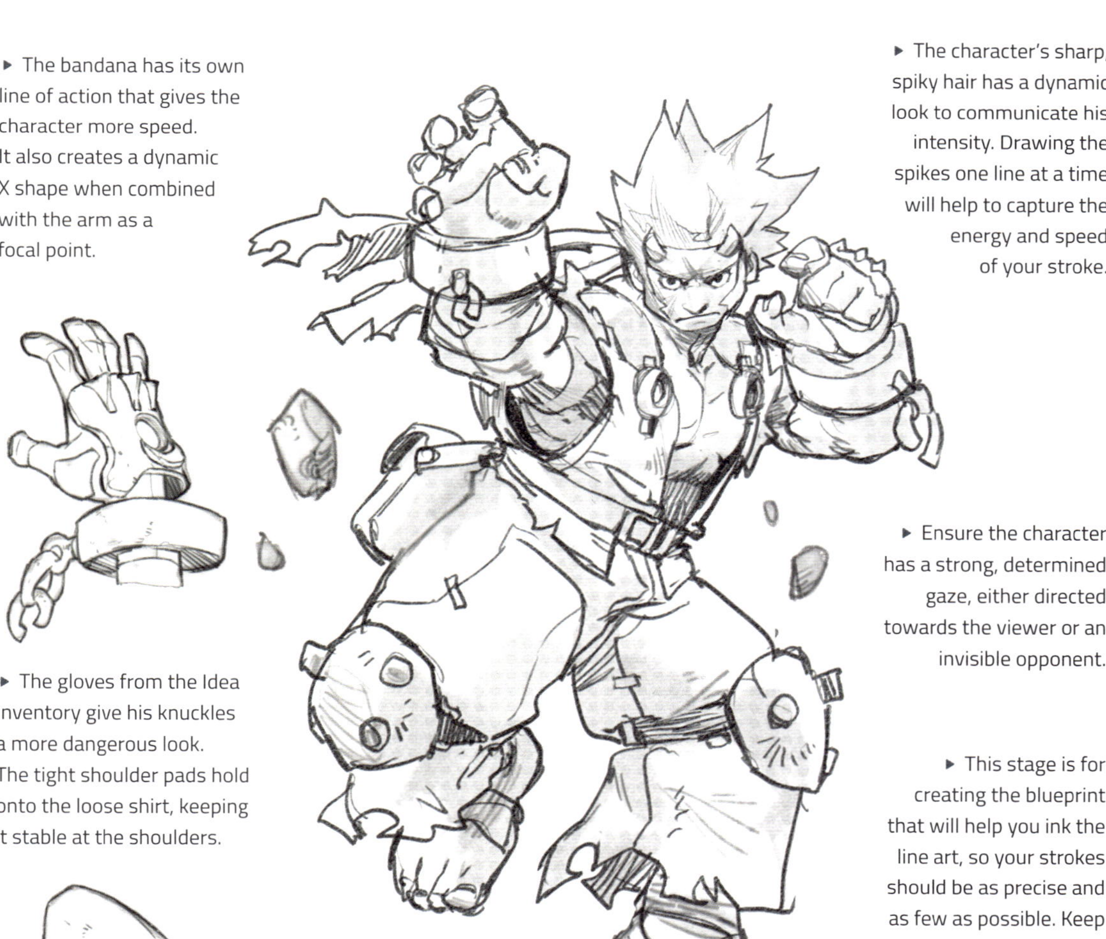

▸ The gloves from the Idea Inventory give his knuckles a more dangerous look. The tight shoulder pads hold onto the loose shirt, keeping it stable at the shoulders.

▸ Ensure the character has a strong, determined gaze, either directed towards the viewer or an invisible opponent.

▸ This stage is for creating the blueprint that will help you ink the line art, so your strokes should be as precise and as few as possible. Keep in mind how objects pass underneath or above one another.

LINE WORK

When drawing over the lines of the final sketch, use the brush pen and varying pen pressure to create a variety of line thicknesses and weights. Tiny details need thinner lines, while larger details require stronger lines. Objects closer to the viewer should have thicker lines, whereas objects that are further away should have thinner lines. This will help you understand how a line can 'travel' from one object to another. Achieving a balance of line thicknesses and weights is key.

▶ Starting with the face will build your confidence as you move on to the rest of the character. Ink the whole face with thin lines, then add deeper pen pressure on areas that have deeper shadows.

▶ His right arm needs thicker lines as it's closer to the viewer. The lines around the fingers should be thicker when the finger is extended towards the viewer, and thinner when it's drawn back into the hand.

▶ Fill any areas that light won't reach with black. This includes the small gap between his chest and shirt, plus the tiny corners of his hair that are close to the bandana's metallic plate.

▶ Ink the hatching on the knee pads in a circular pattern. The direction of the hatching depends on the shape of the object. If the object is flat, the hatching should be straight. If the object is curved, the hatching should curve around the shape to convey its form.

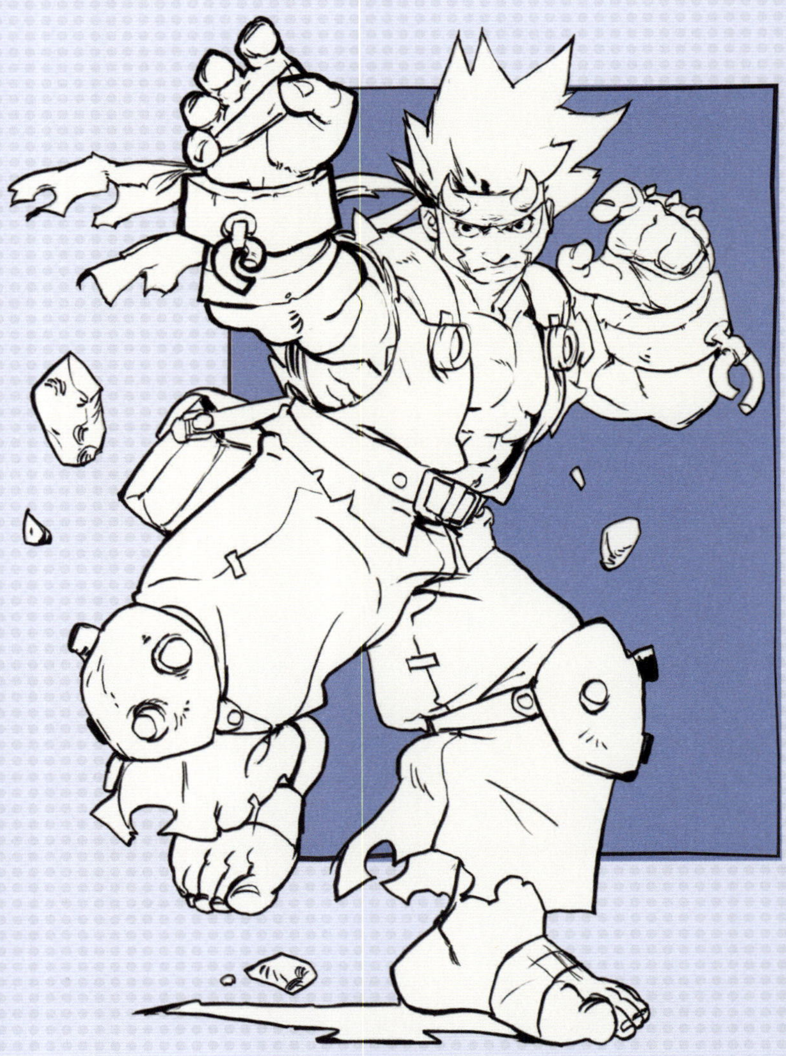

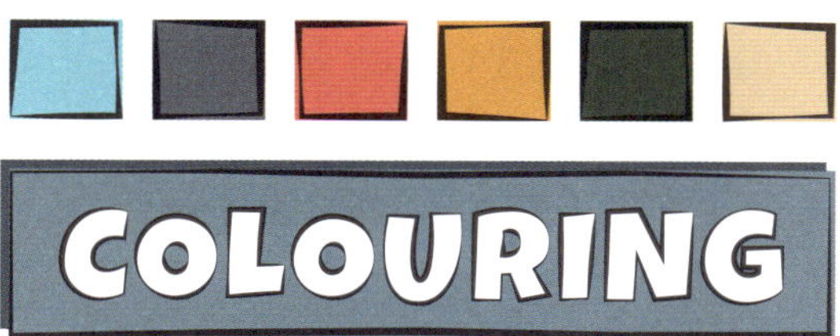

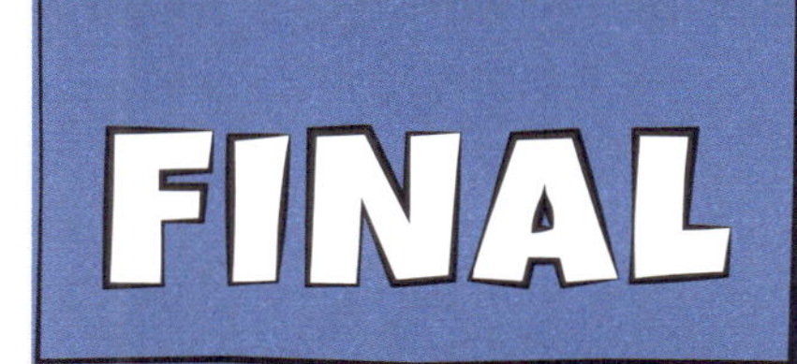

COLOURING

Select the coloured markers you want to use to render the character. Try the colour combination out on a separate piece of paper first before you commit to it. Using complementary colours – such as red and blue, as well as orange and green hues – will enable you to create a character that is calm yet furious. Varying the saturation and value will allow you to guide the viewer's eye through the design.

▶ Start with the first pass of flat colours across the entire body. Plan ahead as to where your highlights will be and leave some white space on the page. Fill in the basic flat colour around it to build a basic rim light.

▶ The character's hair has the highest and strongest saturated colour. Use it as a focal point to attract the viewer's attention. The saturation of the other elements should not be as strong.

▶ Make sure your strokes follow the geometry or the form of each object. For example, the legs are large cylinders, so brushstrokes that follow their shape will help to create a sense of volume.

▶ Use purple as the colour for the shadows. As it's a mix of red and blue, it works well with any coloured surface, whether skin or other materials.

RICH FANTASY VILLAIN

BY RIKA 'BWUSAGI'

This tutorial will teach you how to create a rich fantasy villain and his magical phoenix sidekick. He's a bad guy with expensive clothes, great hair, and an evil agenda. Stylish and arrogant, he looks down on everyone else around him. He often uses underlings as living weapons and is unsympathetic to whatever terrible consequences occur because of his actions. The tutorial will use the 1990s/2000s traditional manga style, as the simple colouring and monotonous tones will fit well with this cold-hearted scoundrel. The heavily stylized lines will make him look like a distinguished, recognizable villain.

TOOLKIT

- ▶ Graphite pencils
- ▶ Eraser
- ▶ Fineliner pen
- ▶ Tracing table (optional)
- ▶ Coloured pencil
- ▶ Blending stump

RESEARCH

To create a rich magical villain, take a look at Giovanni from *Pokémon* and Lelouch from *Code Geass*, or characters with similar vibes. These characters have the evil essence you want to capture for your own villain character. The vintage gentleman aesthetic is a great starting point. The fancy tailcoat suit, walking cane, and tailored trousers all possess interesting shapes to play around with.

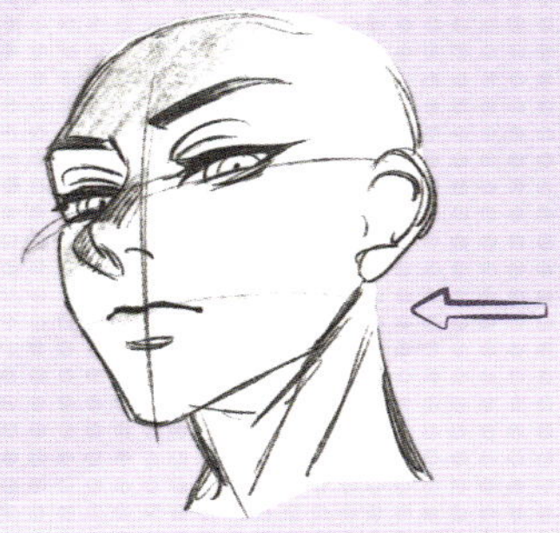

FACE

Villains typically have expressionless faces or intense cold stares, so apply this idea by making his eyes half-lidded. The pupils should be directed downwards to emphasize his arrogance.

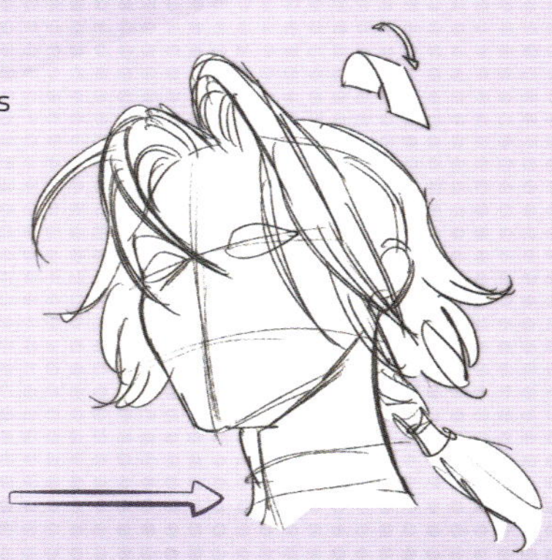

HAIR

Hairstyle is a great way to convey the character's personality. As his clothing will be extravagant, sketch heavily stylized hair to match.

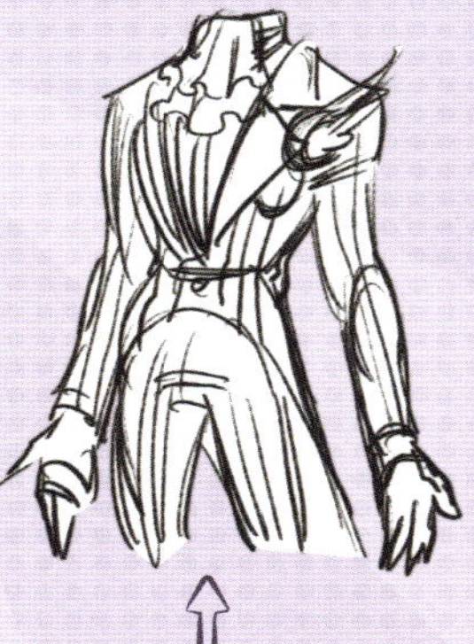

CANE

A walking cane with an animal topper is another great accessory for a villain. It could be purely aesthetic, or perhaps it's a secret weapon.

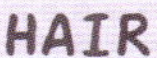

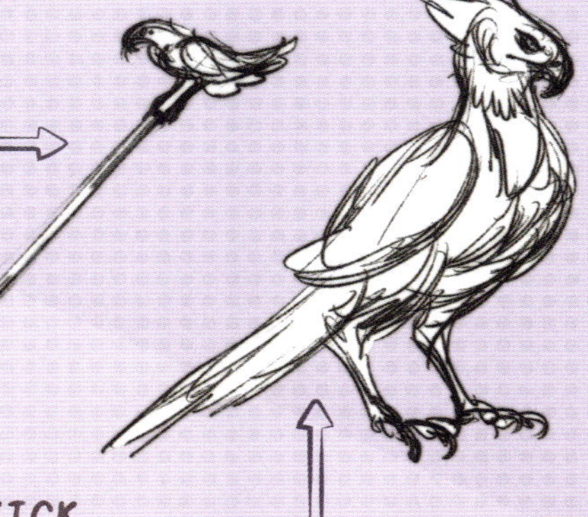

FASHION

A fitted suit with shoulder pads works well with the character's slender body, giving him an iconic silhouette. Accessories like the emblem pin can be used as the character's signature.

SIDEKICK

This exotic-looking fantasy creature is only available to the rich. It's a cross between an apex-predator bird and a phoenix. Its vibrant colour and elegant shape matches the villain's aesthetic, while also showcasing his status.

THUMBNAILS

When exploring thumbnails, look for dramatic poses, slim figures, and extravagant clothes. Ensure your villain has a poised, elegant stance. His body type is fit and lean — no slouching! Experiment with arm poses. For example, arms spread wide can indicate the character's dominance. Consider adding items such as cigars, pets, canes, and other luxurious accessories.

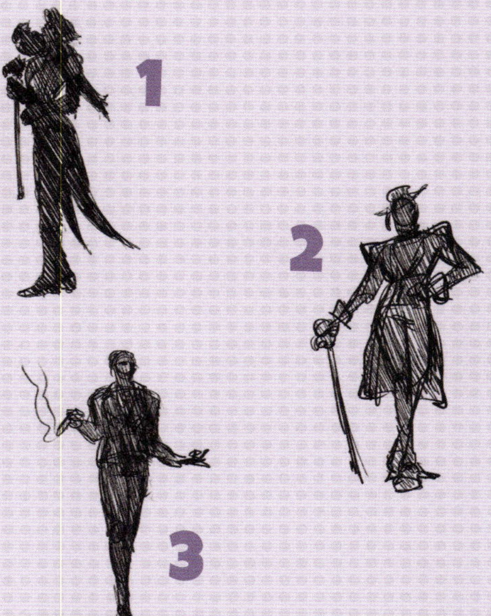
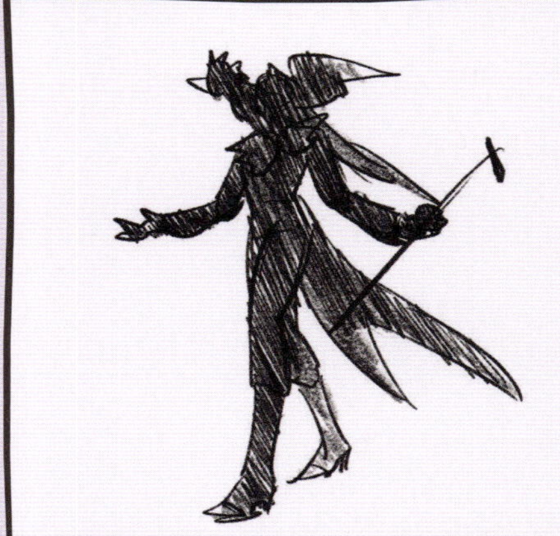
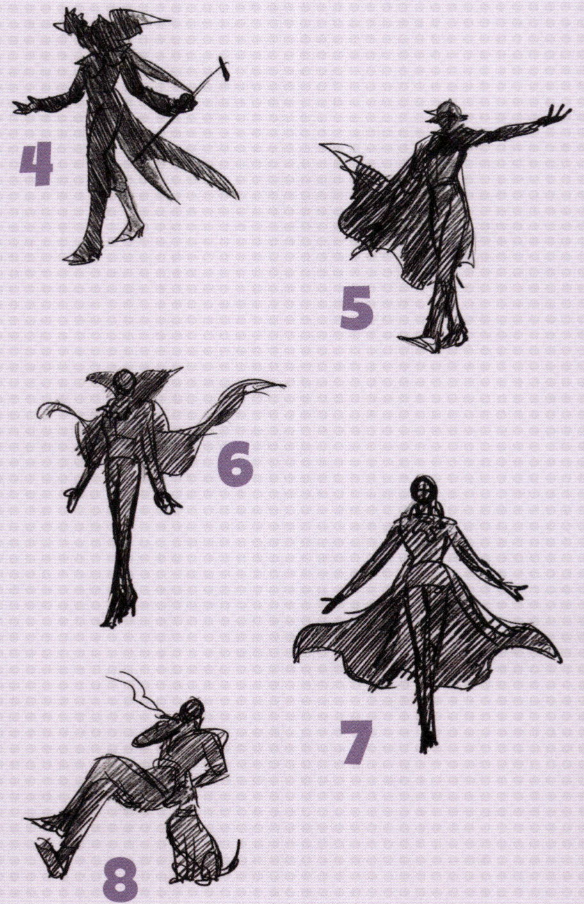

CHOSEN THUMBNAIL

The dramatic pose of thumbnail 4 best captures the villain's theatrical personality. The cane and bird sidekick allow for dynamic shapes and an intriguing yet recognizable silhouette.

FOUNDATIONS

Now that you have a rough shape for the character, sketch a simple stick figure with a coloured pencil, using a trapezium shape for the head and dynamic lines for the body so it doesn't look too stiff. Then add simple, curvy, block-like shapes to carve out the overall body. This will preserve the flow and the intended idea.

BASE

▶ First up, draw three boxes for the head, chest, and hips. Insert crossed lines over these boxes to indicate where the villain is looking. In this case, it's to the upper left.

▶ Sketch simple lines for the arms and legs. Create joints by adding circles on the shoulders, elbows, and wrists. Do the same for where the legs, knees, and ankles begin.

▶ Connect the chest and hips with two curved lines, along with the neck, arms, and legs. To help you envision the shapes, think of them as tubes and add more crossed lines.

LINES

▶ Use your graphite pencil to define the face and hair with big shapes. Make sure the eyes are sharp – you want to give the character a cold stare. Add two triangular shapes for the strands of fringe. This will be an important way of identifying the character.

▶ Shape the suit, trousers, and shoes. Tailor the clothes by using lines to separate each area, such as the shoulders, neck, and where clothing overlaps.

▶ Lastly, define the hands and outline the angle of his fingers. This small feature will help to show off his mannerisms.

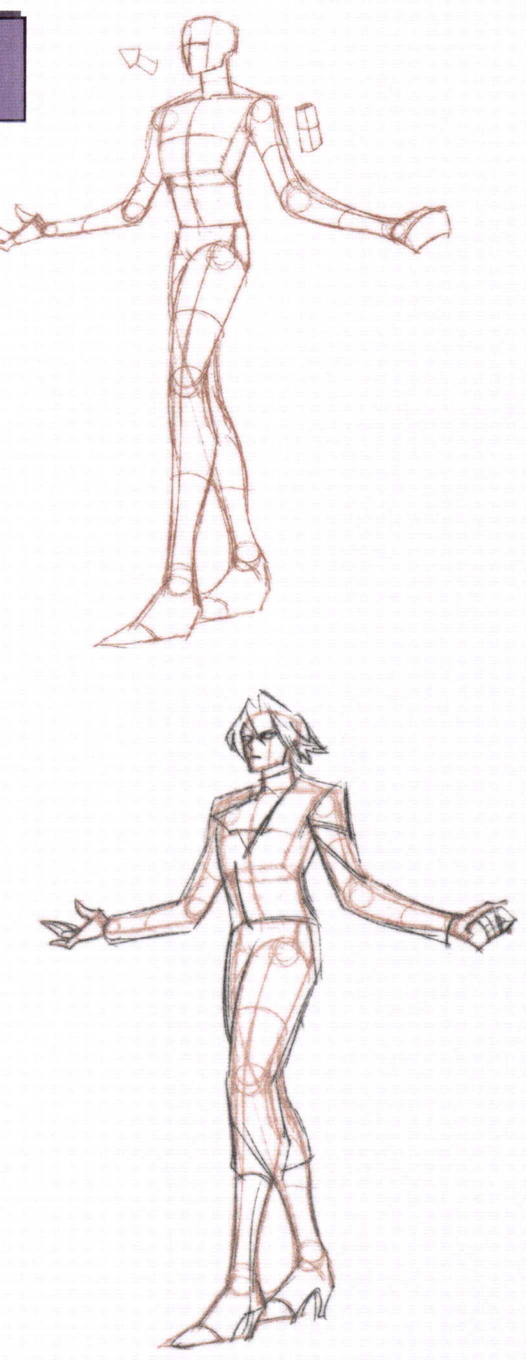

BUILDING UP

In order to bring this villain to life, add more shapes to his face, suit tails, and the emblem shown on the left side of his chest. Refine the face by forming the pupils and eyebrows, but remember to keep his expression slightly stern.

Add folds to make his clothes appear fitted. Make sure to apply pressure with your graphite pencil while drawing these new elements.

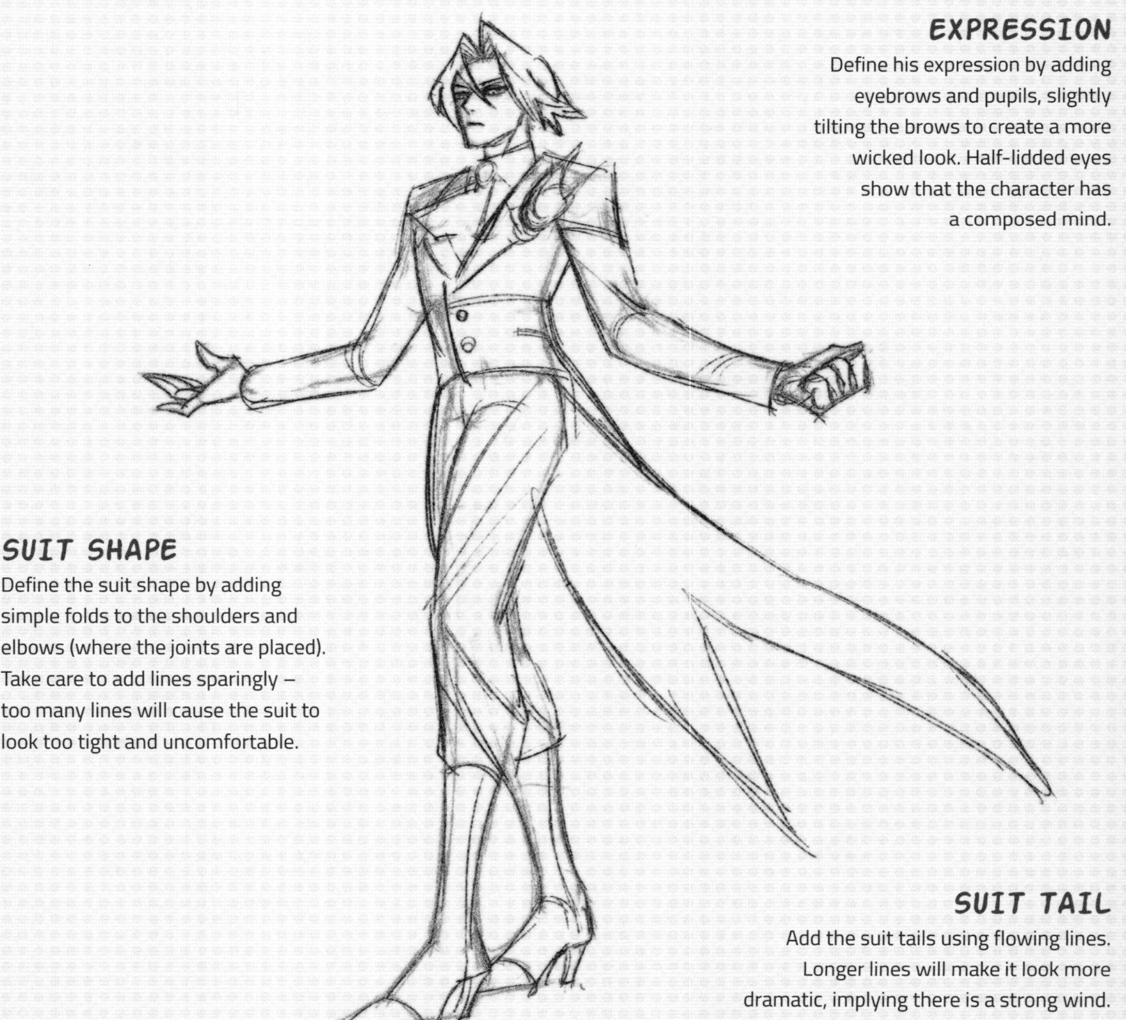

EXPRESSION

Define his expression by adding eyebrows and pupils, slightly tilting the brows to create a more wicked look. Half-lidded eyes show that the character has a composed mind.

SUIT SHAPE

Define the suit shape by adding simple folds to the shoulders and elbows (where the joints are placed). Take care to add lines sparingly – too many lines will cause the suit to look too tight and uncomfortable.

SUIT TAIL

Add the suit tails using flowing lines. Longer lines will make it look more dramatic, implying there is a strong wind.

DESIGN FOCUS

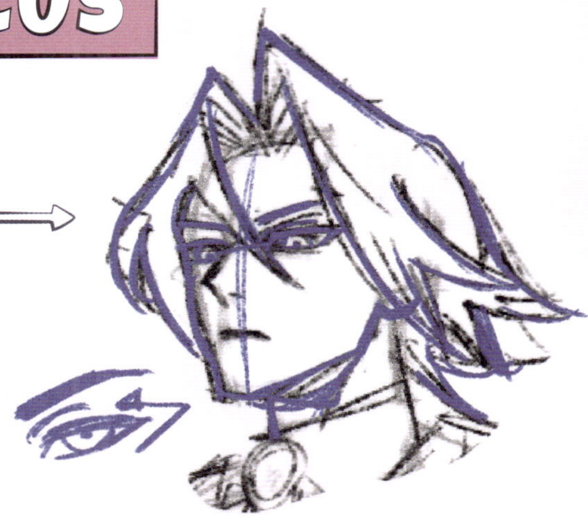

HEAD

Use sharp, angular lines for the eyes, hair, and face shape to convey his evil nature. Some parts of the hair can float, but ensure it isn't too messy. Try to resist including any tiny details.

HANDS

When drawing the hands, use a square shape for the palms and two sections for each finger. His hand should be slim and tapering. Draw his pinky finger pointing out to show his haughty personality.

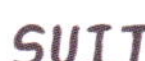

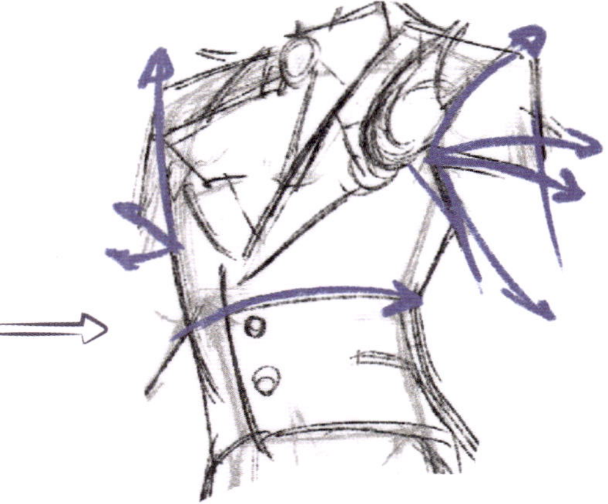

SUIT

The suit should look clean, without too many folds. Areas likely to have creases are the shoulders (especially when the arms are moving) and under the chest. Try to visualize how the character will move. These simple lines will help the overall flow.

IDEA INVENTORY

SIDEKICK

A sidekick or pet reveals a lot about its owner. For example, a canine creature could imply the villain has a strong physique, while a reptilian pet could mean the villain is a cunning liar. Play around with these ideas, incorporating the same shapes used for the main character. Introduce some fantasy elements, such as horns or vibrant colours.

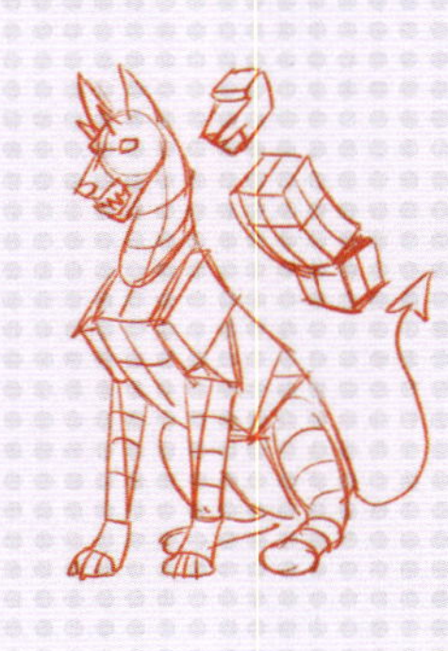

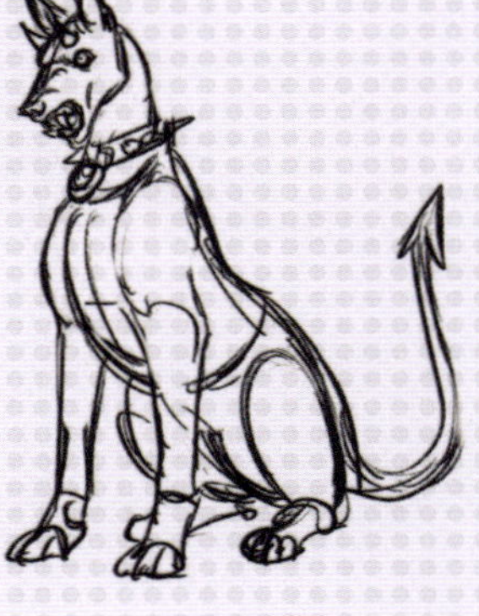

A bird could imply nobility, intelligence, daring, and freedom.

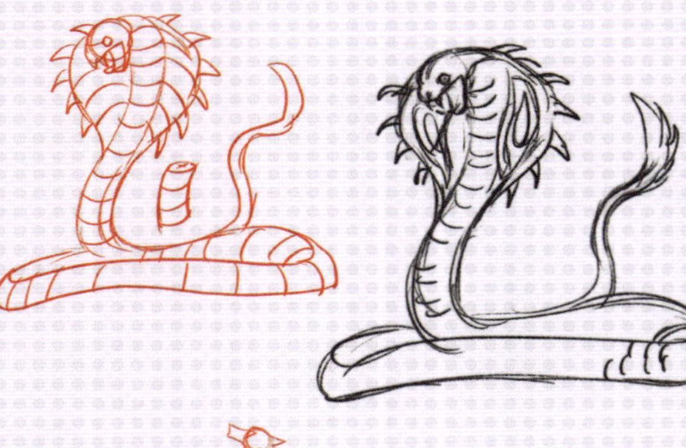

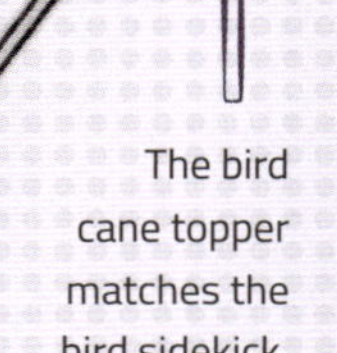

The bird cane topper matches the bird sidekick.

WALKING CANE

This villain is never without his cane. It's also a secret weapon, containing a hidden blade at its tip that's deadly sharp. Use a ruler to draw the length of the canes, then sketch angular animal heads on top.

FINAL SKETCH

Now that you've finalized your ideas, it's time to clean up the sketch to prepare for the line art. Use an eraser to clean any excessive lines and foundation guides. After everything looks polished, add in the phoenix and the bird-head cane.

Use the same pencil to add pressure and refine the sketch. Use this stage to add smaller details, such as the suit pattern and bird feathers.

▶ Lower the eyes and raise the mouth to make his face look more proportional. He's a calm and collected villain, so don't make him look too angry.

▶ Refine the neck ruffle and add another layer underneath by drawing swirly lines to indicate the edges. Make sure all the lines meet at one point. Finally, erase any overlapping lines. For a helpful real-life reference, pinch a piece of tissue paper.

▶ Next, draw a vertical striped pattern onto the suit. Start from the top, ensuring the lines follow the fold shapes to appear more three-dimensional.

▶ Adding a pattern to the suit will give it a fancier look. Start by creating wing-like patterns on the shoulders and inner suit tail. Draw small, continuous curves that follow the shape of the shoulder and flowing tail, then add lines between them.

▶ Draw the bird and walking cane. When drawing the bird's wings, use the same method you used for the wing pattern on the suit's shoulders. Outline the edge of the feathers with small curves, then line them up to attach the wings.

LINE WORK

If you have a tracing table, you can place it beneath your sketch to trace over the lines on a new piece of paper. This will make the inking process cleaner and you won't lose your final sketch. If you don't have a tracing table, ink straight over your sketch on the same paper, and be mindful when erasing the sketch lines to ensure the paper doesn't tear. When inking, remember to imagine your character in three-dimensional rather than flat shapes.

▶ Use a fineliner pen to ink over the whole image, then add weight to the lines. Reline some of the corners to make them thicker and more stylized. Make sure to fill in the tiny gaps too, as this will make the line art look wholly intact.

▶ Create simple textures by adding tiny etchings between the shadows and surface – this will blend the harsh, darker areas to the shape. While etching, make sure to follow the surface shape.

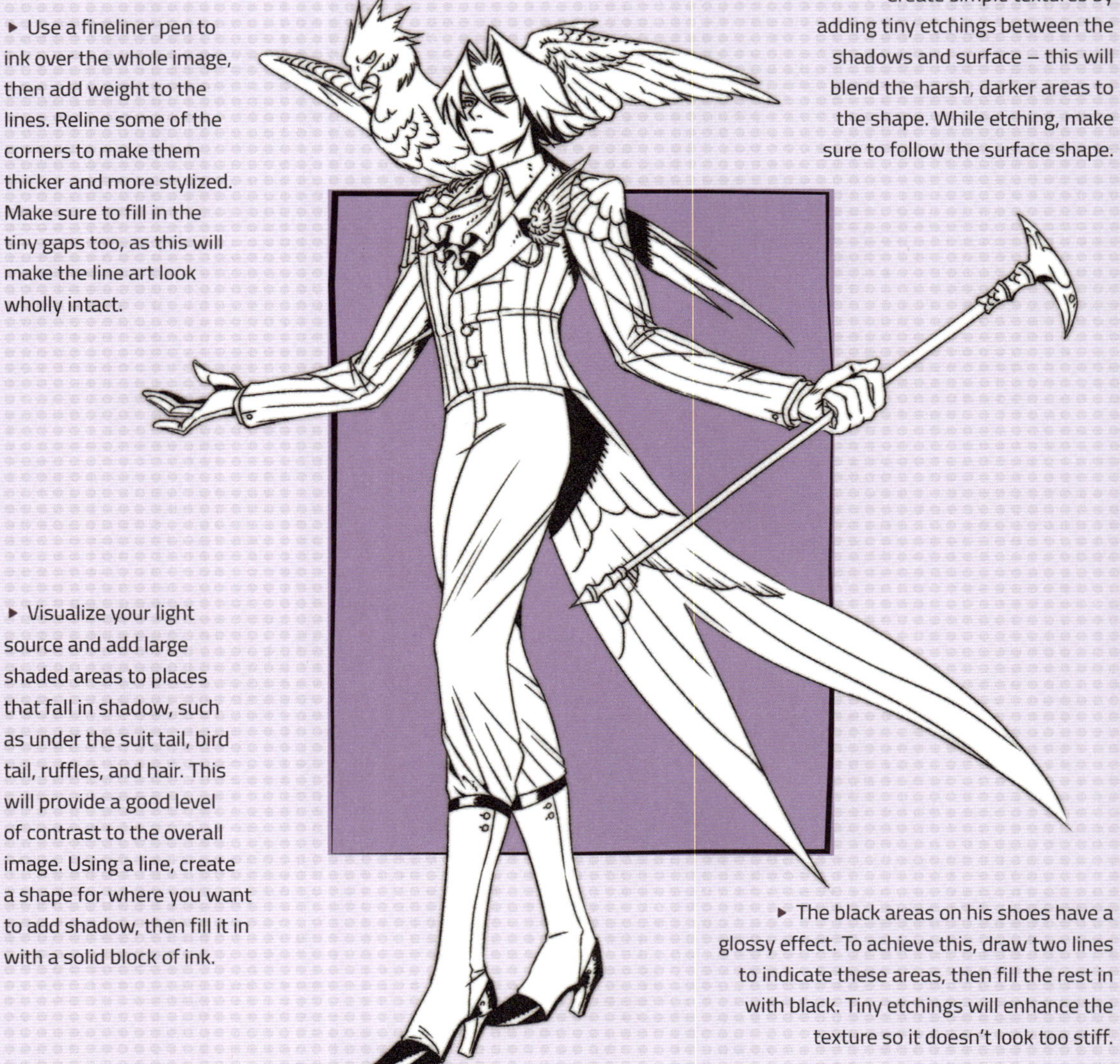

▶ Visualize your light source and add large shaded areas to places that fall in shadow, such as under the suit tail, bird tail, ruffles, and hair. This will provide a good level of contrast to the overall image. Using a line, create a shape for where you want to add shadow, then fill it in with a solid block of ink.

▶ The black areas on his shoes have a glossy effect. To achieve this, draw two lines to indicate these areas, then fill the rest in with black. Tiny etchings will enhance the texture so it doesn't look too stiff.

COLOURING

This villain will have cold colours – such as blue, purple, and pink-maroon – with warmer colours, like gold and orange, on the bird to contrast. Rich and pretentious, he likes to stand out from the crowd. Start by using the cel-shading technique to colour (see page 36), which will make it easier to discern which parts will be bright and which will have shadows.

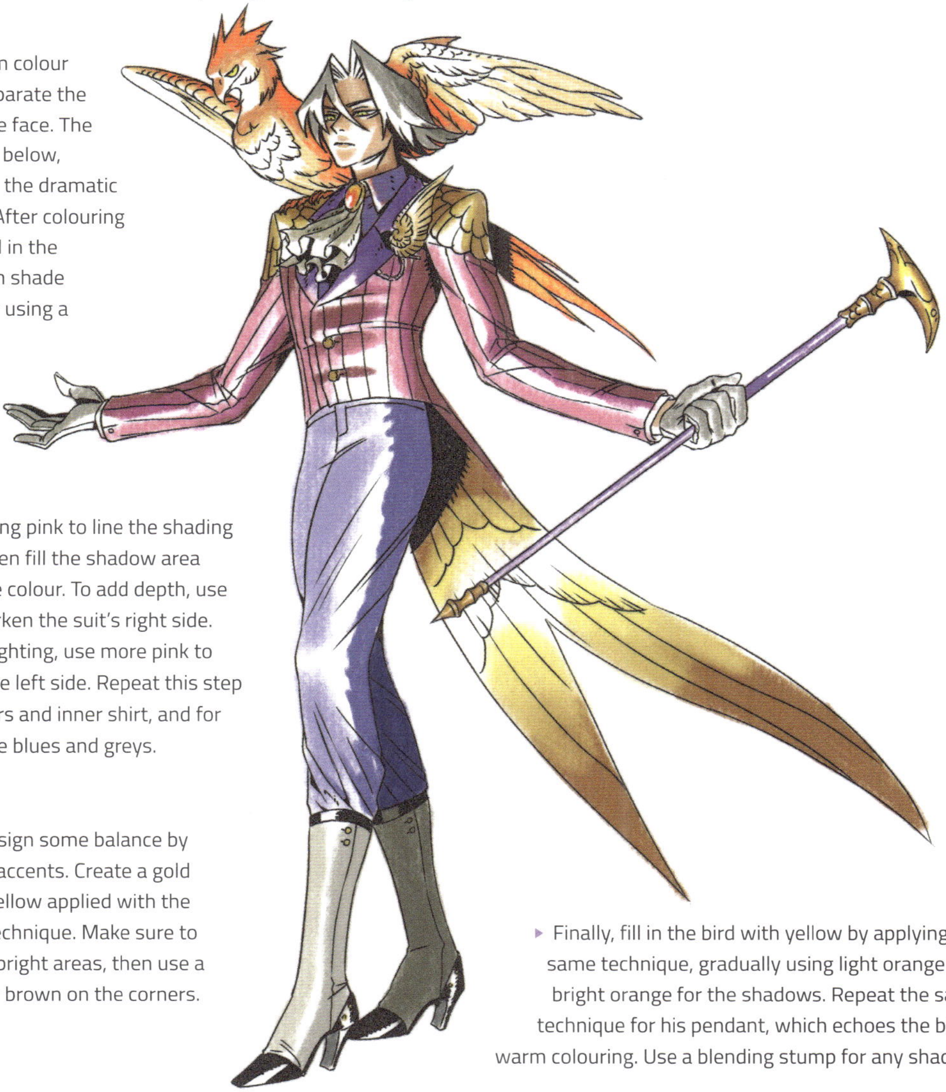

▶ Use a cream colour to line and separate the shading on the face. The light source is below, which adds to the dramatic atmosphere. After colouring these lines, fill in the shadows, then shade under the hair using a brown colour.

▶ Start by using pink to line the shading on the suit, then fill the shadow area with the same colour. To add depth, use maroon to darken the suit's right side. To focus the lighting, use more pink to lightly fill in the left side. Repeat this step for the trousers and inner shirt, and for the gloves, use blues and greys.

▶ Give the design some balance by adding warm accents. Create a gold effect using yellow applied with the cel-shading technique. Make sure to leave out the bright areas, then use a dark yellow or brown on the corners.

▶ Finally, fill in the bird with yellow by applying the same technique, gradually using light orange and bright orange for the shadows. Repeat the same technique for his pendant, which echoes the bird's warm colouring. Use a blending stump for any shading.

▶ Final image © Rika 'BWusagi'

LITTLE MUSHROOM MONSTER

BY CARLES DALMAU

This tutorial will show you how to design a small, friendly companion creature using Clip Studio Paint, though you can follow along in your chosen medium. The style will be inspired by little anime and manga monsters, similar to those that appear in *Pokémon* or *Digimon*. It will begin with a series of sketches to come up with ideas for the creature, before covering steps to develop the character, clean up the sketch, and introduce colour to create the final design.

TOOLKIT

Clip Studio Paint

▸ Texture pen

▸ Soft brush

RESEARCH

When designing a manga character or creature, it can be helpful to start with a theme or subject matter to incorporate into the design, letting it influence the character's shape and form. Mushrooms will be the focus here. Begin by researching mushrooms online or in textbooks to gather a selection of reference material. Next, create a series of small sketches using Clip Studio Paint's Texture pen without pressure, found on the brush panel on the left of the screen.

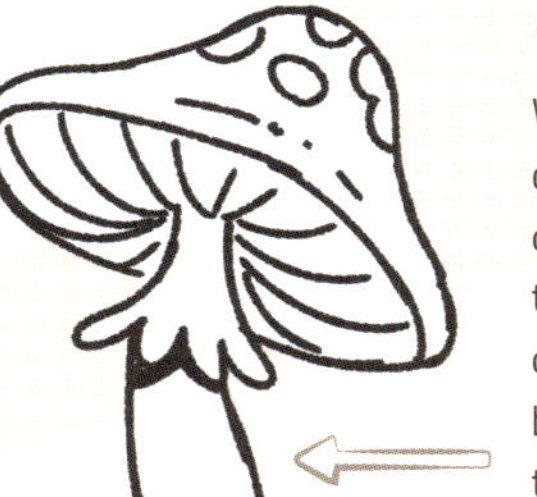

TOADSTOOL

While mushrooms can share similar characteristics, their shapes can drastically differ between the various types. Here is a typical toadstool.

MUSHROOM HAT

Some mushrooms are very simple. The cap of this mushroom looks a little like a hat, which could be incorporated into the character's outfit.

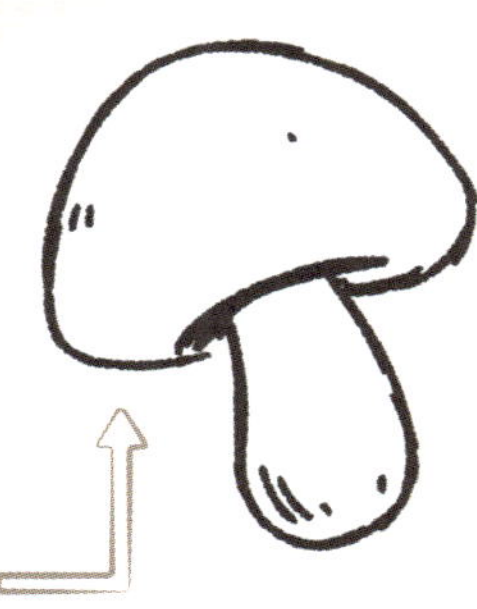

STEM

A mushroom's stem is rooted in the ground. When picked, this stem will be partially covered with dirt. This detail could be included in the character's design and colour.

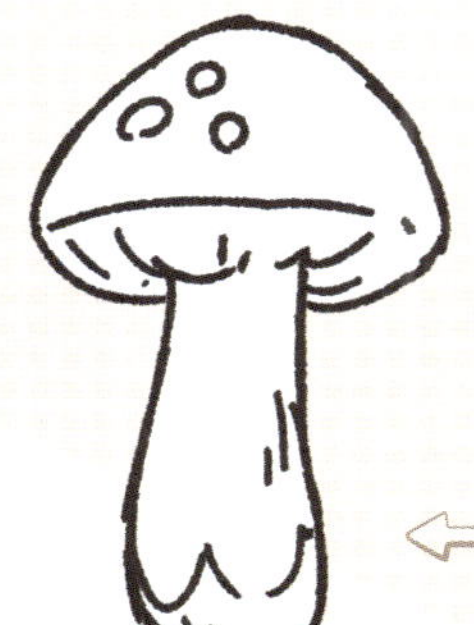

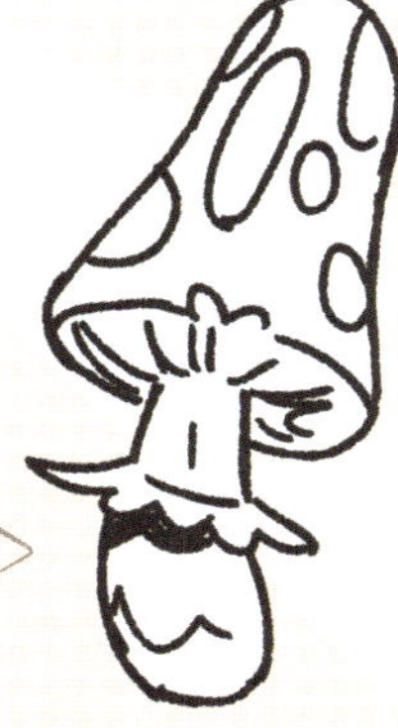

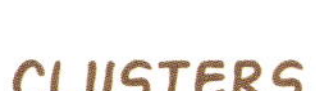

SKIRT

Some mushrooms have a ring midway down the stem that looks like a little skirt. Being able to recognize these details and compare them to fashion elements can add a clever twist to the design.

CLUSTERS

Some types of mushrooms grow clustered together; their long thin stems sprouting from the same root. This offers a different kind of shape and silhouette.

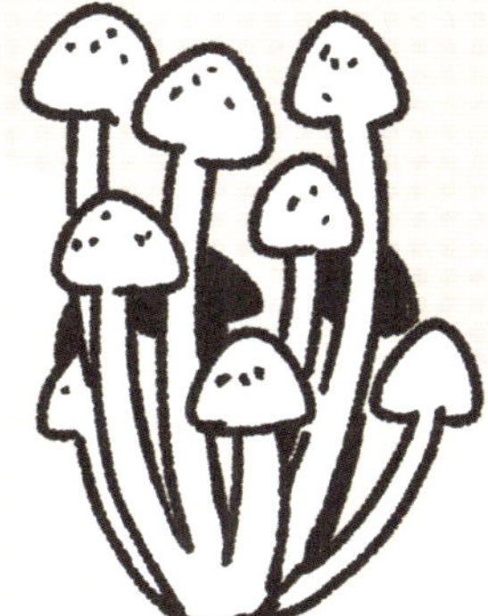

THUMBNAILS

Still using the Texture pen, draw thumbnails of little manga monsters, experimenting with as many shapes as possible. Start with basic geometrical shapes – such as circles, triangles, or rectangles – before adding extra details to make the design look more understandable. Add various elements borrowed from mushrooms to each character – such as a hat-like cap or skirt-like ring – merging these with the designs of different creatures. Some designs could be anthropomorphic, while others could have a closer resemblance to animals.

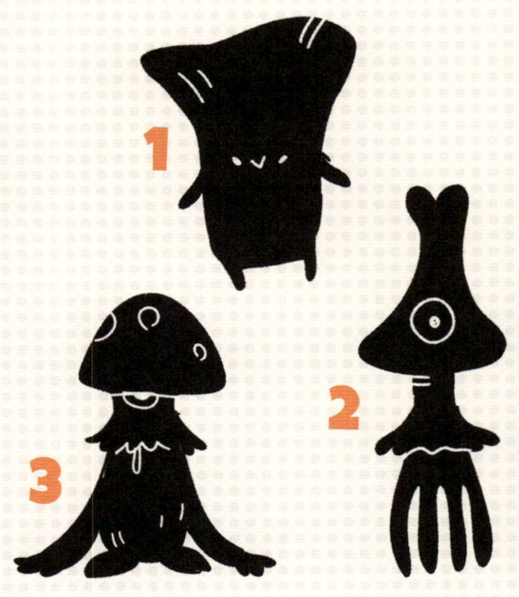

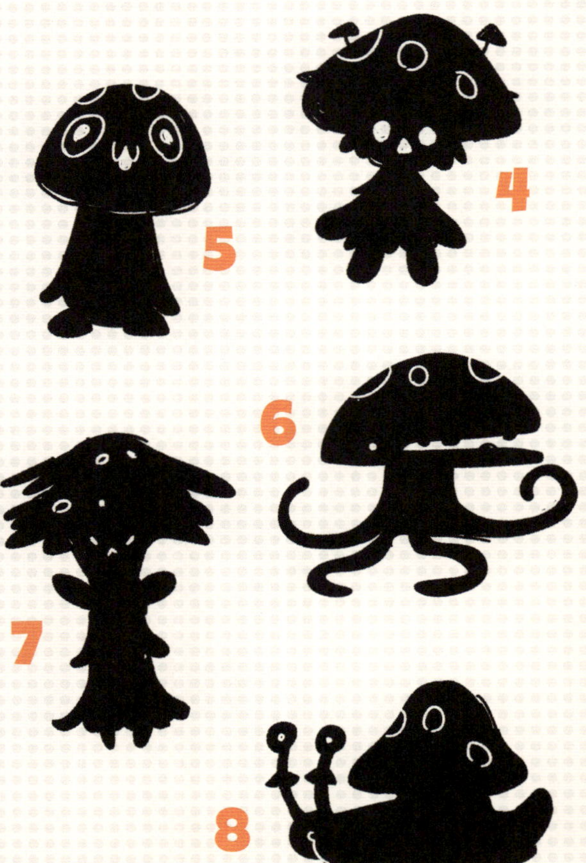

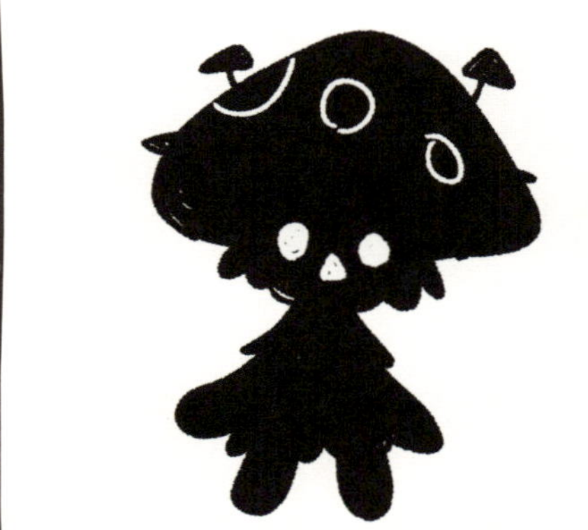

CHOSEN THUMBNAIL

While all of the thumbnails are interesting and could be developed further, thumbnail 4 successfully captures the idea for a mushroom-inspired manga mascot. It's easy to imagine it in a video game or anime show.

FOUNDATIONS

Sketching the foundations involves mapping out the basic shapes. This will make the detailing stage that follows a lot easier. Using the chosen thumbnail as a guide, draw the basic shapes that make up the character. Once this is in place, you can then sketch some variation in shape and form to make the character more interesting.

BASE

▸ When creating a cute monster, it's important to familiarize yourself with shape language. Round shapes will make the character appear more pet-like and friendly, whereas angular shapes can make the character look scarier and more dangerous. To see this in real-life creatures, compare the shapes that make up a cat and a crocodile.

▸ Draw the head so it's almost as big as the body. While no creature would be able to survive with this distorted anatomy in real life, exaggerating this feature will make it appear cuter and more endearing.

▸ Drawing a grid on the surface of each element will allow you to see the shapes of the character more clearly. This will be especially helpful once more details are added.

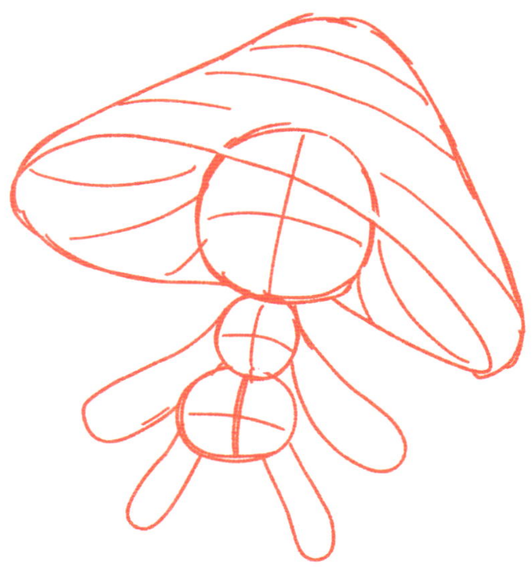

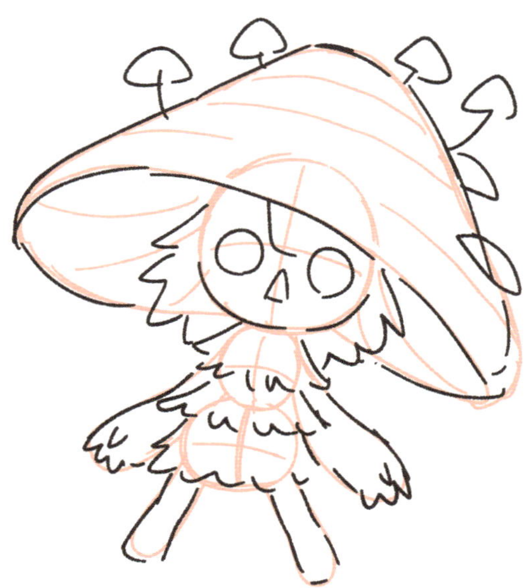

LINES

▸ Start to define the important elements of the final design, such as the little skirt-like rings that wrap around the character's torso. Keeping these base shapes in mind will help as you draw in the body's proportions and volumes.

▸ The character looks too symmetrical in the base sketch. Adding various mushroom shapes on its cap will help to make it more asymmetrical and fun.

▸ When adding details, it's important not to lose the base shape of the character. Have fun drawing in the different elements, but don't add so many that it appears crowded, as this will make the design less readable as a character.

BUILDING UP

Once you have the basic shapes that make the character identifiable, it's time to start refining each element on top of the sketch you already have. Using the Texture pen, focus on adding more volume and weight to the different elements to make them easier to read and identify.

VARIETY

Begin to add variety to the little mushrooms on the character's head – they should vary in size and shape. Try to simplify them in order to understand how their perspective works, and then add more details.

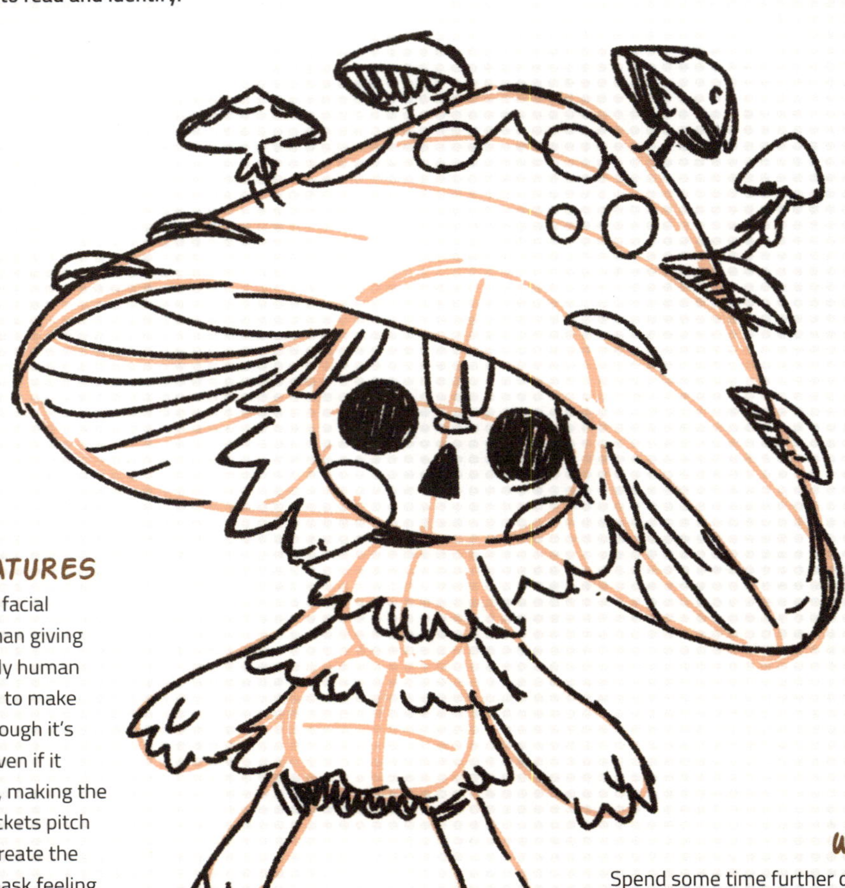

FACIAL FEATURES

Start to define the facial features. Rather than giving the character overly human characteristics, try to make the face look as though it's wearing a mask (even if it isn't). For example, making the mouth and eye sockets pitch black will help to create the deepness of the mask feeling.

WEIGHT

Spend some time further defining the character's 'dress' and 'hair'. Give them some weight by adding curves here and there. Studying the shape of a water droplet can help you to understand how gravity pulls such shapes downwards.

DESIGN FOCUS

SIMPLIFY

Simplifying the different shapes that make up the character right at the beginning is the easiest way to understand the perspective of each element. This will enable you to add more elaborate details afterwards.

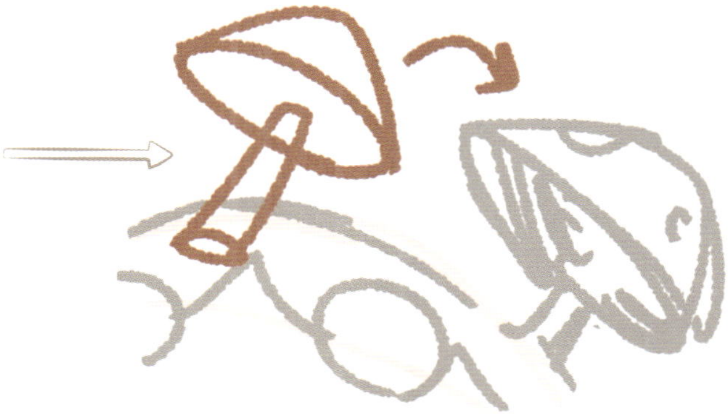

HANDS

When drawing the arms, aim to sketch a wobbly hot-dog shape and then add a few pointy fingers to it. This will make the character look cuter, as well as making the hands easier to draw.

MOUTH

Positioning the character's mouth closer to their eyes will give them a more adorable, childlike look, perfect for a friendly little monster companion. This characteristic is found in babies and puppies alike, and is what makes humans find them so cute.

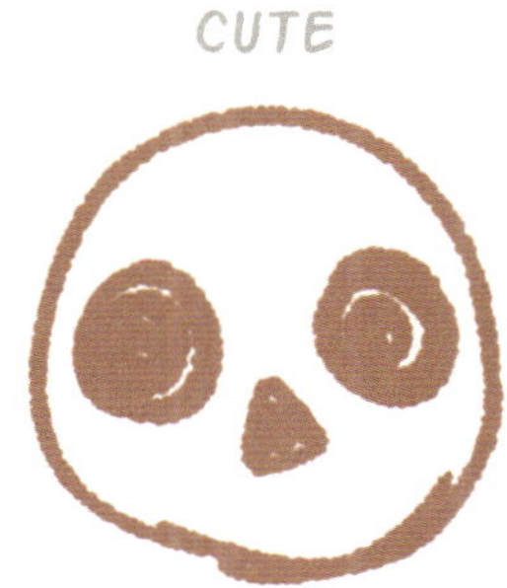

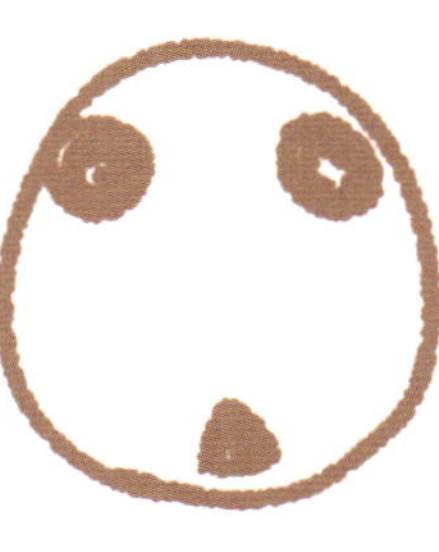

IDEA INVENTORY

MUSHROOM

Using the Texture pen, explore what props or accessories the character could carry to add more story to their design. Consider how you could combine these items with the character's mushroom theme.

This little monster might need a sword for defending itself. A tall pointy mushroom cap acts as the blade, with the skirt-like ring resembling the quillon or cross guard.

Perhaps the character has magical fungi powers. Here a mushroom stem makes up the body of a magic wand. Extra details, such as a couple of bells, give it more visual interest.

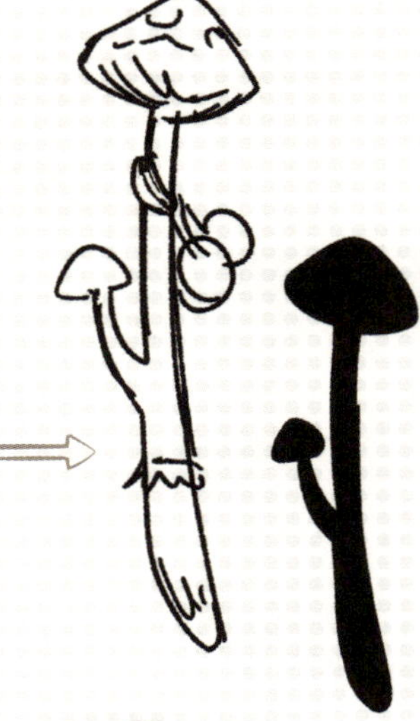

The third prop is a bottle, with the mushroom used as the bottle cap. Maybe it contains a magical fungi potion?

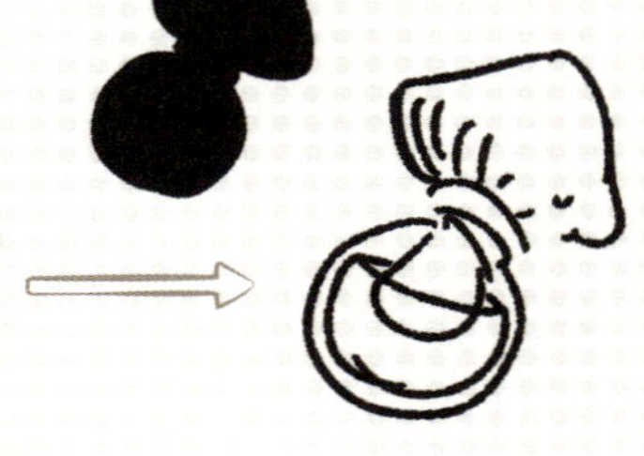

FOREST

Perhaps this little mushroom monster is a forest spirit. It will need forest-themed props crafted from natural elements. Adding leaves and small branch stumps to all three designs helps to give them a rustic look.

A bow and arrows could be used as a weapon. Here a branch is bent to form the body of the bow, bound tight with thread.

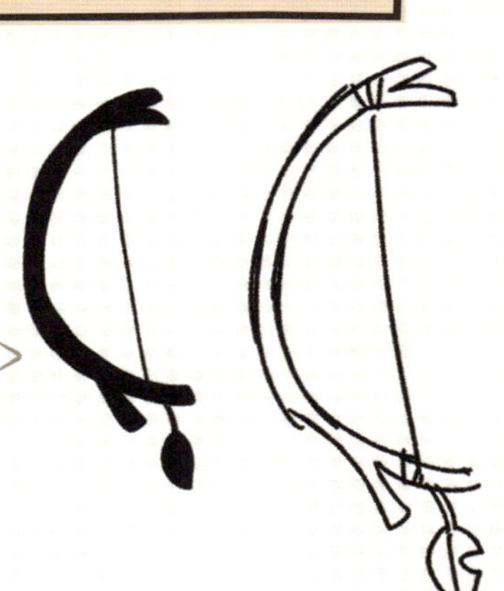

The wand is also crafted from a rustic branch. The lower half resembles the roots of a tree, while the tip is an ornate coil of wood, giving it a fantasy look.

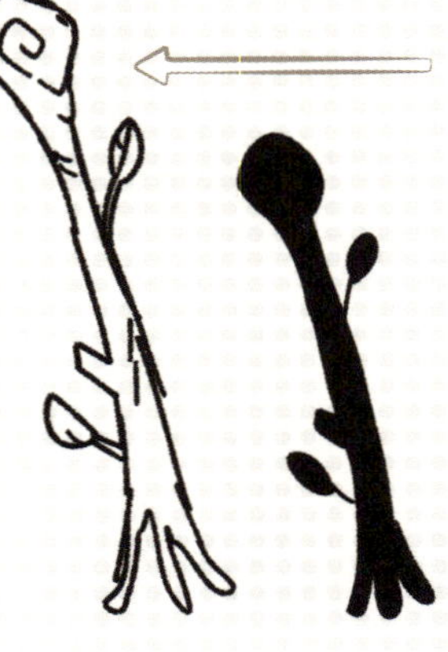

The sword is formed by two branches bound together with cord, rather than any metal elements.

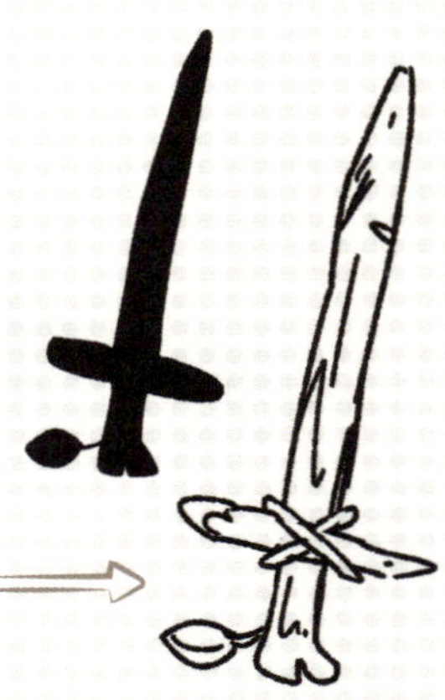

FINAL SKETCH

The final sketch is not the final drawing, so it doesn't have to be perfect. The focus should be on making sure that all the elements of the character are understood, as this will make drawing the line art in the next step much easier.

As you use the Texture pen to add new details and elements, try not to lose sight of the initial geometric shapes of the character. The silhouette must still be recognizable, so avoid overloading the little monster with too many details.

▶ As you refine the character's design, add a little variation to each element to prevent it from looking monotonous. For example, draw little mushrooms on the cap, referring back to your thumbnail studies for ideas for different types of mushroom. Experiment with shape, increasing or decreasing the size of the stem and cap for each little mushroom.

▶ Experiment with shape. The hair looked a little boring in the rough sketch, so I looked up more fungi references to find new shapes that could make the character more interesting.

▶ Add imperfections. It may seem strange, but drawing small stripes and dots in a random manner can lend believability and realism to characters inspired by nature, as nature is rarely perfect.

▶ Avoid perfect symmetry. Even if the character is by design very symmetrical due to its shapes, try to make the details look slightly different on either side. This will give it a more fun and unique look.

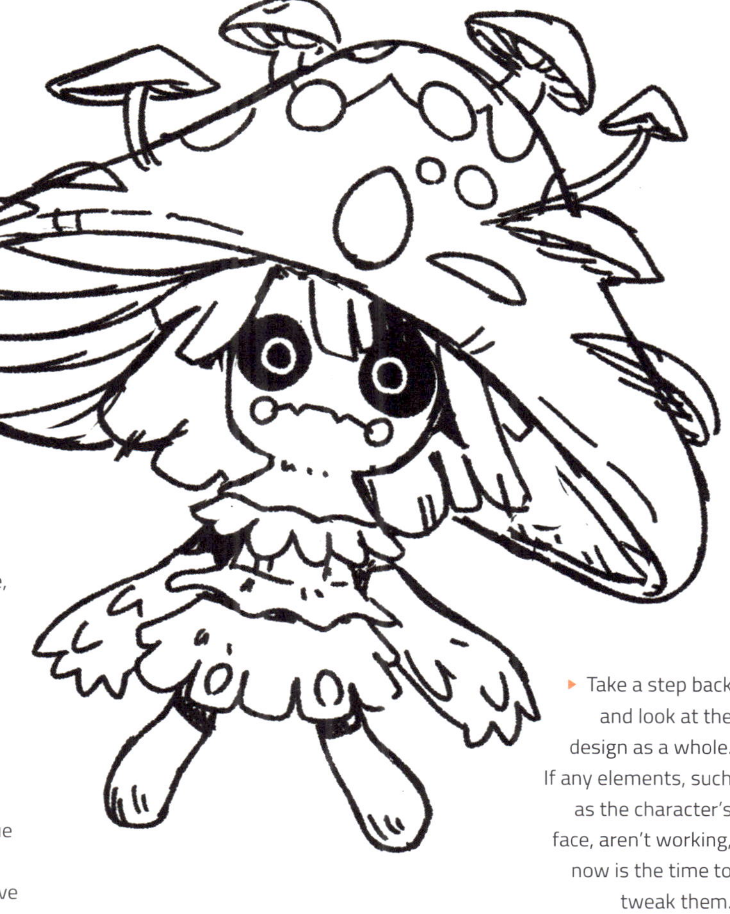

▶ Take a step back and look at the design as a whole. If any elements, such as the character's face, aren't working, now is the time to tweak them.

LINE WORK

Once the final sketch is finished, it's time to clean it up by drawing neat line art over the top. Try using the Texture pen with pressure, making sure the brush stabilizer is set to maximum, which will make the lines as smooth as possible.

(The stabilizer can be found in the tool properties of your brush.) Begin to draw over the top of the final sketch, trying to vary the line thickness throughout the design.

▶ If you struggle with drawing neat line art, make use of Clip Studio Paint's Stabilizer tool. It's also a good idea to make a copy of the brush you're using, keeping one with maximum stabilization and the other without it. Some larger elements will be easier to draw with more stabilization, whereas smaller details are often easier to draw without it.

▶ Fill some areas with black to create contrast between elements, as well as to help draw the viewer's attention to a particular area. With the character's face, the black eyes and a dark area beside the right eye instantly pulls focus.

▶ When it comes to line thickness, try to make the overall shapes thicker, and the smaller details – such as imperfections – thinner. This is achieved by altering the pressure you apply to the brush when drawing. More pressure will produce thicker lines, and less pressure thinner lines.

▶ When adding imperfections, try to improvise a little. Some could look like little strokes, while others may look like slight curves that wrap around an element. They're imperfections, so avoid trying to make them perfect!

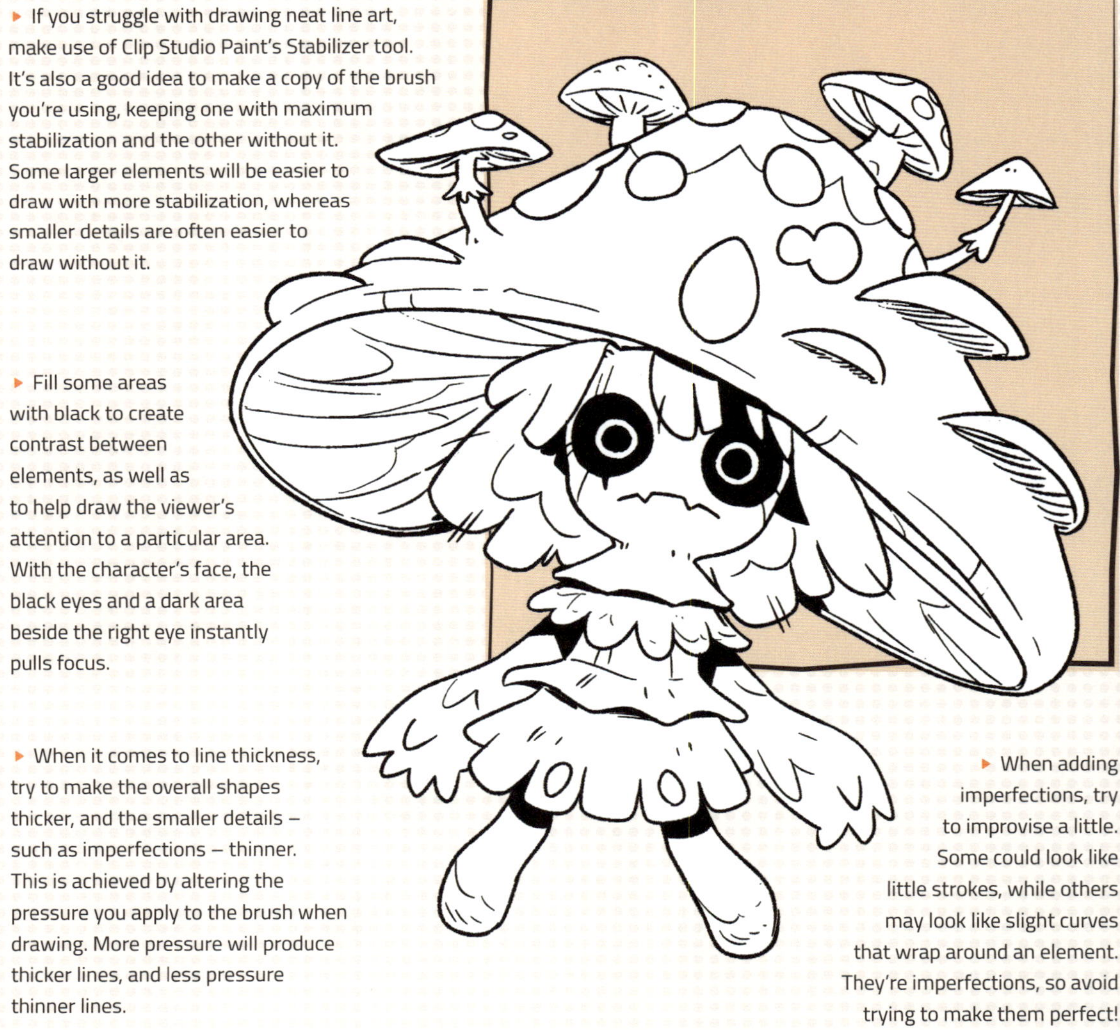

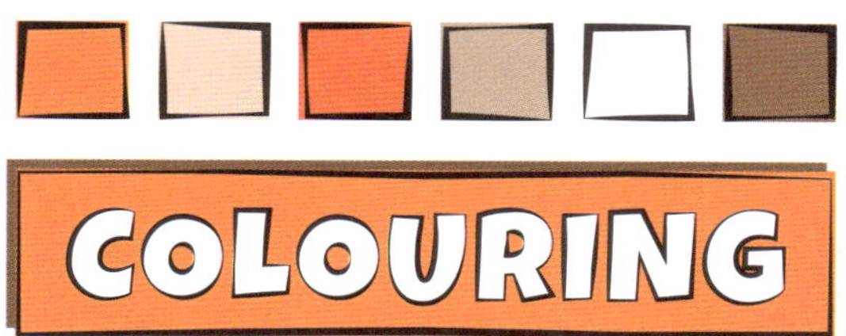

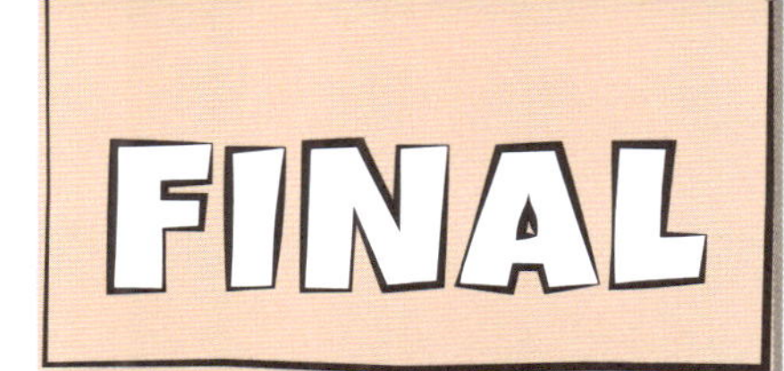

COLOURING

When deciding on colours, refer back to your mushroom reference material. Mushrooms typically have a whitish stem, while the caps come in various colours, though these are often red, brown, or orange. Having a clear reference will help you to choose colours. The colour palette used here has an autumnal tone, as orange colours always work well for characters inspired by nature. Again, use the Texture pen, along with the soft brush to create gradients.

▶ Start by colouring the whole character with a flat colour, on a new layer below the line art. This will help to define the shape, making it easier to apply the colours without having to worry about painting outside of the character.

▶ Once the base colour is down, apply the flat colours based on the autumnal palette. Focus on painting inside each element to avoid it looking muddy. Messy colouring can work for some styles, but it's not the chosen approach for this character.

▶ After the flat colours are painted in, experiment with applying a gradient. Select part of the head, then use the soft brush to paint a gradient over the top, using a reddish tone for the upper part. This creates a subtle variation of tones that make the design more interesting.

▶ Paint shadows on the underside of the character's various layers, such as beneath the skirt-like rings. Next, paint a few highlights on the mushroom's cap. Finish by painting colour over some of the black line work, such as the lines on the top of the head, to give the final drawing a simpler, cleaner feel.

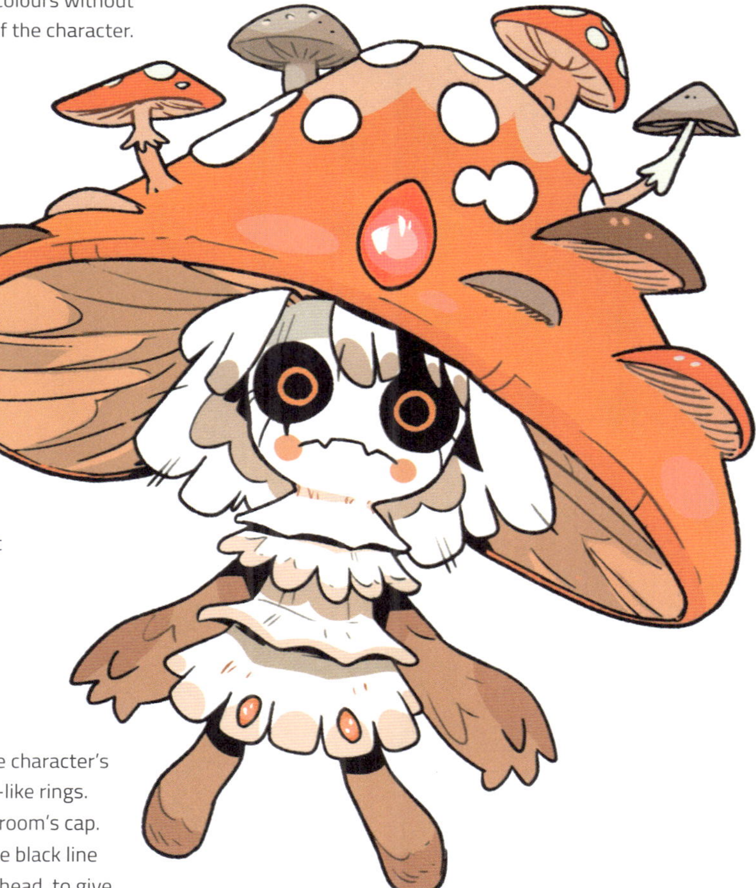

NEKOMIMI GIRL

BY SIMZART

This tutorial will walk you through the process of creating a kemonomimi manga character. A kemonomimi is a humanoid character with animal features, such as a bird's wings or a fox's ears and tail. There are various types of kemonomimi based on different animal themes. This tutorial will focus on creating a nekomimi, which is a manga character with cat features. Starting with assembling the references needed to create the artwork, the tutorial will develop the concept step-by-step, from rough sketches to final image.

TOOLKIT

Clip Studio Paint

▸ Pencil brush

▸ Ink brush

▸ Round brushes

RESEARCH

Begin by researching the kemonomimi subject matter. Often seen in anime and manga, these characters blend human and animal elements. The majority of their body is anthropomorphic, with animal elements added; in this case, cat ears and a tail. (An important aspect to remember is that the animal ears replace the humanoid ears.) It's also not unusual for a kemonomimi character's skin to have a different hue from the typical human skin range.

EARS

One of the most iconic parts of a kemonomimi character is their ears. Using the Pencil brush, sketch different types of animal ears, such as those of a rabbit, deer, and cat.

TAIL

The tail is another recognizable element of a kemonomimi. Research various kinds of animal tails, exploring shape, size, and texture.

HAIRSTYLE

The hairstyle is particularly important, as the area where the human ear is usually located has to be covered.

CLOTHES

Clothes can help to tell the character's story and convey their personality. These clothes make up a modern, urban outfit.

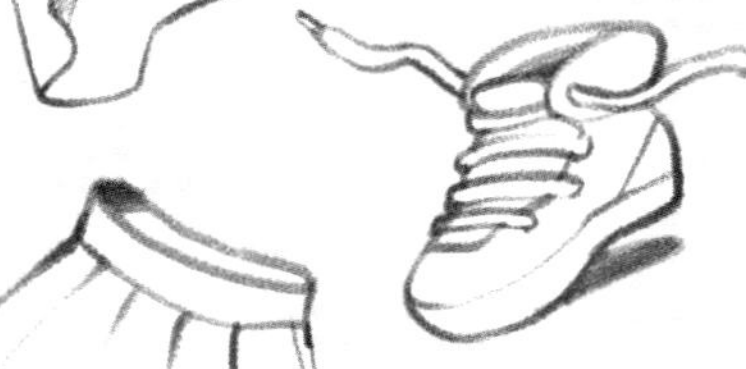

NECKLACE

Kemonomimi characters often have necklaces and chokers. Explore various pendant designs, along with animal collars.

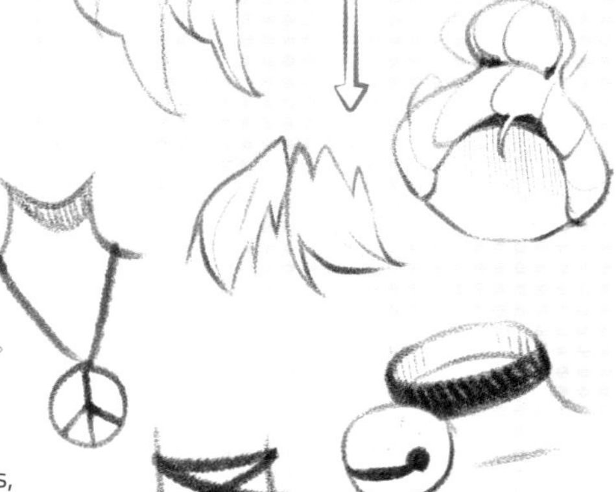

THUMBNAILS

Using the Pencil brush in Clip Studio Paint, create a series of thumbnail explorations to help you to figure out the best pose for the character. Start by drawing iconic manga poses, such as cute, relaxed, fiery, curious, and pin-up. Kemonomimi characters are often drawn in poses that resemble animal movements, so sketch a few of these also. You may decide to go with the typical manga look, or to distance yourself from the usual tropes.

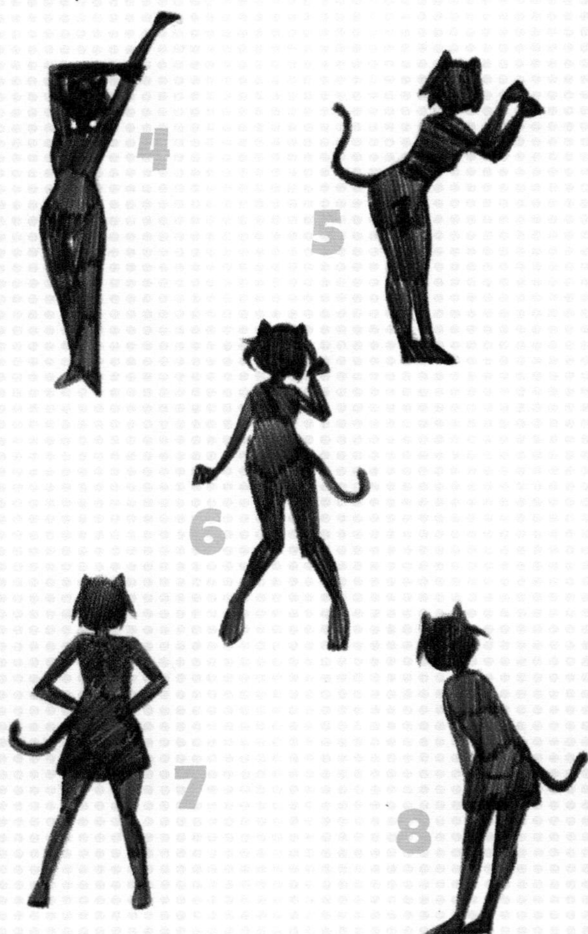

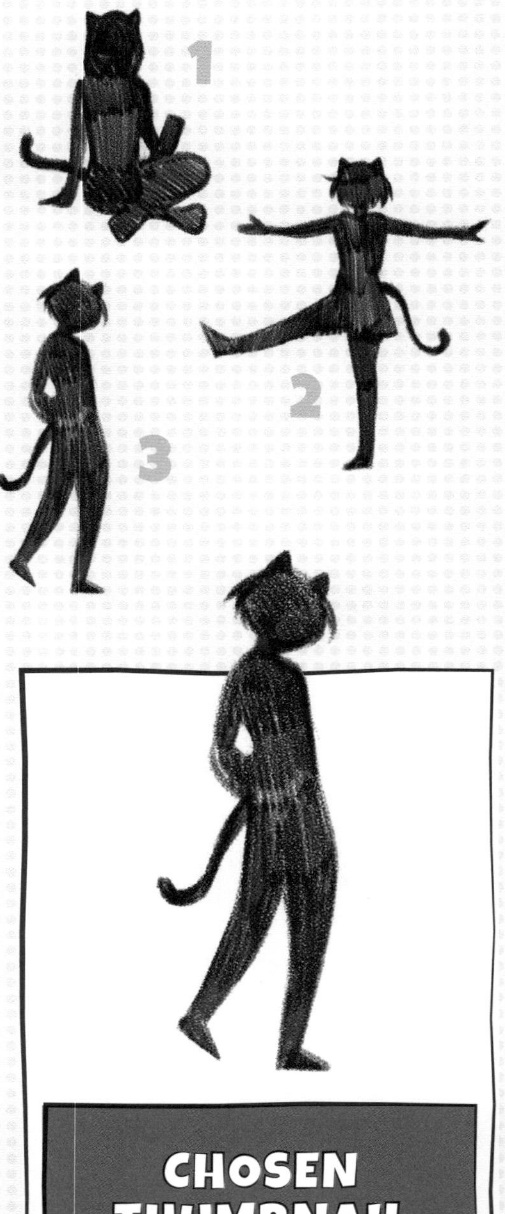

CHOSEN THUMBNAIL

Thumbnail 3 has a shy yet curious posture. This will work well for a nekomimi character with feline personality traits.

FOUNDATIONS

This stage involves developing your chosen thumbnail into a more definite design. On a new layer, lay down the pose of the character, keeping the rhythm as interesting and as close to the thumbnail as possible. If you want to give the character a slight chibi look, draw the head a little bit bigger than the average human head. Consider using a three-quarter angle to show the walking pose more clearly.

BASE

▶ Keep it simple. The focus should be on shape rather than detail at this stage. The most important thing is to make sure the proportions are correct and sit well as a whole.

▶ One approach to simplify the body is to visualize the head and joints as circles, the torso and abdomen as ovals, the legs and arms as cylinders, and the hands and feet as rectangles.

▶ The character's pose doesn't need to be overly dynamic to be interesting. A static pose with a visually pleasing rhythm can be just as engaging with the right proportions.

LINES

▶ Ensure the main shapes are clear and harmonious. Now is the time to start fleshing out the body, removing the basic blocks designed in the previous step. Avoid adding too many details until you're happy with the overall design.

▶ Hair is an important feature for this type of character. Like any other part of the body, it's made up of shapes. Decide how you want it to affect the silhouette.

▶ Erase the overlapping lines drawn for the initial breakdown. This will give the design more depth and make it less confusing. At this stage you want the character to be clear and fairly readable.

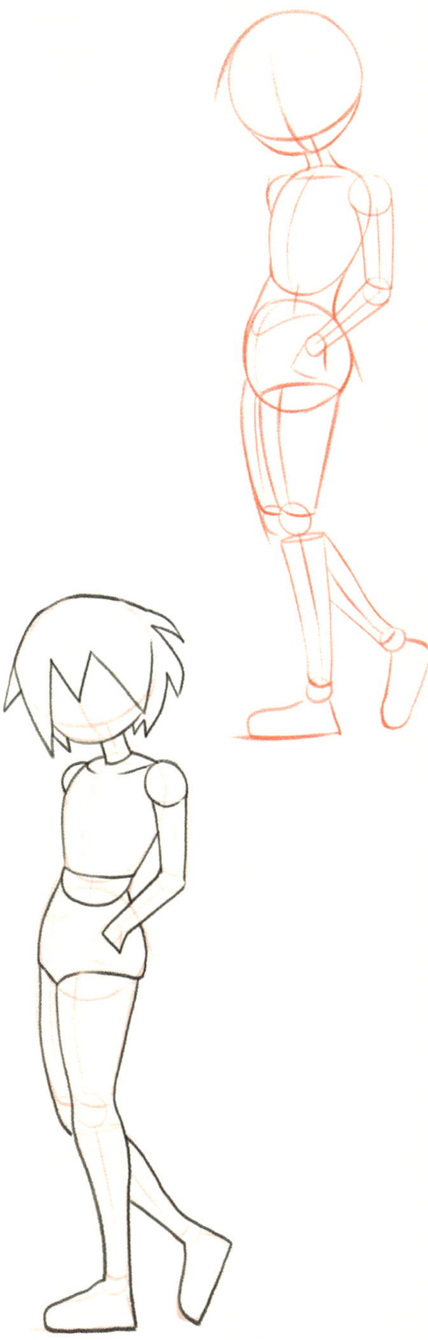

BUILDING UP

On a new layer, keep adding details with the Pencil brush, without losing sight of the original design created in the thumbnail. Add small details that don't break the silhouette. Use cross-hatching and line weight to help you better visualize the shapes and the hierarchy between each element of the drawing. You could also introduce a few shadows at this stage to create an idea of where the light source will be.

EXPRESSION

Start to draw in core elements, such as the eyes, facial features, and hair details. Keep in mind that the character's expression is the most relatable part of the design and one of the first elements the viewer will look at.

FELINE FEATURES

Draw in a cat's tail and ears. These distinctive elements will instantly give the character the iconic nekomimi look. Make sure to give the ears a sense of depth by drawing them in perspective.

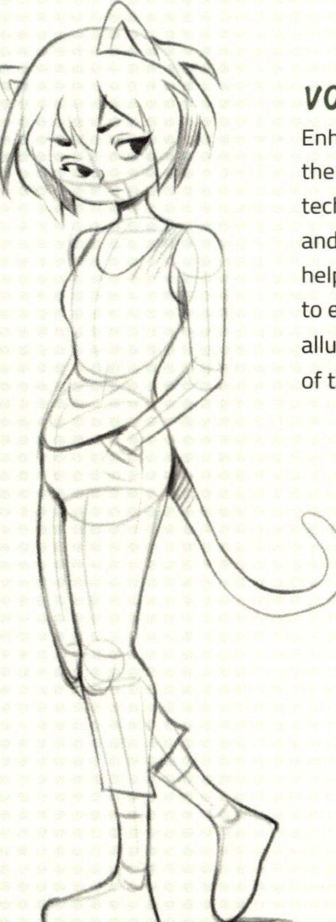

VOLUME

Enhance the design with the use of two key drawing techniques: cross-hatching and line weight. These will help give depth and volume to every shape, as well as alluding to the direction of the light source.

DESIGN FOCUS

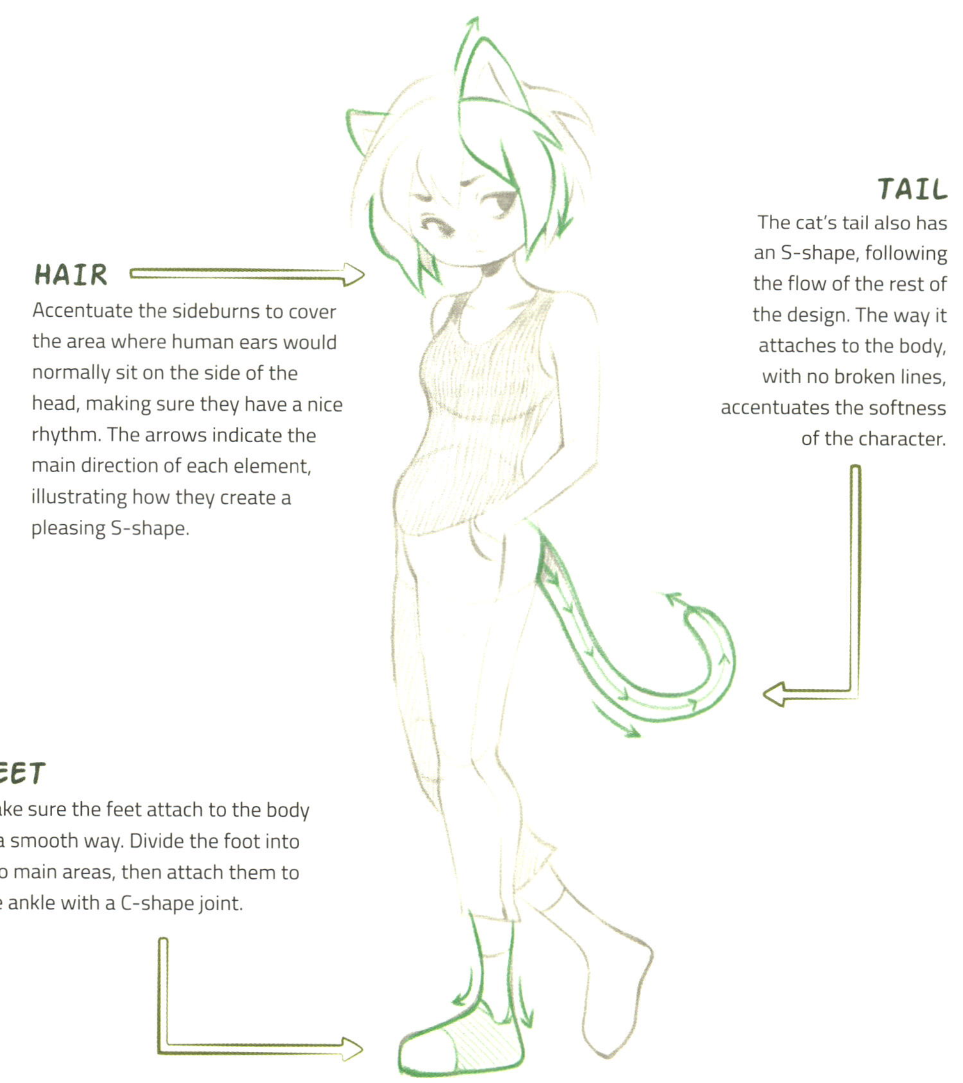

HAIR

Accentuate the sideburns to cover the area where human ears would normally sit on the side of the head, making sure they have a nice rhythm. The arrows indicate the main direction of each element, illustrating how they create a pleasing S-shape.

TAIL

The cat's tail also has an S-shape, following the flow of the rest of the design. The way it attaches to the body, with no broken lines, accentuates the softness of the character.

FEET

Make sure the feet attach to the body in a smooth way. Divide the foot into two main areas, then attach them to the ankle with a C-shape joint.

IDEA INVENTORY

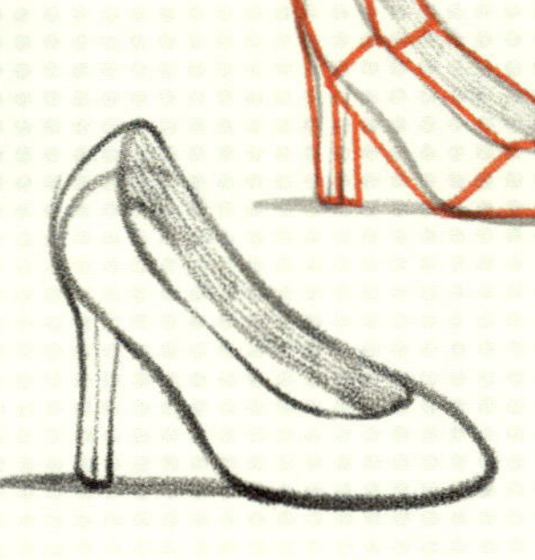

SHOES

Shoes can add a certain weight to the design. Each one of these shoe options will give the character a slightly different look and personality, so choose carefully.

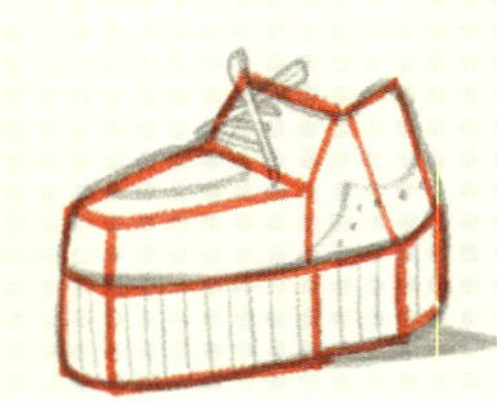
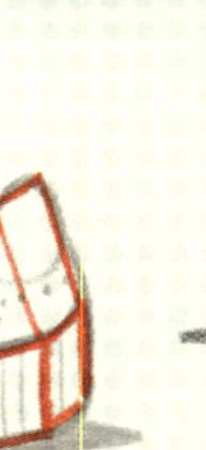

The sneakers are the most casual and laid-back design, which is perfect for this character.

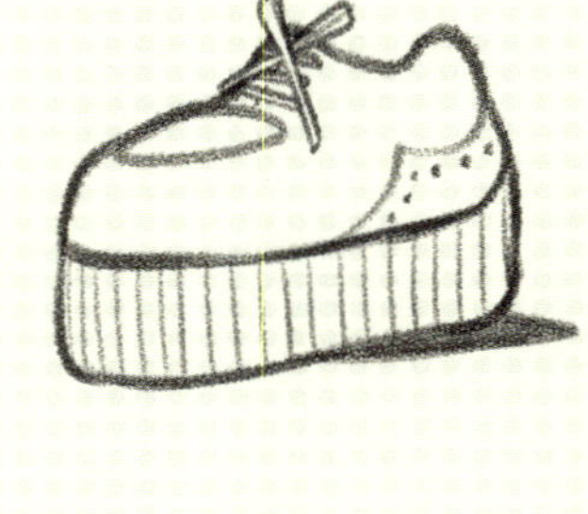
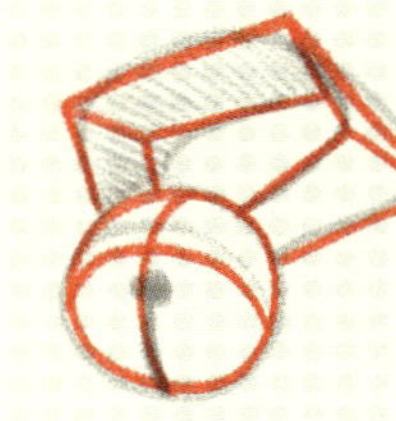

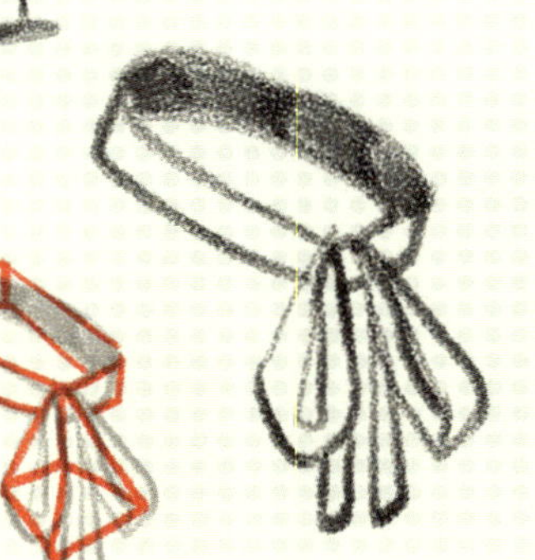
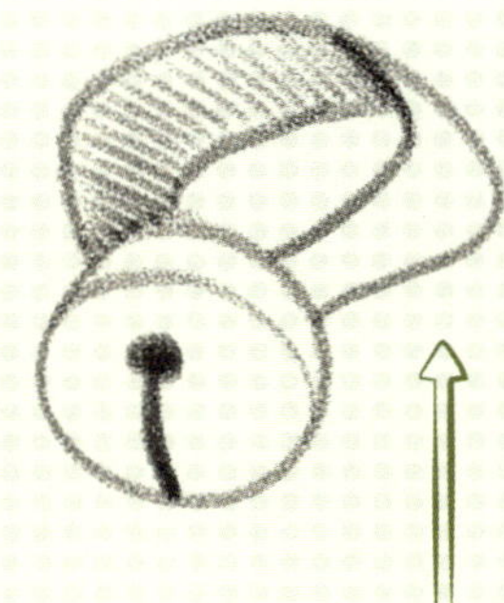

The collar-style bell necklace is a classic when it comes to nekomimi characters and will reinforce the overall theme.

NECKLACE

Necklaces can also influence the persona of the character. Some will give her a cute, feminine look, while others will have the opposite effect.

FINAL SKETCH

Still using the Pencil brush, add your preferred choice of shoe and necklace to the character's design, then build up the sketch with extra cross-hatching and line-weight work. You can also use this stage to add elements that will help communicate the light direction for the final colouring, as well as small details such as the seam on the trousers and socks, plus detailing on the shoes. Feel free to erase some of the circles from the sketch stage if this helps you to visualize the shapes better when inking.

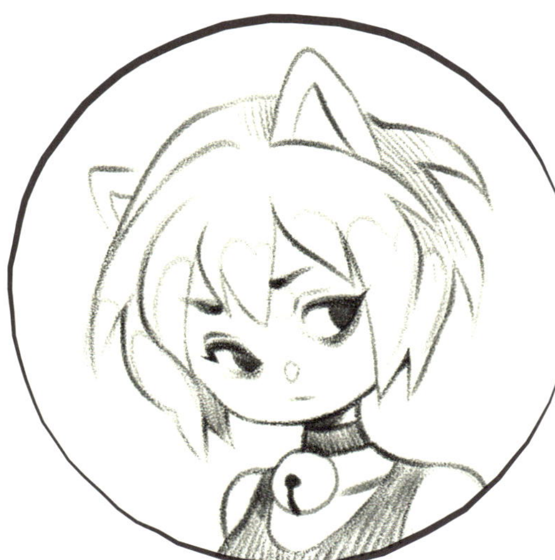

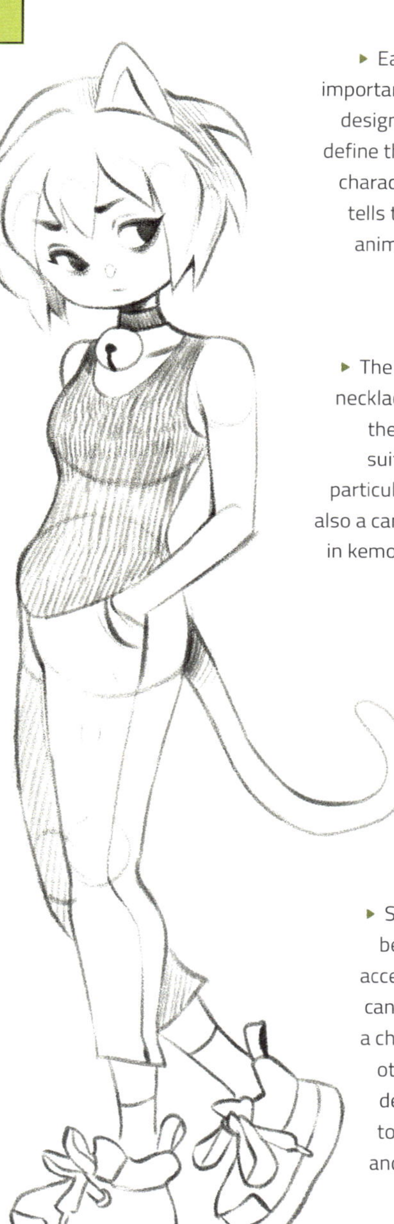

▶ Ears are the most important aspect of this design as they help to define the kemonomimi character. Their shape tells the viewer what animal she is; in this case, a cat.

▶ The collar-style bell necklace, chosen from the Idea Inventory, suits the character particularly well, and is also a canonical element in kemonomimi design.

▶ Use the facial expression, and eyes in particular, to illustrate the mood of the character. Expressions allow the audience to understand the character's personality traits through the lines.

▶ Her clothing – a tank top and jeans – give her a casual look. Simple designs can make the character more relatable for the viewer in a way that complex or highly sophisticated designs rarely are.

▶ Shoes can easily be an overlooked accessory, but they can add interest to a character with an otherwise simple design. Take care to draw the laces and details neatly.

LINE WORK

Create a new layer and use the Ink brush to draw clean line work without destroying the lively look of the pencil sketch. While this can be challenging, try to make your lines as confident as you can. Avoid scratchy lines as much as possible and instead aim to create a smooth and engaging line rhythm. Use the line weight of the ink to emulate the various thicknesses and opacities of the pencil work.

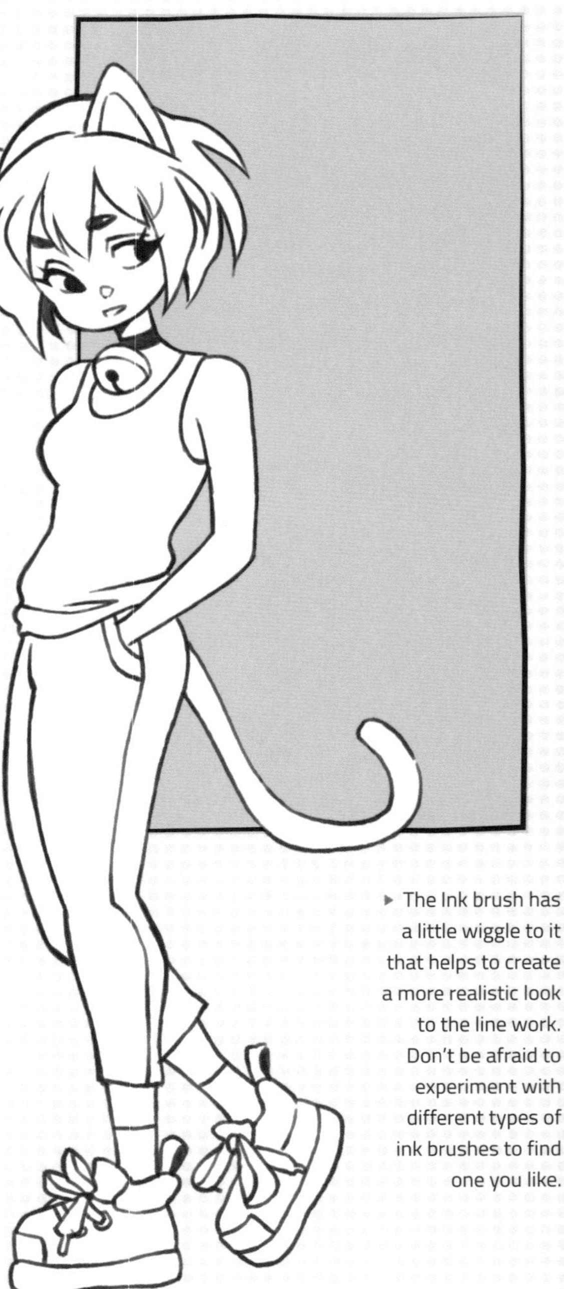

▶ Fill the collar necklace with plain black. Painting a few areas black can provide extra volume and define an initial idea of where shadows will fall, which will help when colouring.

▶ Use a lighter line weight for the face, making sure the facial expression is readable as well as consistent with the final sketch. If the character has delicate facial features, use slightly thinner lines for the eyes, nose, and mouth.

▶ Don't overdo the line work. Keep it clean and simple, avoiding introducing any small details that don't add any visual interest to the final design. The end goal is to create simple line art with clear shapes and enough details that make clear what's important.

▶ The Ink brush has a little wiggle to it that helps to create a more realistic look to the line work. Don't be afraid to experiment with different types of ink brushes to find one you like.

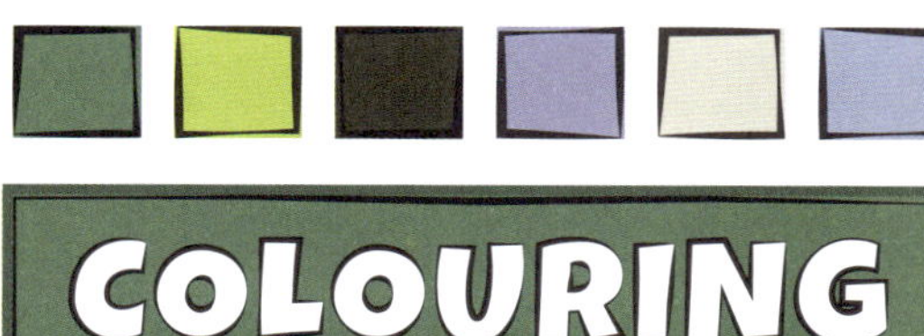

COLOURING

Research colour theory (see page 30) when putting together the colour palette for the character. This knowledge will allow you to use colour to set the mood of the image and tell the character's story. Choosing green tints that represent LED lights seen at night in cities will reinforce the character's urban look and her street style. Purple highlights will add a nice contrast against the green, as it's a complementary colour, and will also help to shape the volumes of the character.

▶ Select default round brushes and a simple flat colouring method using gradients. This will give the character a cartoonlike and almost sticker-like look.

▶ Create the gradient so it's darker at the top of the character, gradually getting lighter as it travels down the design. Not only will this enhance the overall image, but it will help to define the direction of the light source.

▶ Try to limit yourself to the smallest palette of colours as possible. Big colour variations, even if they follow colour theory, often lead to a confusing, scattered look. Less is more in almost every case.

▶ Being creative doesn't mean you always have to pick the boldest, brightest colours. Not everything has to be elaborate or fancy to stand out. The power of a great character design, and great colour, lies in successfully balancing all of the elements together.

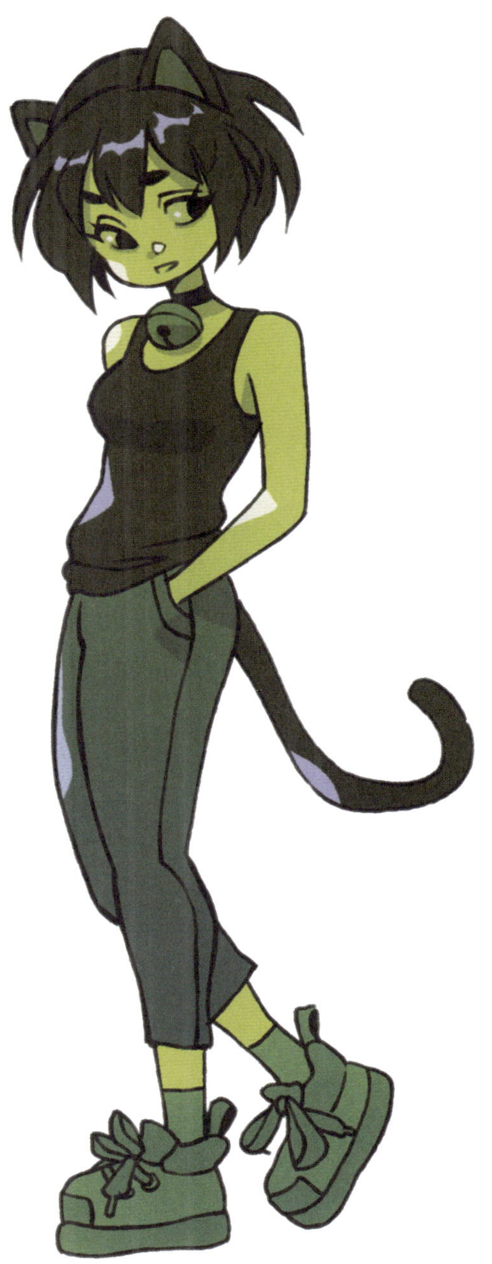

▶ Final image © SimzArt

SCI-FI MECHA PILOT

BY DADOTRONIC

This tutorial will guide you through the process of creating an eye-catching suit for a sci-fi mecha pilot. The story of mecha and tokusatsu is rooted in Japanese pop culture and is the basis for many manga TV shows and video-game franchises that have since become popular around the world. Follow the instructions on these pages and immerse yourself in discovering a cool manga robot design that can be used in a webcomic or indie game.

TOOLKIT

Clip Studio Paint

▸ Soft Airbrush

▸ Real G-Pen

▸ Turnip Pen

RESEARCH

Start by familiarizing yourself with the subject matter, in this case Japanese robot suits and mecha characters. Try to remember where you've seen mecha characters before and what you liked about their designs. Research TV shows in the genre, including what's popular with current audiences.

Select the Soft Airbrush in Clip Studio Paint for drawing initial sketches. Customize the brush by increasing the hardness property so it creates line work that is more defined, yet soft. Experiment with this until it produces a brushstroke you're happy with.

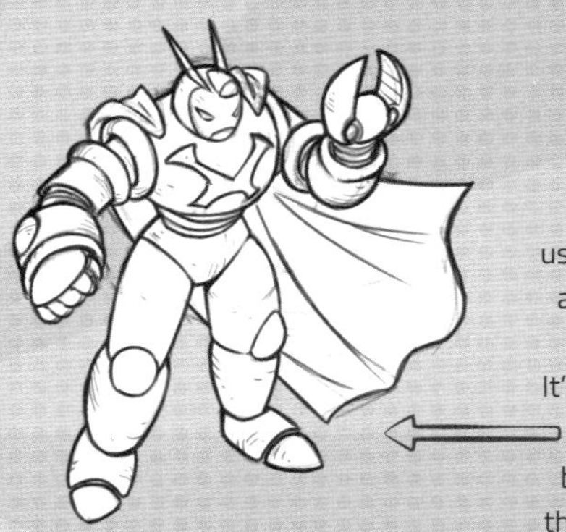

SHAPE & SILHOUETTE

There's nothing wrong with simple shapes; used well, they can build a strong silhouette and memorable character. It's important to capture the deep connection between the robot and the hero that controls it.

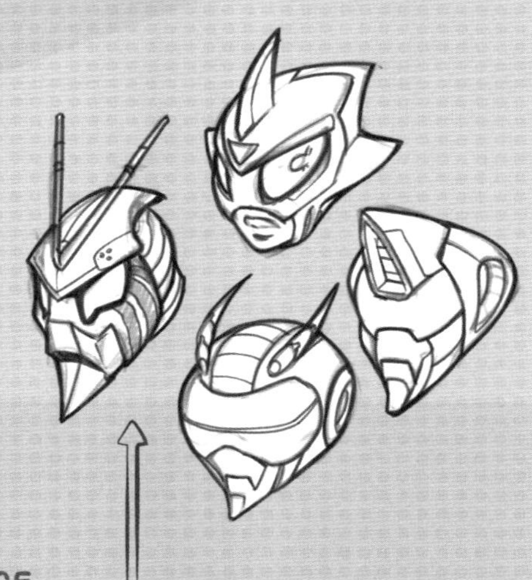

INSECT THEME

The insect theme provides lots of interesting shapes and textures. Find a strong theme and familiarize yourself with its shape language, then use this to inform your design.

FACE

Even on a robot, the face is the most important feature. Sketch out various ideas for the head, exploring the insect theme.

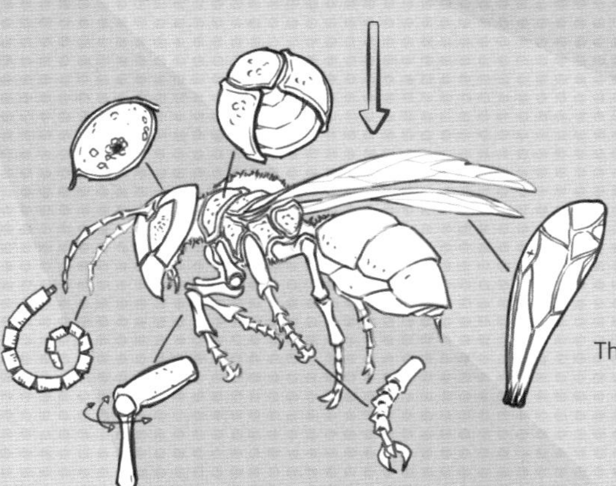

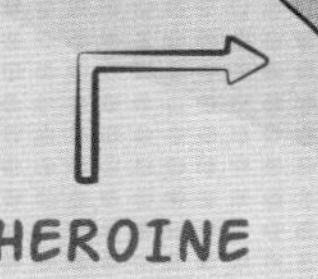

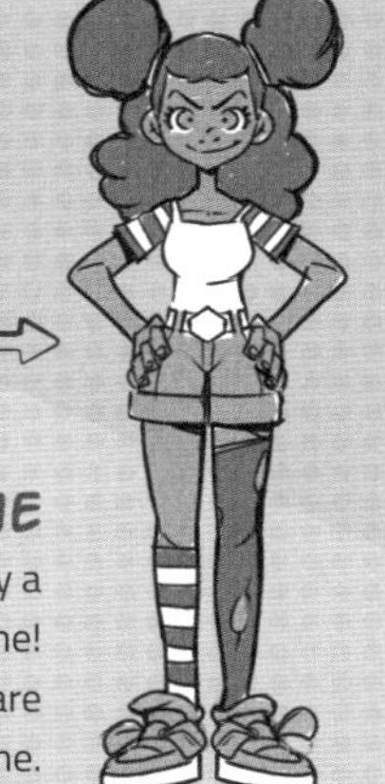

HEROINE

The mecha suit will be controlled by a hero ... or, in this case, a heroine! The striped sock and T-shirt are already starting to echo the theme.

THUMBNAILS

A nifty trick for designing characters is to use symmetry. In Clip Studio Paint, you can draw with symmetry by activating the Symmetrical Ruler. Simply make sure you use the Enable Snapping option for any tool you want to use with the Symmetry Ruler. This is in the Brush Configuration panel, in the Correction category. Thumbnailing with a symmetrical front view allows you to focus on the shapes (size difference and placement) of characters without the distortion caused by poses in perspective.

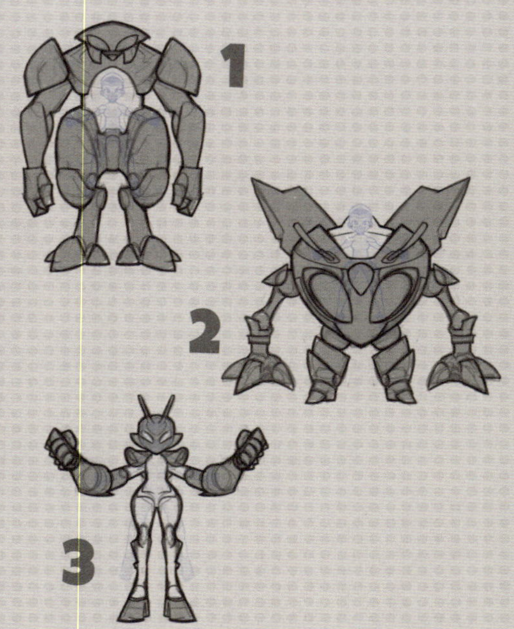

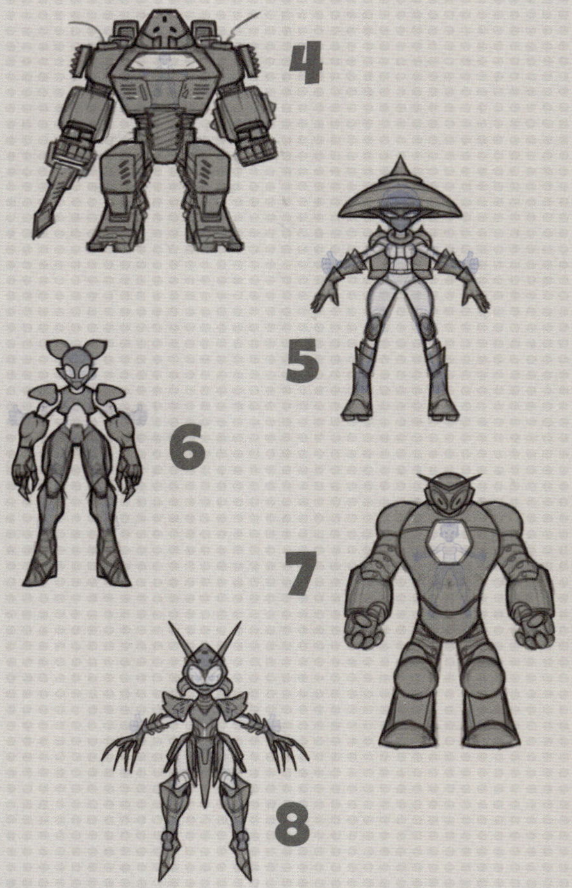

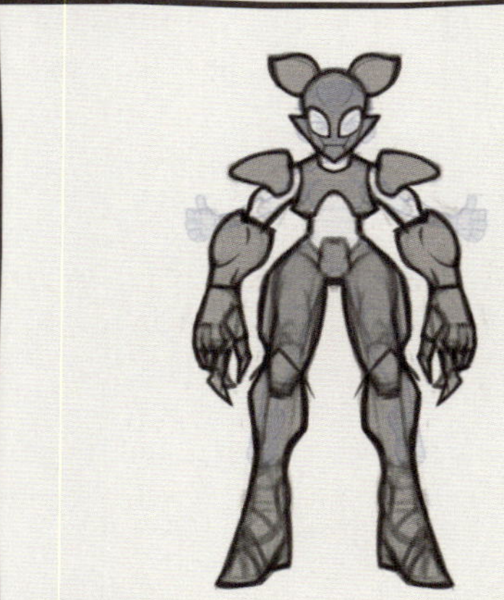

CHOSEN THUMBNAIL

Drawing the mecha suit around the pilot will give you an idea of its size and how the pilot fits inside. The bulky shapes of the armour in thumbnail 6 contrast well against its long proportions.

FOUNDATIONS

The chosen thumbnail is useful for providing a conceptual idea of your design. The next stage is to move on to building the character from the ground up. This is the most technical part of the process. When working digitally, you can use a variety of tools and processes. With Clip Studio Paint, you can also take advantage of being able to combine both 3D and 2D.

BASE

▶ Clip Studio Paint allows you to add 3D mannequins (humanoid figures) to your canvas. From the main menu at the top of the interface, select Window > Material > Body Type. Next, select either a female or male figure to use as a reference.

▶ You can start with any of the poses available in the Pose folder of the Materials Library. Adjust the body parts if necessary and choose a camera angle that is close to a three-quarters frontal view.

▶ Trace over the 3D mannequin to draw your basic figure. This will help you to understand the shapes and proportions, simplifying and adjusting the drawing as you go.

LINES

▶ Using the traced drawing, start to build the mecha suit using basic shapes. As you draw these shapes, try to visualize them as 3D volumes.

▶ You may find it helpful to draw dashed lines through the shapes to indicate different planes; for example, front and side planes.

▶ Select the two small (blue and white) squares icon at the top of the Layers panel. This is a shortcut for colouring any type of layer. It's like a traditional lightbox.

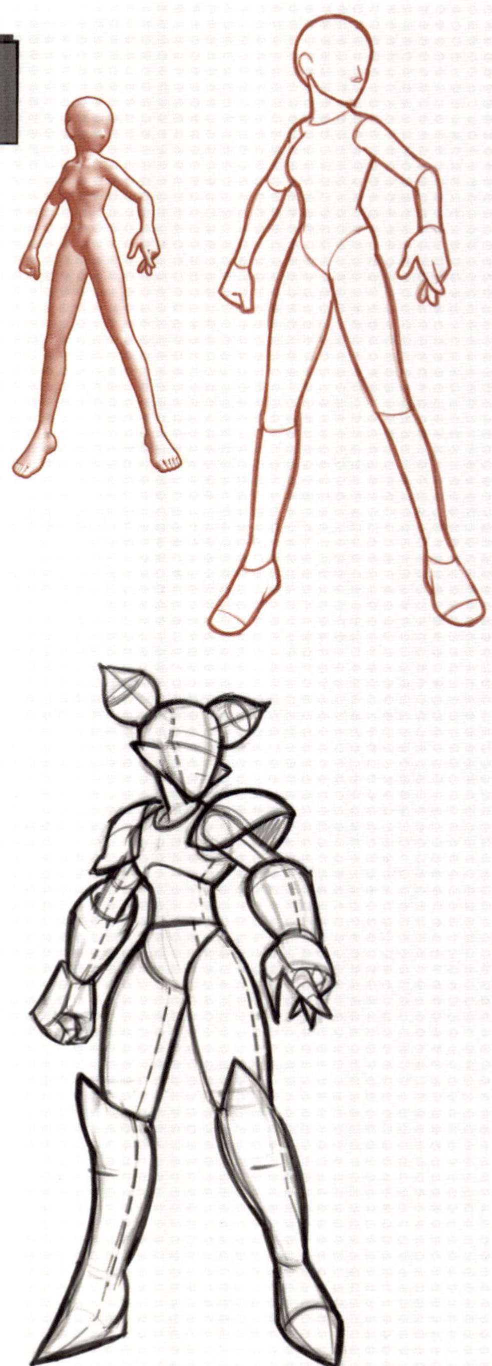

BUILDING UP

Think about how the different shapes of various parts of the human anatomy could be used as armour to protect the body. For example, a breastplate shaped like pectoral muscles, or large shoulder pads shaped like deltoids (shoulder muscles). Use the insect theme to inspire your shape language as you draw. Insects have exoskeletons – an external skeleton or protective shell that shields their inner body from harm, just like a mecha suit!

ADJUST & ROTATE

Don't be afraid to make changes and adjust your design. You can use the Transform command (Edit > Transform > Free Transform) or the Liquify subtool to move, scale up, scale down, or rotate parts of the character to make it more dynamic.

LINE OF ACTION

Use these tools to alter the proportions and tilt the head, torso, and waist, creating a more curved line of action running down from the head to the right foot. Reposition the right arm so it's pointing outwards, opening up the silhouette.

SHAPES

Start to think about the secondary, typically medium, shapes of your character. There's still some room for change, but from now on the design decisions apply to the details and functionality of the suit.

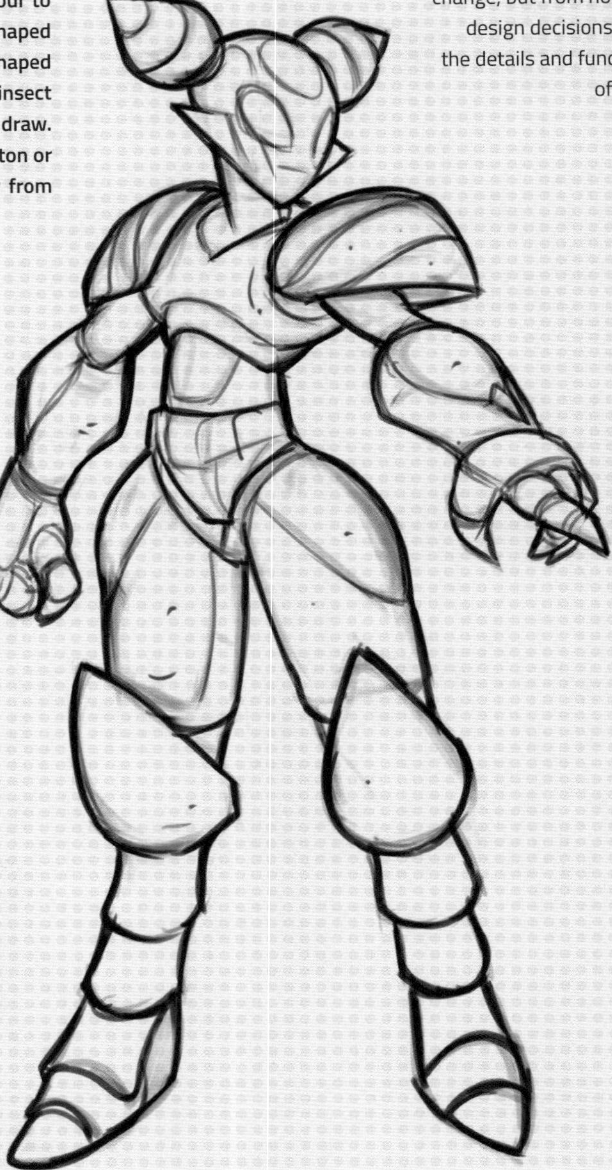

DESIGN FOCUS

ROBOTIC PLATES

Stylize the shapes of human anatomy to look like the mechanical plates of a robot. A basic study of how real muscles and joints work will prove useful for this.

INSECT MARKINGS

Consider how you can incorporate the insect theme, such as by drawing the striped insect markings on the helmet. You could carry this striped ring shape language throughout the design of the mechanical parts.

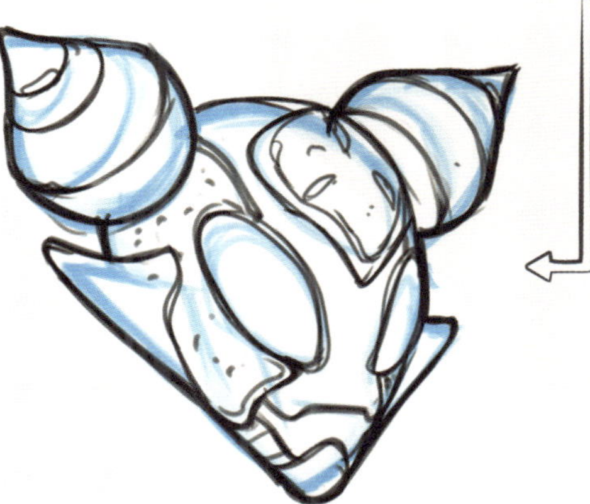

DETAIL VS. SPACE

Leave some elements without detail to balance the more detailed parts. The high-frequency detail on mecha is often hidden under aerodynamic panels, only visible on parts such as joints or connectors.

IDEA INVENTORY

WEAPONS

Consider what the character could use as a weapon. Create a lance by tracing over 3D primitives from the Material Library. Stack boxes and cylinders, rotating them into position to roughly build the object.

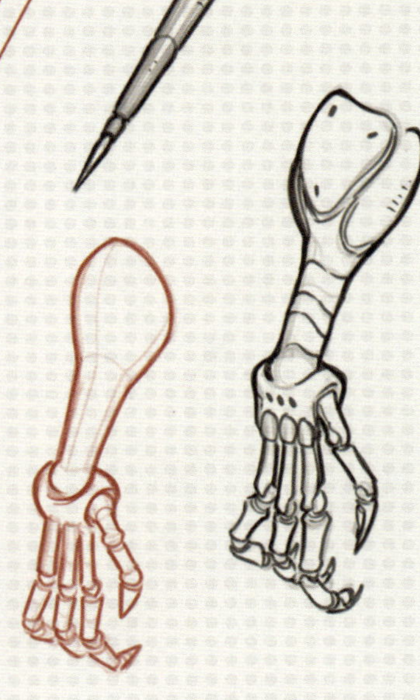

Draw a shield in a front-facing view using the Symmetry Ruler, then transform it into a perspective using the Edit > Transform > Perspective command.

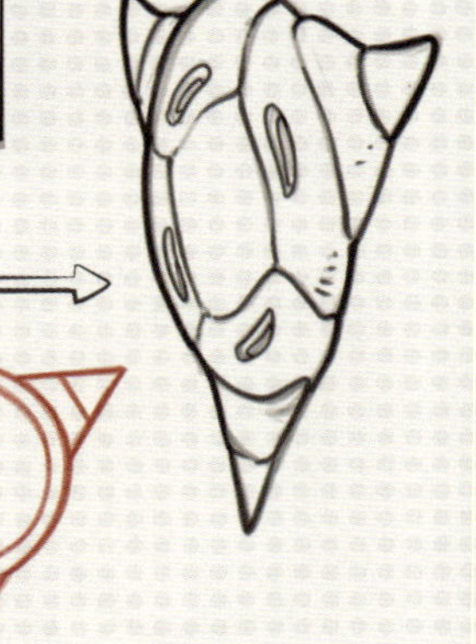

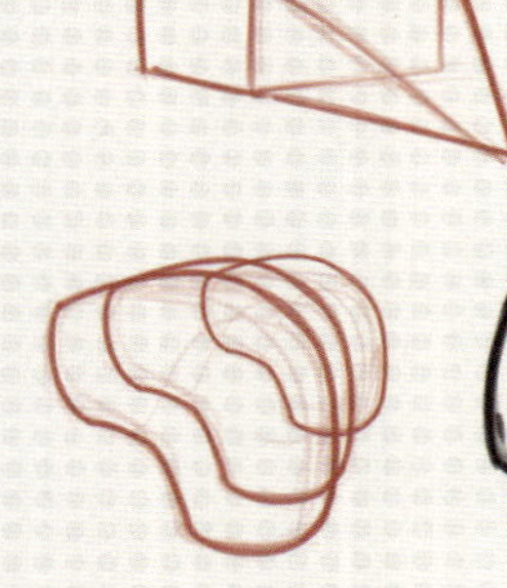

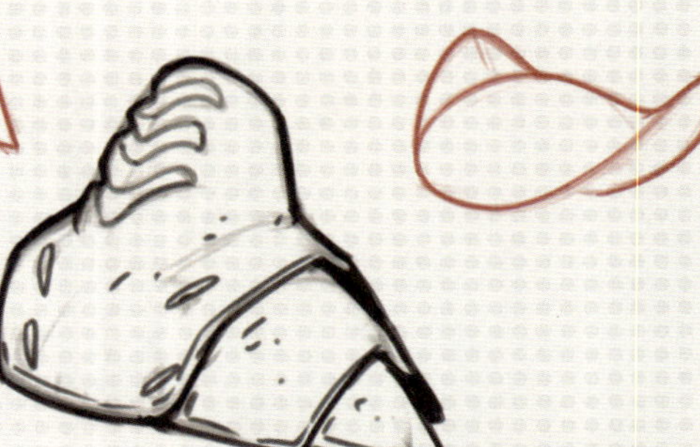

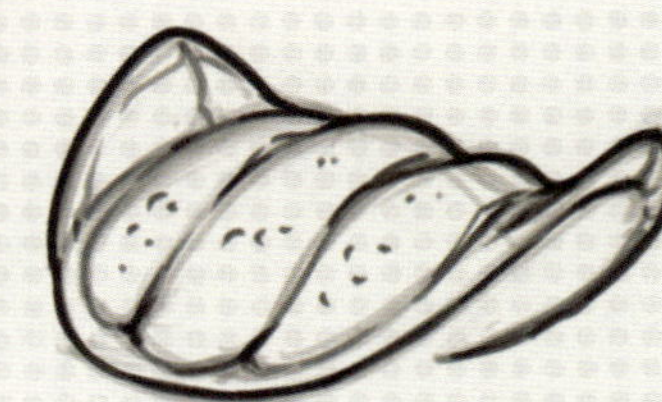

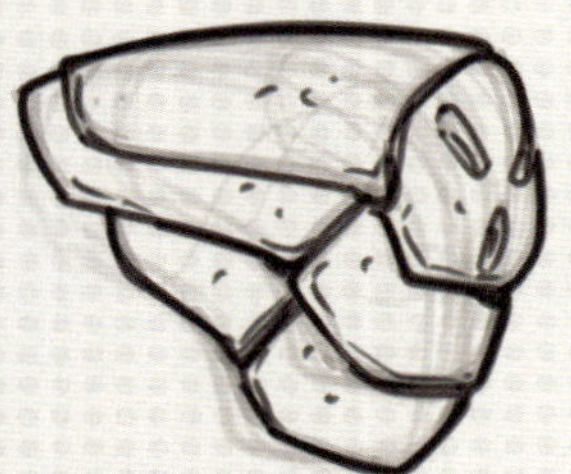

Build up the shape of each shoulder pad, combining natural, exoskeleton forms with metallic, mecha materials.

SHOULDER PADS

Explore ideas for the shoulder pads. Especially if you're new to drawing, force yourself to start with these simple blockouts. The more you practise, the more your basic shapes will become integrated with the actual sketch.

FINAL SKETCH

One of the benefits of working digitally in Clip Studio Paint is that you can work progressively on your drawing, laying down the rough lines and cleaning them up at the same time. This allows you to alternate between drawing and erasing. Check your keyboard shortcuts (File > Shortcut Settings > Options > Drawing Colour) and set a key to use the function 'Switch between main colour and transparent colour', such as the letter 'X'. This configuration will allow you to switch between the pencil and eraser more quickly, enabling you to clean up your lines as you go.

▶ Choose a weapon and shoulder pad style from the previous step to add into the design. When introducing new elements, keep them within the same theme and try to incorporate details from the existing design.

▶ Look back on your early research and initial ideas. Still using the Soft Airbrush, draw curved panels for the mecha suit to give it the organic, exoskeleton look. Following the rhythmic lines of human anatomy will make it easier to find interesting shapes to draw.

▶ Contrast plays an important role in the invention of a design. Areas of high contrast only become focal points when there are clearer, simpler areas to balance them out. Otherwise it's just visual noise and should be avoided.

▶ Build up the drawing layer by layer, drawing through the shapes using long, sweeping lines. If it's difficult to use the entire arm to draw, try zooming out so you can cover more of the page with your lines.

▶ Make sure you have a good, relaxed posture when drawing. For beginner artists, I strongly recommend starting with a tablet without a screen. Though you may lose some speed and spontaneity, you will have better ergonomics.

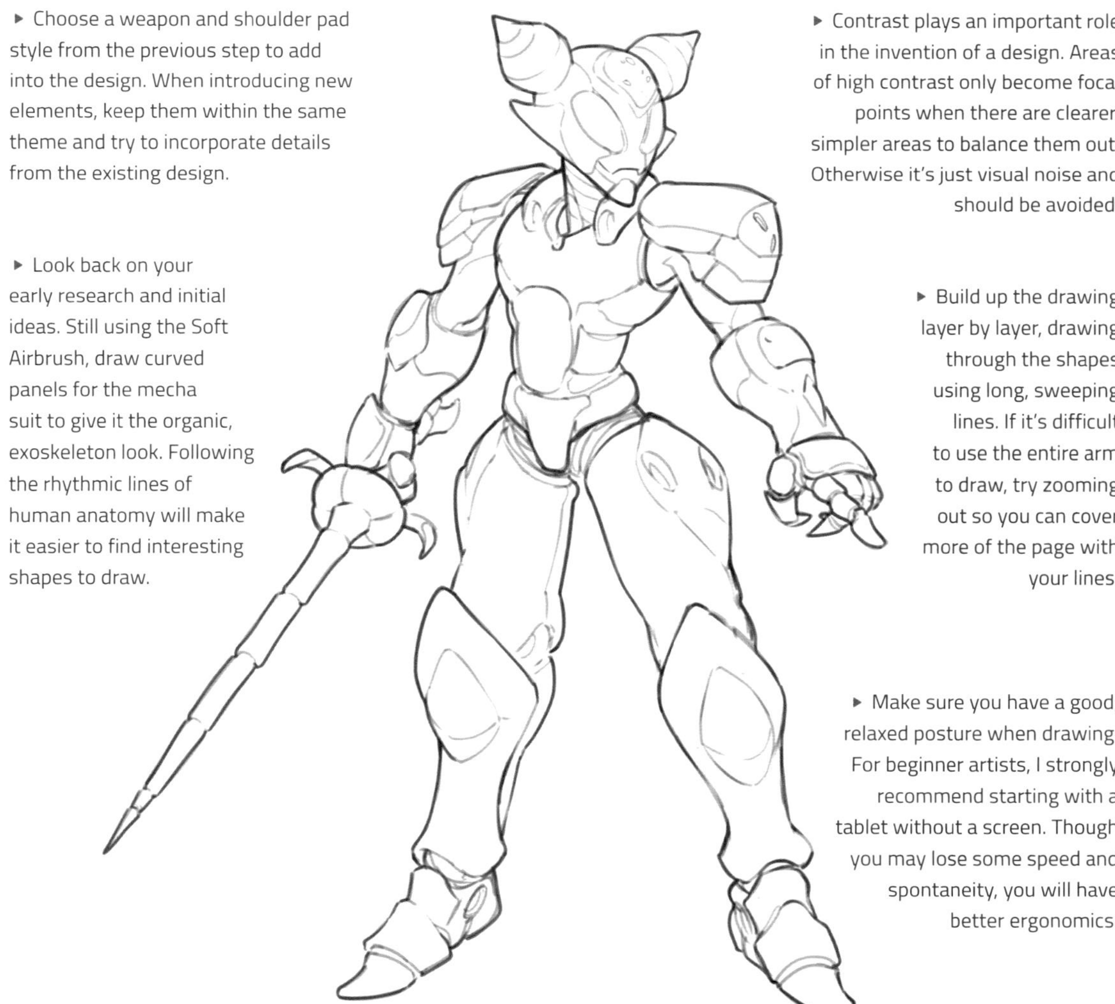

LINE WORK

Known for its drawing and inking tools, Clip Studio Paint has a variety of brushes and pens that can simulate different lines and brushstrokes. Select the Real G-Pen from the Pen category. This brush relies on the pressure of the stylus to create different line thicknesses, but if you don't have such dexterity with your tablet, you can still create interesting line work by breaking the process down into the following steps.

▶ Consider the intended use of your artwork and adjust the scale (zoom level) of the image displayed. For example, place a sheet of paper over the top of your tablet and adjust the zoom in the software until the canvas matches its size. You can now ensure you don't waste time on excessive detail that would likely be lost if the image was reduced or displayed on a smaller screen.

▶ Find a brush size that feels comfortable to draw with, then stick with it. When you combine this practice with the idea of a fixed zoom level, this will enable you to ink faster and more efficiently.

▶ Break it down: start with lines with minimal variation in thickness, ink some hatching to create texture or a three-dimensional feel, then finish with thick lines to convey overlapping shapes.

▶ You can activate the Stabilization option for each brush. If you find it difficult to control the lines – because of the smooth tablet surface or shaking hands, for example – simply increase the stabilization value. However, always remember that imperfections can bring life and character to a drawing.

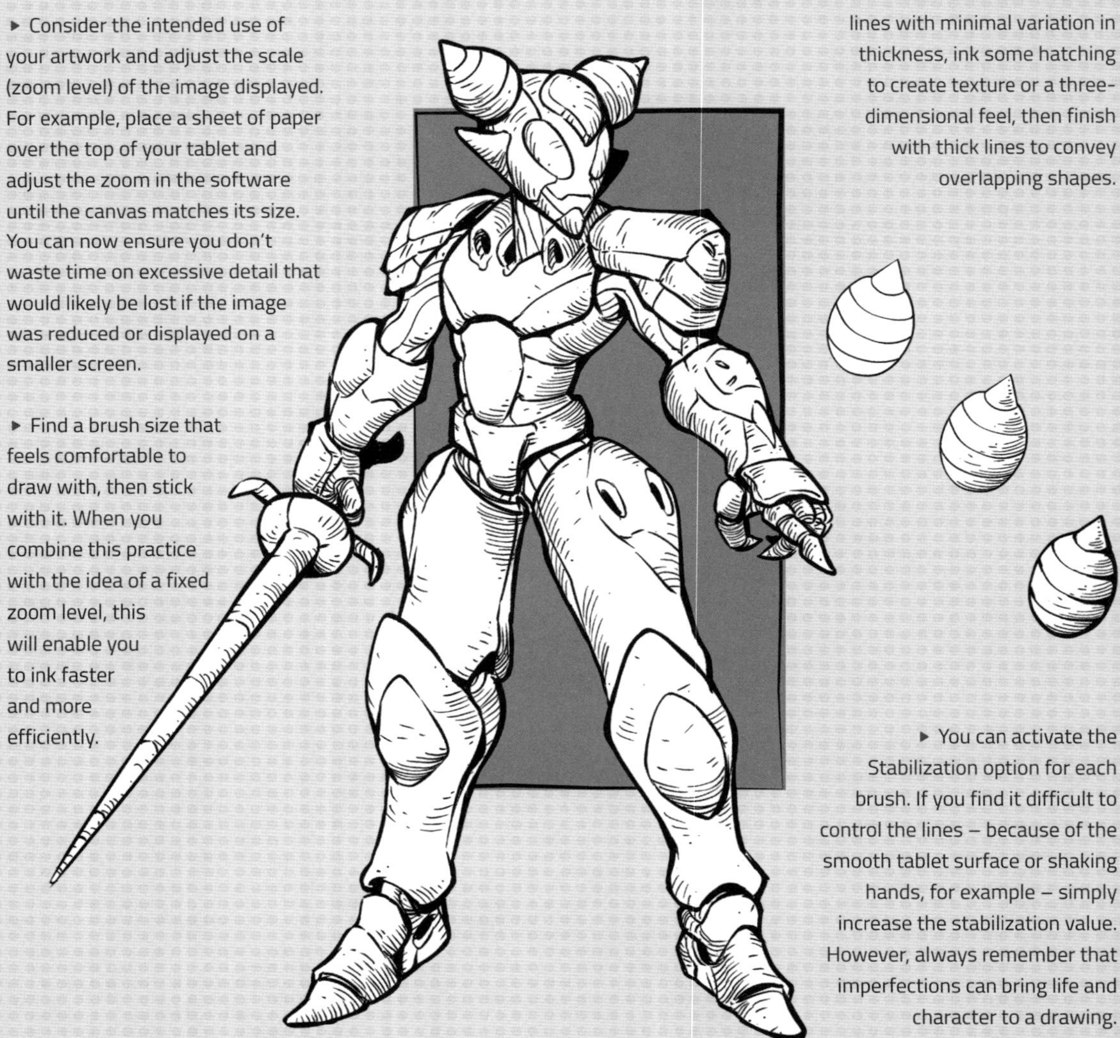

COLOURING

Of the various approaches you can use to colour your work, cel shading is the simplest. Always work on multiple layers and learn how to use masks and clipping masks, as these techniques can be really helpful at this stage. Start by colouring your flat or local colours. Think in terms of colours that are not affected by light or shadow. Choose a palette that is similar to the insect theme you've chosen. If necessary, take colour samples directly from your reference to begin with.

▶ Take a binary approach when shading and avoid blending values too early. Create a new layer over your flat colours in Multiply mode. Reduce the opacity to 50% and use the Turnip Pen to paint over the shaded areas. Any colour will work, but start with a classic desaturated purple.

▶ Paint on highlights by adding a new layer on top and using the Overlay mode. As with the shadows, it's better to simplify and stylize the highlights. Aim for a clean design instead of realistic reflections.

▶ Add some reflections to indicate the smooth surface of the metal suit. Create a layer with low opacity in blend mode to achieve this effect. When adding reflections in the shaded areas, make sure to keep the colours darker than they are in the lighter areas.

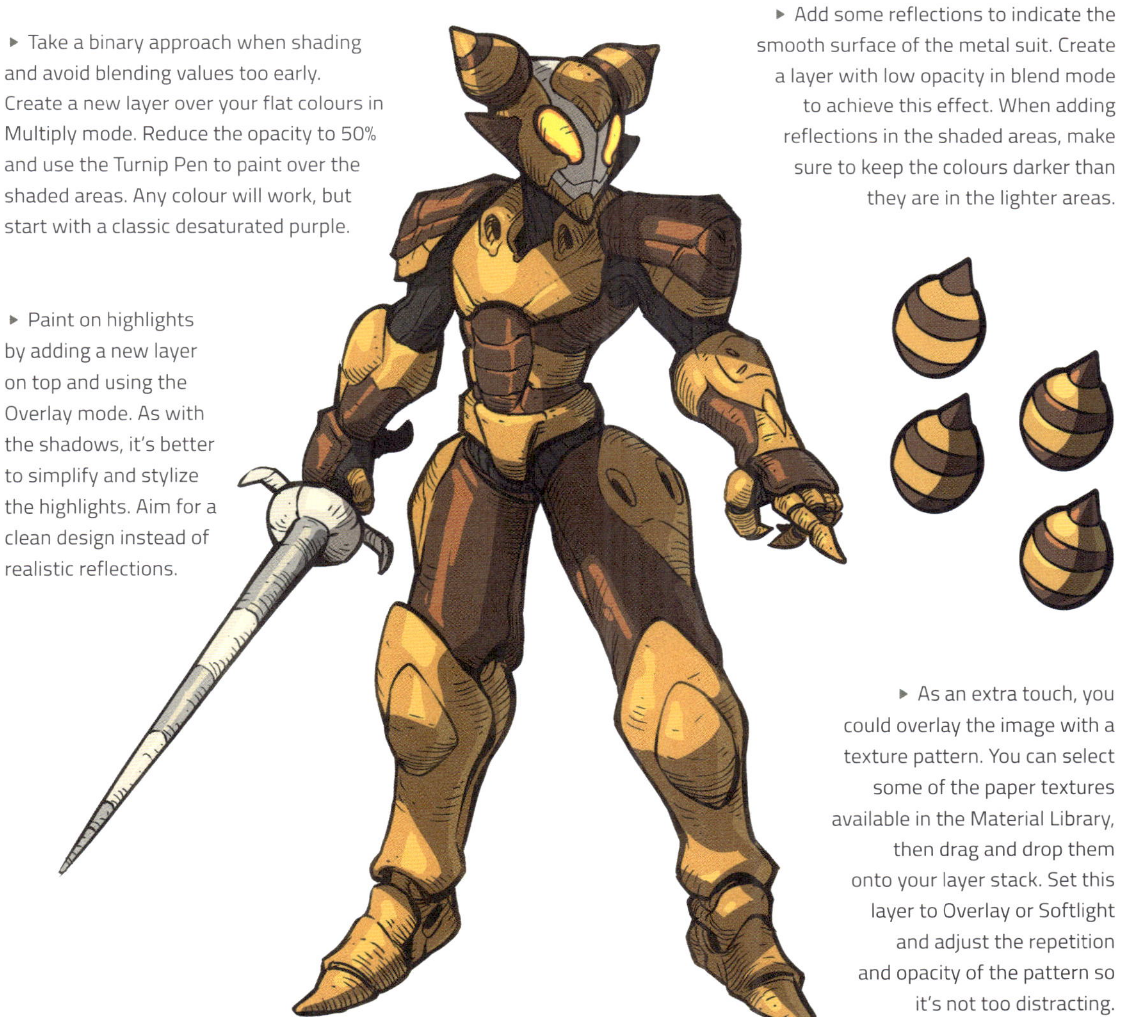

▶ As an extra touch, you could overlay the image with a texture pattern. You can select some of the paper textures available in the Material Library, then drag and drop them onto your layer stack. Set this layer to Overlay or Softlight and adjust the repetition and opacity of the pattern so it's not too distracting.

GOTHIC VAMPIRE

BY LOLITA ALDEA

This tutorial will guide you through the creation of a gothic vampire character who is as dark and menacing as she is stylish and ostentatious. She enjoys adventures under the shadow of night, wearing sumptuous vintage clothing, and sipping fresh blood from her prized goblet. By following the tutorial's steps, you will learn how to use soft, long lines for the line art, followed by strong blocks of colour to create a striking composition. You will also learn how to use details to convey her style and refinement, along with how to create the popular manga aesthetic. By the end, you will have created a formidable yet beautiful vampire character ready to take on the night!

TOOLKIT

Clip Studio Paint

- Any pencil brush
- Vector-type layer (for sketch and inks)
- G-Pen brush
- Paint Bucket tool
- Multiply & Add (Glow) blend modes
- Gradient tool

RESEARCH

Dwelling in the shadows, vampires are shape-shifters who can take the form of a rat, bat, or even a wolf. They are ancient beings, often so old their clothes come from bygone eras, such as late medieval and Victorian styles. With the freedom provided by the modern manga genre, you can add any other details you like to enhance the character in the direction you wish to take the design.

VINTAGE CLOTHING

Vampires' clothing is usually ornate and from past eras. They might wear medieval armour, Victorian corsets, lace jabots, jacquard fabrics, or elegant French-style garments from the eighteenth century. Research these kinds of fabrics and clothing to use as reference material.

BATS

Vampires are often surrounded by bats. Is this due to a natural attraction, or because they're ready and waiting to carry out their mistress's orders?

PREDATOR

When creating a predator, you must capture their intense and powerful presence. Their facial expression, and eyes especially, must communicate this power right away. Feline-shaped pupils can be used to illustrate the character's predatory and animalistic nature.

BAT WINGS

Bat-wing-shaped head ornaments are a staple in vampire representation in manga and anime, so be sure to include this iconic detail to achieve the desired look.

GOBLET

Vampires are often depicted with vivid red eyes to symbolize their thirst for blood. A goblet of blood could convey her slightly more refined personality.

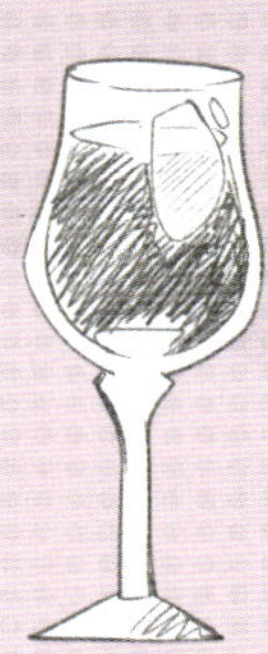

THUMBNAILS

Sketch a variety of different thumbnails to explore your ideas for the character. Her pose should be elegant, her gaze dangerous, and her overall composition wild and supernatural. Look for an interesting shape that's both attractive and easy-to-read. Use S-shaped lines to give movement to her clothes and hair, and Z-shaped or diagonal lines for the general pose of the body. Try to make sure that all of the elements follow different lines, but take care to avoid parallel lines. This will make the drawing more appealing.

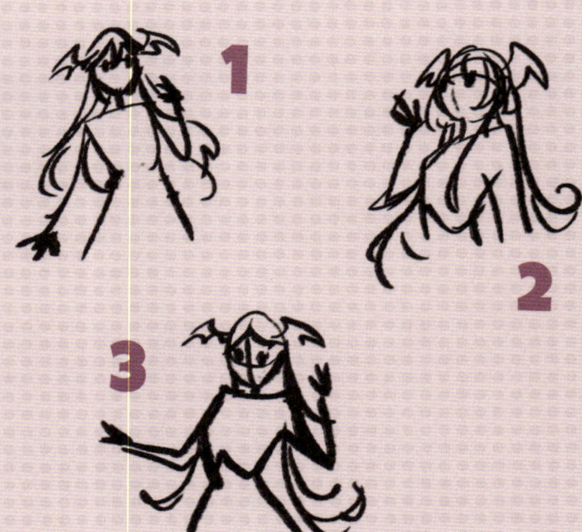

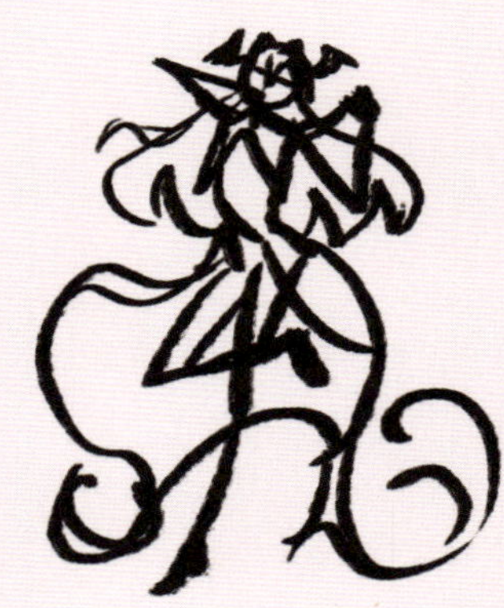

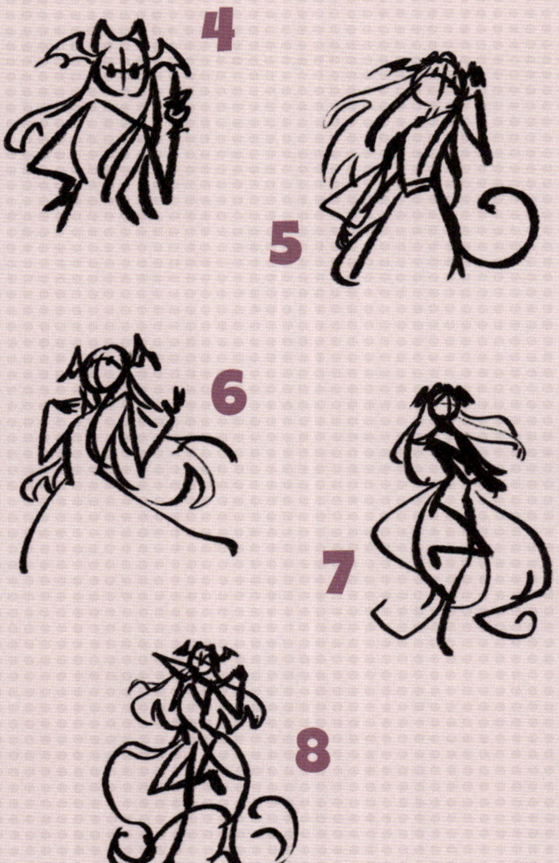

CHOSEN THUMBNAIL

The full-body pose of thumbnail 8 allows for more outfit possibilities and therefore a more alluring and complex composition. The posing of her arms and legs offers more potential to create interesting diagonals and the ethereal way she almost doesn't touch the floor helps to make the pose more dynamic.

FOUNDATIONS

Create a new vector-type layer in Clip Studio Paint to begin your sketch. Using the pencil brush and chosen thumbnail as a reference, start to draw the foundation of the character's skeleton, creating a lose stick figure without details. The sketch doesn't need to be perfect as this is only the base. Focus on capturing the proportions of the figure, as well as the overall composition. Once the proportions are correct, start to sketch in simple geometrical shapes to block out the different parts of her body.

BASE

▶ Draw an oval shape for her head and a triangle for her torso. The hips have an almost diamond-shaped silhouette. Her body is tall and slim, with slender arms and legs that are almost slightly too long, giving the character a supernatural aura.

▶ Draw her hair in a loose triangular S-shape cascading downwards, framing her face. When drawing the strands of her fringe, make sure to leave enough space for her eyes.

▶ The clothing will gracefully fall around her figure, creating an ethereal touch with flowing lines, almost as if the material has a life of its own. Map this out using S-shaped lines, making use of the space around the character.

LINES

▶ To add an extra layer of intensity to the composition, draw the character's face tilted slightly downwards and her eyes looking directly at the viewer. This will introduce a sense of danger and mystery to the already shadowy figure.

▶ To further emphasize the vampire aesthetic, sketch her chin with a slight point and elongate her fingers so they have a predatory, claw-like quality.

▶ Drawing over the stick-figure skeleton, sketch tubes for her arms and legs to give volume to her body. Next, draw in her chest, face, and pointy ears.

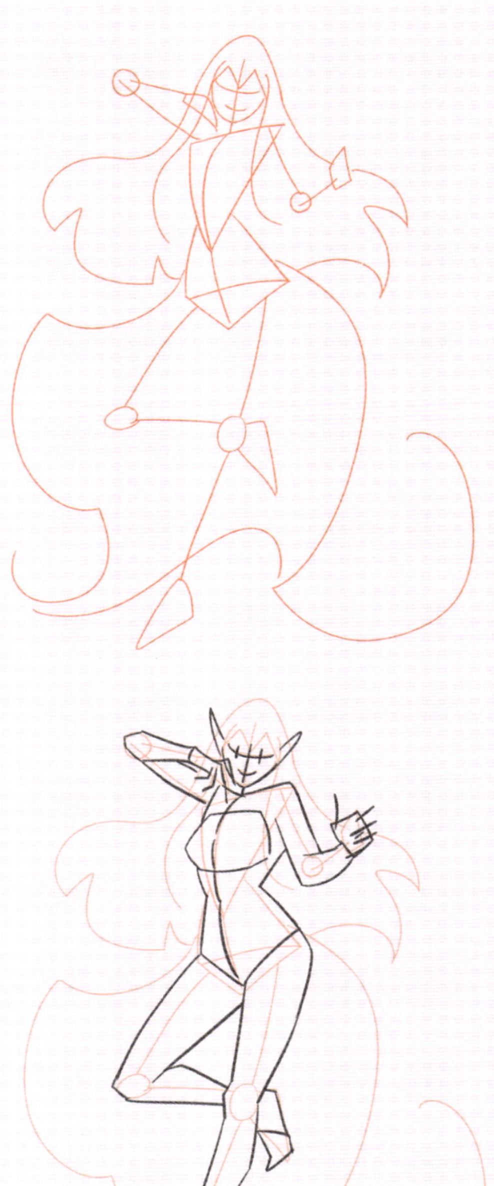

BUILDING UP

Begin to add in more details to your vampire drawing, fleshing out her clothes and face. To give her design flair and flamboyance, you could add sumptuous velvet ribbons or an antique piece of jewellery. You can also consider gothic elements such candles, a goblet, and bats to create a more atmospheric composition.

HEAD PIECE

Emphasize her tall, ominous appearance by adding a velvet ribbon headpiece. And don't forget the small bat-wing-shaped ornaments that are so typical in manga vampire designs.

ANGULAR SHAPES

Include angular shapes throughout the entire design to hint at her lethal nature. Her collar features sharp points, as does the hip section of her vest and her heeled shoes. All these elements work together to evoke fang and bat-wing imagery.

BATS

Draw small bats in different sizes and poses to simulate a colony clustering around their mistress. These bats can be placed throughout the design to fill any empty spaces. Not only will they help to emphasize the bat-wing-inspired design, but they will also provide an extra layer of depth and texture.

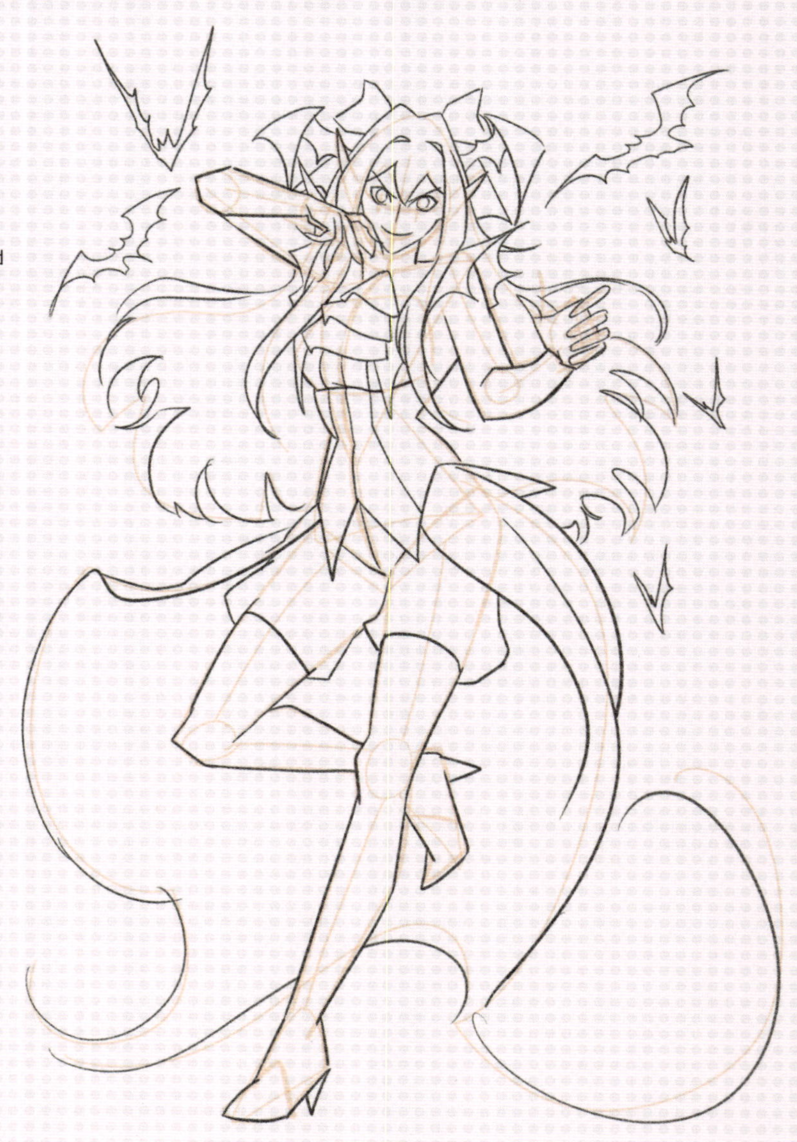

DESIGN FOCUS

FACE & EYES

Draw big, intense, wide-open eyes to give the character the recognizable manga style. To make her gaze more sinister, draw the curve of her iris so it's almost not touching her bottom eyelashes. In anime and manga, this way of drawing eyes is typically used to depict evil and cunning characters. An unusually shaped pupil, such as feline, will achieve a supernatural look, plus a smirk or a sinister smile will let the viewer see her fangs.

HANDS & NAILS

Give her elongated fingers long curved nails to emphasize her claw-like pose. You can also add further details, such as an antique ring or amulet. Drawing hands can be difficult at first, but tricks like drawing the palm as a rectangle and each finger as a three-part stick can make them easier to visualize.

CLOTHING & ACCESSORIES

When designing clothes, let your imagination run wild! Add ribbons, lace, and ornate prints to fashion unique and eye-catching pieces. Think about fabrics that will suit the vampire theme. Consider including velvet, leather, or even fur to give the clothing a historic or lavish look. Be sure to add details such as buckles, buttons, and studs to make the clothing even more interesting.

IDEA INVENTORY

TIGHTS

Decide on a gothic print for the character's tights, such as bats, skulls, stars, bones, or stripes. Details like this are a great way to add a unique and eye-catching element to your character's design.

▶ The gothic patterns can be used to make a statement and tell the character's story. The brighter colours lend a dramatic touch.

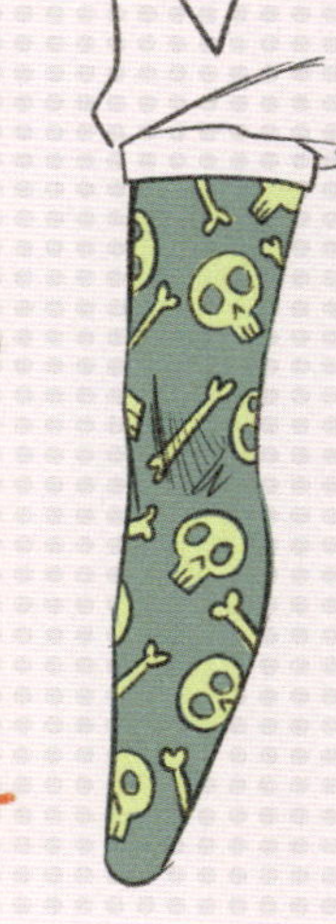

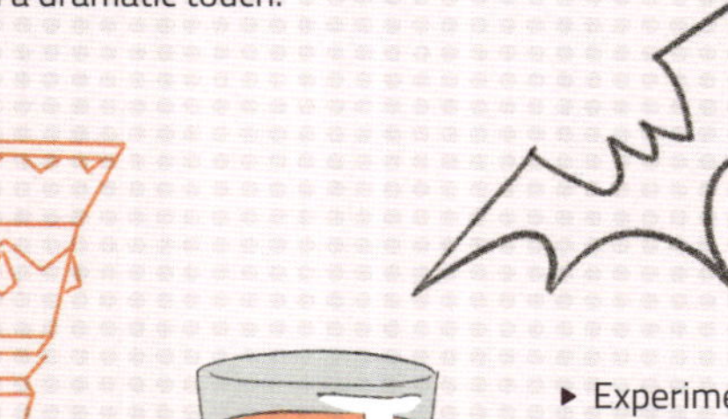

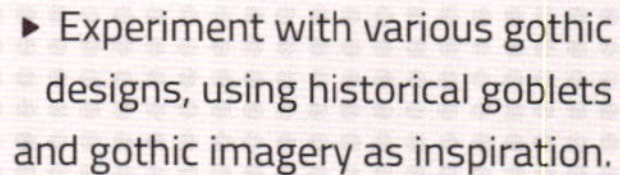

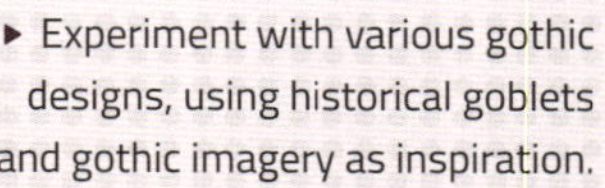

▶ Experiment with various gothic designs, using historical goblets and gothic imagery as inspiration.

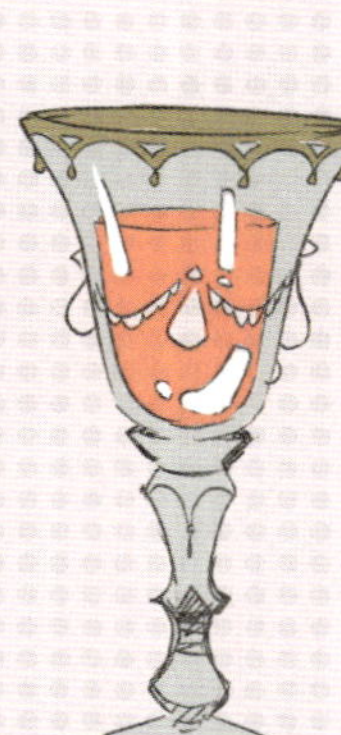

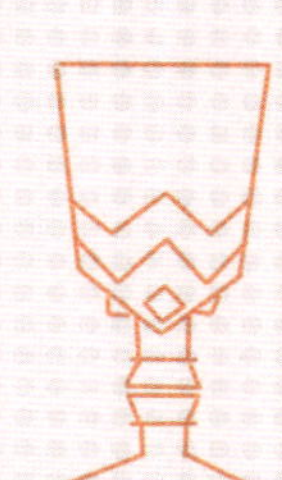

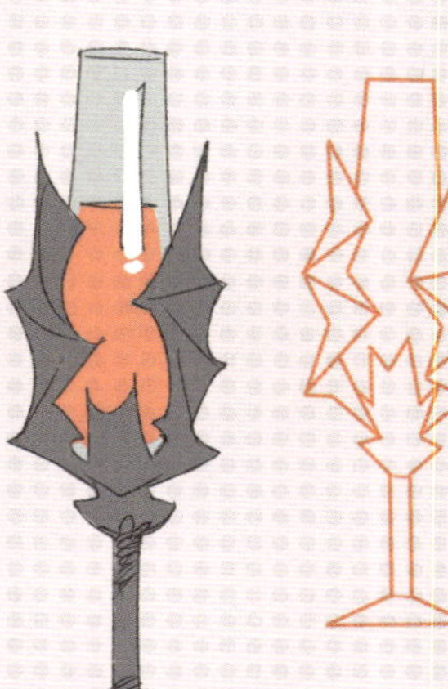

GOBLET

A goblet of blood is an iconic symbol of the dark and mysterious world of vampires, adding a touch of class while also making her look even more menacing. Its inclusion in the scene will be sure to lend an extra layer of horror.

FINAL SKETCH

It's now time to clean up the lines and incorporate all of the elements and final details into the sketch. At this stage you want to make sure to include everything you want in the design before moving on to the inking and colouring steps.

Set your original layers at lesser opacity and create a new vector layer for your final sketch. Set your eraser options to erase just until your lines cross. This will help you to easily rid your sketch of overflow lines.

▶ The ribbon adorning her head should feature delicate lace trim, with an elegant pattern inspired by your earlier historic clothing research. To add visual interest, make sure the shape of the ribbon is slightly different on either side.

▶ Draw the long skirt that drapes down and around the back of the character. Use angular, uneven lines to create a frayed look as the edges brush the floor at varying lengths.

▶ Draw the shoes with a triangular toe-tip and pointed heel to evoke razor-sharp vampire's fangs, then complete them with a decorative bow like the others present on her outfit.

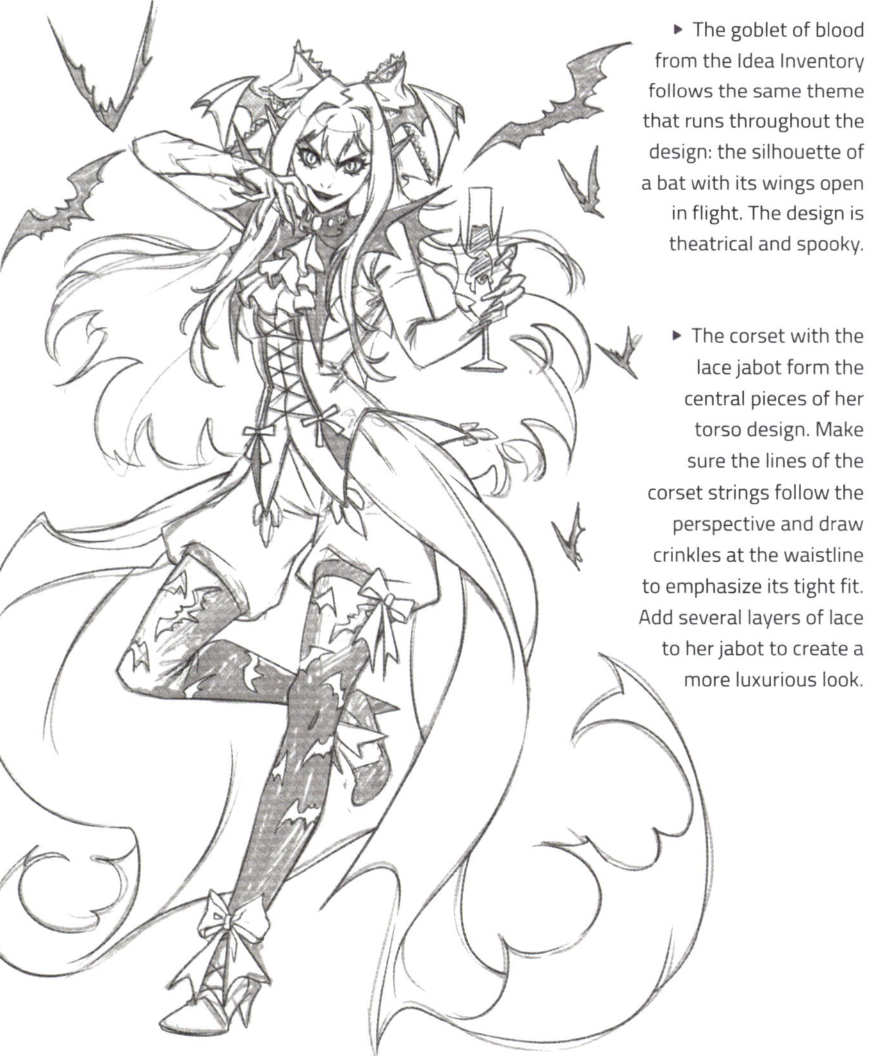

▶ The goblet of blood from the Idea Inventory follows the same theme that runs throughout the design: the silhouette of a bat with its wings open in flight. The design is theatrical and spooky.

▶ The corset with the lace jabot form the central pieces of her torso design. Make sure the lines of the corset strings follow the perspective and draw crinkles at the waistline to emphasize its tight fit. Add several layers of lace to her jabot to create a more luxurious look.

LINE WORK

Create a new vector layer and use the G-Pen as your main brush for inking the line art. It's almost like a calibrated marker, but with more sensitivity than a real one. This will give your lines a controlled thickness variation suitable for a drawing that will be coloured in the next step. As you ink over the final sketch, you can vary the thickness of the lines in different parts of the drawing. Try to make the lines narrower for thin or angular shapes, and thicker where there is an overlap or a shadow cast by the line.

▶ Only use black for the line art. Erase any mistakes with the Eraser tool. You can colour the line art in the next step, but if you do this too early it will cause problems with colouring the character.

▶ It can be tricky to draw long lines in one single brushstroke. Make this easier by temporarily reducing the size of your canvas on your screen. This will decrease the amount of hand movement needed to complete the line.

▶ With vector layers, editing lines is easy. Simply select Control and click your stylus over the line you wish to edit. This will summon an interface to assist you. You can also use the Pinch Line tool.

▶ Ink the bat pattern onto her tights on a separate layer. This will make it much easier to colour the tights in the next step.

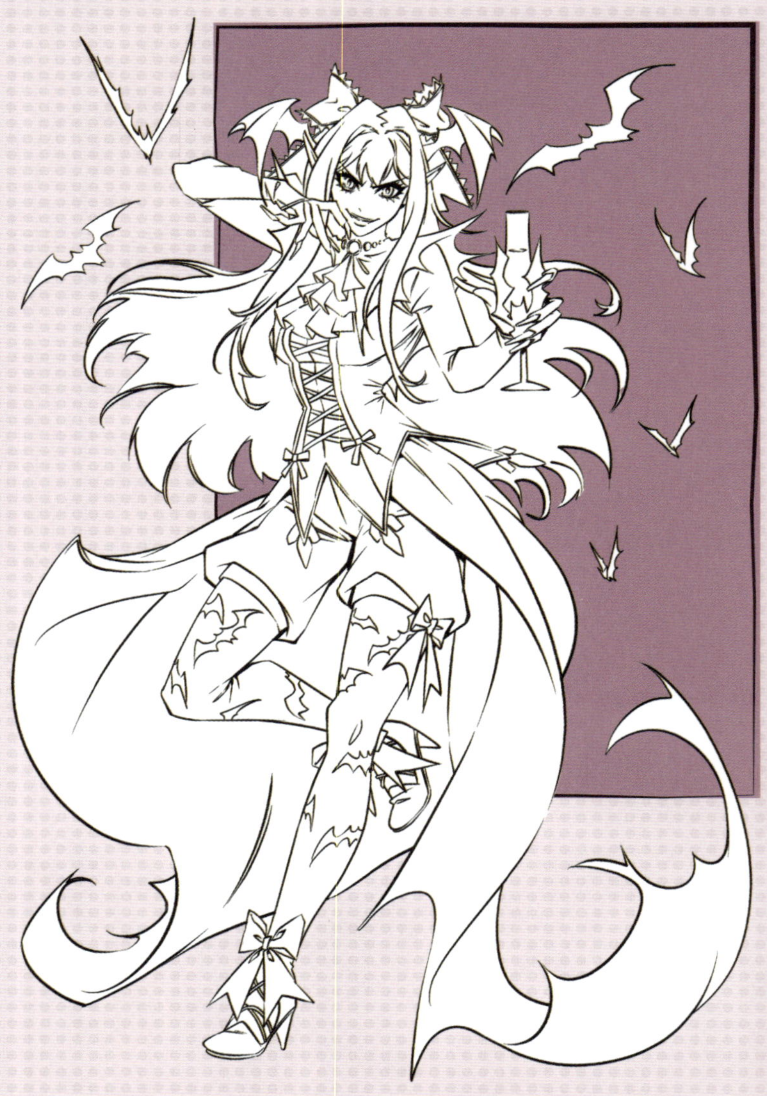

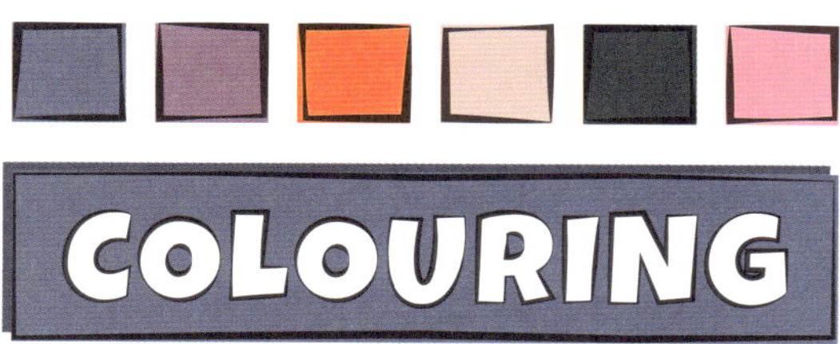

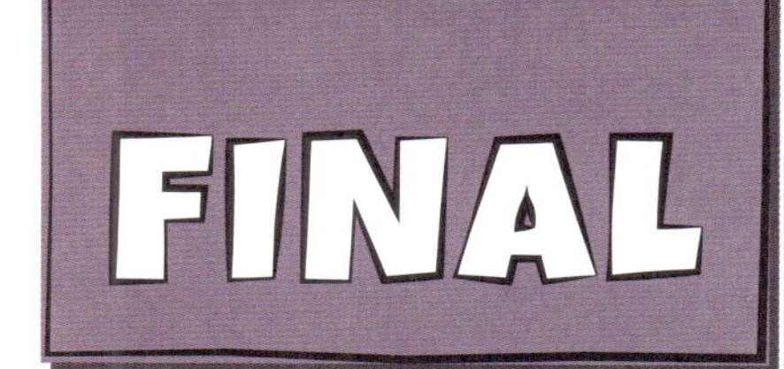

Black and red, symbolizing darkness and blood, best encapsulate the vampiric theme. Use these two colours as the foundation as you choose a colour palette for the character. Consider adding analogous colours, such as blue and purple. Select a neutral white for the hair and a blue-tinged pallid pink tone for the skin. As a vampire, she should have a pale complexion but lips that are a deep red, as if she has been drinking blood for centuries. She will wear a lavish black dress with a high collar, adorned with red velvet ribbons and bows.

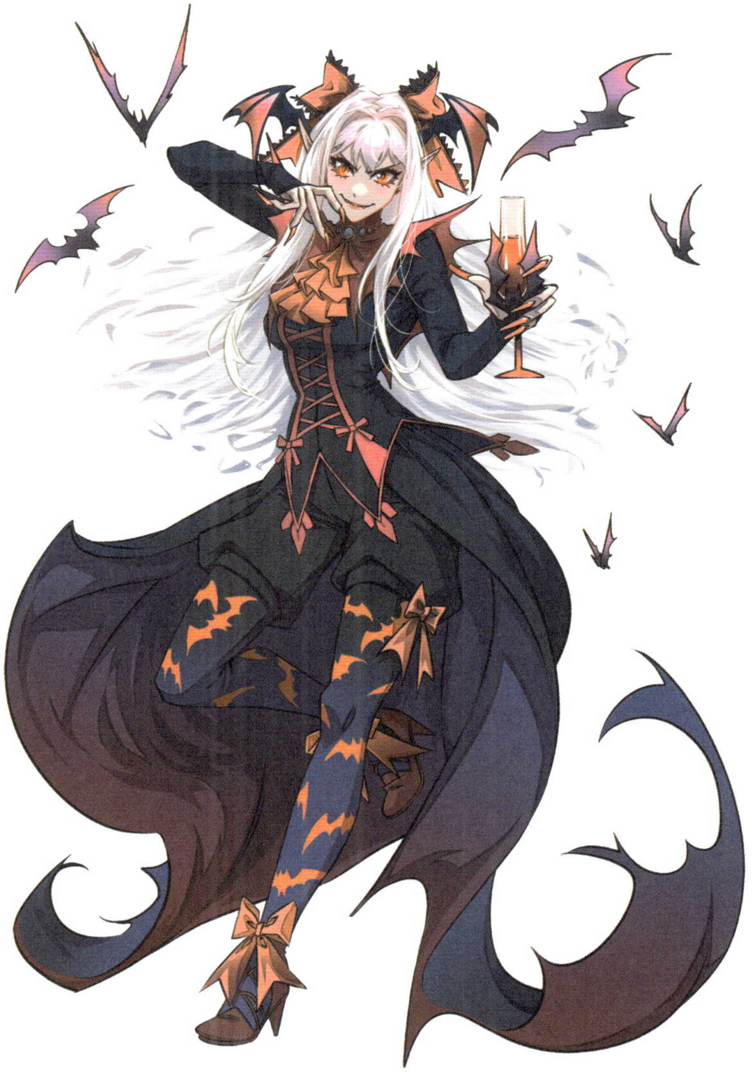

▶ Use the G-Pen and the Paint Bucket tool to fill each area in turn with colour, using the different colours to visually separate each element of the design. For example, the corset strings or the border of the top part of the outfit should be a different colour to clearly differentiate it from the other elements.

▶ Use the Gradient tool to add interest to each section of colour. Start by using the Auto Select tool to select the colour you want to work on, then create a new layer and make a gradient. Use blue over the black parts, and purple over the red areas.

▶ Next create the shadow layer. Make a Multiply layer with opacity set to around 40% and select a purple tone to create the shadows. Arrange this layer on top of all your colour layers.

▶ Erase the lip and hair lines to create a softer look. This way, colour will be the sole protagonist and won't be competing with the black line. Using the Add (Glow) blending mode, add light effects to create visual interest and supernatural flair.

PROJECT BRIEFS

Now you're ready to create your own manga artworks! This page provides a selection of ideas for characters, including a few pointers on backstory or appearance, which you can use to spark your imagination and inspire initial sketches. Using the skills you've picked up over the course of the book, have fun exploring what unique creations you can come up with!

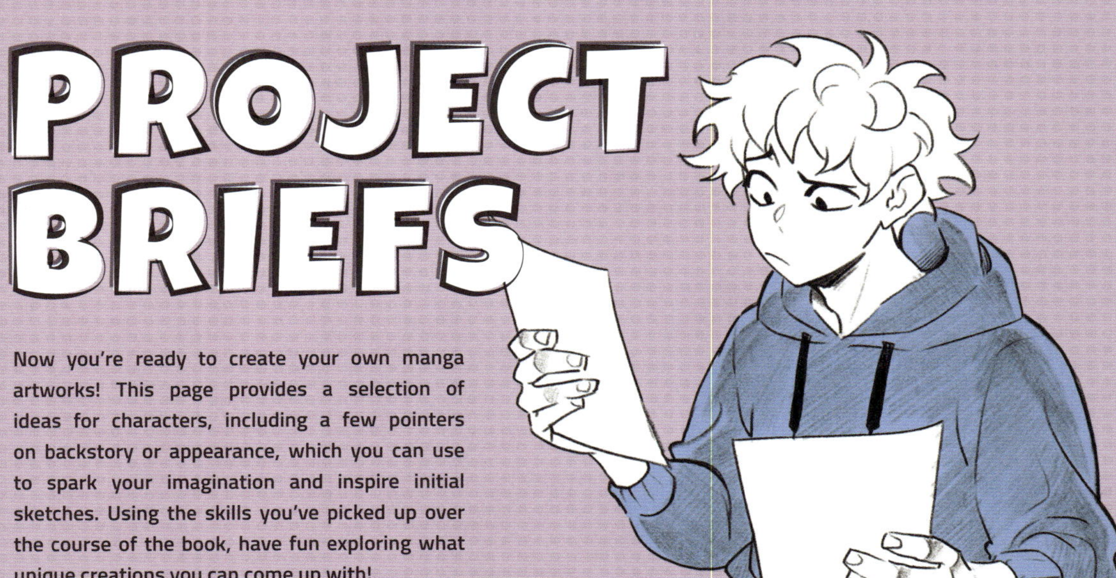

ARISTOCRATIC VILLAIN

Impeccably dressed, this manga mastermind conducts his evil deeds in style. His long locks are perfectly coiffed and his pet chinchilla sits on a cushion on his knee.

GOTHIC WITCH

Tall, dark, and alluring, this witch has wavy violet hair and sharp, talon-like nails. She wears a gothic corseted dress, spider-web tights, and big black boots.

DAISY MASCOT

With wide eyes and sweet smiles, these daisy mascots make cute companions for those picnicking in their fields. But anyone foolish enough to drop litter will invoke their wrath!

MARTIAL ARTIST

Trained by the masters, this character is a skilled martial artist with a slight frame and steely gaze. Silent and swift, he's renowned for his stealthy attacks that catch his opponents unawares.

MAGICAL PRINCESS

The youngest daughter of a noble emperor, by day she wanders the royal palace, bored and alone. But when the gemstones in her tiara begin to glow, she transforms into a magical enchantress, ready to defend the kingdom!

MECHA FIGHTER

Operated by a pilot who sits within, this fighting machine is ready for combat. Expertly crafted to both attack and defend giant threats, this mecha's aerodynamic armour and multiple weapons make it its pilot's pride and joy.

OWL PROFESSOR

This anthropomorphic bird character works at a leading university where she lectures on classical archaeology. Always smartly dressed, she is an imposing figure and cuts a striking silhouette.

TORAMIMI GIRL

Part of the kemonomimi genre, this toramimi girl is fully human except for her tiger ears and tail. She has long auburn hair, large yellow eyes, and a wild streak that can get her in trouble.

GIANT RED PANDA

Though usually small and shy, this red panda is a supersize magical being that lives deep in the heart of the bamboo forest, protecting it from harm and offering wisdom to all who stumble across its path.

VIDEO-GAME CHIBI

Ryu is a normal school boy who likes playing video games, until one day he presses the wrong command and transports himself into the game. Now he's a chibi character on the screen, journeying through the levels to find his freedom!

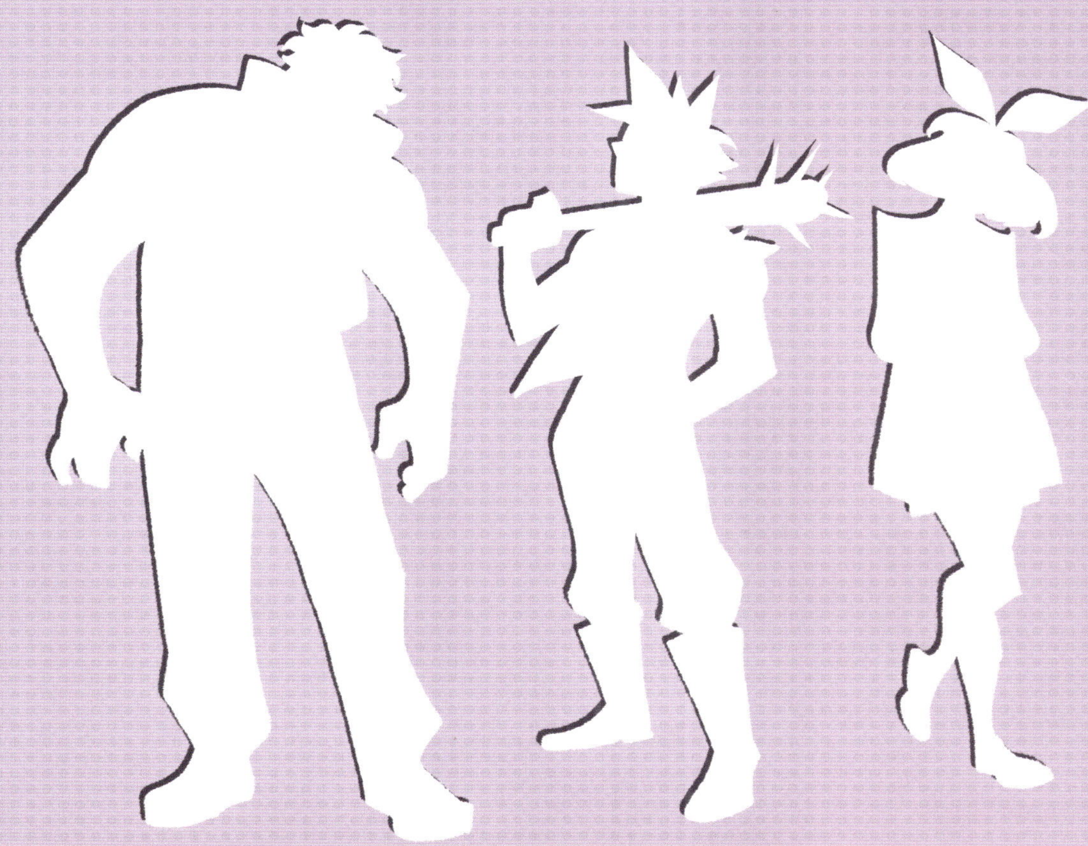

GLOSSARY

ANALOGOUS COLOURS

Colours that sit directly next to each other on the colour wheel, creating a harmonious colour scheme. For example, blue, blue-green, and green produce an analogous colour palette.

ANIME

Anime is an abbreviation for 'animation', which in the West typically refers to animation made in Japan or with a traditionally Japanese look.

CEL SHADING

A colouring technique popular in anime and manga-style artwork that uses a limited amount of colours with solid shapes without gradients. This leads to harder edges and a flat but easily recognizable look.

CHIBI

A form of stylization in manga that makes characters look small, cute, and chubby. Also referred to as 'SD' meaning 'super deformed'.

COMPLEMENTARY COLOURS

These are colours that sit directly opposite each other on the colour wheel, creating a contrasting colour scheme. Used to create visual impact, these include magenta and green, cyan and orange, and yellow and purple.

CONTRAST

The difference between parts of an image, such as bright highlights and dark shadows, small and large shapes, or different colours. Contrast can be used to create visual interest and focal points, drawing the viewer's eye to different areas of an artwork.

FLAT COLOURS

Solid, uniform colours that are consistent in shade, depth, and texture. They create a clean, graphic look, typical of comics.

FOCAL POINT

The area of an image that is the most visually interesting and immediately catches the viewer's attention. It often includes a higher level of detail and contrast, such as a character's face.

FORESHORTENING

A technique used to convey perspective by making parts of the subject appear larger and closer to the viewer. Foreshortening can be used to ensure an image doesn't appear flat and lifeless.

HIGHLIGHTS

The brightest areas of an image, which are painted with the lightest values or colours. These may be the areas closest to the light source, or those made from a glossy material.

JOSEI

Translating to 'woman' in Japanese, josei is created for an older female audience. It contains more mature themes, including romance, fantasy, or office-job related stories.

KODOMO

Meaning 'child' in Japanese, kodomo is manga created for children.

LIGHTING

How an artwork is lit in order to create different atmospheres, moods, and emotions. A scene's lighting might be neutral, natural, artificial, or dramatic, depending on the setting or story.

LINE WEIGHT

The thickness or thinness of a line. An artwork drawn with the same line weight throughout may appear flat and a little boring, whereas an image drawn with varied line weight will have more depth, fluidity, and visual interest.

LINE WORK

Also known as line art. This is often the final line drawing of an image before colour is added. It is a neater, cleaned-up version of the final sketch, though some artists may prefer to have rougher or looser line work.

MANGA

Comics made in Japan or in a Japanese style. Manga is usually printed in black and white and collected in magazines or thick volumes with roughly 200 pages each.

MOOD

The feeling, atmosphere, or emotion an artwork creates, such as spooky and mysterious, or sunny and cheerful. Colour, lighting, character, and composition can all contribute to an artwork's mood.

PERSPECTIVE

A technique used to create the illusion of three-dimensionality on a two-dimensional surface. You can plan out a scene's perspective using a horizon line and one or more vanishing points.

PRIMARY COLOURS

Magenta, yellow, and cyan; these are the three basic colours that can be mixed to create all other colours. Red, yellow, and blue are also considered primary colours, depending on the colour theory you prefer.

REFERENCE

First- or second-hand research for an artist to refer to, such as photographs, videos, or real-life objects. Researching reference imagery is an essential first step in the design process, providing inspiration and ideas that can add interest, believability, and relatability to a design.

SECONDARY COLOURS

Purple, green, and orange; these are created by mixing different variations of the three primary colours.

SEINEN

Meaning 'young man' in Japanese, seinen is created for an older male audience. It usually contains a variety of adult topics and may contain more sexual or violent themes.

SHADOW

The areas of a design that are not lit, perhaps because they are on the underside of an object, or are on the opposite side to the light source. Shadows are sometimes cast by an object blocking the light from reaching another object.

SHOJO

Manga created for a young female audience that often includes romance and slice-of-life stories. It is also known as 'shoujo' or 'shōjo' and means 'young girl' in Japanese.

SHONEN

Manga made for a young male demographic, with stories focusing on action and comedy. Also spelt 'shounen' or 'shōnen', it translates as 'young boy' in Japanese.

THUMBNAILS

Small preliminary, draft versions of your design, used to explore different ideas and compositions. They are simple and quickly made, rather than highly detailed and polished.

CONTRIBUTORS

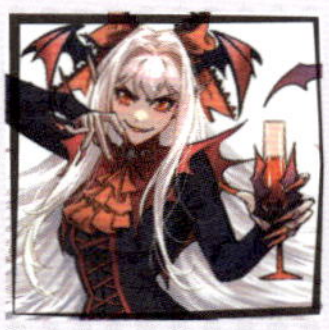 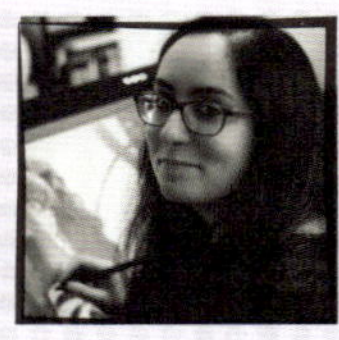

LOLITA ALDEA

Illustrator, comic-book artist, & character designer | lolitaaldea.com

Lolita has been creating manga professionally since 2012 and her books have been translated into multiple languages. She also has experience working in animation, video games, and concept art for miniatures.

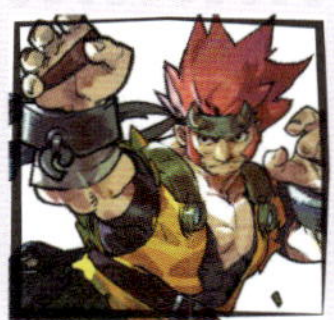 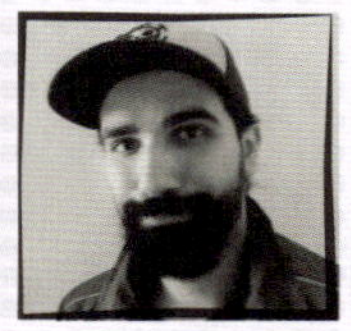

AHMAD BEYROUTHI

Lead artist | artstation.com/madbey

Ahmad is a lead artist, art director, conceptual artist, and animator. He loves video games, especially those from the nineties, and has a passion for tutoring and sharing knowledge.

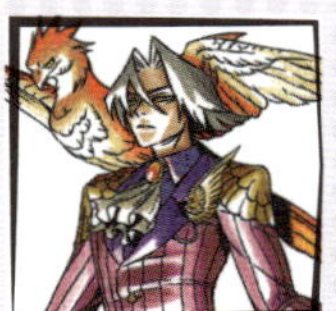 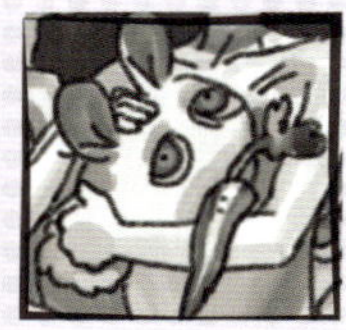

RIKA 'BWUSAGI'

Illustrator | bwusagi.carrd.co

Rika 'BWusagi' is an illustrator based in Indonesia. Her work is focused on designing characters, creatures, and body horror illustrations.

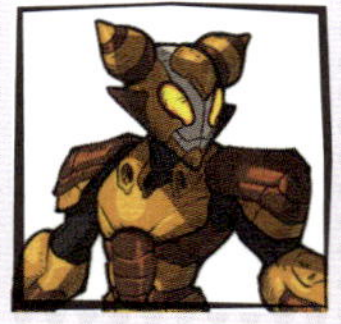 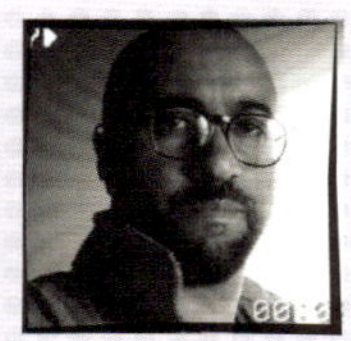

DADOTRONIC

2D artist | dadotronic.com

DADO is an independent visual artist who creates retro video-game-inspired images. His client list includes Celsys, Wacom, Supercell, and Revista Jogo Véio, as well as several indie game studios.

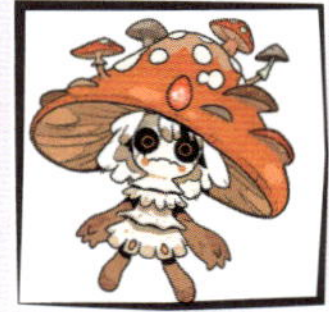 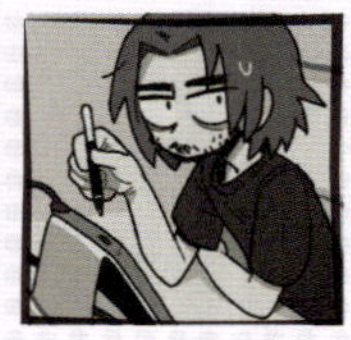

CARLES DALMAU

Illustrator | instagram.com/carles_dalmau

Based in Spain, Carles is an illustrator and comic artist who specializes in creating complex, story-driven illustrations.

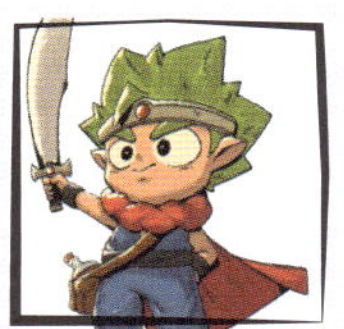 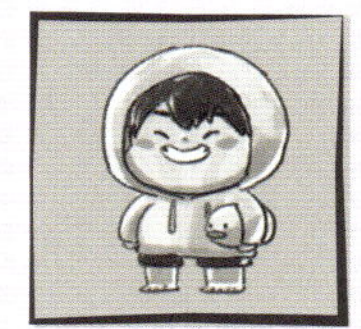

JHON LUIS GAÑAS 'PSYCHORAMEN'

Illustrator | instagram.com/psychoramen

Jhon 'Psychoramen' is a freelance illustrator and character designer from the Philippines.

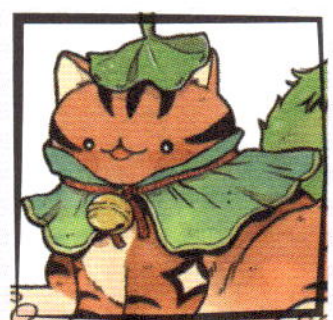 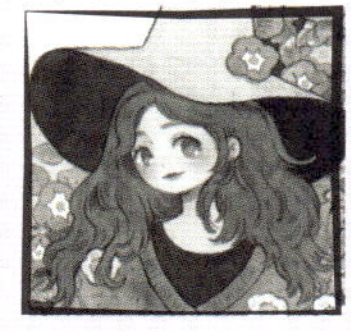

COCO GLEZ

Illustrator | cocoglez.com

Coco is an illustrator from Andalusia, Spain. She loves telling stories through her illustrations, which often portray magical and fantastic environments, and characters inspired by nature.

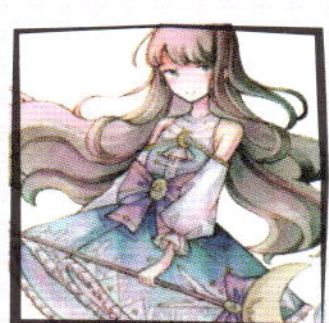 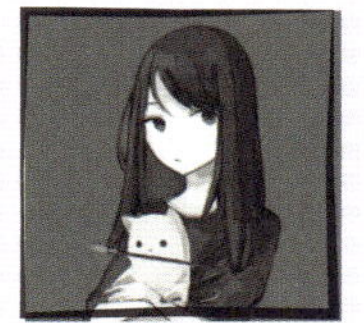

MIO

Illustrator | raemion.carrd.co

Mio is a storytelling watercolour and digital artist based in Germany. She loves expressing emotions through her paintings and is always striving to improve her abilities to translate her rich imagination onto paper.

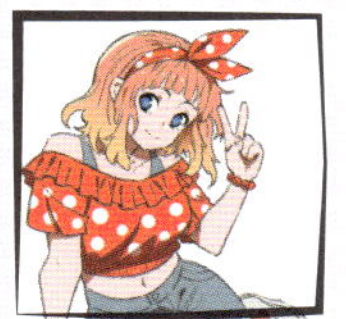 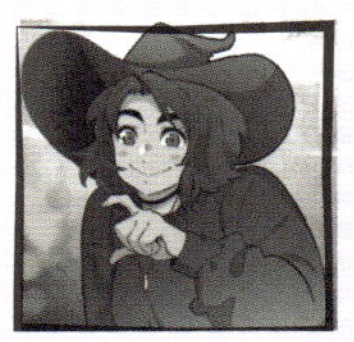

MIYULI

Comic creator & illustrator | miyuliart.com

Miyuli studied 2D animation after experimenting with webcomics in her teens. In addition to working on her Webtoon Original story *Morgana and Oz*, her freelance clients include Wacom and Celsys.

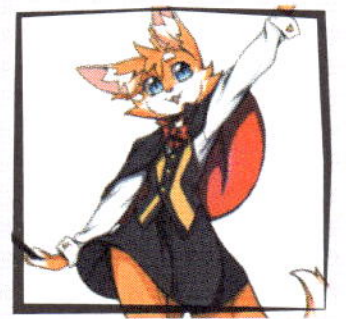 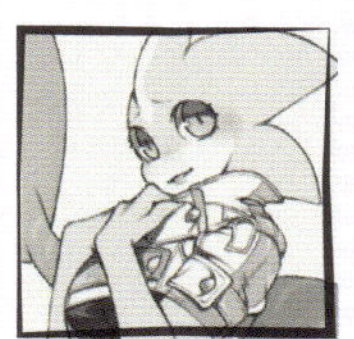

PUNIPAWS

Freelance artist | twitter.com/Punipaws

Punipaws draws anime, manga, and furry-style art, taking inspiration from various cartoons, video games, and media. She enjoys improving her artistic style and trying out new techniques and ideas.

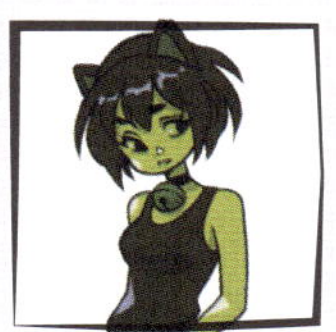 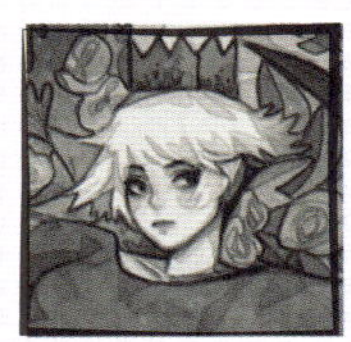

SIMZART

Illustrator | twitter.com/SimzArts

SimzArt, aka Simone Ferriero, is a digital illustrator and comic-book artist based in Italy. His illustrations are inspired by various aesthetics, including euro-manga, Western comics, and manga.

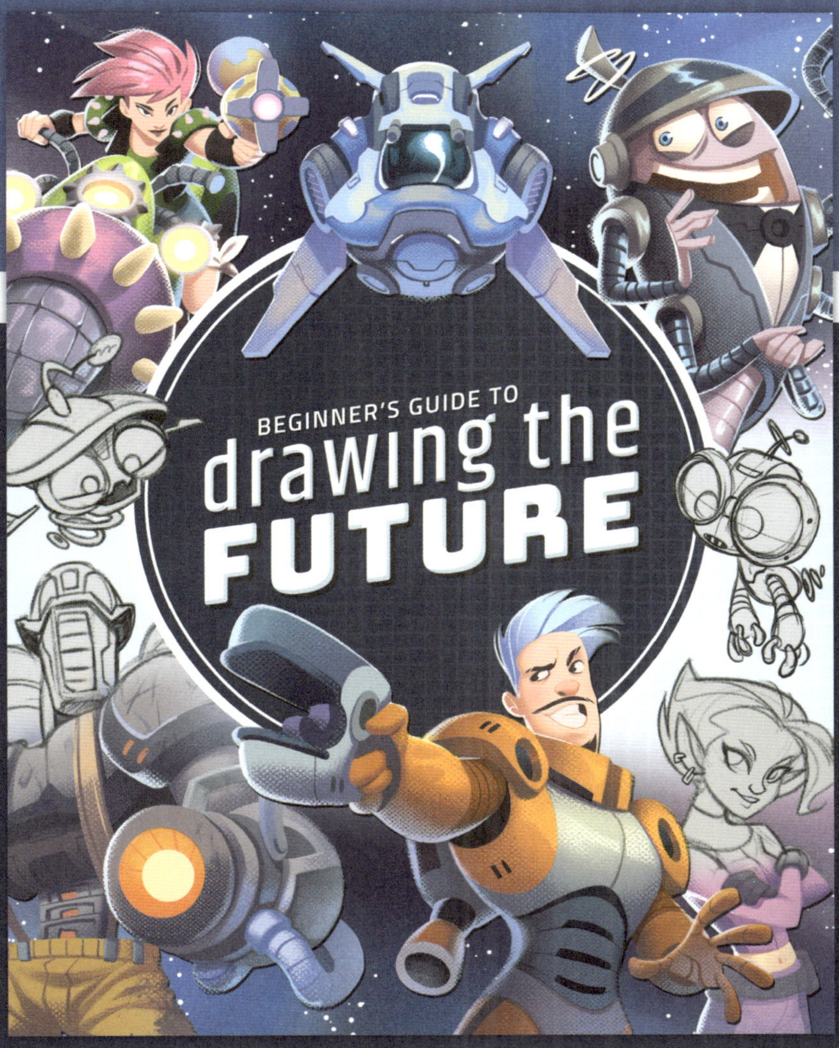

Take a giant leap into a futuristic world of dynamic droids, high-tech vehicles, and space-age characters in this exciting introduction to creating sci-fi drawings. Learn how experienced artists turn the wonders of their imagination into believable concepts, with clear steps, invaluable tips, and art theory made simple.

Available now at
store.3dtotal.com

3dtotalPublishing

3dtotal Publishing is a trailblazing, creative publisher specializing in inspirational and educational resources for artists.

Our titles feature top industry professionals from around the globe who share their experience in skilfully written step-by-step tutorials and fascinating, detailed guides. Illustrated throughout with stunning artwork, these bestselling publications offer creative insight, expert advice, and essential motivation. Fans of digital art will enjoy our comprehensive volumes covering Adobe Photoshop, Procreate, and Blender, as well as our superb titles based around character design, including *Fundamentals of Character Design* and *Creating Characters for the Entertainment Industry*. The dedicated, high-quality blend of instruction and inspiration also extends to traditional art. Titles covering a range of techniques, genres, and abilities allow your creativity to flourish while building essential skills.

Well-established within the industry, we now offer over 100 titles and counting, many of which have been translated into multiple languages around the world. With something for every artist, we are proud to say that our books offer the 3dtotal package:

LEARN · CREATE · SHARE

Visit us at 3dtotalpublishing.com

3dtotal Publishing is part of 3dtotal.com, a leading website for
CG artists founded by Tom Greenway in 1999.